PENGUIN BOOKS

WE, THE CITIZENS

Khyati Pathak is an IT consultant-turned-artist who looks at the world like it's a puzzle waiting to be solved. She creates comic artwork on not-so-comic themes such as politics, feminism, environment and culture. Her work has featured in children's magazines *Pluto* and *Cycle*, and on the comics platform Bakarmax. She co-hosts *Puliyabaazi*, a podcast that features in-depth conversations with experts on policy, politics, technology and more. Her work can be found at The Scribble Bee (www.thescribblebee.com).

Anupam Manur is an assistant professor at the Takshashila Institution. His research interests lie at the intersection of economics, technology and public policy. He writes on platform economics, international trade, India's ongoing jobs crisis and on economic policy. He edits the *Indian Public Policy Review*, a peer-reviewed and open-access journal of economics, public policy and strategy. He has also edited three books under the Takshashila Institution Press. Anupam teaches different variants of economics in all of Takshashila's public policy programmes and is responsible for designing the curriculum for the educational programmes.

Pranay Kotasthane is deputy director at the Takshashila Institution, where he is a researcher and teacher of public policy, foreign policy and public finance. Pranay is the co-author of the public policy bestseller *Missing in Action: Why You Should Care about Public Policy* (2023) and *When the Chips Are Down: A Deep Dive into a Global Crisis* (2023). He co-writes *Anticipating the Unintended*, a newsletter on public policy ideas and frameworks and co-hosts *Puliyabaazi*, a popular Hindi–Urdu podcast on politics, policy and technology.

T0281900

We, the Citizens

STRENGTHENING THE INDIAN REPUBLIC

KHYATI PATHAK,
ANUPAM MANUR
and
PRANAY KOTASTHANE

PENGUIN BOOKS

An imprint of Penguin Random House

PENGUIN BOOKS

USA | Canada | UK | Ireland | Australia
New Zealand | India | South Africa | China| Singapore

Penguin Books is part of the Penguin Random House group of companies
whose addresses can be found at global.penguinrandomhouse.com

Published by Penguin Random House India Pvt. Ltd
4th Floor, Capital Tower 1, MG Road,
Gurugram 122 002, Haryana, India

First published in Penguin Books by Penguin Random House India 2024

Copyright © Khyati Pathak, Anupam Manur and Pranay Kotasthane 2024

ISBN 9780143463559

Typeset in Tw Cen MT
Printed at Thomson Press India Ltd, New Delhi

www.penguin.co.in

We salute those who strive to strengthen the Indian republic
in ways small and big

Contents

Preface

'Koi bhi desh perfect nahi hota,
Usse perfect banana padta hai'

[No nation is perfect,
It needs to be made perfect.]

—*dialogue from Rang De Basanti*
(2006)

At the stroke of the midnight hour on 15 August 1947, few believed that India would really 'awake to life and freedom'. The Republic of India, created in 1950, seemed like an unwieldy experiment, an unstable structure that would collapse under the load of its own people. After all, how could such a populous country with innumerable differences and problems stay together as a democratic republic?

Yet somehow, India and Indians have managed to prove everyone wrong. Not only has India stayed together as one nation state, but it has also thrived despite its many contradictions.

But our problems do not seem to be over yet. Some days, it feels like so much has changed, yet nothing has changed. We may be the world's largest democracy, but we still need to work towards strengthening the foundations of our republic. We often find ourselves embroiled in petty debates while the most fundamental questions that affect us remain overlooked. We do not demand more from our legislators because of a lack of understanding on how public policy choices affect all of us. That's why, the three of us feel that India needs an informed discourse in public affairs.

What should the State do? What should it not do? These questions are often perceived as dull and boring, fit to be limited to academic discussions. This book is our attempt to change that perception. We have taken the core concepts of public policy and presented them in a manner relatable for readers of all ages. This book is for anyone who wants to be an engaged citizen, a positive change maker, or simply wants to grasp the basics of public policy.

This book was conceptualized because of our interactions during the Graduate Certificate in Public Policy (GCPP) programme at the Takshashila Institution, Bengaluru. We borrow heavily from the concepts and frameworks we learned there.

We are three people with very different skill sets and often differing points of view, but the openness of discourse at Takshashila enabled an exchange of ideas that led to this book. A writer-cartoonist, a public policy researcher and an economics professor is a combo hard to come by! Somehow, we felt that we could put together a comic book that could simplify public policy in the Indian context.

We borrow from many academicians and authors we admire and whose ideas have influenced us. We have taken the core concepts, distilled them and weaved them into a narrative. There is a generous sprinkling of references from pop culture and some laments from our lived experiences. Be mindful that this is not an academic book that covers all nuances of the topic. There may be some simplification—our bias is towards clarity and simplicity. If there are any inadvertent slips, it is the cartoonist's fault. Consider this book as the first step in the realm of public policy.

We write this book with immense hope for the future of India, tempered only by the realization that progress cannot happen overnight. We do not believe in quick fixes. We see policymaking as a marathon. We believe in the power of an engaged citizenry. Call it our vain idealism, but we believe in the mantra, *koshish karne walon ki haar nahi hoti* [Those who try never lose].

This little book is just that—a *koshish*, an attempt at adding something useful to the civic discourse. We hope our words can infect you with some of our optimism.

Introduction

It's a Sisyphean Marathon

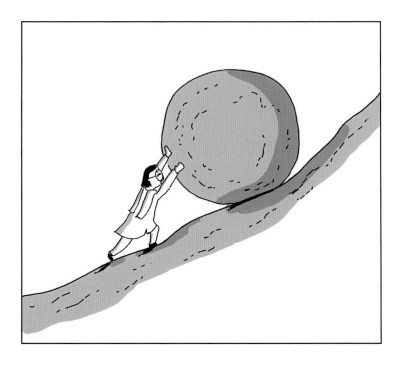

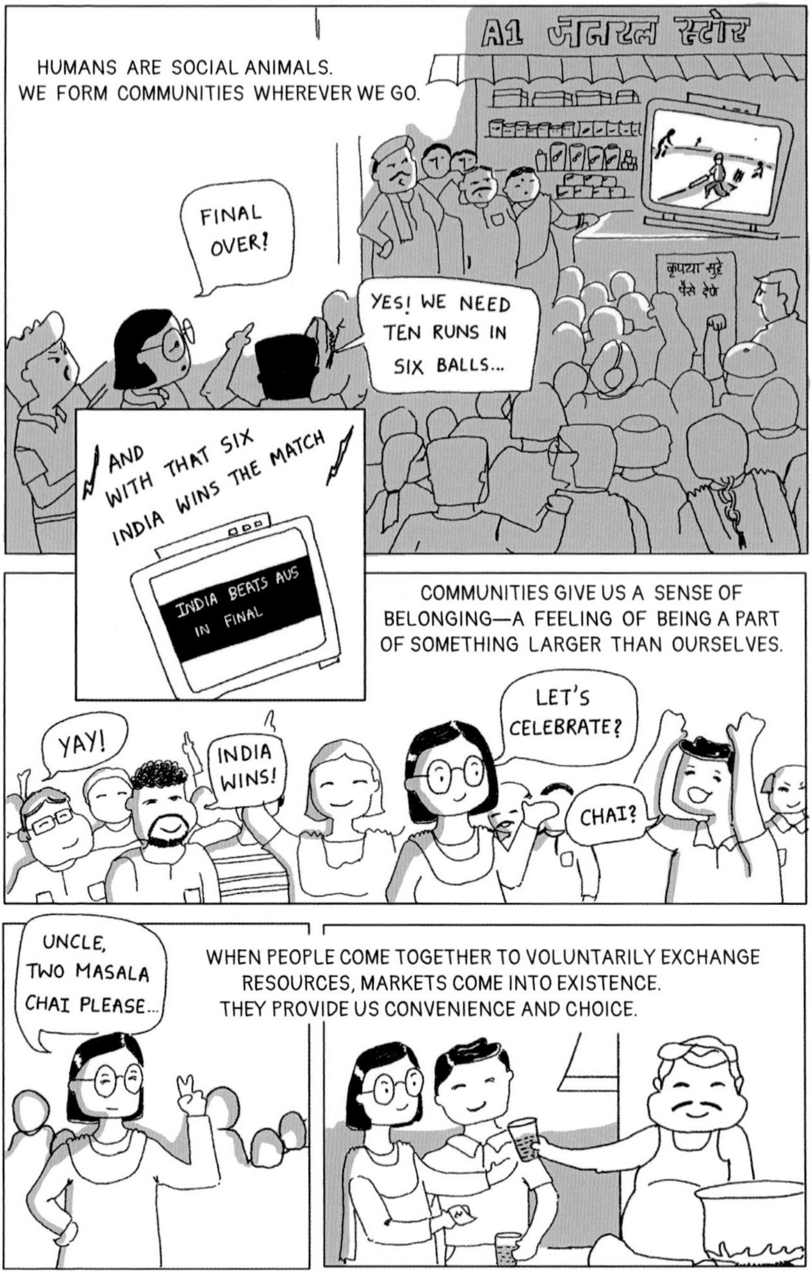
A1 जनरल स्टोर
HUMANS ARE SOCIAL ANIMALS.
WE FORM COMMUNITIES WHEREVER WE GO.
FINAL OVER?
YES! WE NEED TEN RUNS IN SIX BALLS...
AND WITH THAT SIX INDIA WINS THE MATCH
INDIA BEATS AUS IN FINAL
COMMUNITIES GIVE US A SENSE OF BELONGING—A FEELING OF BEING A PART OF SOMETHING LARGER THAN OURSELVES.
YAY!
INDIA WINS!
LET'S CELEBRATE?
CHAI?
UNCLE, TWO MASALA CHAI PLEASE...
WHEN PEOPLE COME TOGETHER TO VOLUNTARILY EXCHANGE RESOURCES, MARKETS COME INTO EXISTENCE.
THEY PROVIDE US CONVENIENCE AND CHOICE.

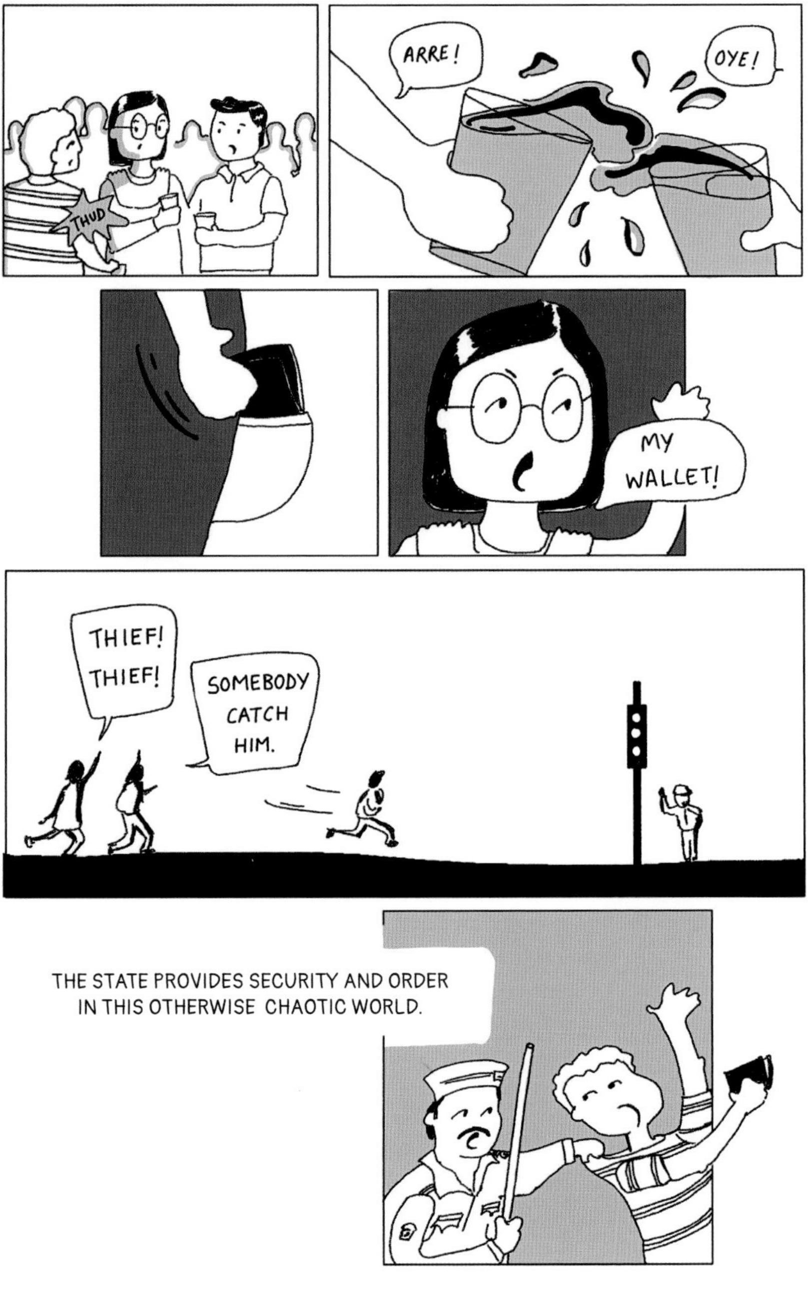
THUD
ARRE!
OYE!
MY WALLET!
THIEF! THIEF!
SOMEBODY CATCH HIM.
THE STATE PROVIDES SECURITY AND ORDER IN THIS OTHERWISE CHAOTIC WORLD.

WE LIVE AT THE INTERSECTION OF THE STATE, MARKET AND SOCIETY.
THEY AFFECT THE BIG AND SMALL DECISIONS OF OUR LIFE.

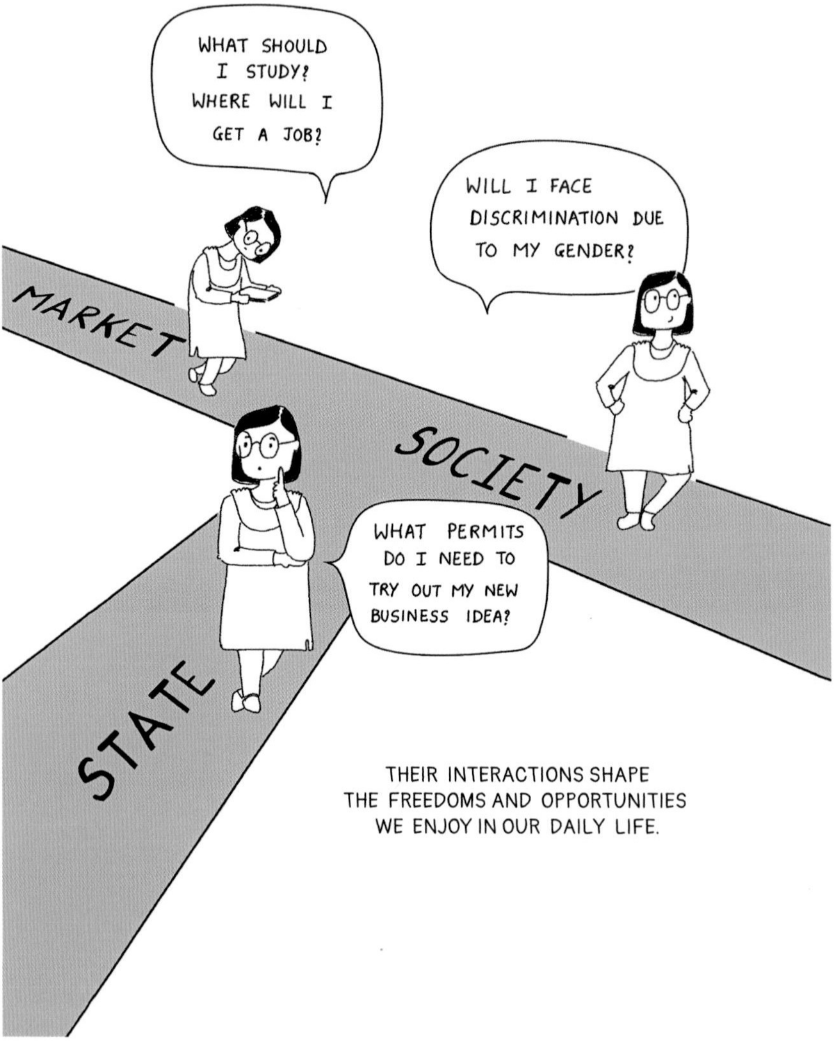
WHAT SHOULD I STUDY? WHERE WILL I GET A JOB?
WILL I FACE DISCRIMINATION DUE TO MY GENDER?
MARKET
SOCIETY
WHAT PERMITS DO I NEED TO TRY OUT MY NEW BUSINESS IDEA?
STATE

THEIR INTERACTIONS SHAPE
THE FREEDOMS AND OPPORTUNITIES
WE ENJOY IN OUR DAILY LIFE.

NOW, THE STATE IS UNIQUE AMONGST THE THREE
BECAUSE IT COMMANDS DISPROPORTIONATE POWER OVER US.

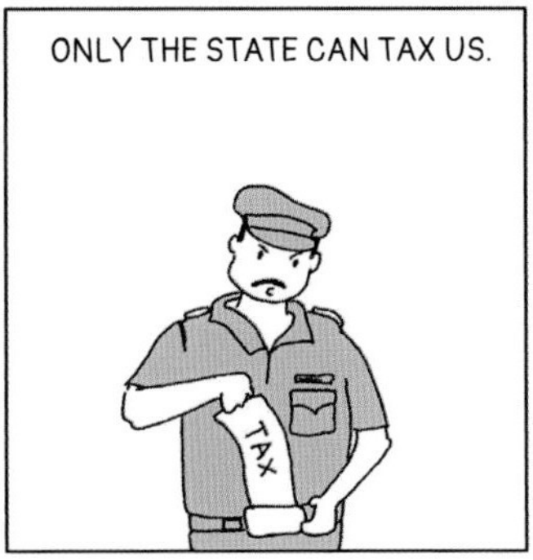
ONLY THE STATE CAN TAX US.
TAX

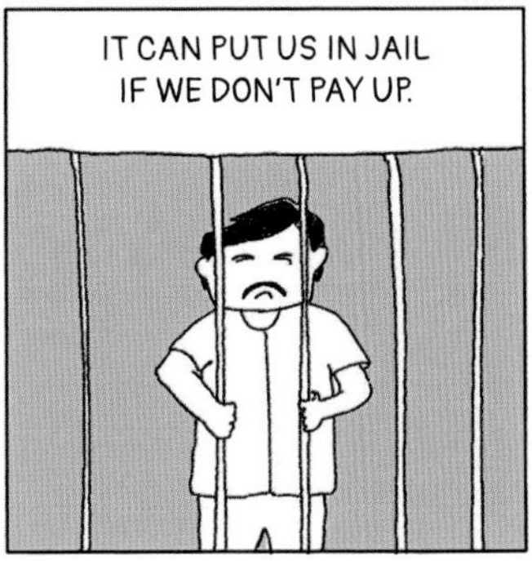
IT CAN PUT US IN JAIL
IF WE DON'T PAY UP.

ONLY THE STATE HAS THE LEGITIMACY TO DO CERTAIN THINGS.

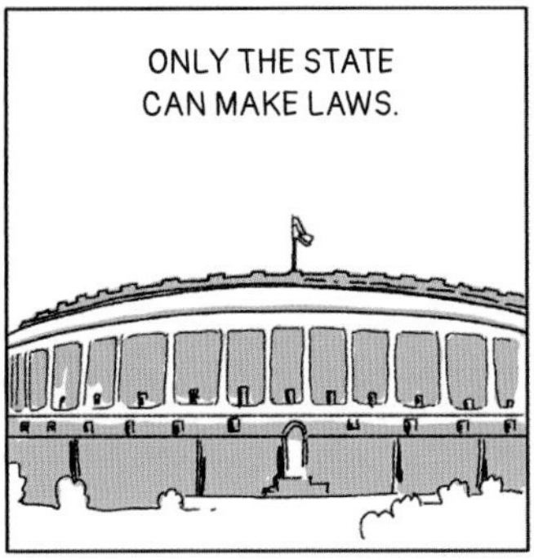
ONLY THE STATE
CAN MAKE LAWS.

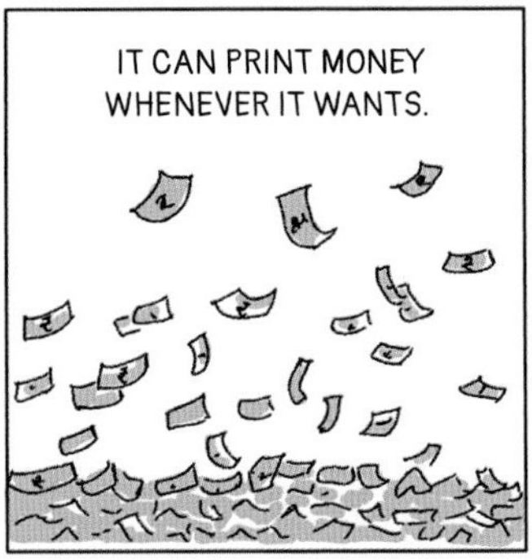
IT CAN PRINT MONEY
WHENEVER IT WANTS.

WITH THESE VAST POWERS COME GREAT RESPONSIBILITIES LIKE

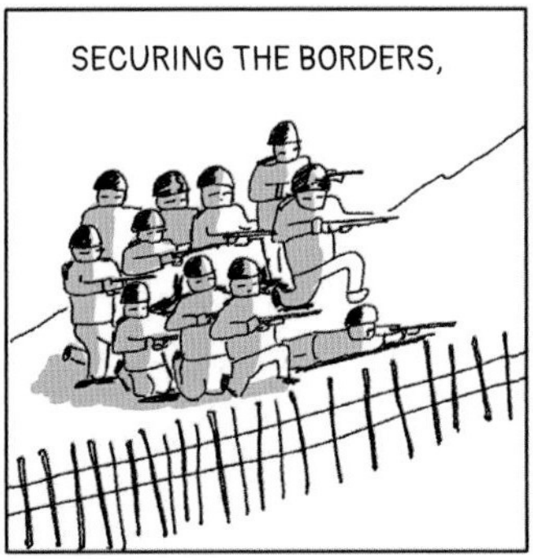
SECURING THE BORDERS,

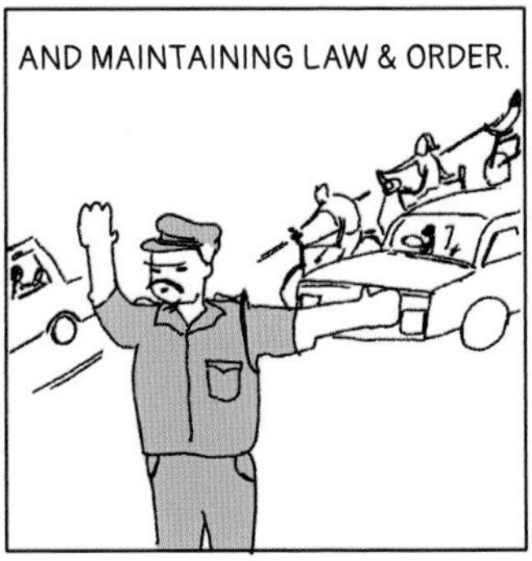
AND MAINTAINING LAW & ORDER.

WHEN POLICIES ARE DONE RIGHT, THE STATE CAN MAKE GREAT THINGS HAPPEN
THAT MARKETS AND SOCIETY WOULD NOT BE ABLE TO ACHIEVE BY THEMSELVES.

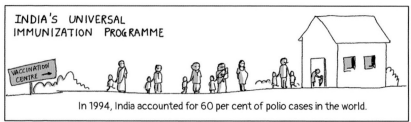

INDIA'S UNIVERSAL IMMUNIZATION PROGRAMME

VACCINATION CENTRE →

In 1994, India accounted for 60 per cent of polio cases in the world.

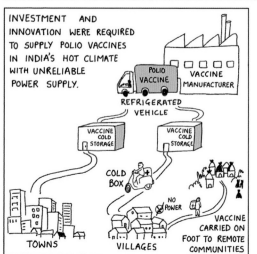

INVESTMENT AND INNOVATION WERE REQUIRED TO SUPPLY POLIO VACCINES IN INDIA'S HOT CLIMATE WITH UNRELIABLE POWER SUPPLY.

POLIO VACCINE

VACCINE MANUFACTURER

REFRIGERATED VEHICLE

VACCINE COLD STORAGE

VACCINE COLD STORAGE

COLD BOX

NO POWER

VACCINE CARRIED ON FOOT TO REMOTE COMMUNITIES

TOWNS

VILLAGES

POLIO RAVIVAR

ENSURING NOT A SINGLE CHILD IS LEFT BEHIND.

INDIA DECLARED POLIO FREE IN 2014

IMPROVEMENTS IN INFANT MORTALITY & UNDER-5 MORTALITY

BUT, IF POLICIES ARE NOT THOUGHT THROUGH,
THEN THEY CAN HAVE DISASTROUS CONSEQUENCES TOO.

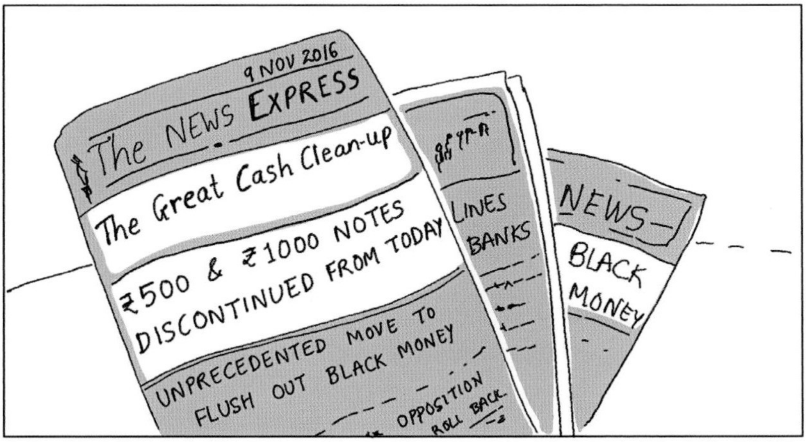

9 NOV 2016
The NEWS EXPRESS
The Great Cash Clean-up
₹500 & ₹1000 NOTES DISCONTINUED FROM TODAY
UNPRECEDENTED MOVE TO FLUSH OUT BLACK MONEY
OPPOSITION
ROLL BACK
LINES
BANKS
NEWS
BLACK MONEY

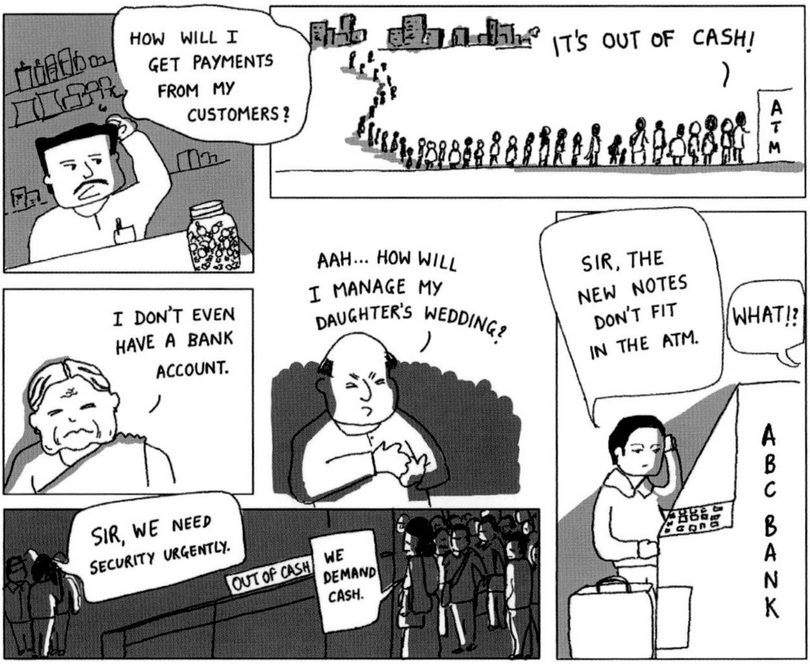

HOW WILL I GET PAYMENTS FROM MY CUSTOMERS?
IT'S OUT OF CASH!
ATM
I DON'T EVEN HAVE A BANK ACCOUNT.
AAH... HOW WILL I MANAGE MY DAUGHTER'S WEDDING?
SIR, THE NEW NOTES DON'T FIT IN THE ATM.
WHAT!?
ABC BANK
SIR, WE NEED SECURITY URGENTLY.
OUT OF CASH
WE DEMAND CASH.

AND SO IT'S IMPORTANT THAT WE UNDERSTAND STATE ACTIONS AND ANALYSE THEIR EFFECTS AND SIDE EFFECTS.

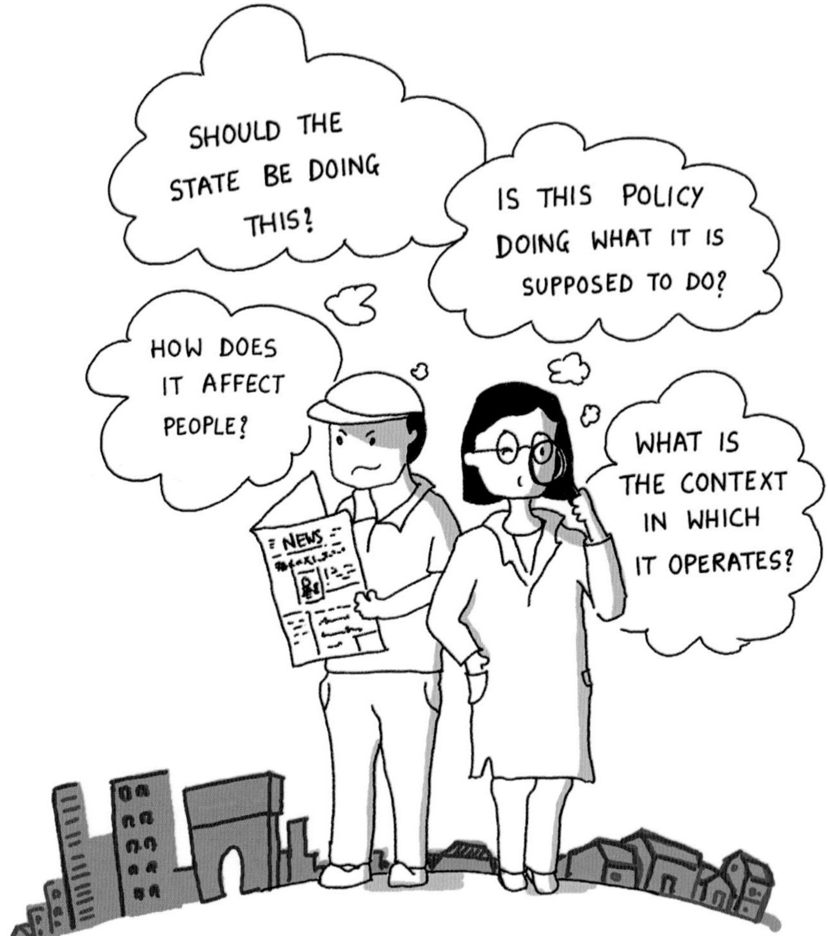
SHOULD THE STATE BE DOING THIS?
IS THIS POLICY DOING WHAT IT IS SUPPOSED TO DO?
HOW DOES IT AFFECT PEOPLE?
WHAT IS THE CONTEXT IN WHICH IT OPERATES?
NEWS

THIS DOESN'T MEAN THAT MARKETS AND SOCIETY ARE BYSTANDERS IN THIS SYSTEM. THEY ARE ACTIVE PLAYERS WITH THEIR OWN STRENGTHS AND WEAKNESSES.

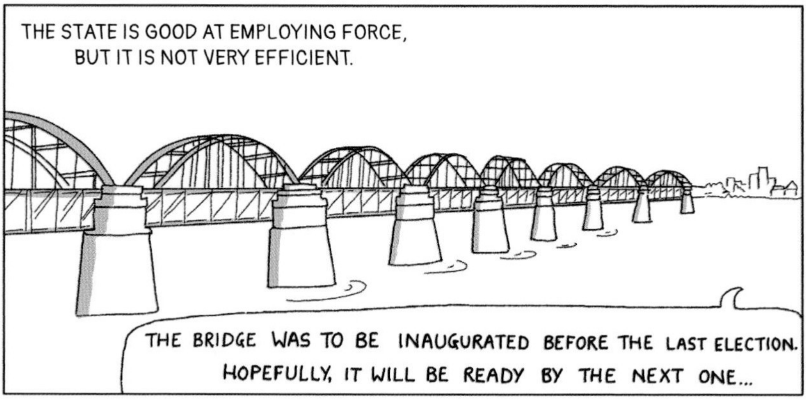
THE STATE IS GOOD AT EMPLOYING FORCE, BUT IT IS NOT VERY EFFICIENT.
THE BRIDGE WAS TO BE INAUGURATED BEFORE THE LAST ELECTION. HOPEFULLY, IT WILL BE READY BY THE NEXT ONE...

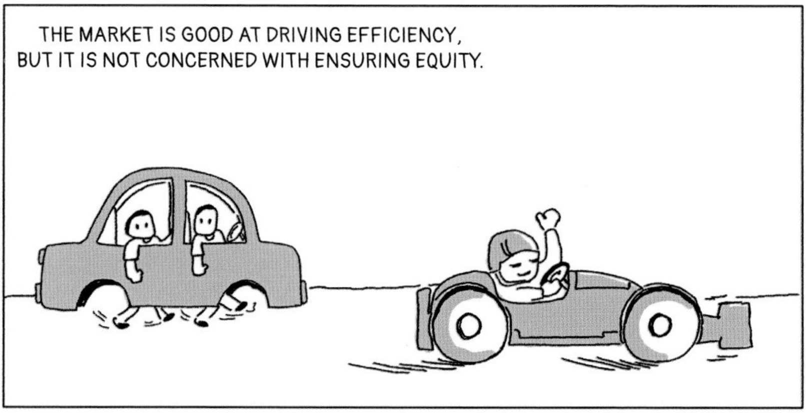
THE MARKET IS GOOD AT DRIVING EFFICIENCY, BUT IT IS NOT CONCERNED WITH ENSURING EQUITY.

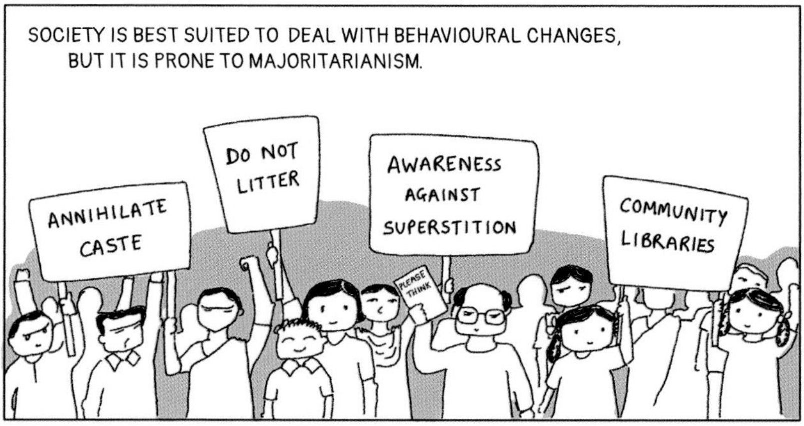
SOCIETY IS BEST SUITED TO DEAL WITH BEHAVIOURAL CHANGES, BUT IT IS PRONE TO MAJORITARIANISM.
ANNIHILATE CASTE
DO NOT LITTER
AWARENESS AGAINST SUPERSTITION
PLEASE THINK
COMMUNITY LIBRARIES

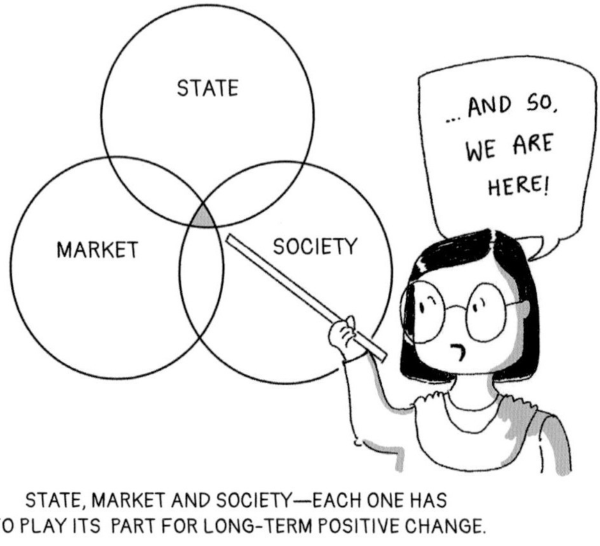
STATE
MARKET
SOCIETY
... AND SO, WE ARE HERE!

STATE, MARKET AND SOCIETY—EACH ONE HAS TO PLAY ITS PART FOR LONG-TERM POSITIVE CHANGE.

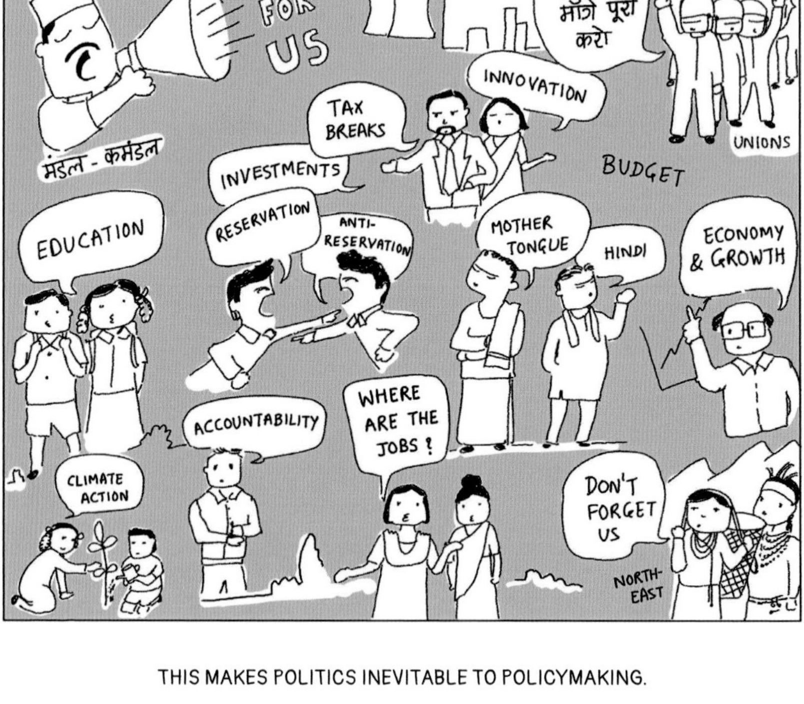
VOTE FOR US
हमारी मॉंगे पूरी करो
मंडल - कमंडल
INNOVATION
TAX BREAKS
INVESTMENTS
UNIONS
BUDGET
EDUCATION
RESERVATION
ANTI-RESERVATION
MOTHER TONGUE
HINDI
ECONOMY & GROWTH
ACCOUNTABILITY
WHERE ARE THE JOBS ?
CLIMATE ACTION
DON'T FORGET US
NORTH-EAST

THIS MAKES POLITICS INEVITABLE TO POLICYMAKING.

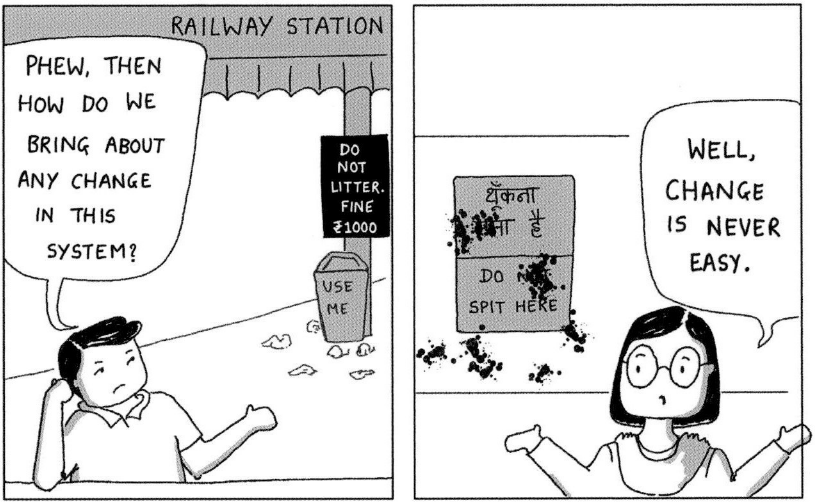
RAILWAY STATION
PHEW, THEN HOW DO WE BRING ABOUT ANY CHANGE IN THIS SYSTEM?
DO NOT LITTER. FINE ₹1000
USE ME
WELL, CHANGE IS NEVER EASY.

SOMETIMES, IT MAY SEEM LIKE A SISYPHEAN* MARATHON
WITH NO END IN SIGHT, BUT WE MUST STILL PERSIST.

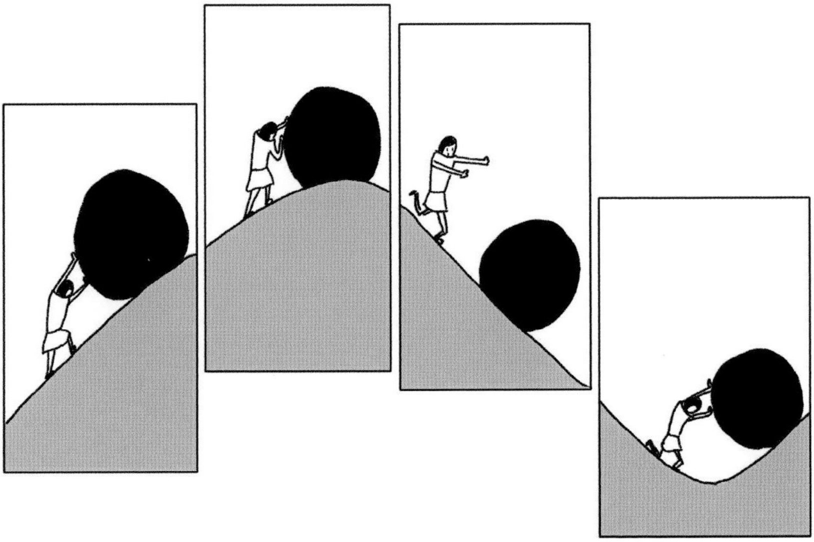

* In Greek mythology, Sisyphus was condemned to a never-ending punishment to push a boulder up a hill, only to watch it roll down everytime he reached the peak, thereby making it an endless task.

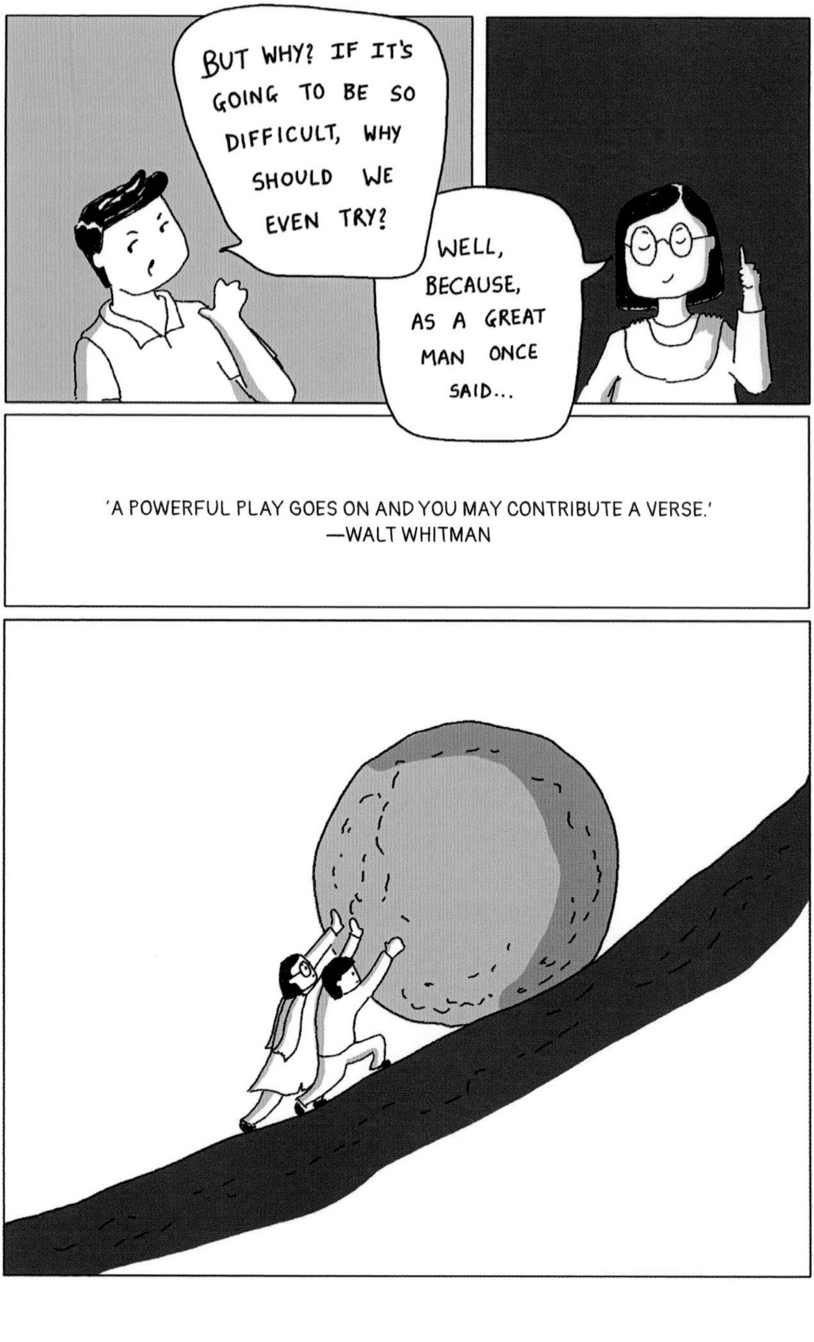
BUT WHY? IF IT'S GOING TO BE SO DIFFICULT, WHY SHOULD WE EVEN TRY?
WELL, BECAUSE, AS A GREAT MAN ONCE SAID...
'A POWERFUL PLAY GOES ON AND YOU MAY CONTRIBUTE A VERSE.'
—WALT WHITMAN

Chapter 1

Birbal Stands Up for the Left-Handers

The rule of law

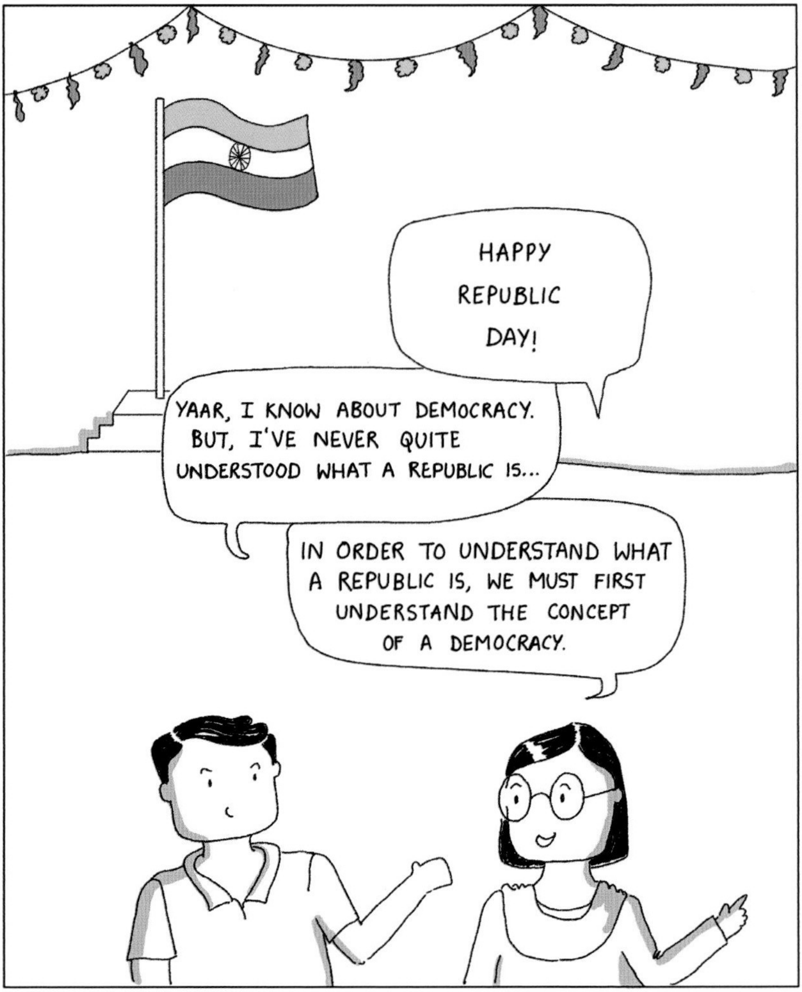
HAPPY REPUBLIC DAY!
YAAR, I KNOW ABOUT DEMOCRACY. BUT, I'VE NEVER QUITE UNDERSTOOD WHAT A REPUBLIC IS...
IN ORDER TO UNDERSTAND WHAT A REPUBLIC IS, WE MUST FIRST UNDERSTAND THE CONCEPT OF A DEMOCRACY.

DEMOCRACY IS WHEN PEOPLE ELECT THEIR REPRESENTATIVES THROUGH FREE AND FAIR ELECTIONS.

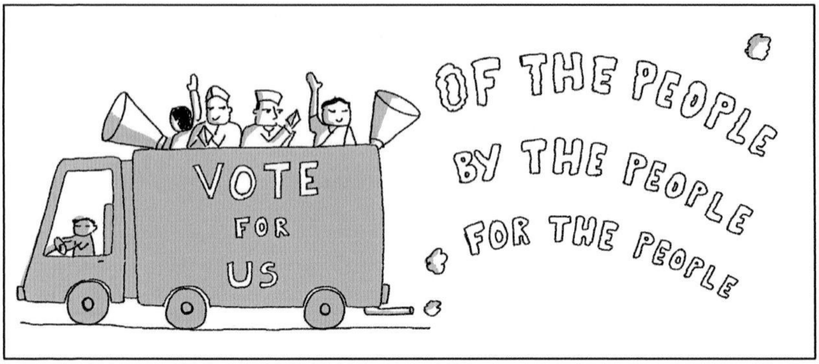
VOTE
FOR
US
OF THE PEOPLE
BY THE PEOPLE
FOR THE PEOPLE

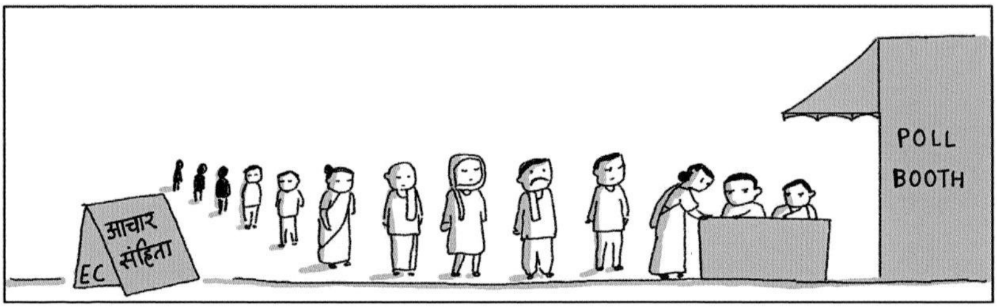
EC आचार संहिता
POLL BOOTH

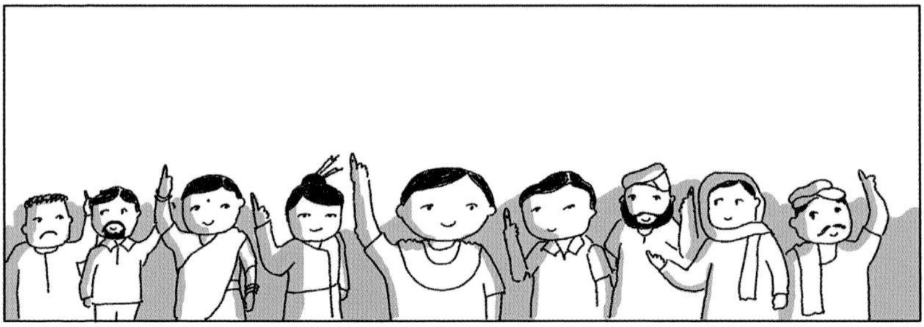

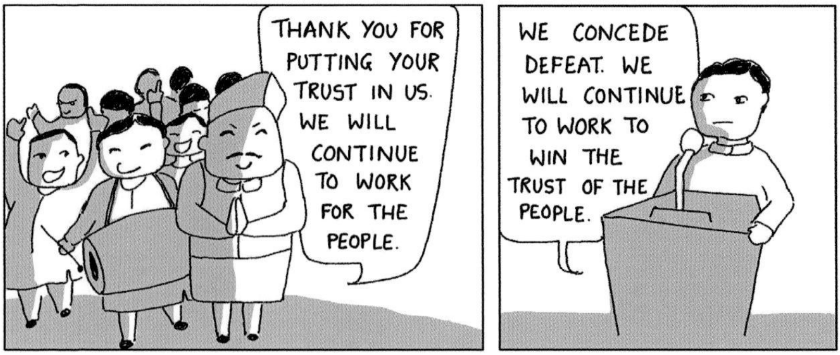
THANK YOU FOR PUTTING YOUR TRUST IN US. WE WILL CONTINUE TO WORK FOR THE PEOPLE.
WE CONCEDE DEFEAT. WE WILL CONTINUE TO WORK TO WIN THE TRUST OF THE PEOPLE.

NOTE THAT DEMOCRACY IS A PROCEDURAL CONCEPT.

AN UNDEMOCRATIC PROCESS IS ONE WHERE ONE PERSON OR A SMALL GROUP MAKES THE DECISION, WHILE A MAJORITY OF THE PEOPLE AFFECTED BY IT DO NOT GET TO PARTICIPATE.

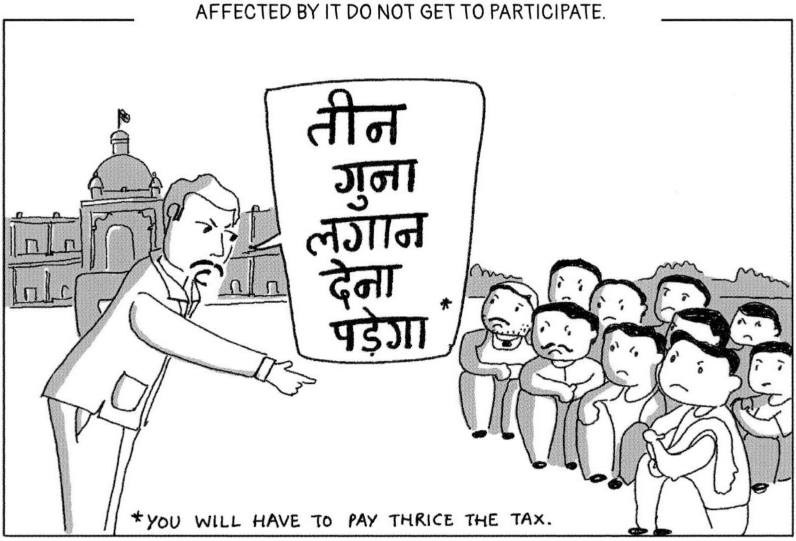

तीन गुना लगान देना पड़ेगा*
*YOU WILL HAVE TO PAY THRICE THE TAX.

A DEMOCRATIC PROCESS MEANS THAT EVERYONE INVOLVED HAS AGREED TO A PROCEDURE AND THE PROCEDURE HAS BEEN FOLLOWED IN THE DECISION-MAKING.

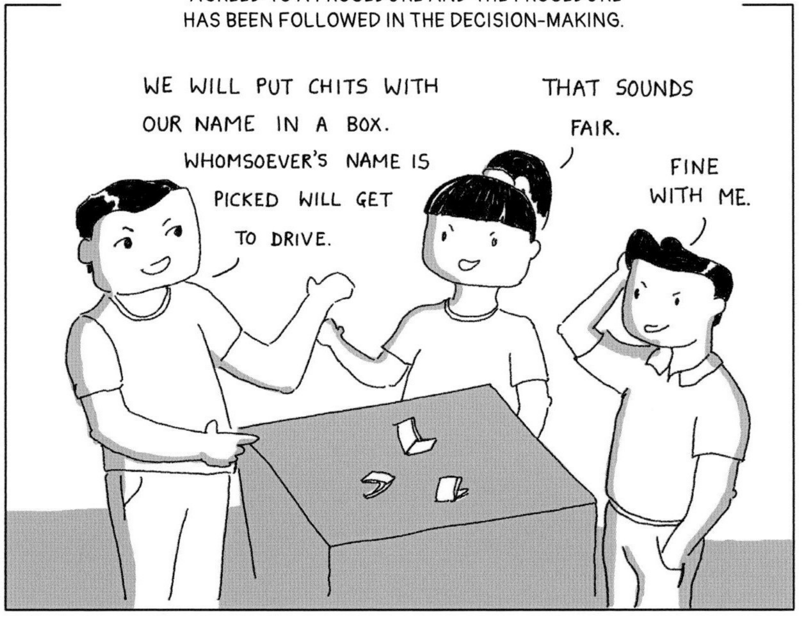

WE WILL PUT CHITS WITH OUR NAME IN A BOX. WHOMSOEVER'S NAME IS PICKED WILL GET TO DRIVE.
THAT SOUNDS FAIR.
FINE WITH ME.

DEMOCRACY ALLOWS THE PEOPLE TO HAVE A SAY IN THE DECISION-MAKING. BUT, DEMOCRACY ALONE IS NOT ENOUGH.

A DEMOCRACY WITHOUT ANY GUARD RAILS CAN ALSO LEAD TO 'MAJORITARIAN RULE'. THINK ABOUT THIS HYPOTHETICAL SCENARIO...

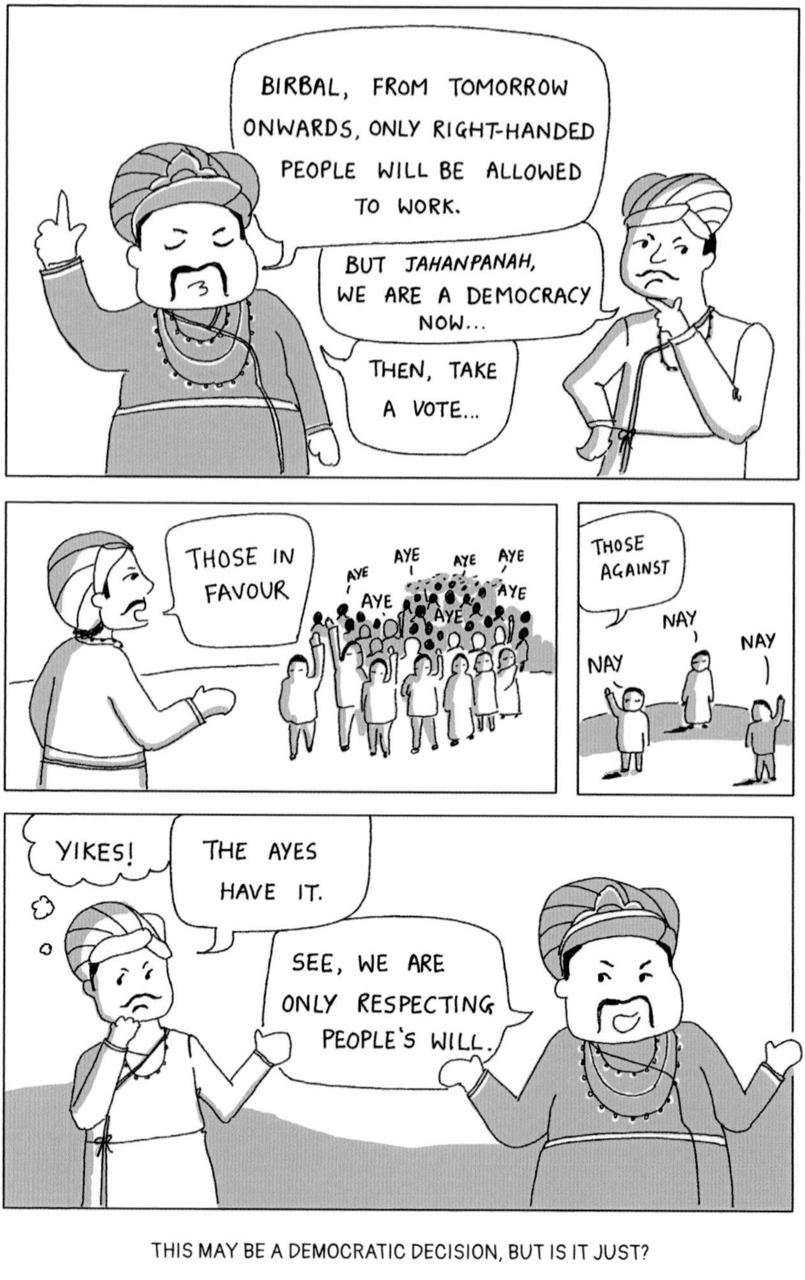
BIRBAL, FROM TOMORROW ONWARDS, ONLY RIGHT-HANDED PEOPLE WILL BE ALLOWED TO WORK.
BUT JAHANPANAH, WE ARE A DEMOCRACY NOW...
THEN, TAKE A VOTE...
THOSE IN FAVOUR
AYE
AYE
AYE
AYE
AYE
AYE
AYE
THOSE AGAINST
NAY
NAY
NAY
YIKES!
THE AYES HAVE IT.
SEE, WE ARE ONLY RESPECTING PEOPLE'S WILL.

THIS MAY BE A DEMOCRATIC DECISION, BUT IS IT JUST?

THIS IS WHERE THE REPUBLIC COMES TO OUR RESCUE.
NOW, THE ORIGINAL MEANING OF THE WORD 'REPUBLIC' MEANT
A TYPE OF STATE THAT IS NOT A MONARCHY.

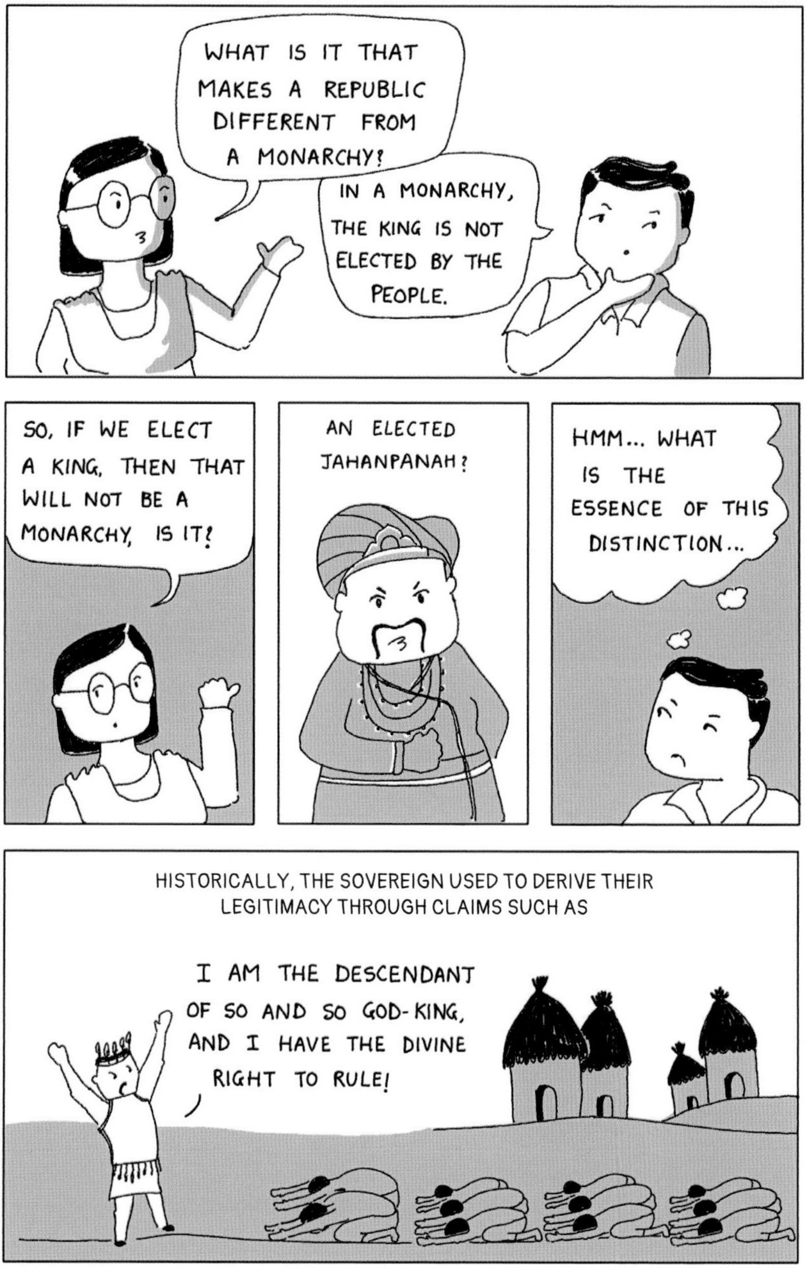
WHAT IS IT THAT MAKES A REPUBLIC DIFFERENT FROM A MONARCHY?
IN A MONARCHY, THE KING IS NOT ELECTED BY THE PEOPLE.
SO, IF WE ELECT A KING, THEN THAT WILL NOT BE A MONARCHY, IS IT?
AN ELECTED JAHANPANAH?
HMM... WHAT IS THE ESSENCE OF THIS DISTINCTION...
HISTORICALLY, THE SOVEREIGN USED TO DERIVE THEIR LEGITIMACY THROUGH CLAIMS SUCH AS
I AM THE DESCENDANT OF SO AND SO GOD-KING, AND I HAVE THE DIVINE RIGHT TO RULE!

IN A MONARCHY, IT IS ASSUMED THAT THE HEAD OF STATE (AKA THE KING) HAS ABSOLUTE POWER AND DOES NOT HAVE TO ABIDE BY ANY RULE OF LAW.

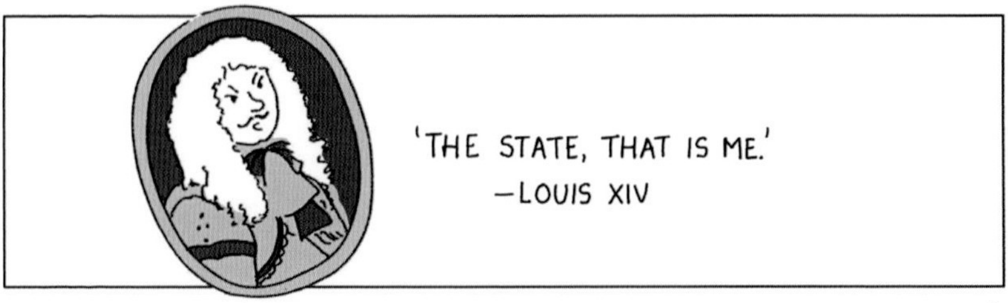
'THE STATE, THAT IS ME.'
—LOUIS XIV

OVER THE CENTURIES, THIS IDEA THAT THE SOVEREIGN CAN HAVE ABSOLUTE POWERS WAS CHALLENGED.

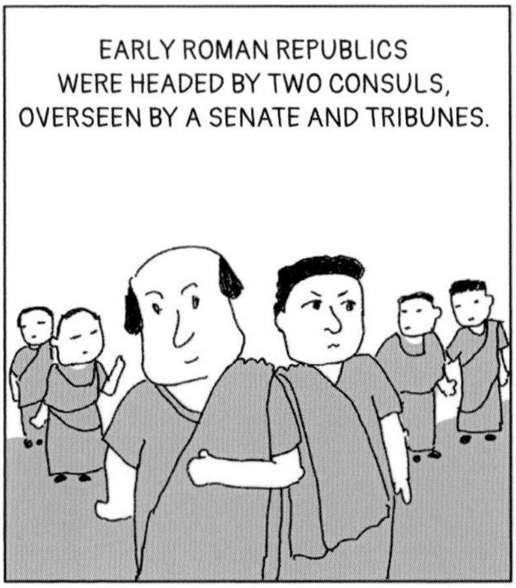
EARLY ROMAN REPUBLICS WERE HEADED BY TWO CONSULS, OVERSEEN BY A SENATE AND TRIBUNES.

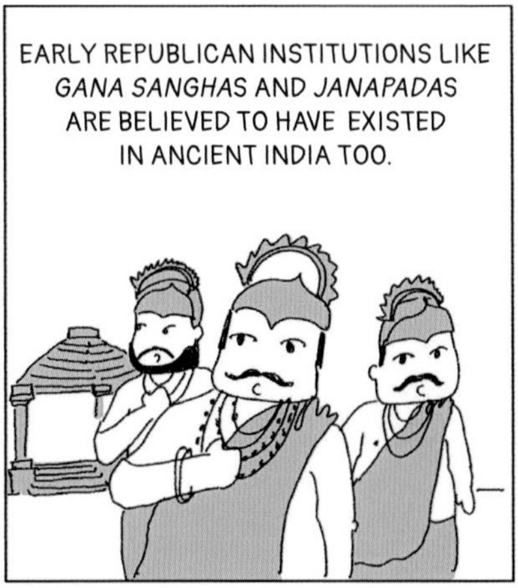
EARLY REPUBLICAN INSTITUTIONS LIKE *GANA SANGHAS* AND *JANAPADAS* ARE BELIEVED TO HAVE EXISTED IN ANCIENT INDIA TOO.

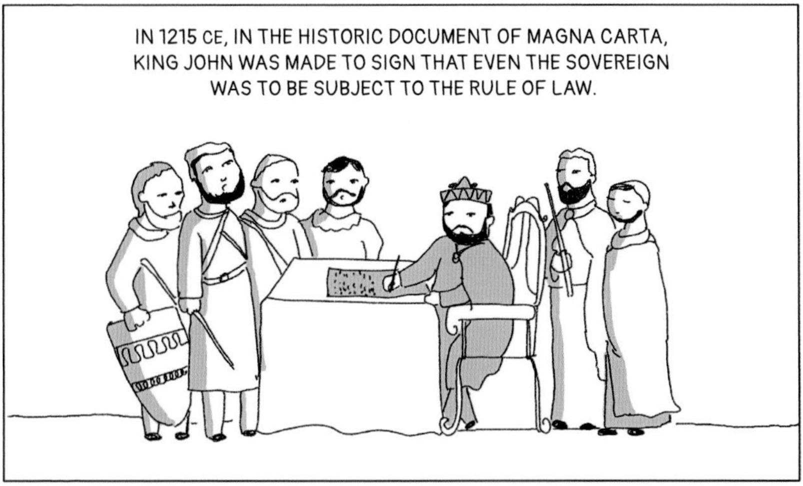
IN 1215 CE, IN THE HISTORIC DOCUMENT OF MAGNA CARTA, KING JOHN WAS MADE TO SIGN THAT EVEN THE SOVEREIGN WAS TO BE SUBJECT TO THE RULE OF LAW.

LATER, IT BECAME THE BASIS OF THE UNIVERSAL DECLARATION OF HUMAN RIGHTS AND SEVERAL CONSTITUTIONS.

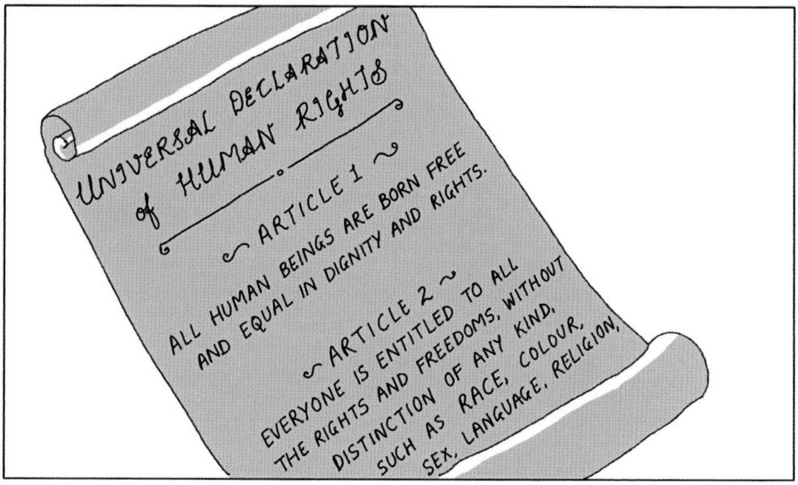
UNIVERSAL DECLARATION of HUMAN RIGHTS
ARTICLE 1
ALL HUMAN BEINGS ARE BORN FREE AND EQUAL IN DIGNITY AND RIGHTS.
ARTICLE 2
EVERYONE IS ENTITLED TO ALL THE RIGHTS AND FREEDOMS, WITHOUT DISTINCTION OF ANY KIND, SUCH AS RACE, COLOUR, SEX, LANGUAGE, RELIGION,

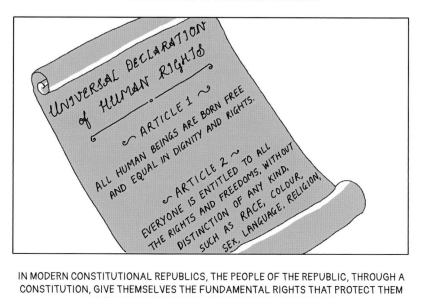

IN MODERN CONSTITUTIONAL REPUBLICS, THE PEOPLE OF THE REPUBLIC, THROUGH A CONSTITUTION, GIVE THEMSELVES THE FUNDAMENTAL RIGHTS THAT PROTECT THEM AND PLACE RESTRICTIONS ON THE POWER OF THE STATE.

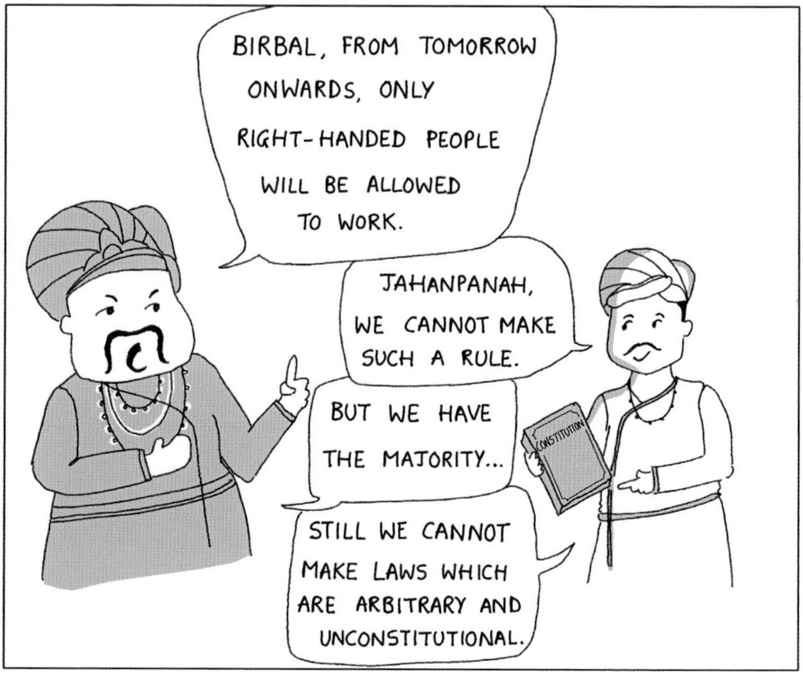
BIRBAL, FROM TOMORROW ONWARDS, ONLY RIGHT-HANDED PEOPLE WILL BE ALLOWED TO WORK.
JAHANPANAH, WE CANNOT MAKE SUCH A RULE.
CONSTITUTION
BUT WE HAVE THE MAJORITY...
STILL WE CANNOT MAKE LAWS WHICH ARE ARBITRARY AND UNCONSTITUTIONAL.

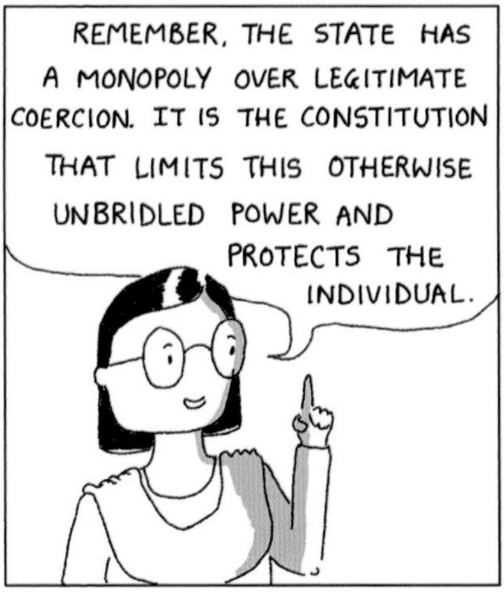
REMEMBER, THE STATE HAS A MONOPOLY OVER LEGITIMATE COERCION. IT IS THE CONSTITUTION THAT LIMITS THIS OTHERWISE UNBRIDLED POWER AND PROTECTS THE INDIVIDUAL.

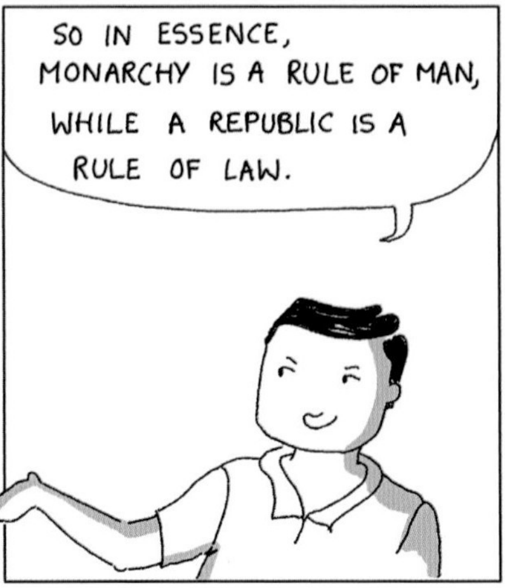
SO IN ESSENCE, MONARCHY IS A RULE OF MAN, WHILE A REPUBLIC IS A RULE OF LAW.

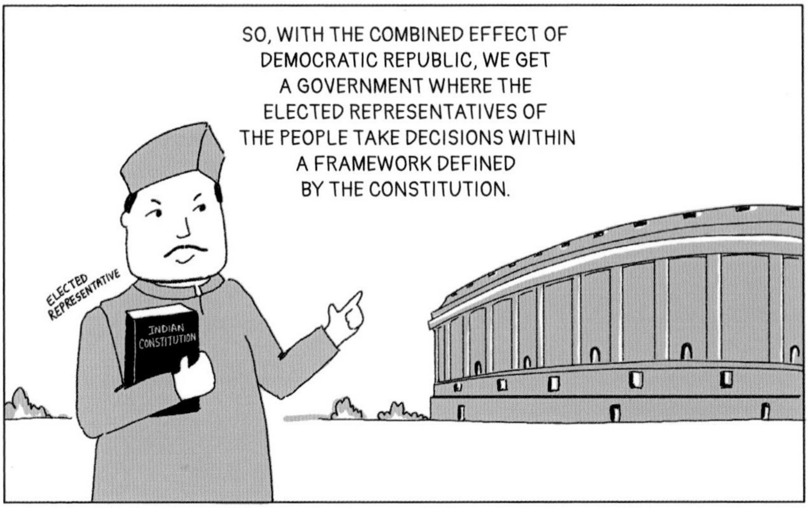
SO, WITH THE COMBINED EFFECT OF DEMOCRATIC REPUBLIC, WE GET A GOVERNMENT WHERE THE ELECTED REPRESENTATIVES OF THE PEOPLE TAKE DECISIONS WITHIN A FRAMEWORK DEFINED BY THE CONSTITUTION.
ELECTED REPRESENTATIVE
INDIAN CONSTITUTION

BUT LET'S NOT MAKE THE MISTAKE OF THINKING OF THE INDIAN CONSTITUTION AS JUST A RULE BOOK.

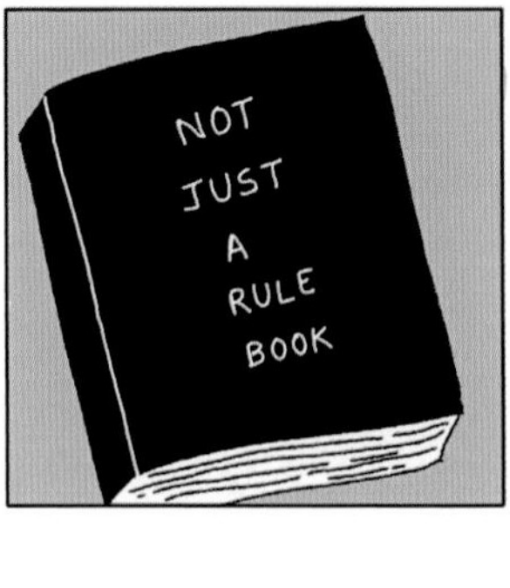
NOT JUST A RULE BOOK

EVEN THOUGH INDIA WAS A DEEPLY HIERARCHICAL SOCIETY,
THE INDIAN CONSTITUTION PROMISED EQUAL FUNDAMENTAL RIGHTS
TO ALL ITS PEOPLE, RIGHT AT THE OUTSET.

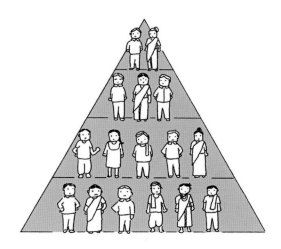

TO ADOPT UNIVERSAL SUFFRAGE IRRESPECTIVE OF CASTE, GENDER, RELIGION
AND RACE WAS NOTHING SHORT OF A REVOLUTION.

WOMEN   SCHEDULED CASTES   RELIGIOUS   ETHNIC
          SCHEDULED TRIBES   MINORITIES   MINORITIES

TO GET A BETTER PERSPECTIVE, COMPARE THIS.

USA, THE OLDEST DEMOCRACY IN THE WORLD, REMOVED THE RACIAL BARRIER TO VOTING ONLY IN 1965.

I HAVE A DREAM...

DR MARTIN LUTHER KING JR, 1963 SPEECH.

WOMEN IN SWITZERLAND GAINED VOTING RIGHTS ONLY IN 1971.

HMM... OUR FOUNDING FATHERS WERE THINKING QUITE AHEAD OF THEIR TIME.

DON'T FORGET, WE HAD 15 FOUNDING MOTHERS TOO AS MEMBERS OF OUR CONSTITUENT ASSEMBLY.

VIJAYA LAKSHMI PANDIT
SUCHETA KRIPLANI
SAROJINI NAIDU
RENUKA RAY
AMRIT KAUR
RAJKUMARI
PURNIMA BANERJEE
MALATI CHOUDHURY
LEELA ROY
KAMLA CHAUDHARY
HANSA MEHTA
DURGABAI DESHMUKH
BEGUM AIZAZ RASUL
DAKSHAYANI VELAYUDHAN
ANNIE MASCARENE
AMMU SWAMINATHAN

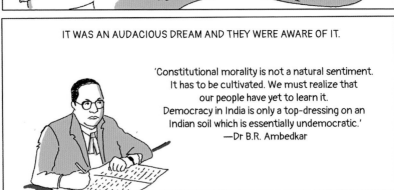

IT WAS AN AUDACIOUS DREAM AND THEY WERE AWARE OF IT.

'Constitutional morality is not a natural sentiment. It has to be cultivated. We must realize that our people have yet to learn it. Democracy in India is only a top-dressing on an Indian soil which is essentially undemocratic.'
—Dr B.R. Ambedkar

WE HAVE ACHIEVED A POLITICAL DEMOCRACY.
WE STILL HAVE A LONG WAY TO GO BEFORE WE ACHIEVE TRUE SOCIAL DEMOCRACY WHERE LIBERTY, EQUALITY AND FRATERNITY ARE PRACTISED IN THE TRUE SENSE.

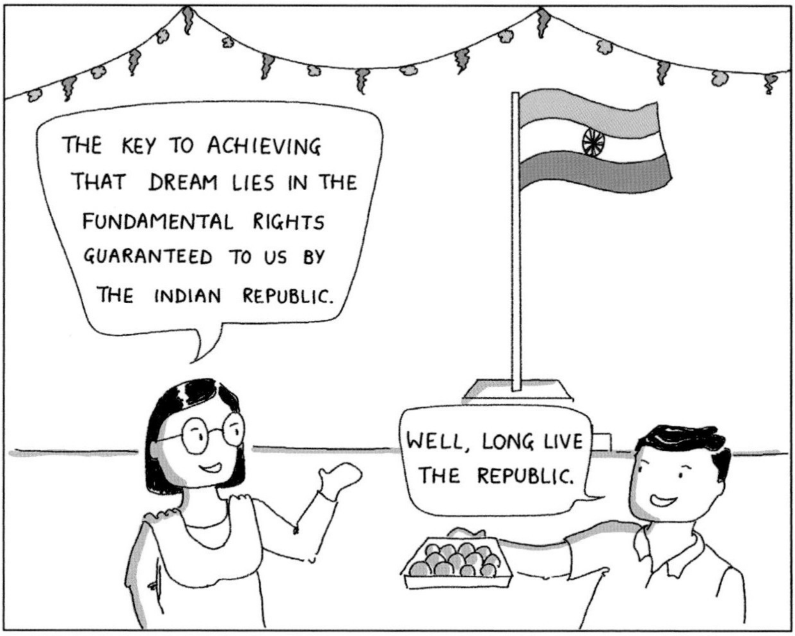
THE KEY TO ACHIEVING THAT DREAM LIES IN THE FUNDAMENTAL RIGHTS GUARANTEED TO US BY THE INDIAN REPUBLIC.
WELL, LONG LIVE THE REPUBLIC.

Chapter 2

Much Like Football Fan Clubs

Nations and States

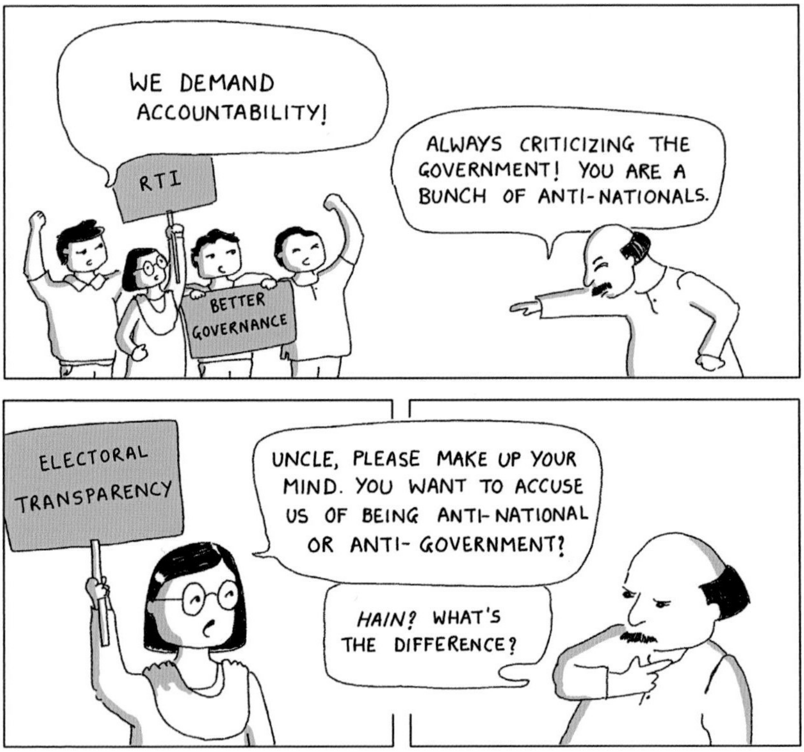

WE DEMAND ACCOUNTABILITY!
RTI
BETTER GOVERNANCE
ALWAYS CRITICIZING THE GOVERNMENT! YOU ARE A BUNCH OF ANTI-NATIONALS.
ELECTORAL TRANSPARENCY
UNCLE, PLEASE MAKE UP YOUR MIND. YOU WANT TO ACCUSE US OF BEING ANTI-NATIONAL OR ANTI-GOVERNMENT?
HAIN? WHAT'S THE DIFFERENCE?

NATIONS AND GOVERNMENTS ARE TWO VERY DIFFERENT CONCEPTS.
IT IS VERY HARD TO DEFINE WHAT MAKES A NATION. THINK ABOUT THIS. . .

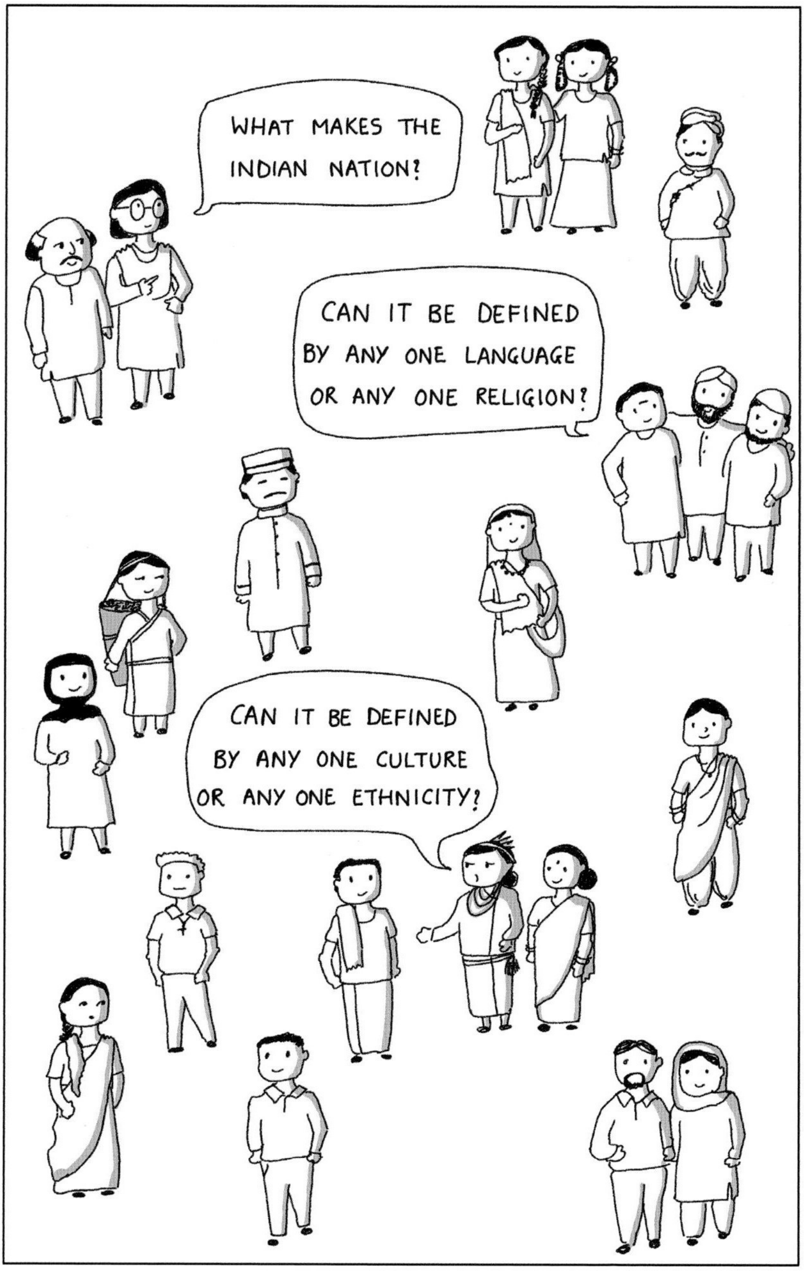
WHAT MAKES THE INDIAN NATION?
CAN IT BE DEFINED BY ANY ONE LANGUAGE OR ANY ONE RELIGION?
CAN IT BE DEFINED BY ANY ONE CULTURE OR ANY ONE ETHNICITY?

POLITICAL SCIENTIST BENEDICT ANDERSON DEFINES NATIONS AS 'IMAGINED COMMUNITIES'—THEY ARE IMAGINED BECAUSE THE MEMBERS OF A NATION WILL NEVER KNOW ALL THE OTHER MEMBERS, BUT STILL FEEL A KINSHIP WITH THEM.

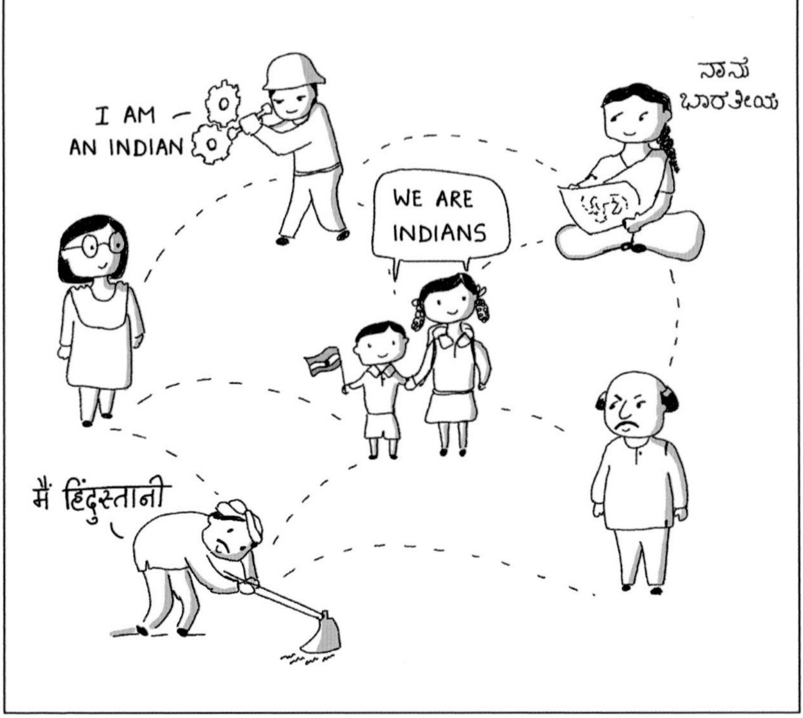
I AM AN INDIAN
ನಾನು ಭಾರತೀಯ
WE ARE INDIANS
मैं हिंदुस्तानी

NATIONS MAY BE IMAGINED, BUT THEY ARE NOT IMAGINARY. NATIONHOOD IS A REAL SENTIMENT FOR WHICH PEOPLE ARE READY TO MAKE GREAT SACRIFICES.

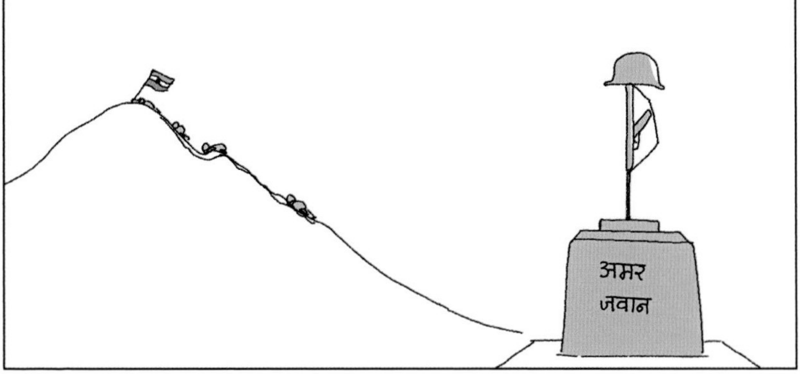
अमर
जवान

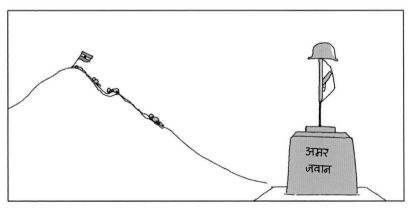

AT THE SAME TIME, ANY STRICT CRITERION FOR NATIONHOOD IS HARD TO DEFINE.

NATIONS ARE LIKE LARGE AND INTENSE VERSIONS OF FOOTBALL FAN CLUBS.

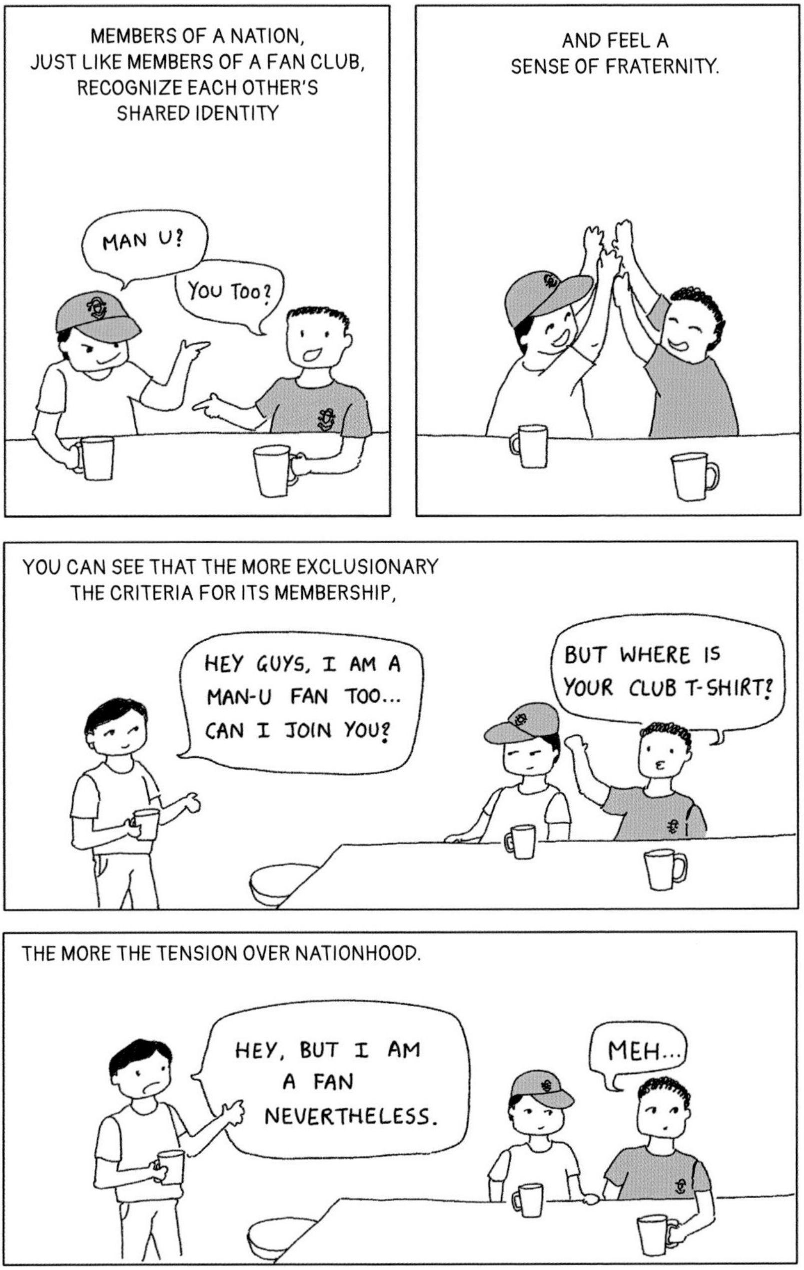
MEMBERS OF A NATION, JUST LIKE MEMBERS OF A FAN CLUB, RECOGNIZE EACH OTHER'S SHARED IDENTITY
MAN U?
YOU TOO?
AND FEEL A SENSE OF FRATERNITY.
YOU CAN SEE THAT THE MORE EXCLUSIONARY THE CRITERIA FOR ITS MEMBERSHIP,
HEY GUYS, I AM A MAN-U FAN TOO... CAN I JOIN YOU?
BUT WHERE IS YOUR CLUB T-SHIRT?
THE MORE THE TENSION OVER NATIONHOOD.
HEY, BUT I AM A FAN NEVERTHELESS.
MEH...

ALSO, SUB-NATIONS CAN AND OFTEN DO EXIST WITHIN A NATION.

THE STATE, ON THE OTHER HAND, IS A POLITICAL ENTITY.

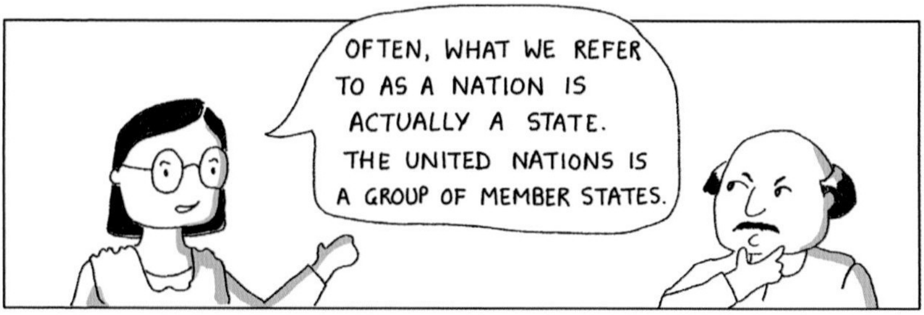
OFTEN, WHAT WE REFER TO AS A NATION IS ACTUALLY A STATE. THE UNITED NATIONS IS A GROUP OF MEMBER STATES.

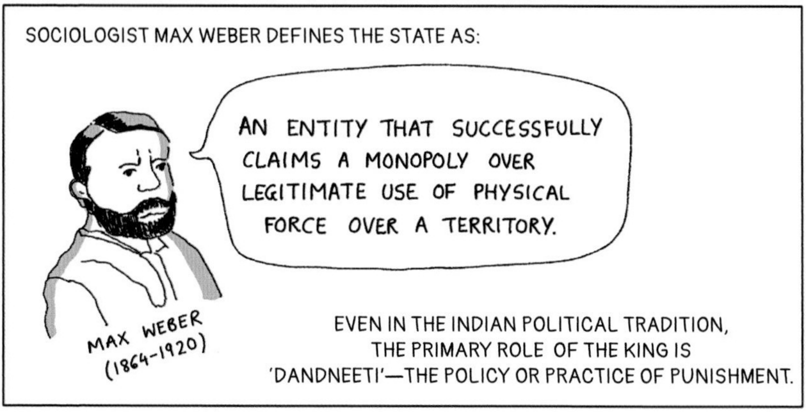
SOCIOLOGIST MAX WEBER DEFINES THE STATE AS:
AN ENTITY THAT SUCCESSFULLY CLAIMS A MONOPOLY OVER LEGITIMATE USE OF PHYSICAL FORCE OVER A TERRITORY.
MAX WEBER (1864-1920)
EVEN IN THE INDIAN POLITICAL TRADITION, THE PRIMARY ROLE OF THE KING IS 'DANDNEETI'—THE POLICY OR PRACTICE OF PUNISHMENT.

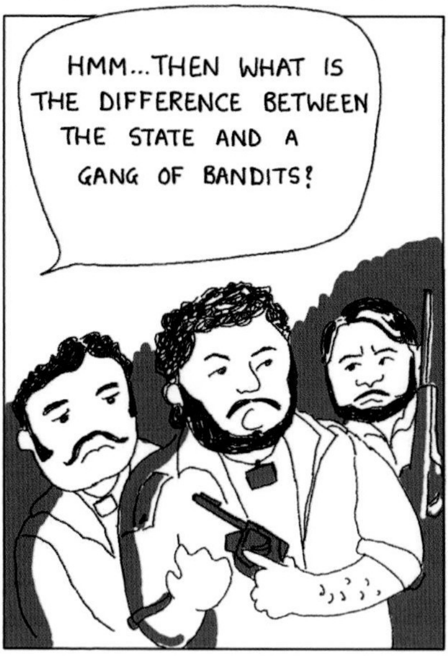
HMM... THEN WHAT IS THE DIFFERENCE BETWEEN THE STATE AND A GANG OF BANDITS?

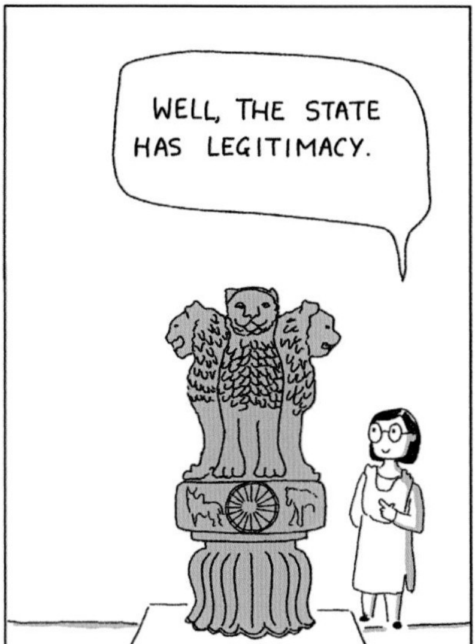
WELL, THE STATE HAS LEGITIMACY.

THE STATE DERIVES ITS LEGITIMACY FROM THIS TERM CALLED 'THE SOCIAL CONTRACT'. THE IDEA IS THIS— IN THE ABSENCE OF A POWERFUL STATE, WE ARE IN A STATE OF NATURE.

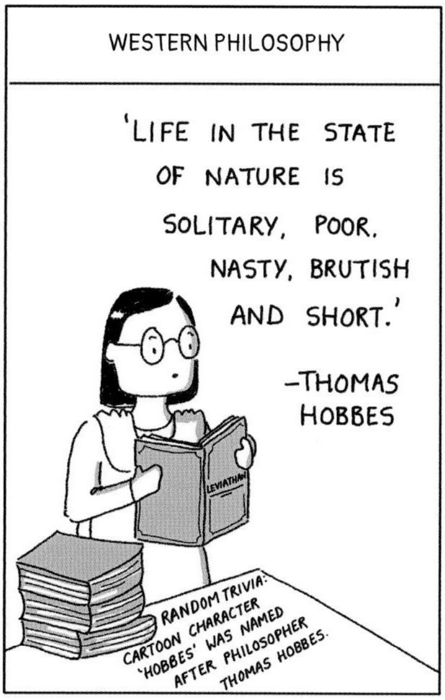
WESTERN PHILOSOPHY
'LIFE IN THE STATE OF NATURE IS SOLITARY, POOR, NASTY, BRUTISH AND SHORT.'
–THOMAS HOBBES
LEVIATHAN
RANDOM TRIVIA: CARTOON CHARACTER 'HOBBES' WAS NAMED AFTER PHILOSOPHER THOMAS HOBBES.

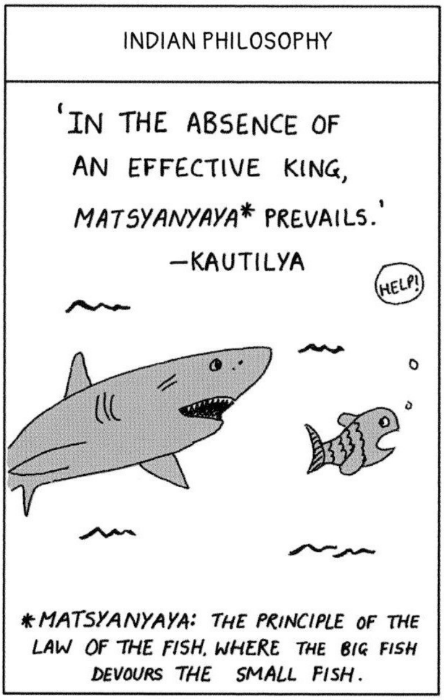
INDIAN PHILOSOPHY
'IN THE ABSENCE OF AN EFFECTIVE KING, *MATSYANYAYA** PREVAILS.'
—KAUTILYA
HELP!
**MATSYANYAYA*: THE PRINCIPLE OF THE LAW OF THE FISH, WHERE THE BIG FISH DEVOURS THE SMALL FISH.

AND SO, INDIVIDUALS ENTER INTO A (TACIT) CONTRACT WITH THE STATE, SUBMITTING SOME OF THEIR FREEDOMS IN RETURN FOR SECURITY AND PROTECTION OF THEIR REMAINING FREEDOMS.

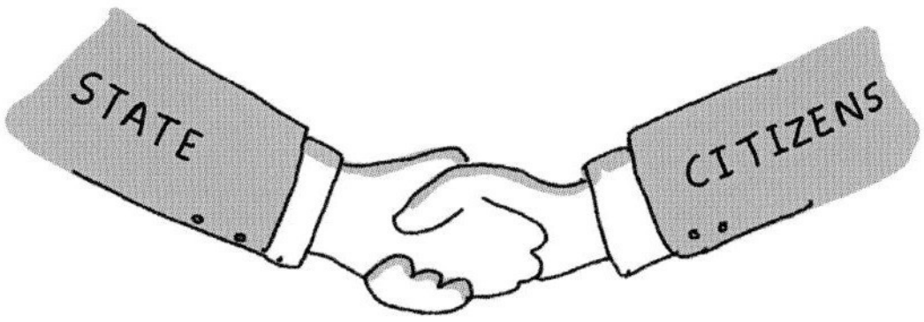
STATE
CITIZENS

'THE PURPOSE OF SOCIAL CONTRACT IS TO PROTECT THE NATURAL RIGHTS OF CITIZENS SUCH AS LIFE, LIBERTY AND PROPERTY.'

—JOHN LOCKE

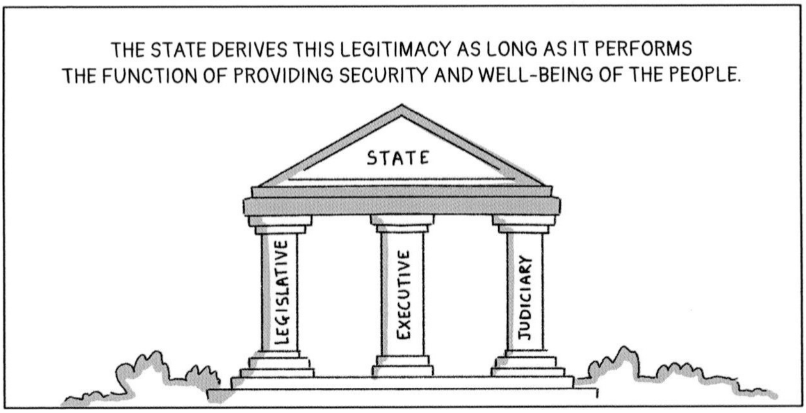
THE STATE DERIVES THIS LEGITIMACY AS LONG AS IT PERFORMS THE FUNCTION OF PROVIDING SECURITY AND WELL-BEING OF THE PEOPLE.
STATE
LEGISLATIVE
EXECUTIVE
JUDICIARY

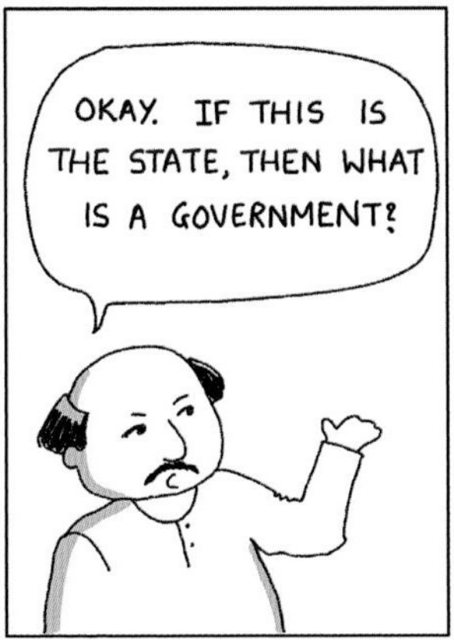
OKAY. IF THIS IS THE STATE, THEN WHAT IS A GOVERNMENT?

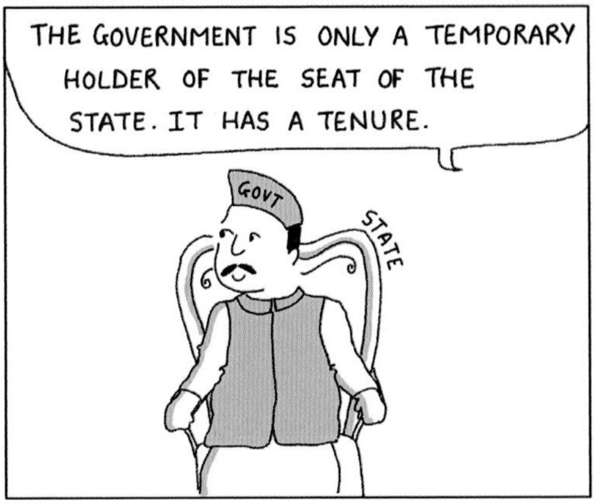
THE GOVERNMENT IS ONLY A TEMPORARY HOLDER OF THE SEAT OF THE STATE. IT HAS A TENURE.
GOVT
STATE

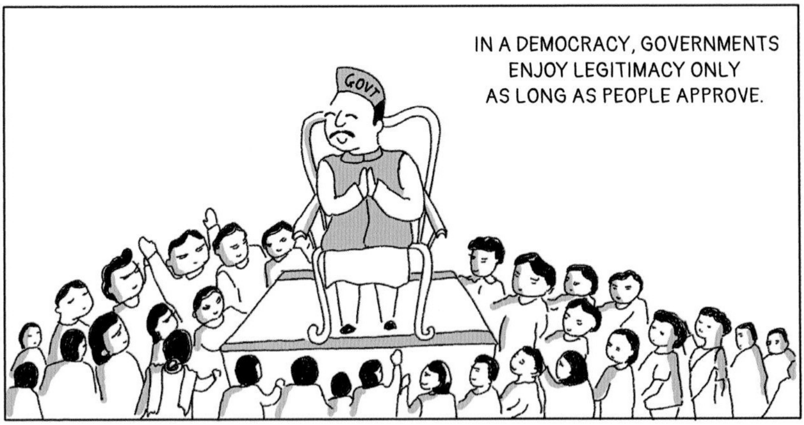
IN A DEMOCRACY, GOVERNMENTS ENJOY LEGITIMACY ONLY AS LONG AS PEOPLE APPROVE.
GOVT

CRITICISM OF THE GOVERNMENT IS A LEGITIMATE TOOL FOR CITIZENS TO NEGOTIATE THEIR OWN FREEDOMS AND DEMANDS IN THE TACIT 'SOCIAL CONTRACT'.

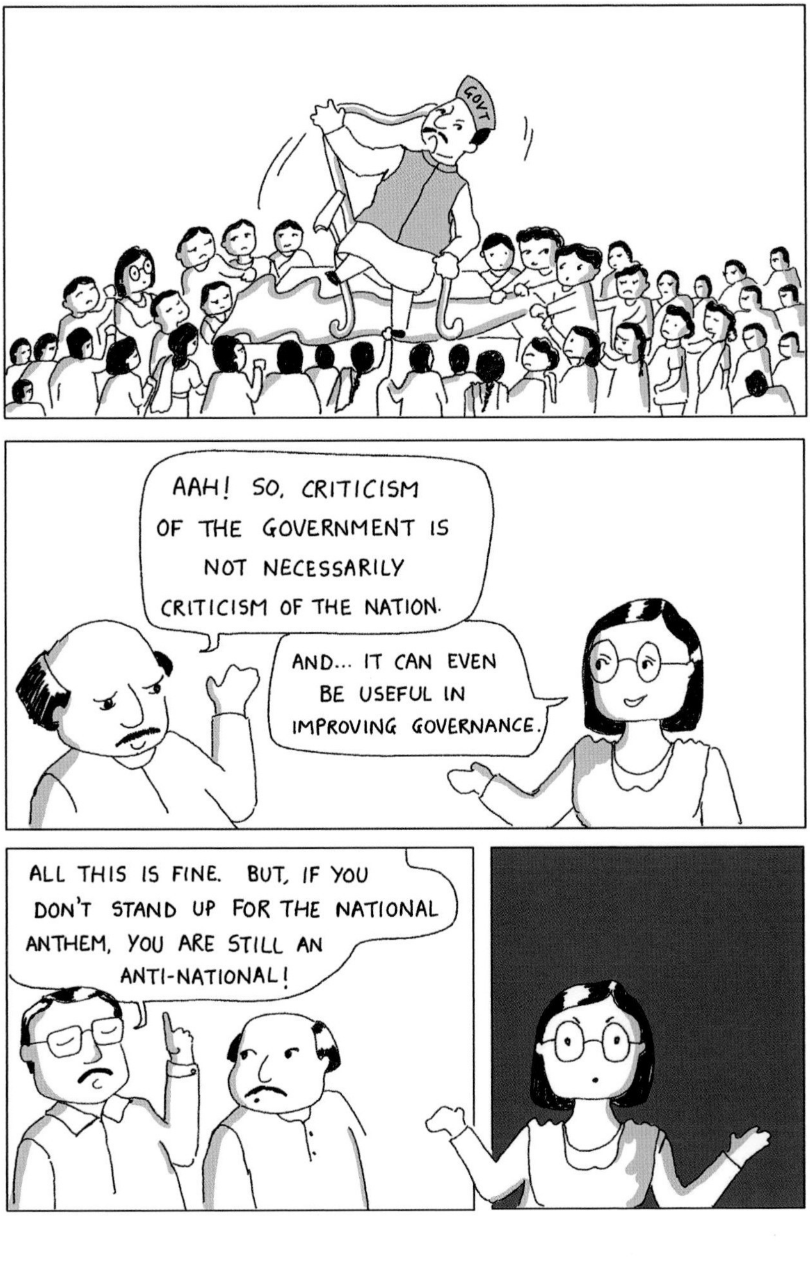
GOVT
AAH! SO, CRITICISM OF THE GOVERNMENT IS NOT NECESSARILY CRITICISM OF THE NATION.
AND... IT CAN EVEN BE USEFUL IN IMPROVING GOVERNANCE.
ALL THIS IS FINE. BUT, IF YOU DON'T STAND UP FOR THE NATIONAL ANTHEM, YOU ARE STILL AN ANTI-NATIONAL!

Chapter 3

Long Hands but Short Feet

Too big, yet too small

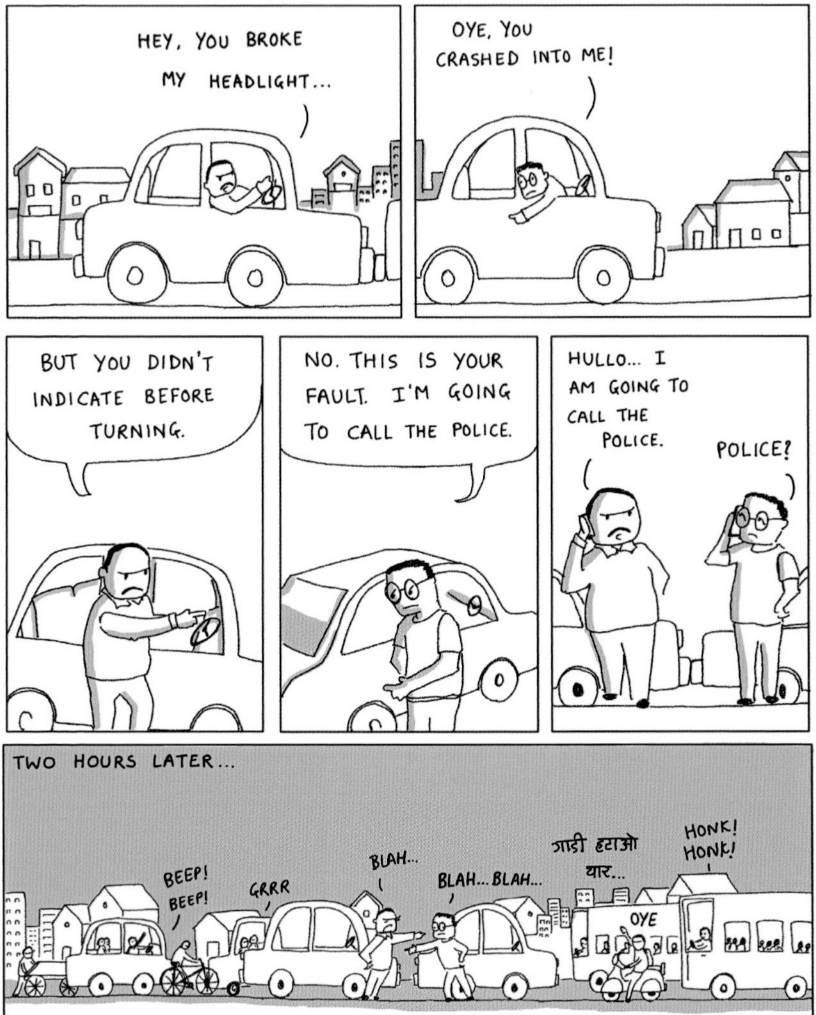
HEY, YOU BROKE MY HEADLIGHT...
OYE, YOU CRASHED INTO ME!
BUT YOU DIDN'T INDICATE BEFORE TURNING.
NO. THIS IS YOUR FAULT. I'M GOING TO CALL THE POLICE.
HULLO... I AM GOING TO CALL THE POLICE.
POLICE?
TWO HOURS LATER...
BEEP! BEEP!
GRRR
BLAH...
BLAH... BLAH...
गाड़ी हटाओ यार...
OYE
HONK! HONK!
POLICE NOWHERE TO BE SEEN!

THIS IS OUR EXPERIENCE OF THE INDIAN STATE.
THE MOMENT WE NEED IT THE MOST, IT GOES MISSING.

THE POPULAR PERCEPTION IS THAT THE INDIAN STATE IS OVERSTAFFED WITH INEFFICIENT GOVERNMENT EMPLOYEES.

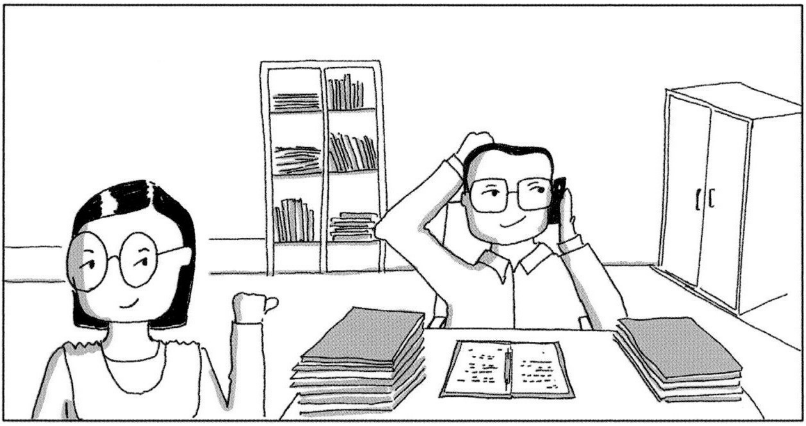

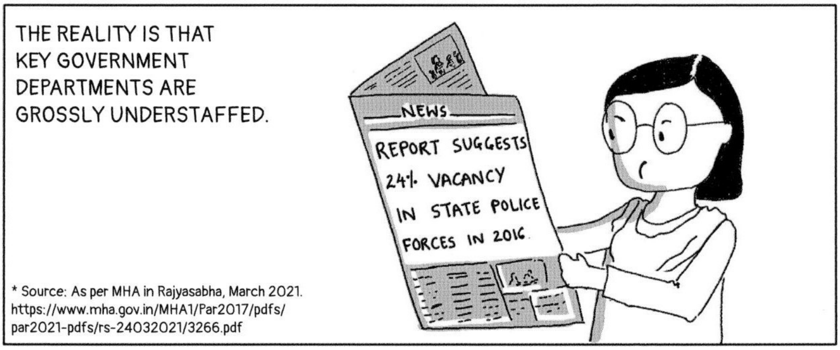
THE REALITY IS THAT KEY GOVERNMENT DEPARTMENTS ARE GROSSLY UNDERSTAFFED.
NEWS
REPORT SUGGESTS 24% VACANCY IN STATE POLICE FORCES IN 2016
* Source: As per MHA in Rajyasabha, March 2021. https://www.mha.gov.in/MHA1/Par2017/pdfs/par2021-pdfs/rs-24032021/3266.pdf

WHILE THE UNITED NATIONS RECOMMENDS 222 POLICE PER LAKH PERSONS, INDIA'S ACTUAL POLICE STRENGTH IS JUST 155.78 POLICE PER LAKH PERSONS.*

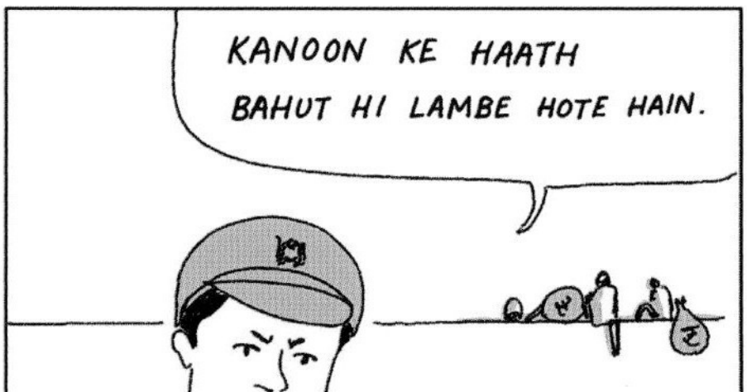
KANOON KE HAATH BAHUT HI LAMBE HOTE HAIN.

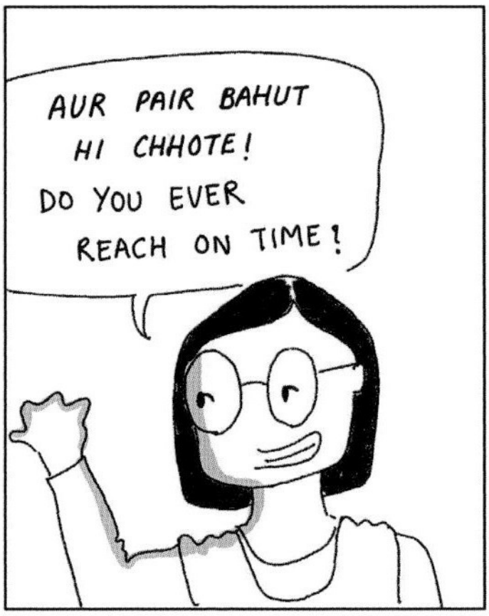
AUR PAIR BAHUT HI CHHOTE! DO YOU EVER REACH ON TIME?

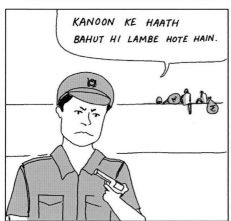

THE INDIAN STATE IS SMALL AS MEASURED BY THE NUMBER OF GOVERNMENT EMPLOYEES.

IT IS ALSO RELATIVELY SMALL WHEN MEASURED BY PUBLIC EXPENDITURE.

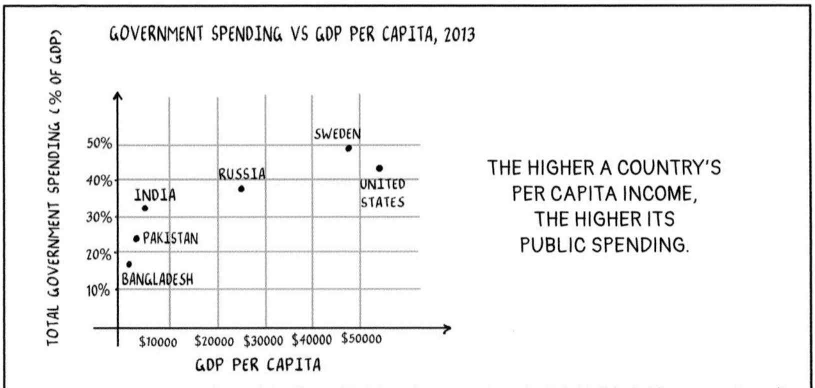
GOVERNMENT SPENDING VS GDP PER CAPITA, 2013
TOTAL GOVERNMENT SPENDING (% OF GDP)
50%
40%
30%
20%
10%
SWEDEN
RUSSIA
UNITED STATES
INDIA
PAKISTAN
BANGLADESH
$10000 $20000 $30000 $40000 $50000
GDP PER CAPITA
THE HIGHER A COUNTRY'S PER CAPITA INCOME, THE HIGHER ITS PUBLIC SPENDING.
Source: https://ourworldindata.org/government-spending#what-is-linked-with-government-spending

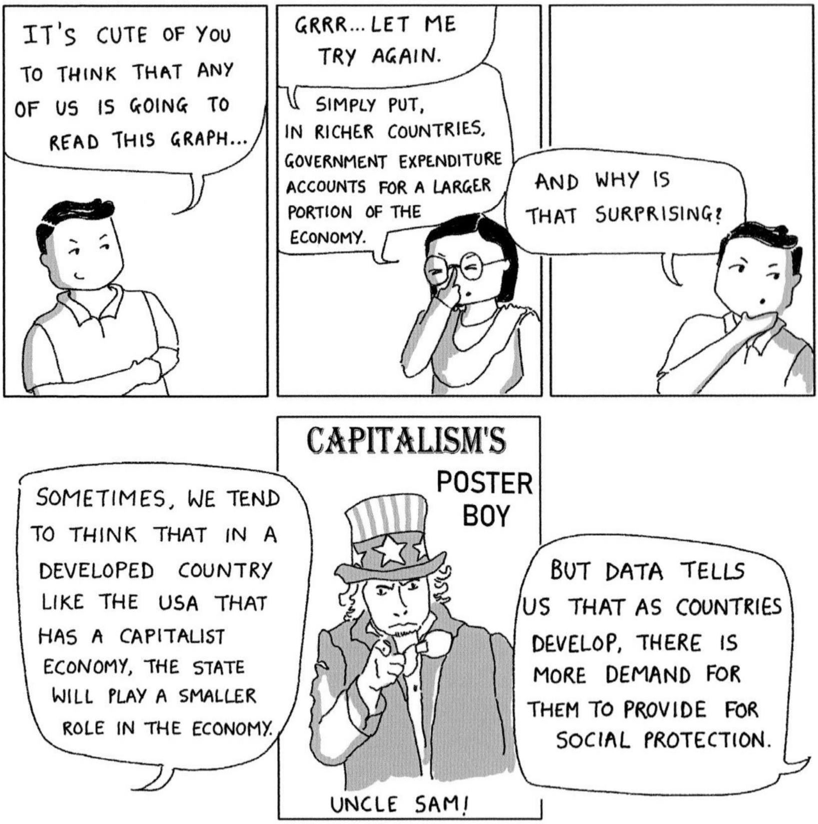
IT'S CUTE OF YOU TO THINK THAT ANY OF US IS GOING TO READ THIS GRAPH...
GRRR... LET ME TRY AGAIN.
SIMPLY PUT, IN RICHER COUNTRIES, GOVERNMENT EXPENDITURE ACCOUNTS FOR A LARGER PORTION OF THE ECONOMY.
AND WHY IS THAT SURPRISING?
SOMETIMES, WE TEND TO THINK THAT IN A DEVELOPED COUNTRY LIKE THE USA THAT HAS A CAPITALIST ECONOMY, THE STATE WILL PLAY A SMALLER ROLE IN THE ECONOMY.
CAPITALISM'S
POSTER BOY
UNCLE SAM!
BUT DATA TELLS US THAT AS COUNTRIES DEVELOP, THERE IS MORE DEMAND FOR THEM TO PROVIDE FOR SOCIAL PROTECTION.

THE STATE IS NOT ABSENT, BUT ACTUALLY PLAYS A
BIGGER ROLE IN FEWER AREAS AND DOES THEM WELL.

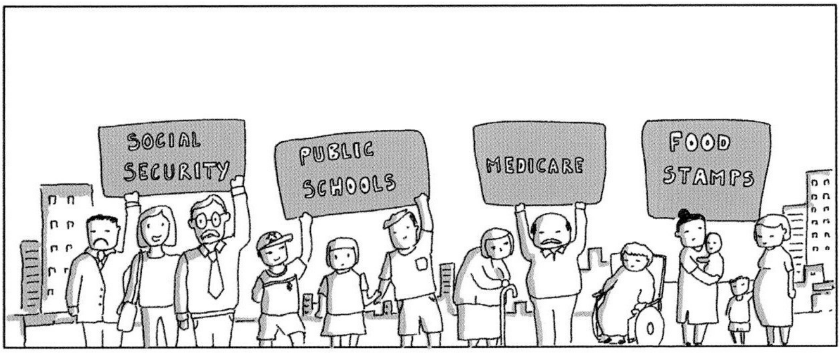
SOCIAL SECURITY
PUBLIC SCHOOLS
MEDICARE
FOOD STAMPS

ON THE OTHER HAND, THE INDIAN STATE, WHICH HAS LESSER
INCOME AND HENCE LESSER MONEY TO SPEND, IS ALSO THINLY SPREAD OUT ACROSS
SUNDRY DEPARTMENTS AND A LONG LIST OF PUBLIC-SECTOR UNITS (PSUs).

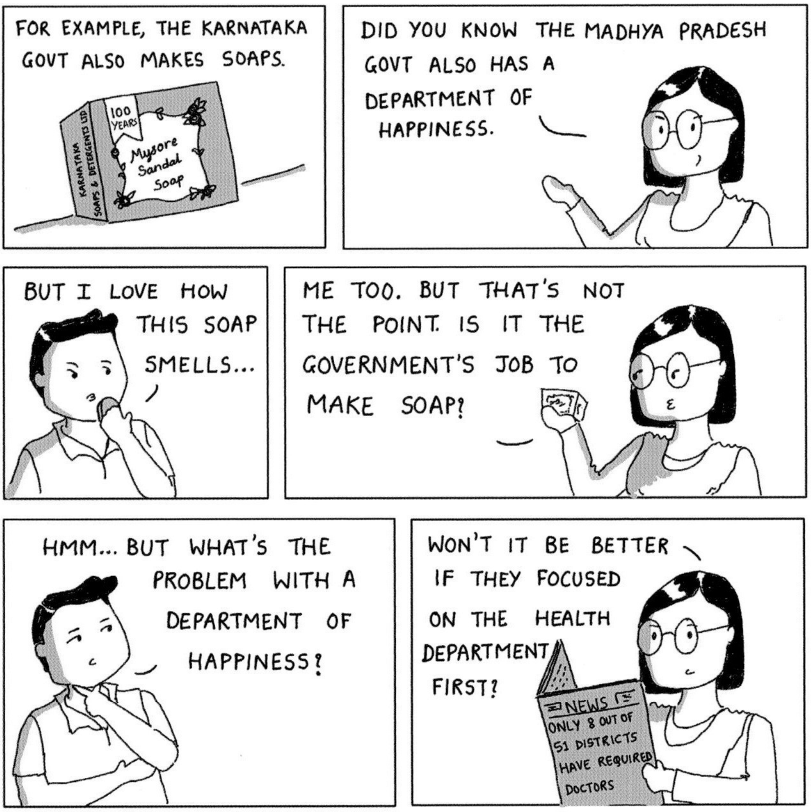
FOR EXAMPLE, THE KARNATAKA GOVT ALSO MAKES SOAPS.
100 YEARS
Mysore Sandal Soap
KARNATAKA SOAPS & DETERGENTS LTD
DID YOU KNOW THE MADHYA PRADESH GOVT ALSO HAS A DEPARTMENT OF HAPPINESS.
BUT I LOVE HOW THIS SOAP SMELLS...
ME TOO. BUT THAT'S NOT THE POINT. IS IT THE GOVERNMENT'S JOB TO MAKE SOAP?
HMM... BUT WHAT'S THE PROBLEM WITH A DEPARTMENT OF HAPPINESS?
WON'T IT BE BETTER IF THEY FOCUSED ON THE HEALTH DEPARTMENT FIRST?
NEWS
ONLY 8 OUT OF 51 DISTRICTS HAVE REQUIRED DOCTORS

IT IS ALSO VERY TOP-HEAVY. IT HAS MORE EMPLOYEES AT THE CENTRE AND THE STATE LEVELS, BUT IS GROSSLY UNDERSTAFFED AT THE LOCAL LEVEL.

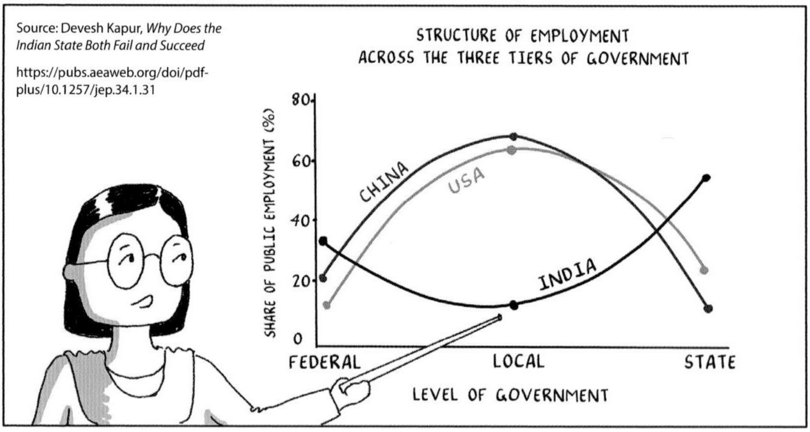
Source: Devesh Kapur, *Why Does the Indian State Both Fail and Succeed*
https://pubs.aeaweb.org/doi/pdf-plus/10.1257/jep.34.1.31
STRUCTURE OF EMPLOYMENT
ACROSS THE THREE TIERS OF GOVERNMENT
SHARE OF PUBLIC EMPLOYMENT (%)
80
60
40
20
0
CHINA
USA
INDIA
FEDERAL
LOCAL
STATE
LEVEL OF GOVERNMENT

THIS ABSENCE OF STATE CAPACITY AT THE LOCAL GOVERNMENT LEVEL IS ALL TOO APPARENT TO US.

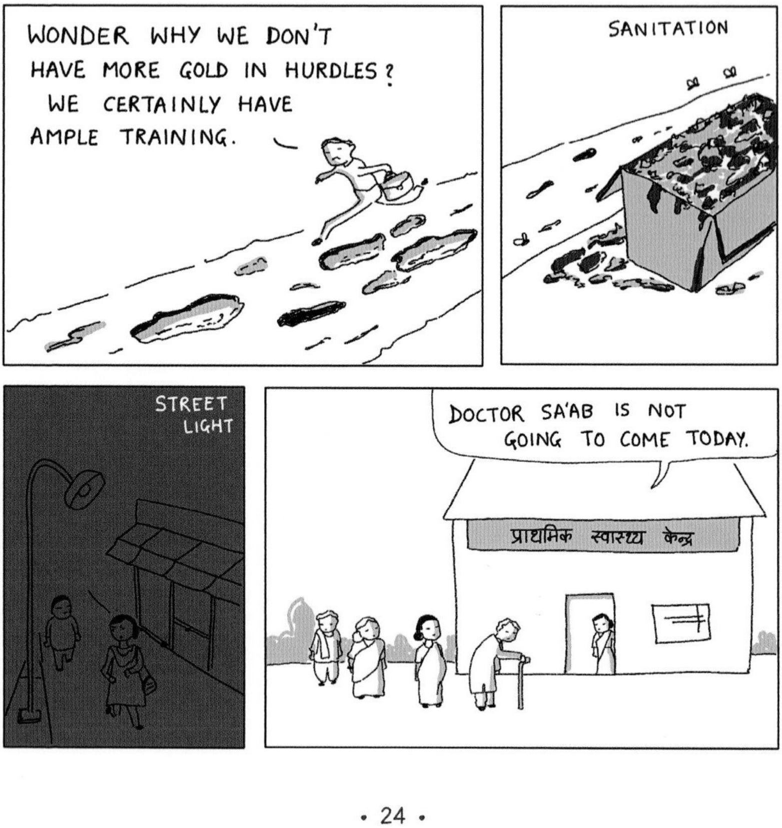
WONDER WHY WE DON'T HAVE MORE GOLD IN HURDLES? WE CERTAINLY HAVE AMPLE TRAINING.
SANITATION
STREET LIGHT
DOCTOR SA'AB IS NOT GOING TO COME TODAY.
प्राथमिक स्वास्थ्य केन्द्र

IN SPITE OF ITS LIMITATIONS IN TERMS OF PUBLIC EXPENDITURE, THE NUMBER OF EMPLOYEES AND STATE CAPACITY, THE INDIAN STATE IS QUITE BIG ON AMBITION.

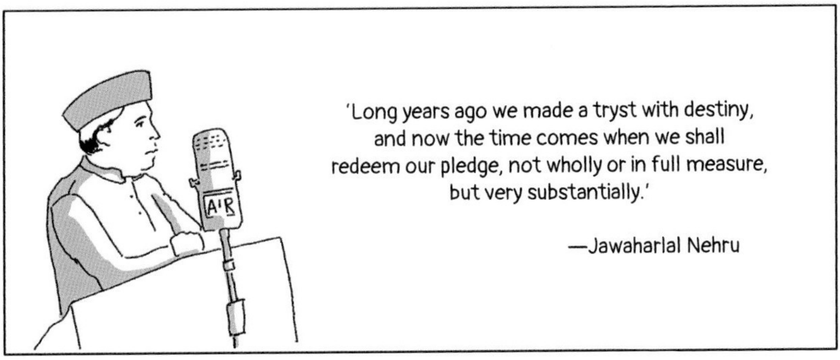
AIR
'Long years ago we made a tryst with destiny, and now the time comes when we shall redeem our pledge, not wholly or in full measure, but very substantially.'
—Jawaharlal Nehru

IN 1947, LOOKING AT THE REALITIES OF CASTE, CLASS AND RELIGION, THE INDIAN STATE CONSCIOUSLY SET OUT TO TRANSFORM THE SOCIETY—POLITICALLY, ECONOMICALLY AND SOCIALLY.

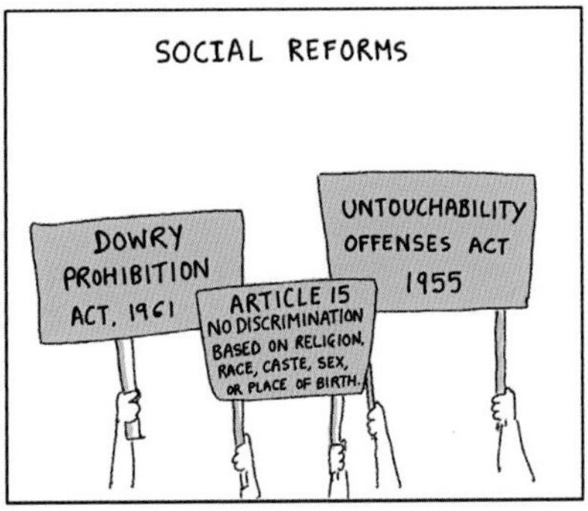
SOCIAL REFORMS
DOWRY PROHIBITION ACT, 1961
ARTICLE 15 NO DISCRIMINATION BASED ON RELIGION, RACE, CASTE, SEX, OR PLACE OF BIRTH.
UNTOUCHABILITY OFFENSES ACT 1955

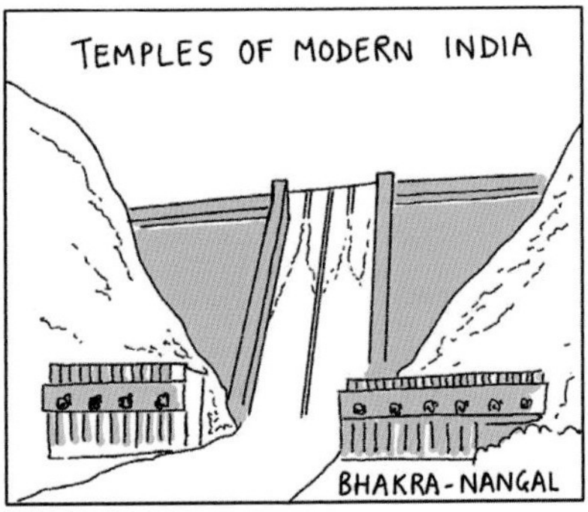
TEMPLES OF MODERN INDIA
BHAKRA-NANGAL

THIS ALSO MEANT THAT IT SET VERY LOFTY GOALS FOR ITSELF.

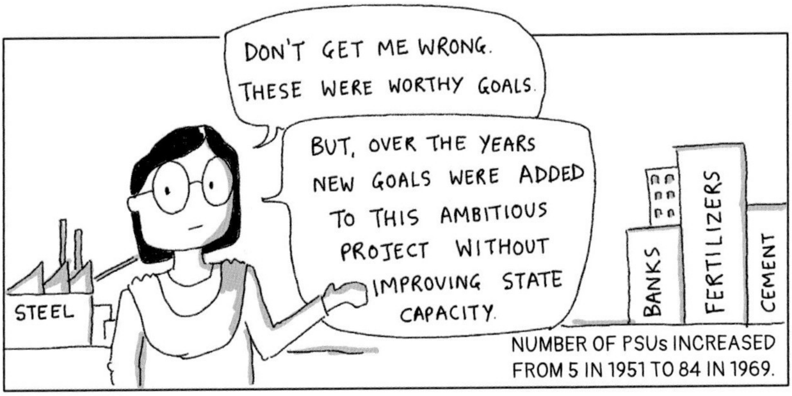
DON'T GET ME WRONG. THESE WERE WORTHY GOALS.
BUT, OVER THE YEARS NEW GOALS WERE ADDED TO THIS AMBITIOUS PROJECT WITHOUT IMPROVING STATE CAPACITY.
STEEL
BANKS
FERTILIZERS
CEMENT
NUMBER OF PSUs INCREASED FROM 5 IN 1951 TO 84 IN 1969.

ALTHOUGH WE HAVE STRONG LAWS TO DEAL WITH EVERYTHING FROM HEINOUS CRIMES TO SOCIAL REFORM, SOME OF THESE REMAIN PAPER TIGERS.

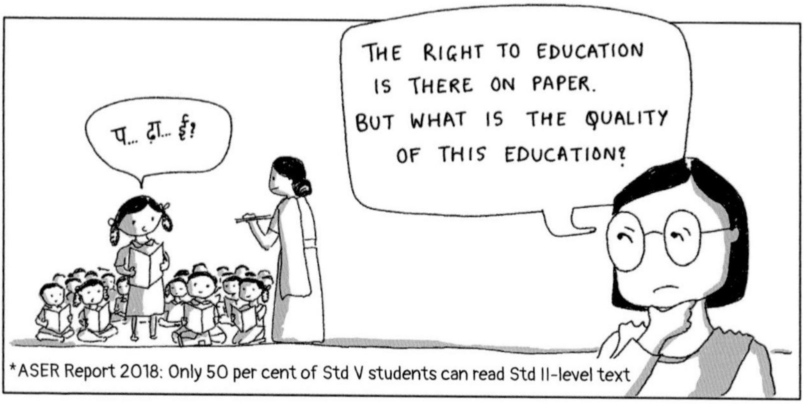
प... ढ़ा... ई?
THE RIGHT TO EDUCATION IS THERE ON PAPER. BUT WHAT IS THE QUALITY OF THIS EDUCATION?
*ASER Report 2018: Only 50 per cent of Std V students can read Std II-level text

SOME OF THESE LAWS PERMEATE INTO OUR PRIVATE LIVES, CONTROLLING US RATHER THAN GOVERNING.

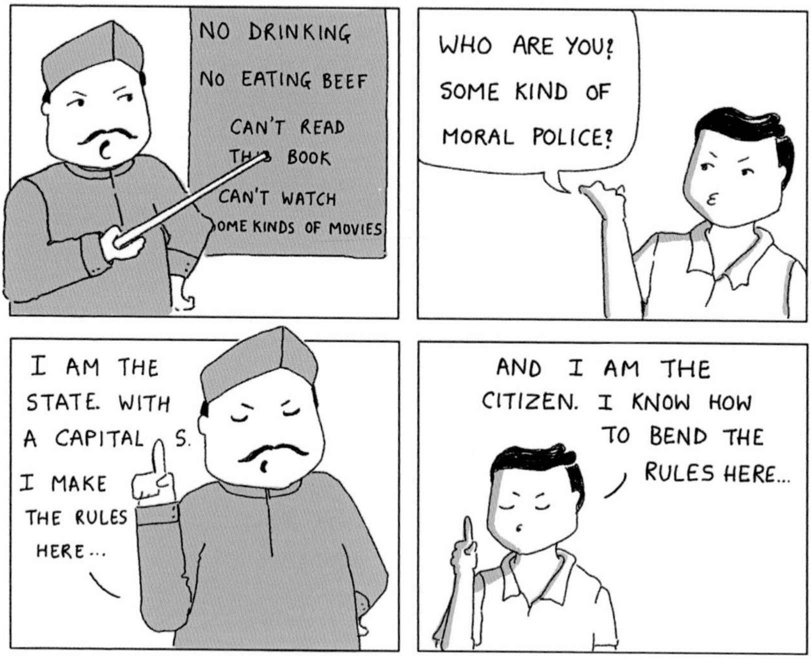
NO DRINKING
NO EATING BEEF
CAN'T READ TH BOOK
CAN'T WATCH
OME KINDS OF MOVIES
WHO ARE YOU? SOME KIND OF MORAL POLICE?
I AM THE STATE. WITH A CAPITAL S. I MAKE THE RULES HERE...
AND I AM THE CITIZEN. I KNOW HOW TO BEND THE RULES HERE...

THE PARADOX OF THE INDIAN STATE IS THAT IT IS VERY BIG IN ITS AMBITION, BUT VERY SMALL IN ITS CAPACITY TO ENFORCE THE RULES IT MAKES. RESOLVING THIS PARADOX IS THE KEY TO BETTER GOVERNANCE.

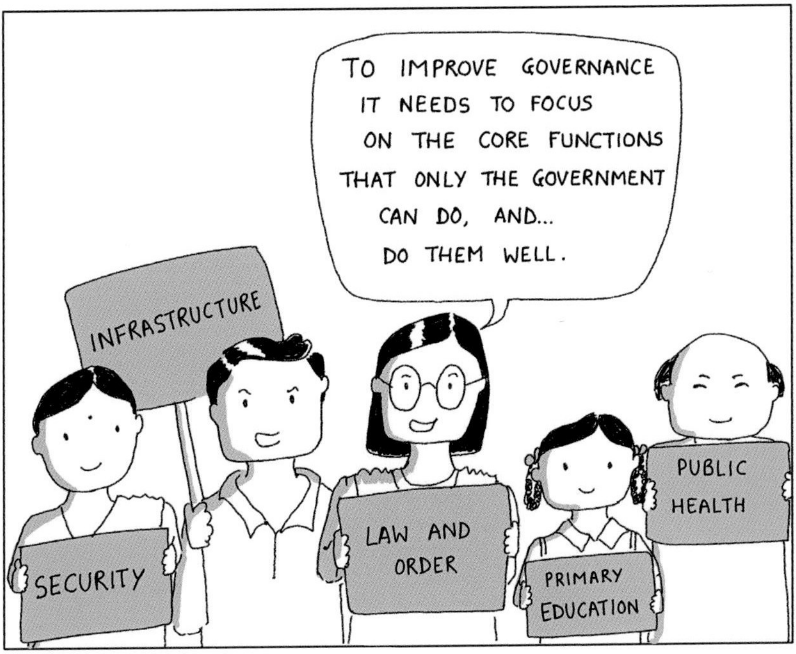
TO IMPROVE GOVERNANCE IT NEEDS TO FOCUS ON THE CORE FUNCTIONS THAT ONLY THE GOVERNMENT CAN DO, AND... DO THEM WELL.
INFRASTRUCTURE
SECURITY
LAW AND ORDER
PRIMARY EDUCATION
PUBLIC HEALTH

Chapter 4

Spontaneous Vadas Trump Planned Idlis

The invisible hand

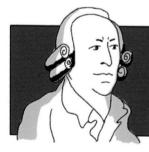

'It is not from the benevolence of the butcher,
the brewer, or the baker that we expect our dinner,
but from their regard to their own self-interest.'
—Adam Smith

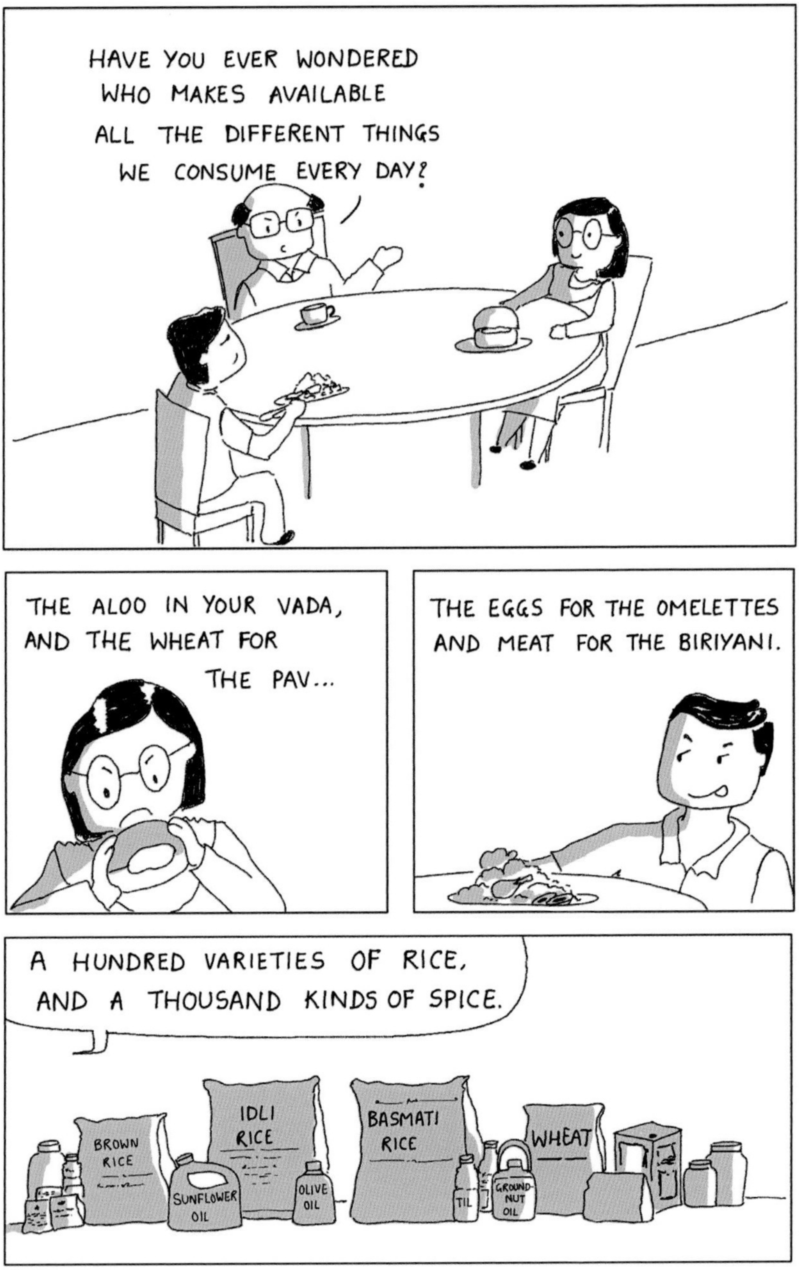
HAVE YOU EVER WONDERED WHO MAKES AVAILABLE ALL THE DIFFERENT THINGS WE CONSUME EVERY DAY?
THE ALOO IN YOUR VADA, AND THE WHEAT FOR THE PAV...
THE EGGS FOR THE OMELETTES AND MEAT FOR THE BIRIYANI.
A HUNDRED VARIETIES OF RICE, AND A THOUSAND KINDS OF SPICE.
BROWN RICE
IDLI RICE
SUNFLOWER OIL
OLIVE OIL
BASMATI RICE
TIL
GROUND-NUT OIL
WHEAT

EVERYTHING FROM A SIMPLE PEN TO HIGH-TECH GADGETS...

THERE IS NO CENTRAL PLANNER INSTRUCTING PEOPLE ON WHAT THEY SHOULD DO EACH DAY.

STILL, EVERY EVENING THE VADA-PAV WALA SETS UP HIS STALL. WHAT IS IT THAT DRIVES HIM?

I WANT TO END WORLD HUNGER!

SAID NO VADA-PAV WALA EVER.

I WANT TO SEND MY CHILDREN TO COLLEGE.

बाबू वडेवाले

#streetfood
#bestvadapav

THIS APPLIES TO EVERYONE—YOU AND ME.
EACH ONE OF US IS DRIVEN BY OUR OWN SELF-INTEREST.

THIS SYSTEM WORKS BECAUSE PEOPLE VOLUNTARILY COME TOGETHER TO EXCHANGE THEIR GOODS OR SERVICES.

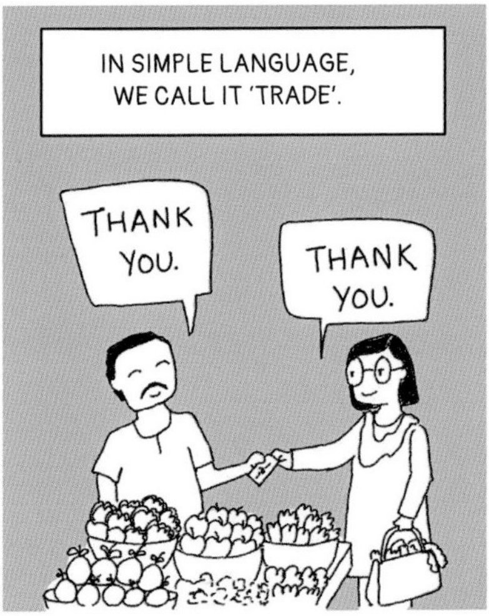
IN SIMPLE LANGUAGE, WE CALL IT 'TRADE'.
THANK YOU.
THANK YOU.

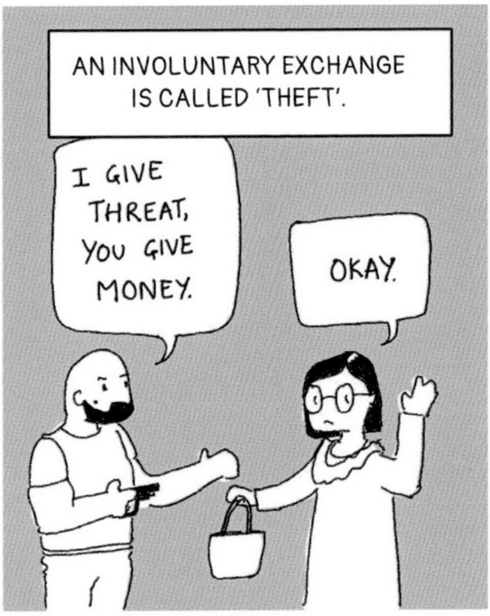
AN INVOLUNTARY EXCHANGE IS CALLED 'THEFT'.
I GIVE THREAT, YOU GIVE MONEY.
OKAY.

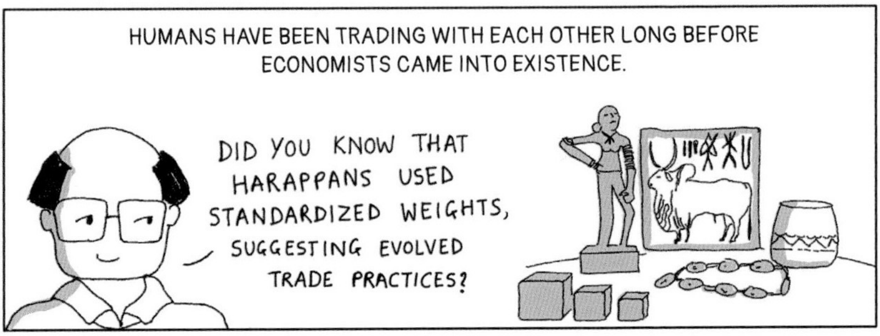
HUMANS HAVE BEEN TRADING WITH EACH OTHER LONG BEFORE ECONOMISTS CAME INTO EXISTENCE.
DID YOU KNOW THAT HARAPPANS USED STANDARDIZED WEIGHTS, SUGGESTING EVOLVED TRADE PRACTICES?

PEOPLE TRADE ONLY WHEN THEY ARE BENEFITTING FROM IT.

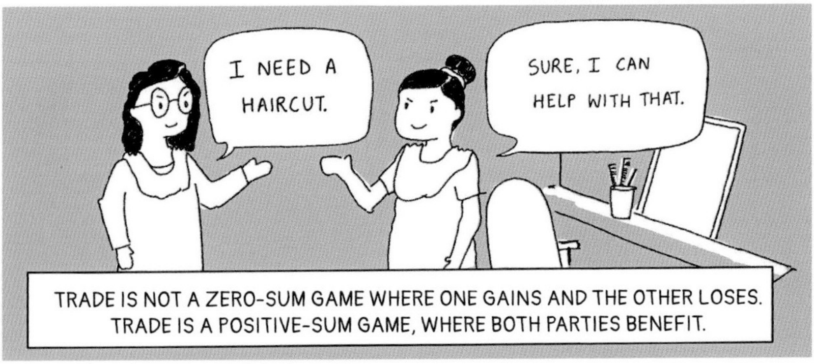
I NEED A HAIRCUT.
SURE, I CAN HELP WITH THAT.
TRADE IS NOT A ZERO-SUM GAME WHERE ONE GAINS AND THE OTHER LOSES. TRADE IS A POSITIVE-SUM GAME, WHERE BOTH PARTIES BENEFIT.

THE HAIRDRESSER VALUES THE Rs 200 MORE THAN THE TIME SPENT ON A HAIRCUT, WHILE THE CUSTOMER VALUES A SWANKY HAIRCUT MORE THAN Rs 200.

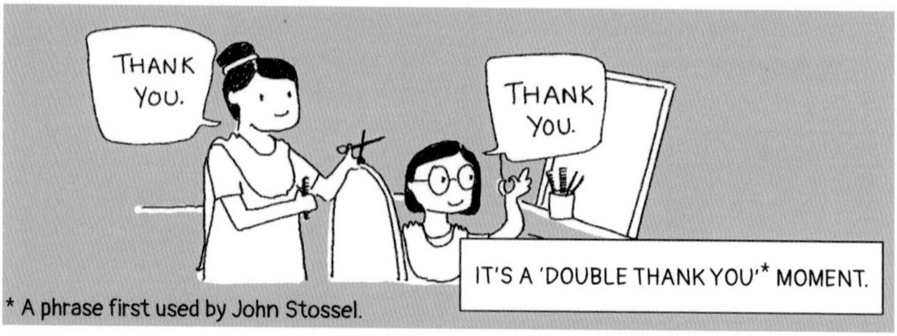
THANK YOU.
THANK YOU.
IT'S A 'DOUBLE THANK YOU'* MOMENT.
* A phrase first used by John Stossel.

TRADE ALSO LEADS TO SPECIALIZATION.

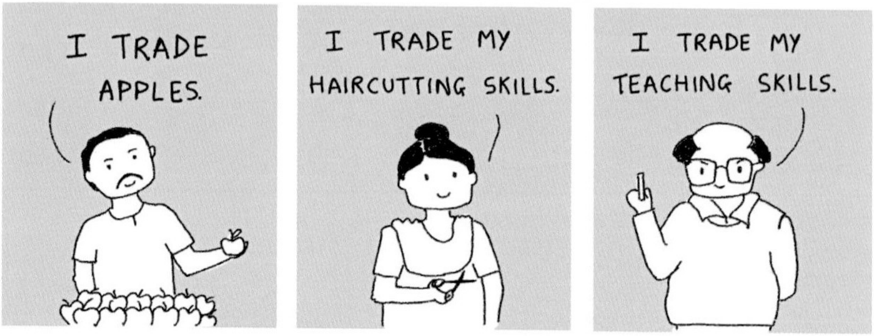
I TRADE APPLES.
I TRADE MY HAIRCUTTING SKILLS.
I TRADE MY TEACHING SKILLS.

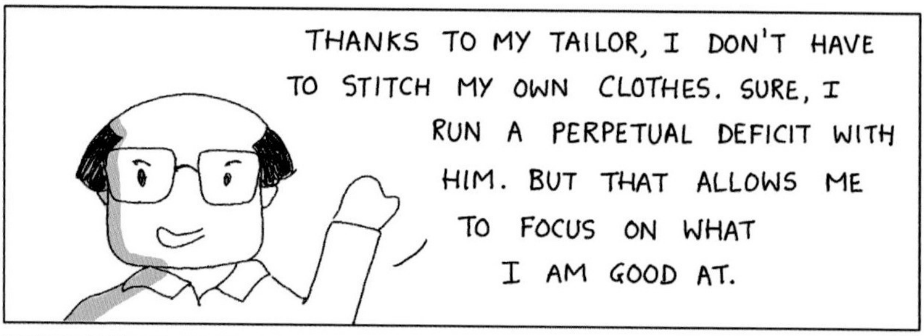
THANKS TO MY TAILOR, I DON'T HAVE TO STITCH MY OWN CLOTHES. SURE, I RUN A PERPETUAL DEFICIT WITH HIM. BUT THAT ALLOWS ME TO FOCUS ON WHAT I AM GOOD AT.

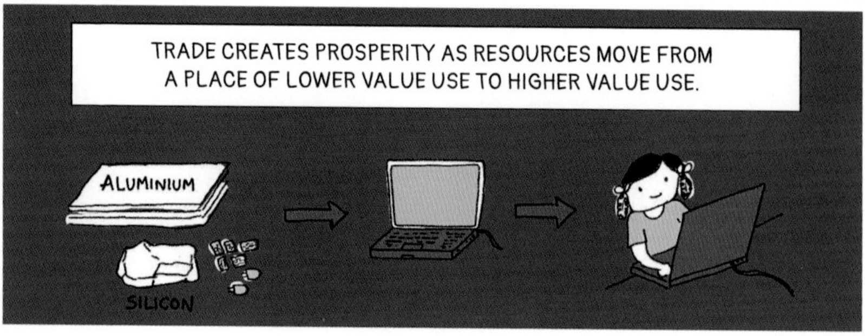
TRADE CREATES PROSPERITY AS RESOURCES MOVE FROM A PLACE OF LOWER VALUE USE TO HIGHER VALUE USE.
ALUMINIUM
SILICON

HUMAN BEINGS DOING THIS OVER AND OVER AGAIN HAS RESULTED IN MUCH OF THE WEALTH AND PROSPERITY WE SEE AROUND US.

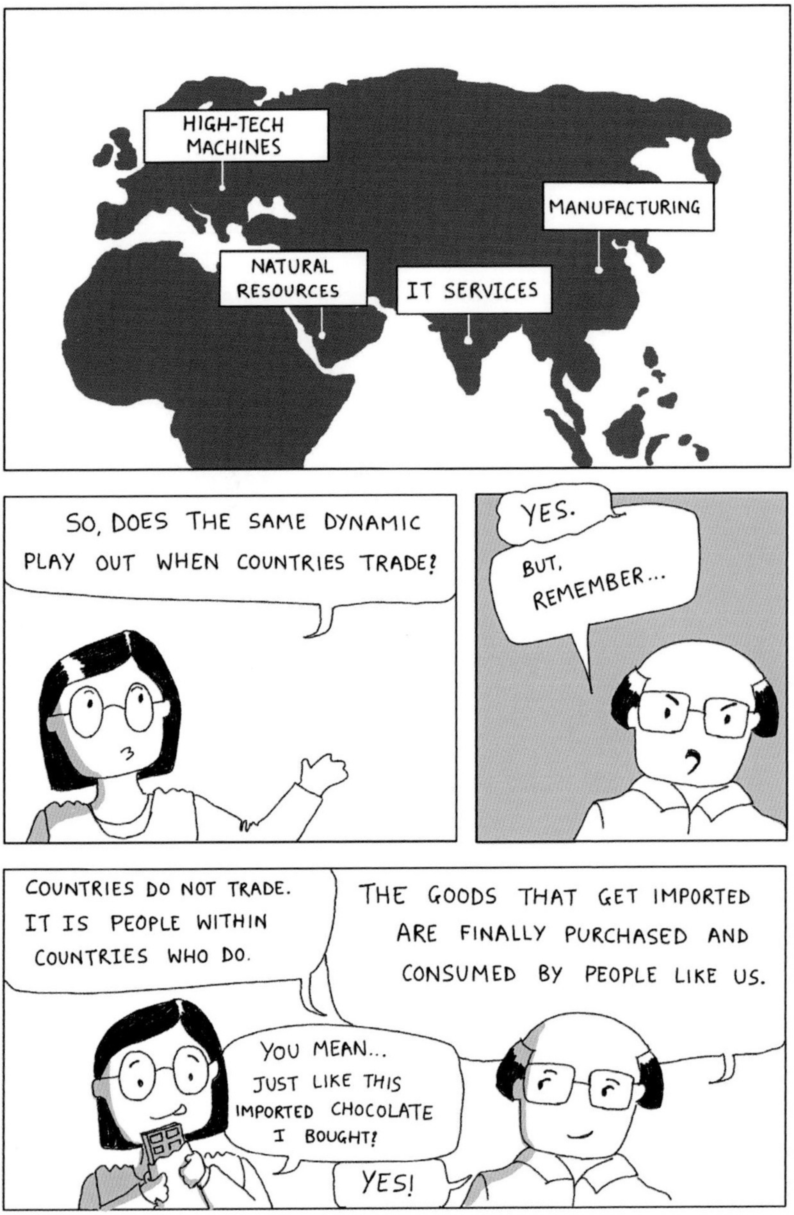

HIGH-TECH MACHINES
MANUFACTURING
NATURAL RESOURCES
IT SERVICES
SO, DOES THE SAME DYNAMIC PLAY OUT WHEN COUNTRIES TRADE?
YES.
BUT, REMEMBER...
COUNTRIES DO NOT TRADE. IT IS PEOPLE WITHIN COUNTRIES WHO DO.
THE GOODS THAT GET IMPORTED ARE FINALLY PURCHASED AND CONSUMED BY PEOPLE LIKE US.
YOU MEAN... JUST LIKE THIS IMPORTED CHOCOLATE I BOUGHT?
YES!

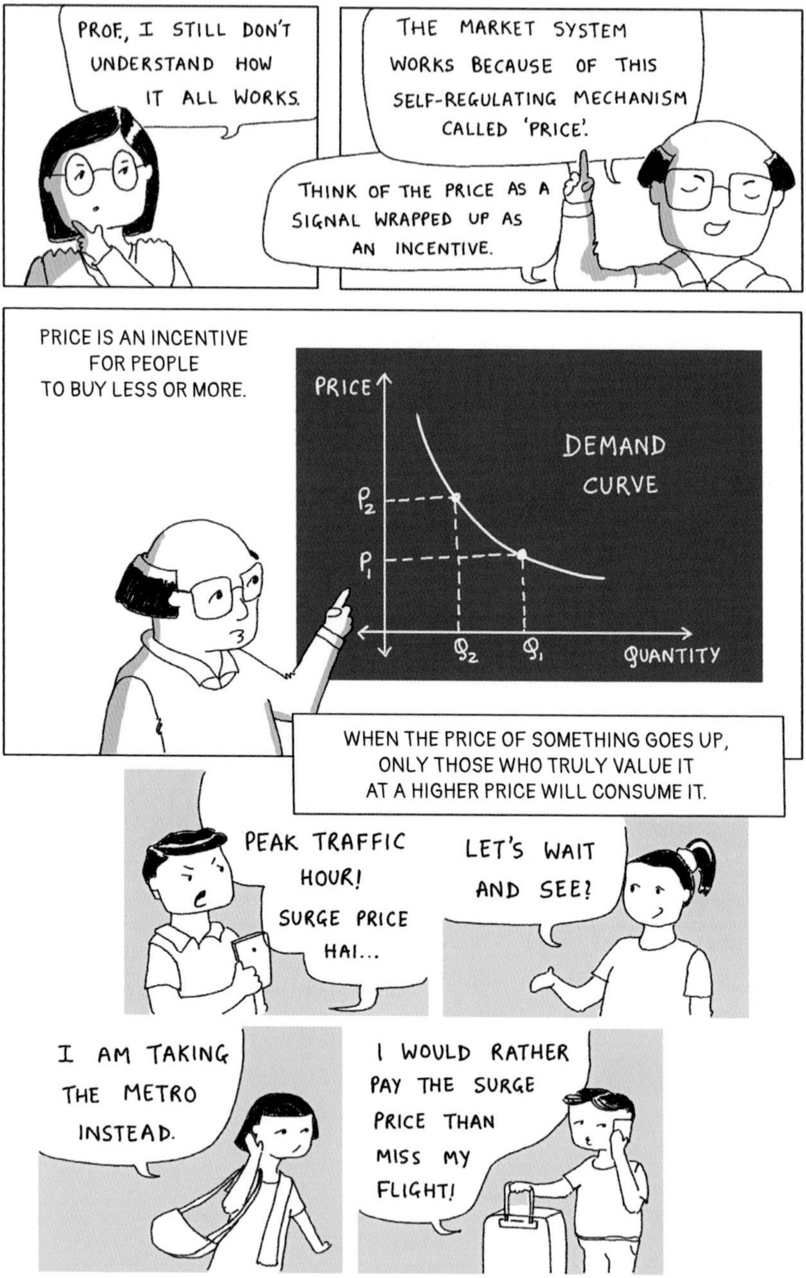

PROF., I STILL DON'T UNDERSTAND HOW IT ALL WORKS.
THE MARKET SYSTEM WORKS BECAUSE OF THIS SELF-REGULATING MECHANISM CALLED 'PRICE'.
THINK OF THE PRICE AS A SIGNAL WRAPPED UP AS AN INCENTIVE.
PRICE IS AN INCENTIVE FOR PEOPLE TO BUY LESS OR MORE.
PRICE
DEMAND CURVE
P2
P1
Q2
Q1
QUANTITY
WHEN THE PRICE OF SOMETHING GOES UP, ONLY THOSE WHO TRULY VALUE IT AT A HIGHER PRICE WILL CONSUME IT.
PEAK TRAFFIC HOUR! SURGE PRICE HAI...
LET'S WAIT AND SEE?
I AM TAKING THE METRO INSTEAD.
I WOULD RATHER PAY THE SURGE PRICE THAN MISS MY FLIGHT!

THOSE WHO DO NOT VALUE IT AT THAT PRICE WILL FIND ALTERNATIVES.
THE NET EFFECT IS A MORE EFFICIENT ALLOCATION OF SCARCE RESOURCES.

AT THE SAME TIME, IT SIGNALS TO EVERYONE ELSE THAT THERE IS A GAP IN THE SUPPLY THAT NEEDS TO BE FILLED.

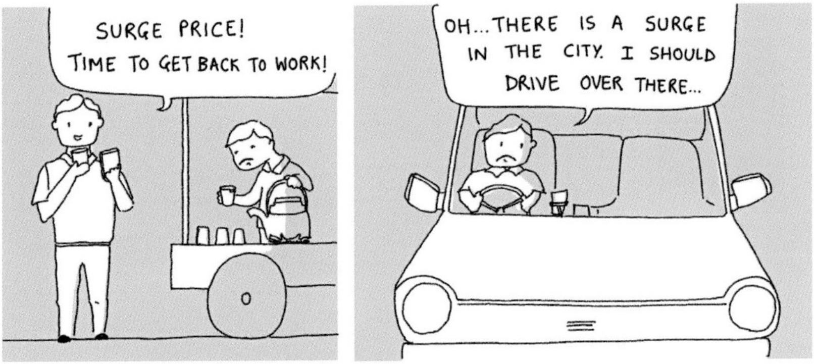
SURGE PRICE!
TIME TO GET BACK TO WORK!
OH... THERE IS A SURGE IN THE CITY. I SHOULD DRIVE OVER THERE...

WHEN ENOUGH DRIVERS HAVE MOVED TO THE AREA, THE MISMATCH IS RESOLVED AND THE SURGE GETS OVER.

THE BEAUTY OF THIS IS THAT ALL OF THIS HAPPENS THROUGH A SPONTANEOUS ORDER, WITHOUT ANY CENTRAL PLANNER DICTATING ANYTHING.

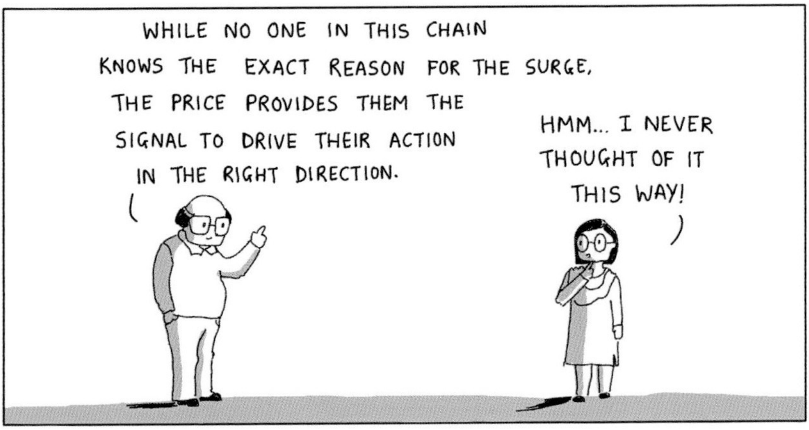
WHILE NO ONE IN THIS CHAIN KNOWS THE EXACT REASON FOR THE SURGE, THE PRICE PROVIDES THEM THE SIGNAL TO DRIVE THEIR ACTION IN THE RIGHT DIRECTION.
HMM... I NEVER THOUGHT OF IT THIS WAY!

IT CAN BE ARGUED THAT NO AUTHORITY WILL BE ABLE TO DO EVEN HALF AS GOOD A JOB BECAUSE THE KNOWLEDGE REQUIRED TO MAKE EFFICIENT DECISIONS DOES NOT LIE WITH ANY INDIVIDUAL.

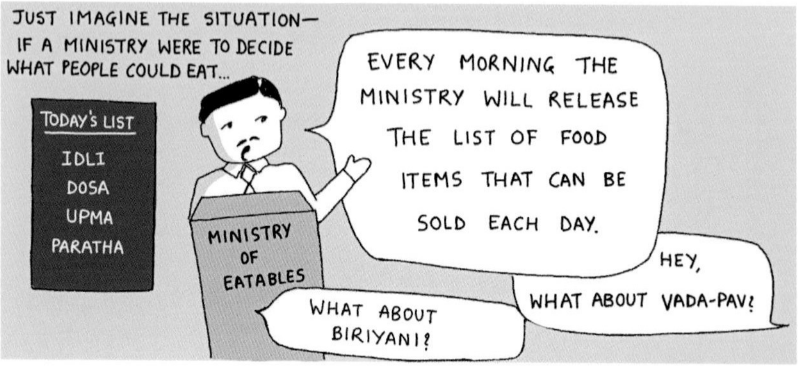
JUST IMAGINE THE SITUATION— IF A MINISTRY WERE TO DECIDE WHAT PEOPLE COULD EAT...
TODAY'S LIST
IDLI
DOSA
UPMA
PARATHA
MINISTRY OF EATABLES
EVERY MORNING THE MINISTRY WILL RELEASE THE LIST OF FOOD ITEMS THAT CAN BE SOLD EACH DAY.
HEY, WHAT ABOUT VADA-PAV?
WHAT ABOUT BIRIYANI?

THIS KNOWLEDGE IS DISPERSED IN SOCIETY. EACH ONE UNDERSTANDS THE WORK THEY DO THE BEST.

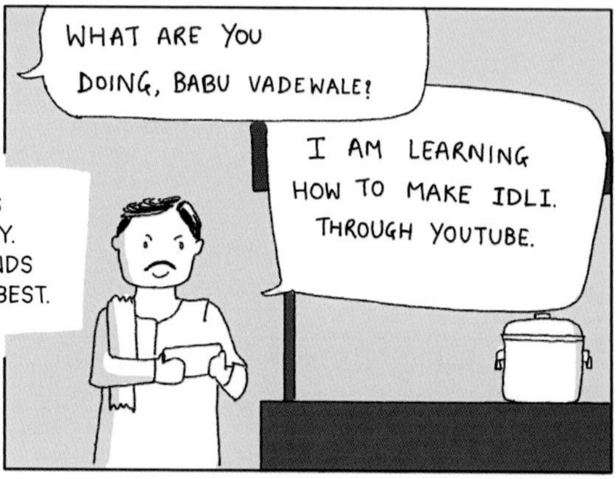
WHAT ARE YOU DOING, BABU VADEWALE?
I AM LEARNING HOW TO MAKE IDLI. THROUGH YOUTUBE.

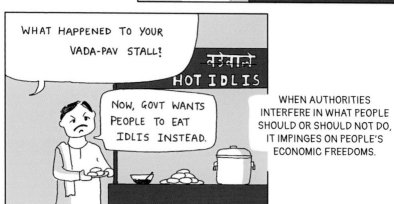

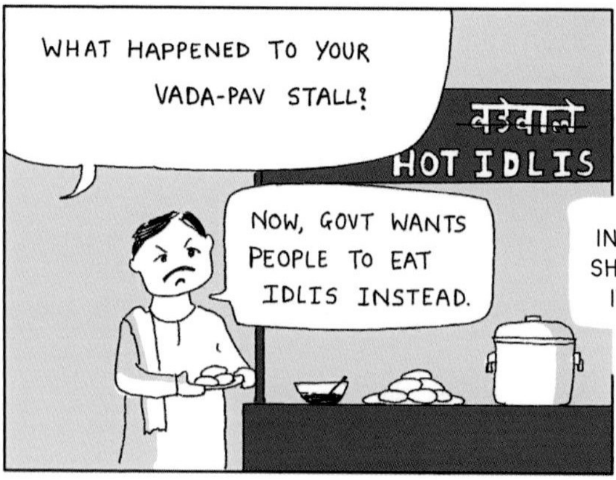
WHAT HAPPENED TO YOUR VADA-PAV STALL?
वडेवाले
HOT IDLIS
NOW, GOVT WANTS PEOPLE TO EAT IDLIS INSTEAD.

WHEN AUTHORITIES INTERFERE IN WHAT PEOPLE SHOULD OR SHOULD NOT DO, IT IMPINGES ON PEOPLE'S ECONOMIC FREEDOMS.

THE PRICE MECHANISM, DRIVEN BY SUPPLY AND DEMAND, GIVES USEFUL INFORMATION TO INDIVIDUALS TO MAKE THE BEST DECISION FOR THEMSELVES.

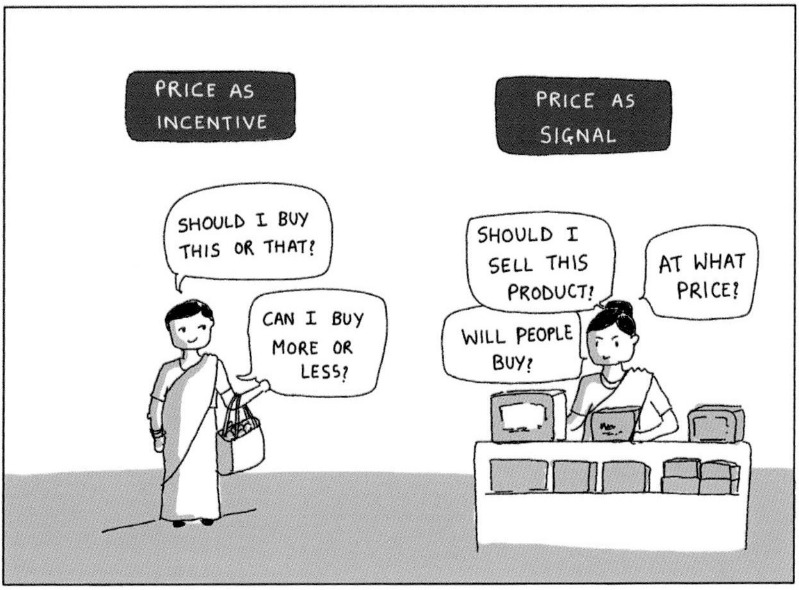

PRICE AS INCENTIVE
PRICE AS SIGNAL
SHOULD I BUY THIS OR THAT?
CAN I BUY MORE OR LESS?
SHOULD I SELL THIS PRODUCT?
AT WHAT PRICE?
WILL PEOPLE BUY?

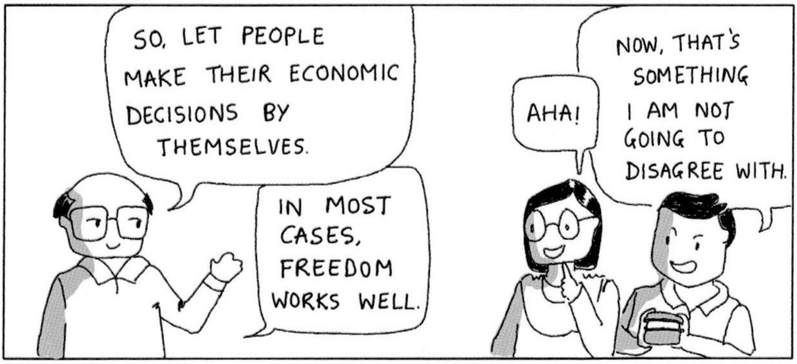

SO, LET PEOPLE MAKE THEIR ECONOMIC DECISIONS BY THEMSELVES.
IN MOST CASES, FREEDOM WORKS WELL.
AHA!
NOW, THAT'S SOMETHING I AM NOT GOING TO DISAGREE WITH.

Chapter 5

Superhero Wants to Eliminate All Crime

Incentives matter

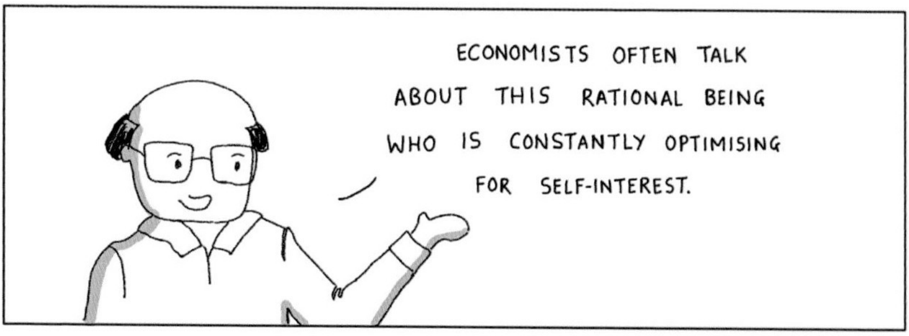
ECONOMISTS OFTEN TALK ABOUT THIS RATIONAL BEING WHO IS CONSTANTLY OPTIMISING FOR SELF-INTEREST.

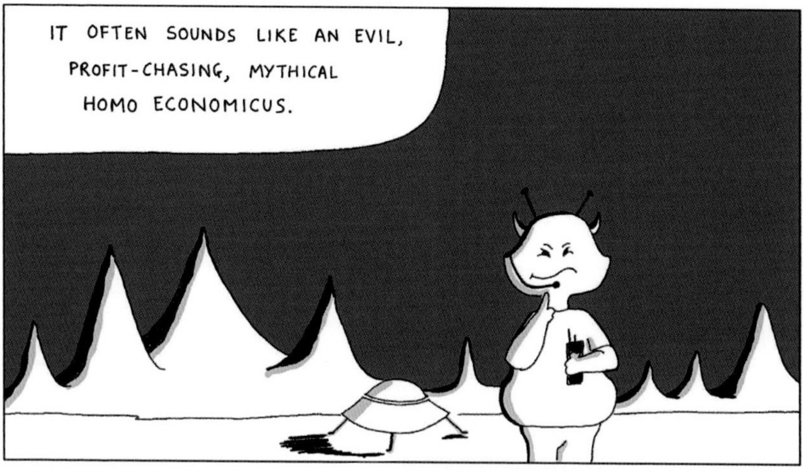
IT OFTEN SOUNDS LIKE AN EVIL, PROFIT-CHASING, MYTHICAL HOMO ECONOMICUS.

LOOK CLOSELY AND THEY WILL LOOK A LOT LIKE YOU AND ME.

ET TU?

EACH ONE OF US IS A RATIONAL BEING.

WE LOOK FOR OUR SELF-INTEREST AND MAKE CHOICES TO OPTIMIZE VALUE IN EVERYTHING WE DO.

LIKE HOW I MAKE A DECISION ON WHETHER TO STUDY OR NOT?

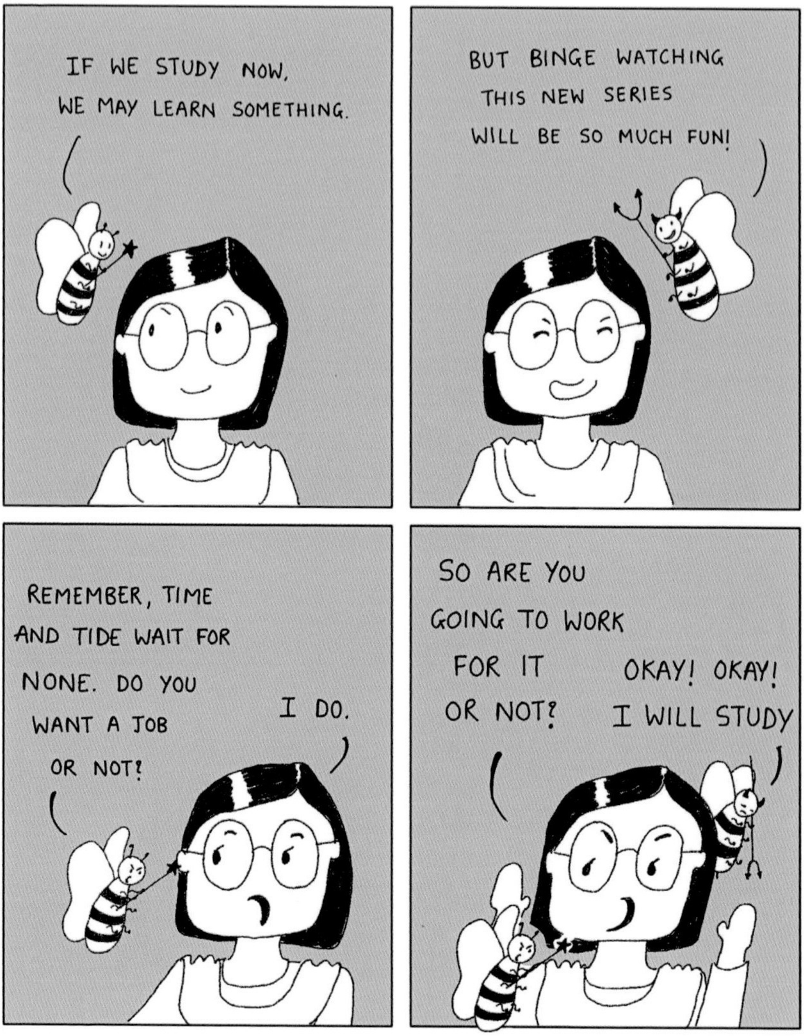
IF WE STUDY NOW, WE MAY LEARN SOMETHING.
BUT BINGE WATCHING THIS NEW SERIES WILL BE SO MUCH FUN!
REMEMBER, TIME AND TIDE WAIT FOR NONE. DO YOU WANT A JOB OR NOT?
I DO.
SO ARE YOU GOING TO WORK FOR IT OR NOT?
OKAY! OKAY! I WILL STUDY

AS RATIONAL BEINGS, ALL OF US TRY TO MAXIMIZE OUR UTILITY AND MINIMIZE OUR COSTS. WELL, AT LEAST MOST OF THE TIME.*

* Behavioural Economics tells us that humans don't act rationally all the time. In fact, sometimes they act pretty irrationally and against their own self-interest. But that discussion is out of the scope of this book.

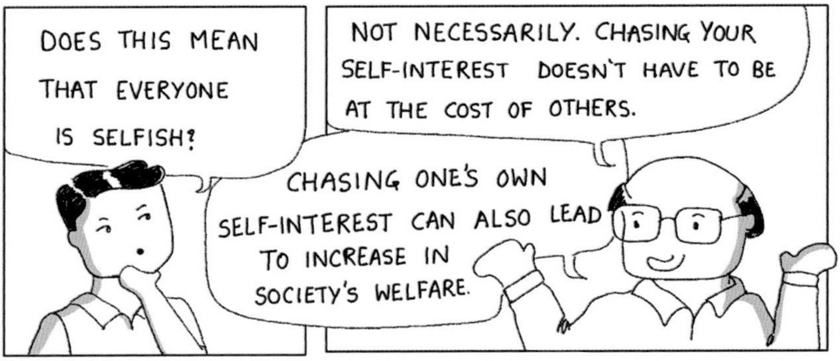
DOES THIS MEAN THAT EVERYONE IS SELFISH?
NOT NECESSARILY. CHASING YOUR SELF-INTEREST DOESN'T HAVE TO BE AT THE COST OF OTHERS.
CHASING ONE'S OWN SELF-INTEREST CAN ALSO LEAD TO INCREASE IN SOCIETY'S WELFARE.

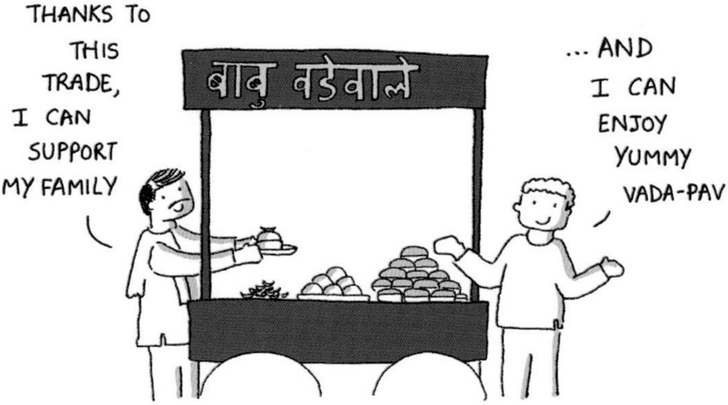
THANKS TO THIS TRADE, I CAN SUPPORT MY FAMILY
बाबु वडेवाले
... AND I CAN ENJOY YUMMY VADA-PAV

ALSO, DIFFERENT PEOPLE VALUE DIFFERENT THINGS AND MAY RESPOND TO DIFFERENT INCENTIVES.

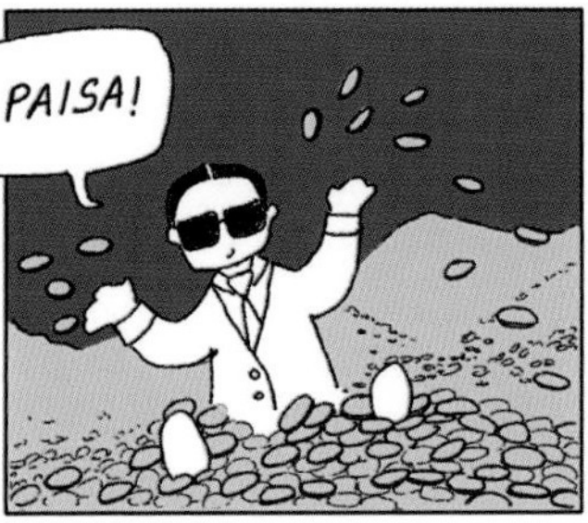
PAISA!

SURE, SOME PEOPLE FIND UTILITY IN MONEY.

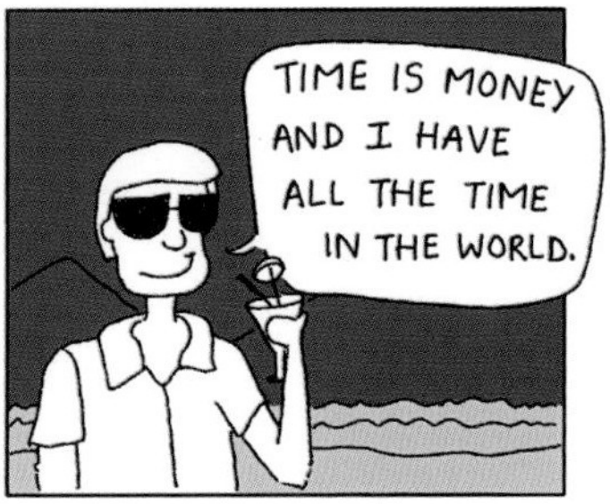
TIME IS MONEY AND I HAVE ALL THE TIME IN THE WORLD.

OTHERS MAY FIND UTILITY IN LEISURE.

WHAT WE KNOW IS THAT WHEN INCENTIVES ARE WELL-DEFINED, RATIONAL BEINGS RESPOND TO THEM.

SALE SALE SALE
50% OFF - END OF
CUSTOMERS CHASE DISCOUNTS
EMPLOYEES CARE ABOUT THE OUTCOMES WHEN THEIR SALARIES DEPEND ON IT.
SALARY STRUCTURE
FIXED
PERFORMANCE LINKED

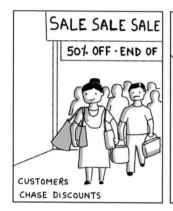

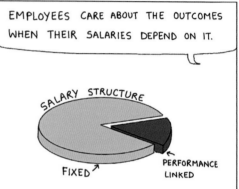

WHEN INCENTIVES ARE MISSING, PEOPLE RESPOND TO THAT TOO.

WE TEND TO WASTE THINGS MORE WHEN WE DON'T HAVE TO PAY FOR THEM.
GOVERNMENT EMPLOYEES ARE ACCUSED OF BEING OBLIVIOUS TO CUSTOMER SATISFACTION.
SIR, JUST NEED YOUR SIGN.
COME AFTER LUNCH HOUR.
LUNCH BREAK

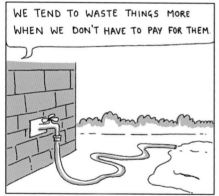

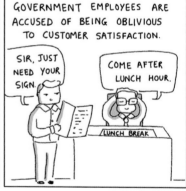

BUT RATIONAL BEINGS DON'T JUST CHASE INCENTIVES BLINDLY. THEY ALSO ACCOUNT FOR COSTS.

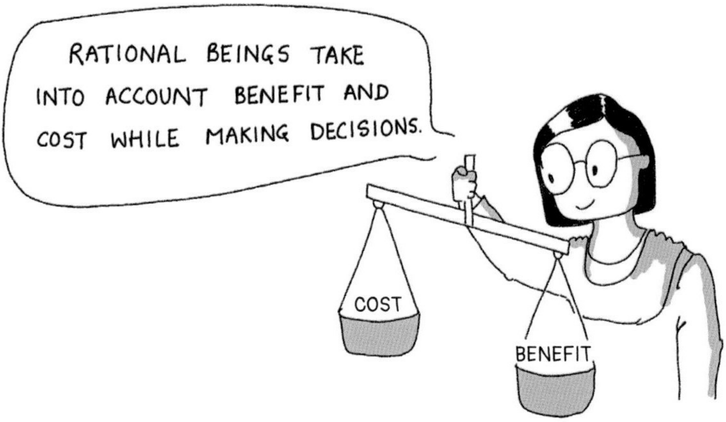
RATIONAL BEINGS TAKE INTO ACCOUNT BENEFIT AND COST WHILE MAKING DECISIONS.
COST
BENEFIT

JUST LIKE INCENTIVES, COSTS COME IN DIFFERENT FORMS TOO. THERE IS AN EXPLICIT COST WHICH IS ALSO CALLED ACCOUNTING COST, AND THEN THERE IS AN IMPLICIT COST CALLED OPPORTUNITY COST.

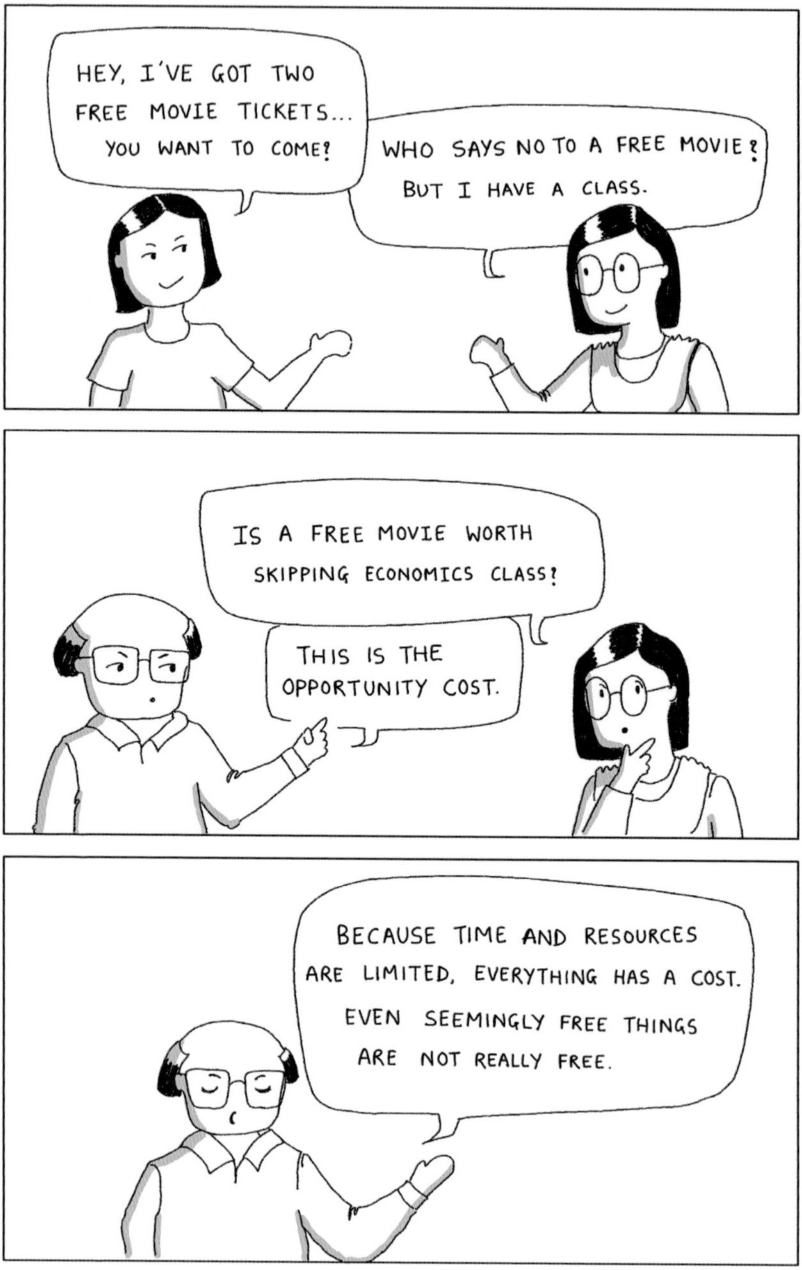
HEY, I'VE GOT TWO FREE MOVIE TICKETS... YOU WANT TO COME?
WHO SAYS NO TO A FREE MOVIE? BUT I HAVE A CLASS.
IS A FREE MOVIE WORTH SKIPPING ECONOMICS CLASS?
THIS IS THE OPPORTUNITY COST.
BECAUSE TIME AND RESOURCES ARE LIMITED, EVERYTHING HAS A COST. EVEN SEEMINGLY FREE THINGS ARE NOT REALLY FREE.

```
                            ┌─────────────────────┐
                            │   ACCOUNTING COST   │
                            └─────────────────────┘
                               (costs that get
                              accounted or billed)
                                      +
┌─────────────────┐         ┌─────────────────────┐
│  ECONOMIC COST  │         │  OPPORTUNITY COST   │
└─────────────────┘         └─────────────────────┘
                              (the foregone benefit
                              that could have been
                                derived by choosing
                               another alternative)
```

INTERESTINGLY, WE FOLLOW THIS QUITE INTUITIVELY IN OUR PERSONAL LIVES, BUT TEND TO FORGET IT WHILE THINKING ABOUT PUBLIC POLICY QUESTIONS.

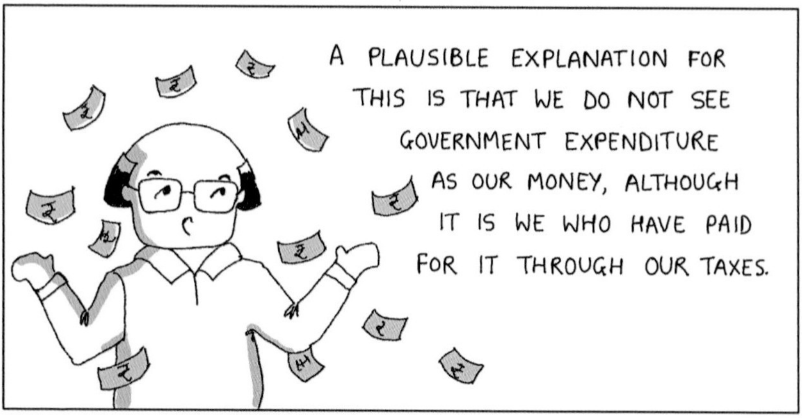
A PLAUSIBLE EXPLANATION FOR THIS IS THAT WE DO NOT SEE GOVERNMENT EXPENDITURE AS OUR MONEY, ALTHOUGH IT IS WE WHO HAVE PAID FOR IT THROUGH OUR TAXES.

EVERY RUPEE THAT THE GOVERNMENT SPENDS ON ONE PROGRAMME IS A RUPEE NOT AVAILABLE FOR ANOTHER PROGRAMME.

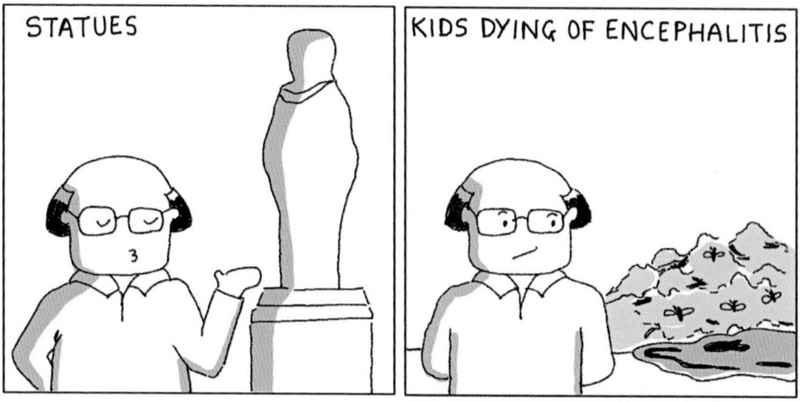
STATUES
KIDS DYING OF ENCEPHALITIS

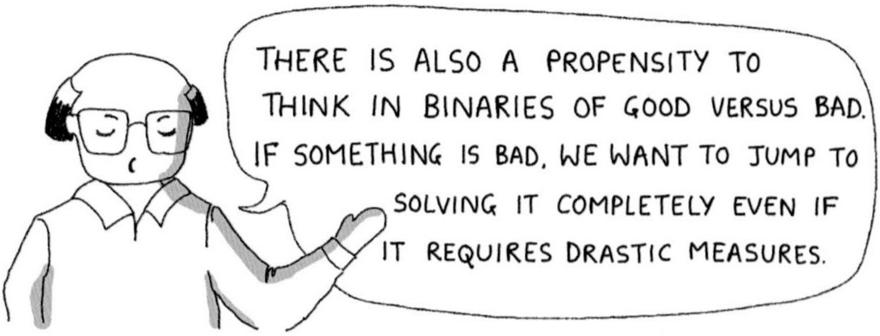
THERE IS ALSO A PROPENSITY TO THINK IN BINARIES OF GOOD VERSUS BAD. IF SOMETHING IS BAD, WE WANT TO JUMP TO SOLVING IT COMPLETELY EVEN IF IT REQUIRES DRASTIC MEASURES.

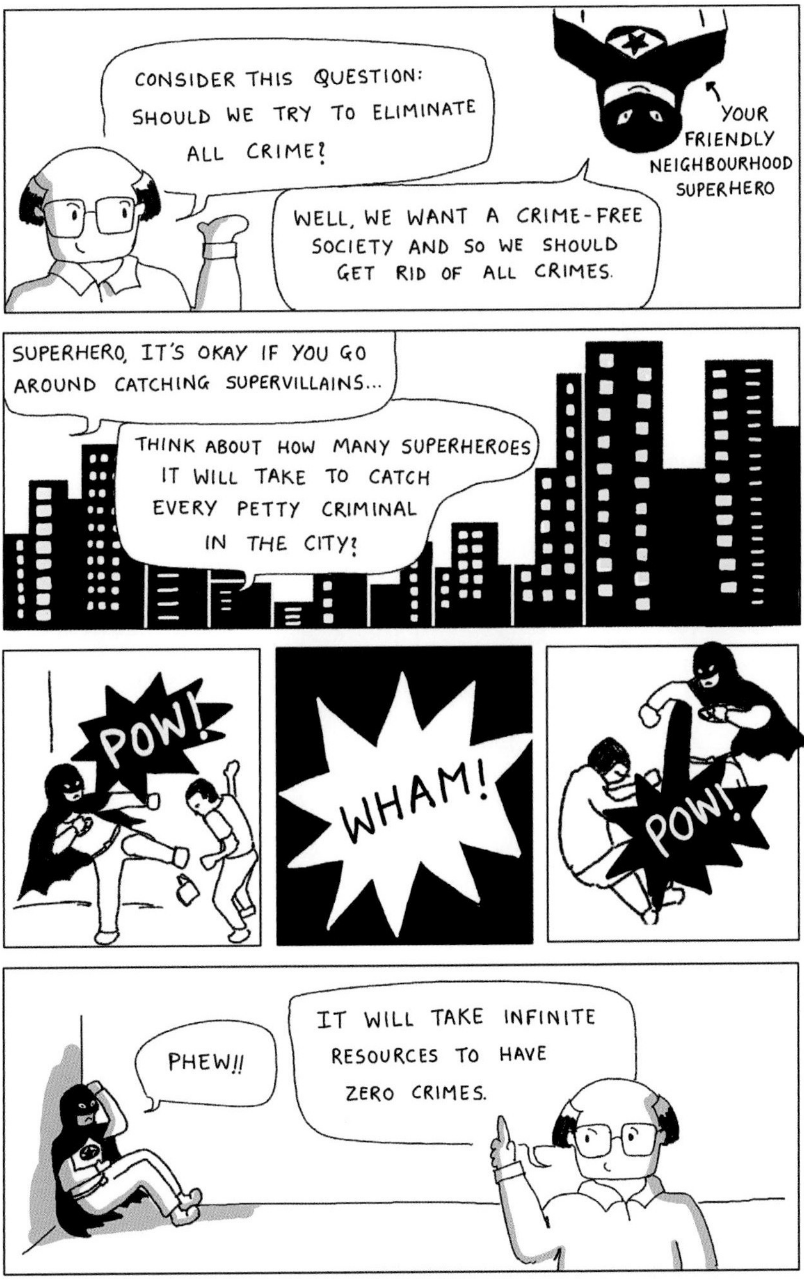
CONSIDER THIS QUESTION: SHOULD WE TRY TO ELIMINATE ALL CRIME?
YOUR FRIENDLY NEIGHBOURHOOD SUPERHERO
WELL, WE WANT A CRIME-FREE SOCIETY AND SO WE SHOULD GET RID OF ALL CRIMES.
SUPERHERO, IT'S OKAY IF YOU GO AROUND CATCHING SUPERVILLAINS...
THINK ABOUT HOW MANY SUPERHEROES IT WILL TAKE TO CATCH EVERY PETTY CRIMINAL IN THE CITY?
POW!
WHAM!
POW!
PHEW!!
IT WILL TAKE INFINITE RESOURCES TO HAVE ZERO CRIMES.

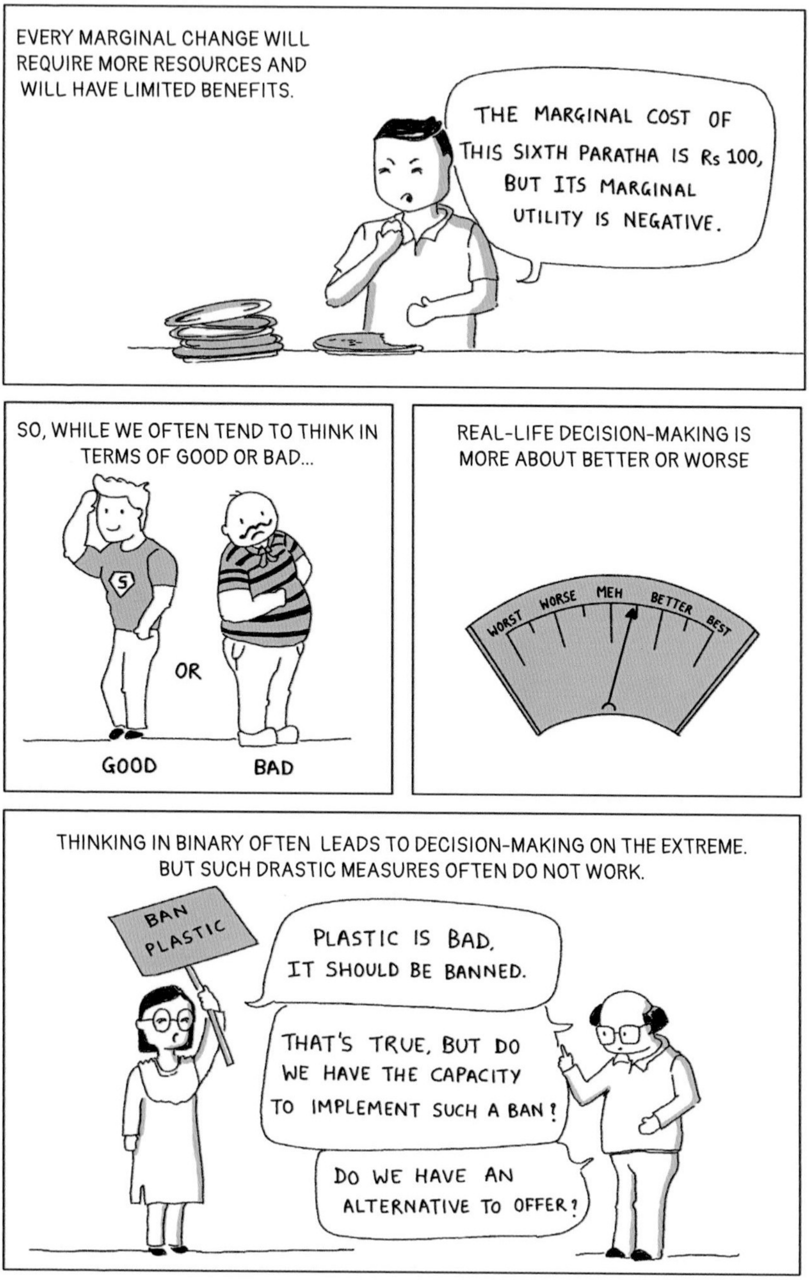
EVERY MARGINAL CHANGE WILL REQUIRE MORE RESOURCES AND WILL HAVE LIMITED BENEFITS.
THE MARGINAL COST OF THIS SIXTH PARATHA IS Rs 100, BUT ITS MARGINAL UTILITY IS NEGATIVE.
SO, WHILE WE OFTEN TEND TO THINK IN TERMS OF GOOD OR BAD...
S
OR
GOOD
BAD
REAL-LIFE DECISION-MAKING IS MORE ABOUT BETTER OR WORSE
WORST
WORSE
MEH
BETTER
BEST
THINKING IN BINARY OFTEN LEADS TO DECISION-MAKING ON THE EXTREME. BUT SUCH DRASTIC MEASURES OFTEN DO NOT WORK.
BAN PLASTIC
PLASTIC IS BAD, IT SHOULD BE BANNED.
THAT'S TRUE, BUT DO WE HAVE THE CAPACITY TO IMPLEMENT SUCH A BAN?
DO WE HAVE AN ALTERNATIVE TO OFFER?

INSTEAD WE SHOULD THINK ABOUT
HOW TO MAKE THE SITUATION BETTER.

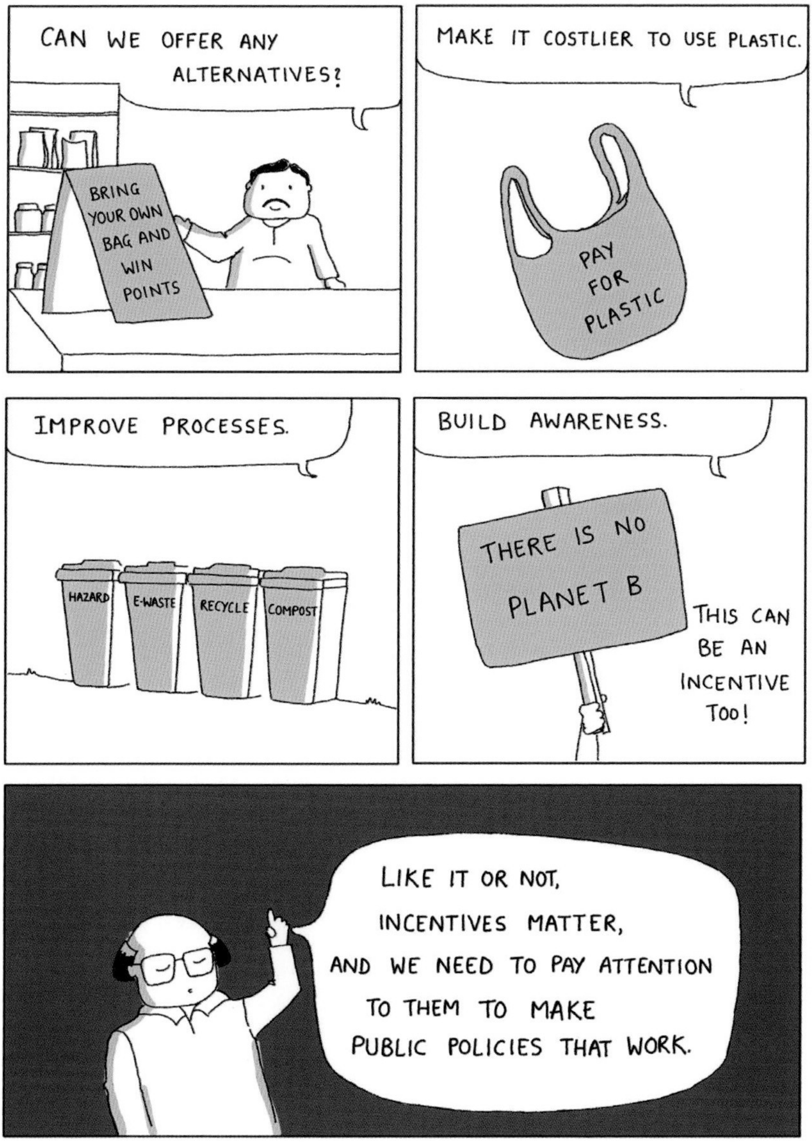
CAN WE OFFER ANY ALTERNATIVES?
BRING YOUR OWN BAG AND WIN POINTS
MAKE IT COSTLIER TO USE PLASTIC.
PAY FOR PLASTIC
IMPROVE PROCESSES.
HAZARD
E-WASTE
RECYCLE
COMPOST
BUILD AWARENESS.
THERE IS NO PLANET B
THIS CAN BE AN INCENTIVE TOO!
LIKE IT OR NOT, INCENTIVES MATTER, AND WE NEED TO PAY ATTENTION TO THEM TO MAKE PUBLIC POLICIES THAT WORK.

Chapter 6

Government's Toolkit

Things governments do

WE OFTEN HEAR PEOPLE SAYING...

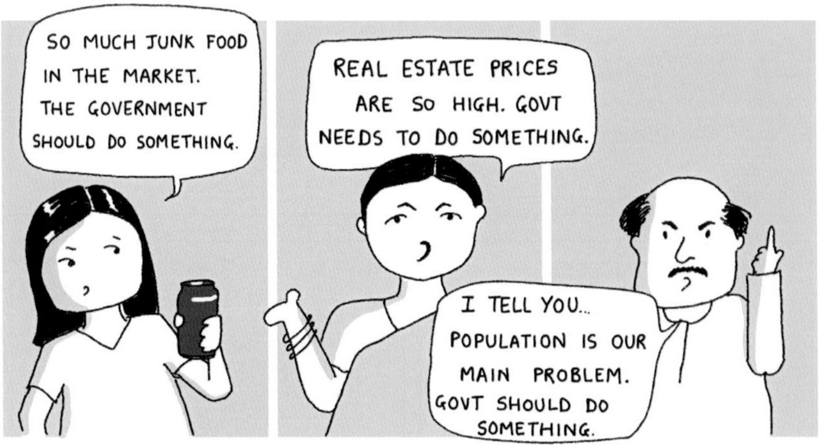
SO MUCH JUNK FOOD IN THE MARKET. THE GOVERNMENT SHOULD DO SOMETHING.
REAL ESTATE PRICES ARE SO HIGH. GOVT NEEDS TO DO SOMETHING.
I TELL YOU... POPULATION IS OUR MAIN PROBLEM. GOVT SHOULD DO SOMETHING.

BUT WHEN ASKED WHAT THEY THINK THE GOVERNMENT SHOULD DO...
WE OFTEN HEAR THIS KIND OF RESPONSES.

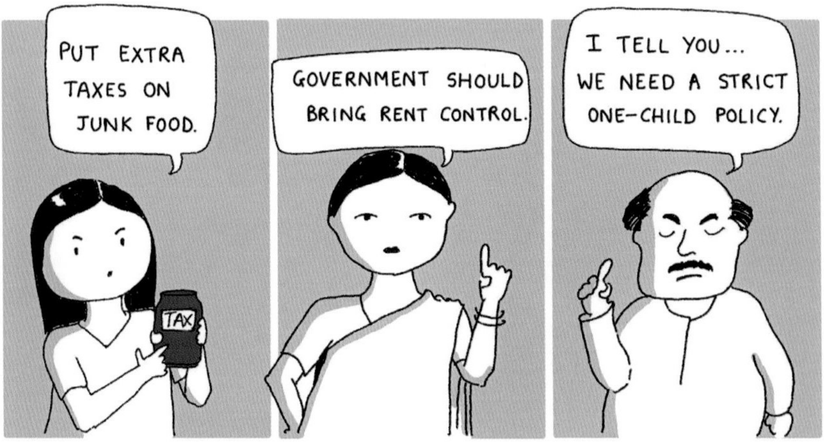
PUT EXTRA TAXES ON JUNK FOOD.
TAX
GOVERNMENT SHOULD BRING RENT CONTROL.
I TELL YOU... WE NEED A STRICT ONE-CHILD POLICY.

IN SHORT, THREE QUICK RESPONSES COME TO MIND AS THE SOLUTION TO EVERY POLICY PROBLEM.

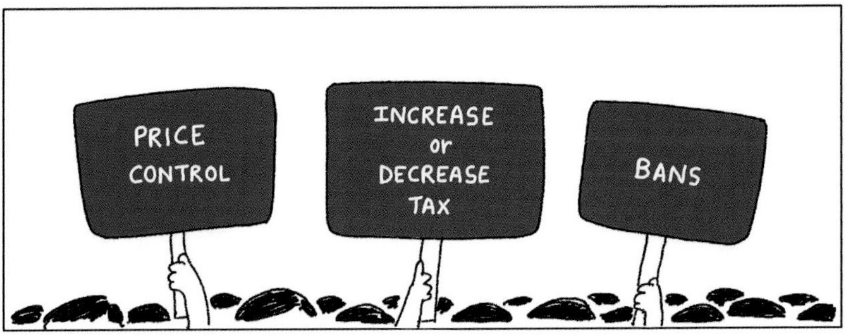
PRICE CONTROL
INCREASE or DECREASE TAX
BANS

WHAT WE DON'T REALIZE IS THAT THE GOVERNMENT HAS MANY OTHER TOOLS IN ITS POLICY ARMOUR THAT IT CAN (AND DOES) USE.

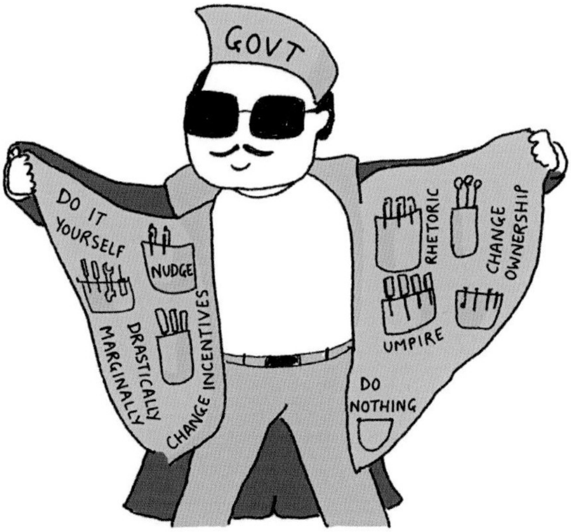
GOVT
DO IT YOURSELF
NUDGE
DRASTICALLY MARGINALLY
CHANGE INCENTIVES
RHETORIC
CHANGE OWNERSHIP
UMPIRE
DO NOTHING

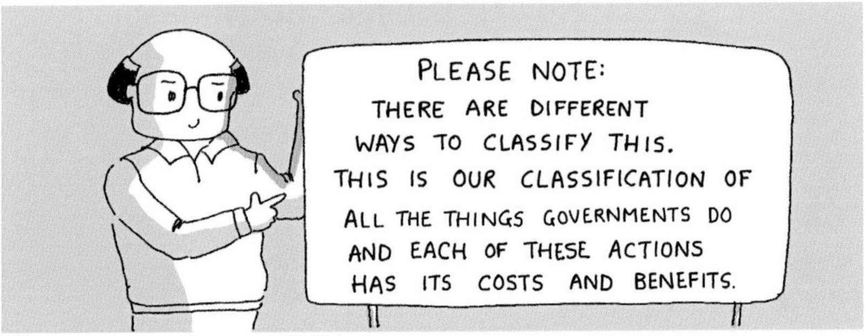
PLEASE NOTE:
THERE ARE DIFFERENT WAYS TO CLASSIFY THIS.
THIS IS OUR CLASSIFICATION OF ALL THE THINGS GOVERNMENTS DO AND EACH OF THESE ACTIONS HAS ITS COSTS AND BENEFITS.

WE CLASSIFY ALL THAT THE GOVERNMENT DOES INTO EIGHT CATEGORIES:

#1. DO NOTHING

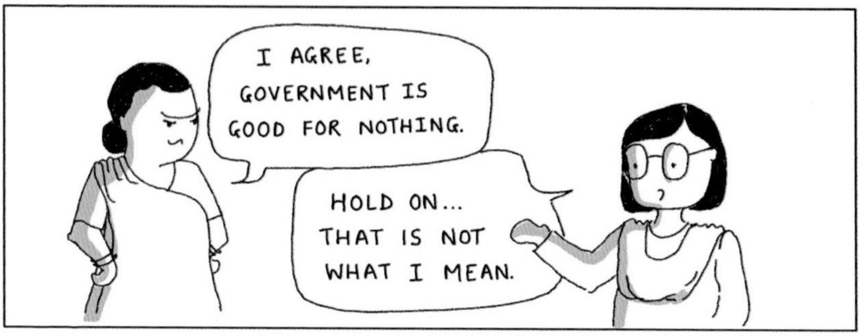
I AGREE, GOVERNMENT IS GOOD FOR NOTHING.
HOLD ON... THAT IS NOT WHAT I MEAN.

SOMETIMES THE GOVERNMENT CHOOSES NOT TO DO ANYTHING ABOUT AN ISSUE IF IT THINKS THAT THE MARKET OR THE SOCIETY CAN SOLVE THE PROBLEM BY ITSELF.

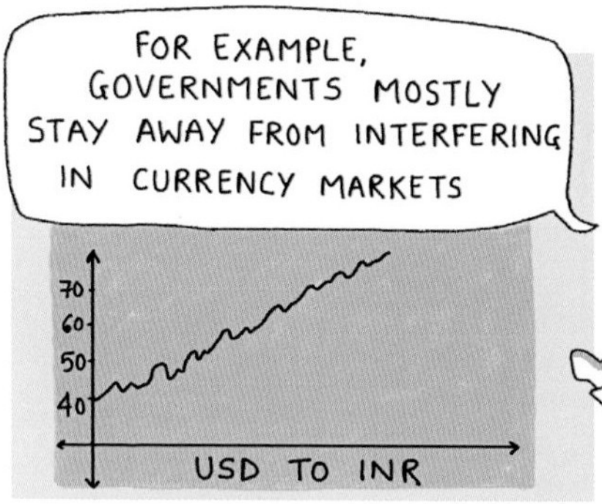
FOR EXAMPLE, GOVERNMENTS MOSTLY STAY AWAY FROM INTERFERING IN CURRENCY MARKETS
70
60
50
40
USD TO INR

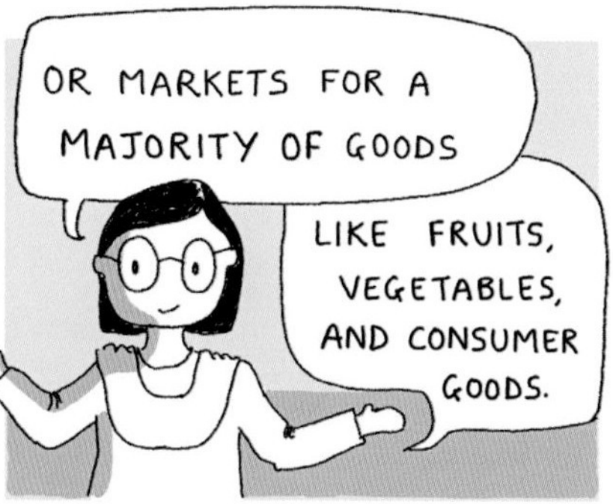
OR MARKETS FOR A MAJORITY OF GOODS
LIKE FRUITS, VEGETABLES, AND CONSUMER GOODS.

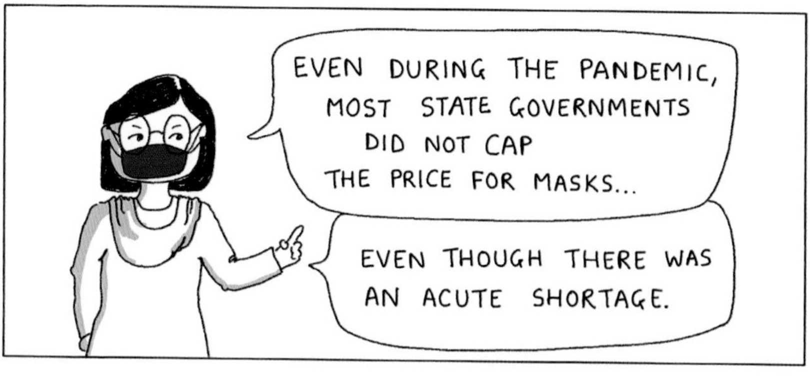
EVEN DURING THE PANDEMIC, MOST STATE GOVERNMENTS DID NOT CAP THE PRICE FOR MASKS...
EVEN THOUGH THERE WAS AN ACUTE SHORTAGE.

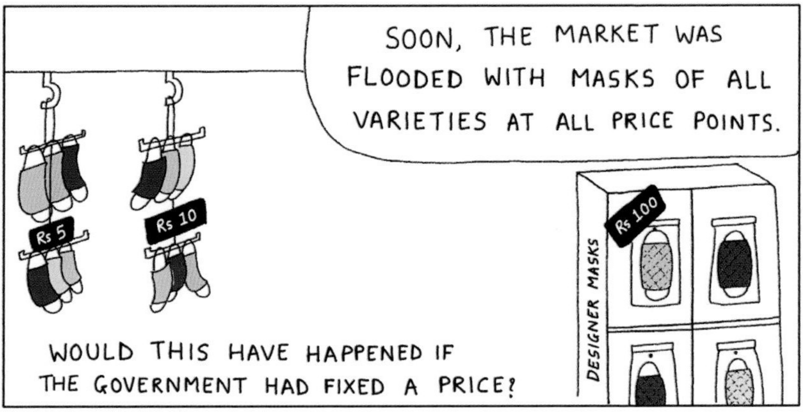
SOON, THE MARKET WAS FLOODED WITH MASKS OF ALL VARIETIES AT ALL PRICE POINTS.
Rs 5
Rs 10
DESIGNER MASKS
Rs 100
WOULD THIS HAVE HAPPENED IF THE GOVERNMENT HAD FIXED A PRICE?

THE GOVERNMENT DOES NOT NEED TO SOLVE EVERY PROBLEM.
SOME ISSUES ARE BEST RESOLVED BY EITHER THE MARKET OR THE SOCIETY.

HOWEVER...

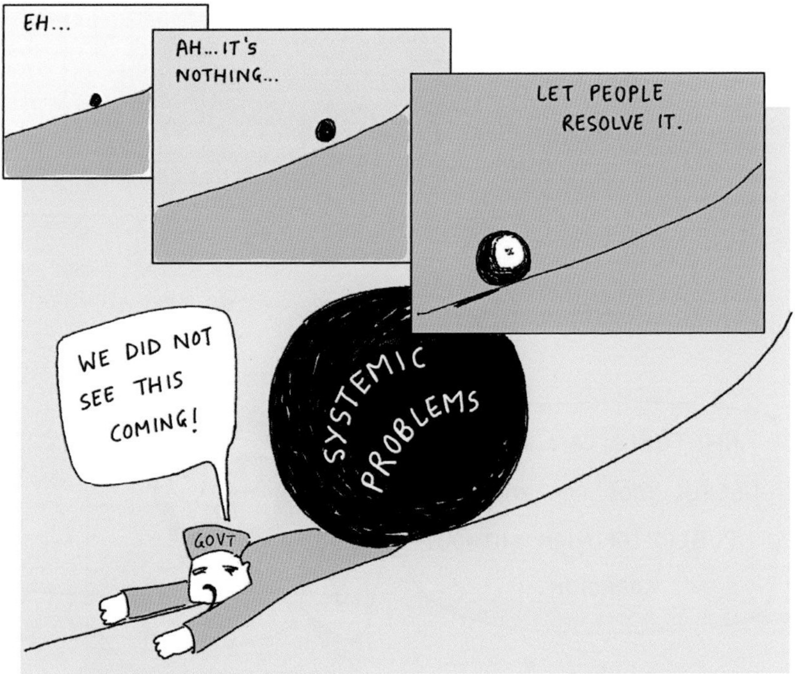
EH...
AH... IT'S NOTHING...
LET PEOPLE RESOLVE IT.
WE DID NOT SEE THIS COMING!
SYSTEMIC PROBLEMS
GOVT

THE RISK WITH DOING NOTHING IS THAT IF SYSTEMIC PROBLEMS ARE IGNORED, THEY MAY SNOWBALL LATER AND BECOME EVEN HARDER TO SOLVE.

#2. ENGAGE IN RHETORIC

SOMETIMES, THE GOVERNMENT DOESN'T WANT TO ACTIVELY TACKLE AN ISSUE, BUT STILL WANTS TO STEER PUBLIC OPINION.

IN SUCH CASES, IT CAN ENGAGE IN RHETORIC.

'TOILETS ARE MORE IMPORTANT THAN TEMPLES'

'हम दो हमारे दो'

'WE TWO, OUR TWO'

RHETORIC CAN BE A USEFUL TOOL FOR INFLUENCING PUBLIC OPINION WITHOUT COERCION.

ENGAGING IN RHETORIC DOES NOT REQUIRE AS MUCH STATE CAPACITY OR RESOURCES.

RHETORIC WORKS WHEN PEOPLE HAVE TRUST IN THE PERSON ENGAGING IN RHETORIC.

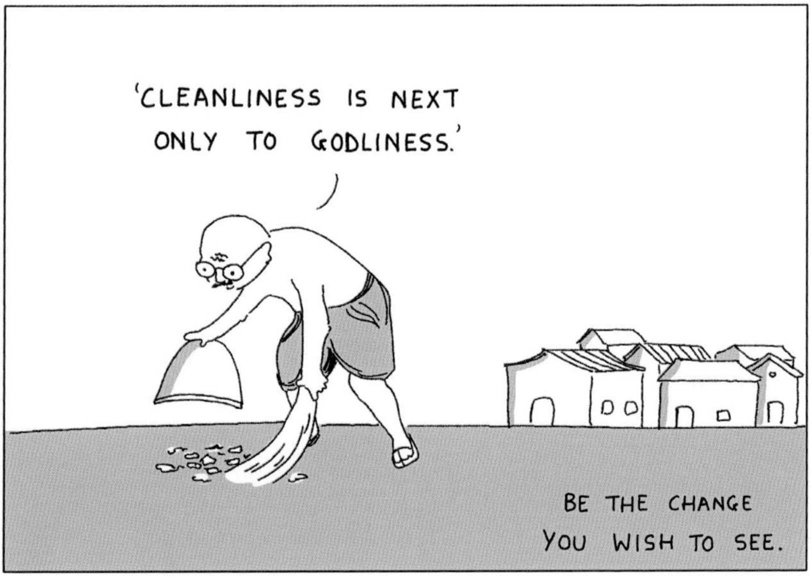
'CLEANLINESS IS NEXT ONLY TO GODLINESS.'
BE THE CHANGE YOU WISH TO SEE.

BUT IT MAY FALL FLAT IF THE SOURCE OF THE RHETORIC HAS NO CREDIBILITY IN PEOPLE'S MINDS.

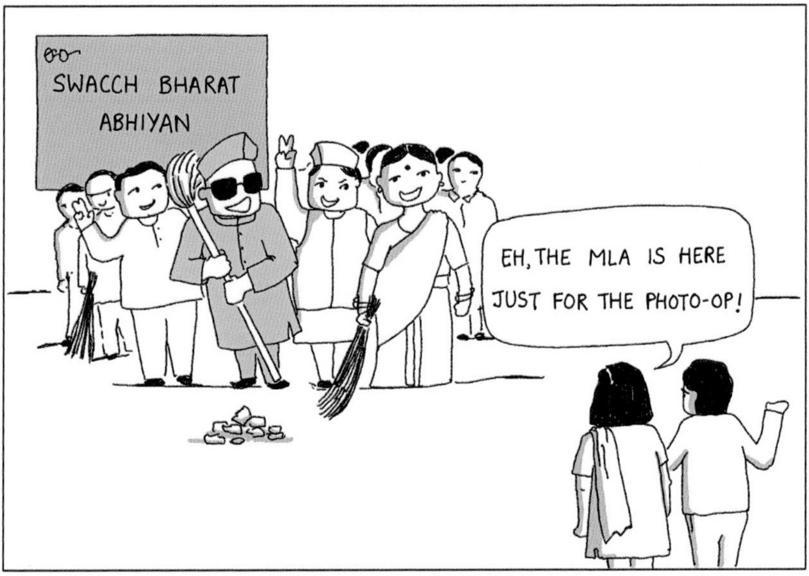
SWACCH BHARAT ABHIYAN
EH, THE MLA IS HERE JUST FOR THE PHOTO-OP!

#3. NUDGE

WHEN THE GOVERNMENT WANTS TO INFLUENCE PEOPLE'S BEHAVIOUR, ONE TOOL IN ITS ARMOUR IS TO NUDGE THEM.

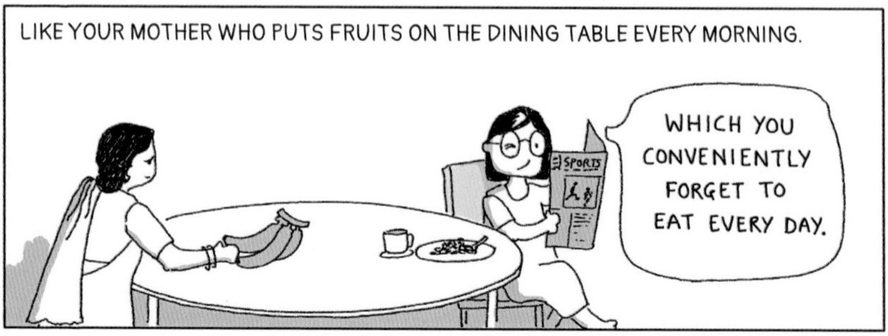
LIKE YOUR MOTHER WHO PUTS FRUITS ON THE DINING TABLE EVERY MORNING.
SPORTS
WHICH YOU CONVENIENTLY FORGET TO EAT EVERY DAY.

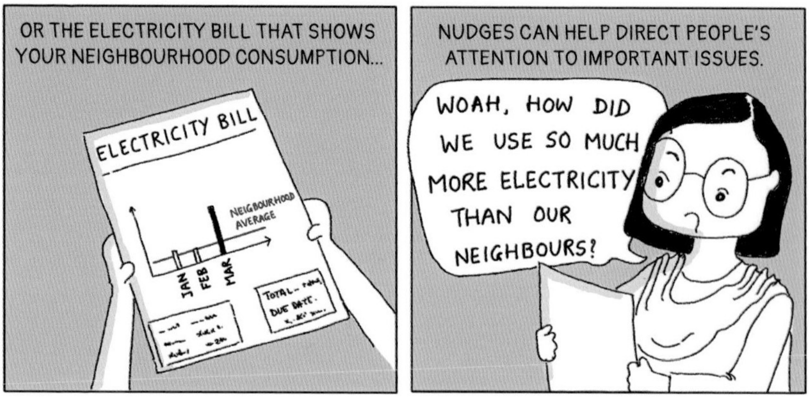
OR THE ELECTRICITY BILL THAT SHOWS YOUR NEIGHBOURHOOD CONSUMPTION...
ELECTRICITY BILL
NEIGBOURHOOD AVERAGE
JAN
FEB
MAR
NUDGES CAN HELP DIRECT PEOPLE'S ATTENTION TO IMPORTANT ISSUES.
WOAH, HOW DID WE USE SO MUCH MORE ELECTRICITY THAN OUR NEIGHBOURS?

NUDGES ARE EASY FOR GOVERNMENTS TO IMPLEMENT AS THEY DON'T REQUIRE A LOT OF STATE CAPACITY.

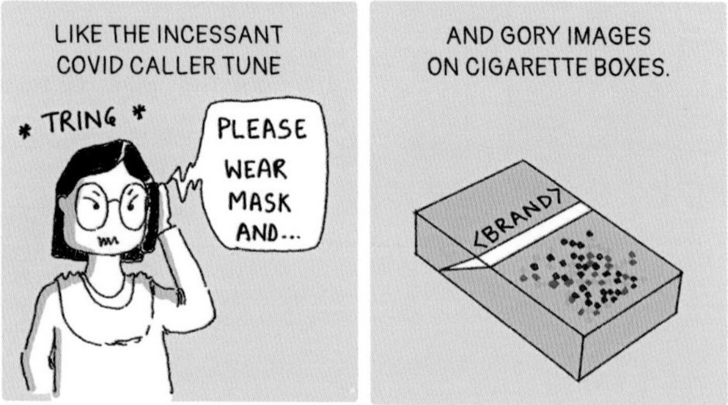
LIKE THE INCESSANT COVID CALLER TUNE
* TRING *
PLEASE WEAR MASK AND...
AND GORY IMAGES ON CIGARETTE BOXES.
<BRAND>

THEY ARE ALSO LESS COERCIVE ON THE PEOPLE AS THEY CAN BE EASILY IGNORED. BUT BEYOND A POINT, PEOPLE GET DESENSITIZED WITH NUDGES.

#4. UMPIRE

UMPIRING IS AN IMPORTANT FUNCTION IN GOVERNANCE.
MOST REGULATING BODIES LIKE SEBI AND THE RBI FALL UNDER THIS.

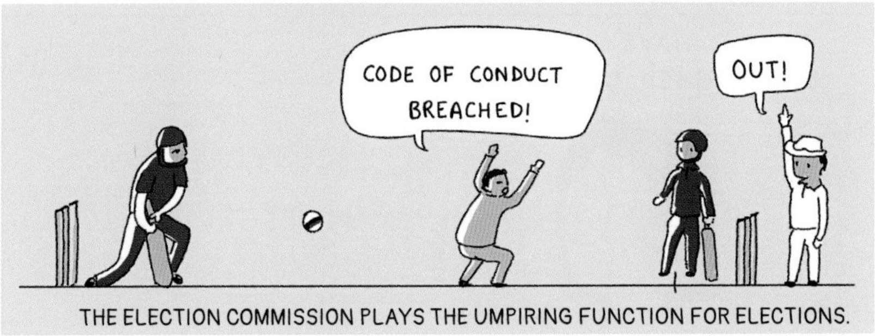
CODE OF CONDUCT BREACHED!
OUT!
THE ELECTION COMMISSION PLAYS THE UMPIRING FUNCTION FOR ELECTIONS.

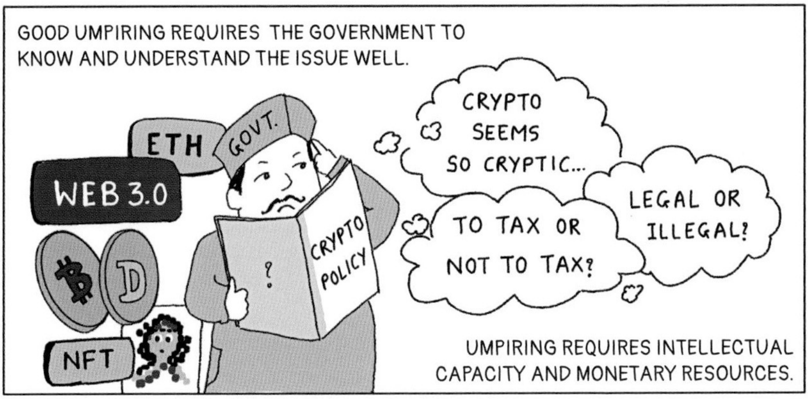
GOOD UMPIRING REQUIRES THE GOVERNMENT TO KNOW AND UNDERSTAND THE ISSUE WELL.
ETH
WEB 3.0
NFT
GOVT.
CRYPTO POLICY
CRYPTO SEEMS SO CRYPTIC...
LEGAL OR ILLEGAL?
TO TAX OR NOT TO TAX?
UMPIRING REQUIRES INTELLECTUAL CAPACITY AND MONETARY RESOURCES.

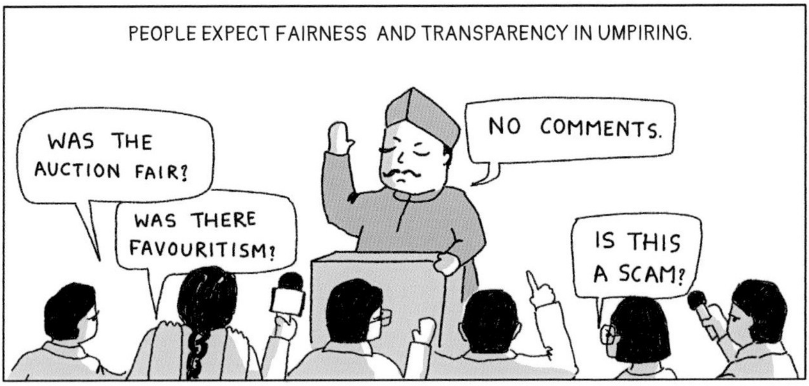
PEOPLE EXPECT FAIRNESS AND TRANSPARENCY IN UMPIRING.
WAS THE AUCTION FAIR?
WAS THERE FAVOURITISM?
NO COMMENTS.
IS THIS A SCAM?

IF THE GOVERNMENT CANNOT UMPIRE WELL,
IT STANDS TO LOSE CREDIBILITY.

#5. MARGINALLY CHANGING INCENTIVES

THE NEXT TOOL IN THE GOVERNMENT'S ARMOUR TO CHANGE PEOPLE'S BEHAVIOUR IS TO MARGINALLY CHANGE THEIR INCENTIVES.

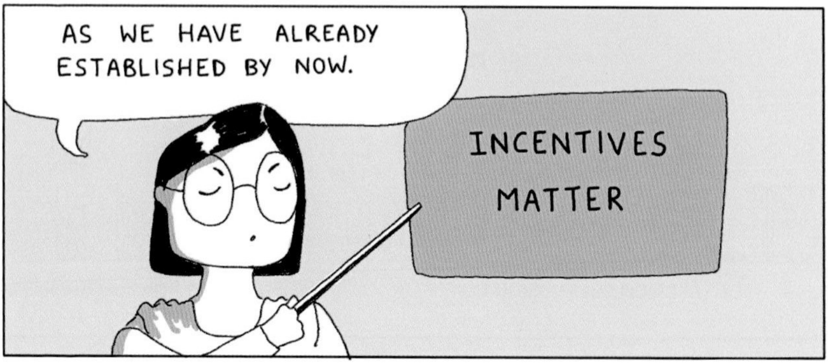
AS WE HAVE ALREADY ESTABLISHED BY NOW.
INCENTIVES MATTER

BY APPLYING SIN TAXES, IT CAN DISCOURAGE PEOPLE FROM USING CERTAIN GOODS.

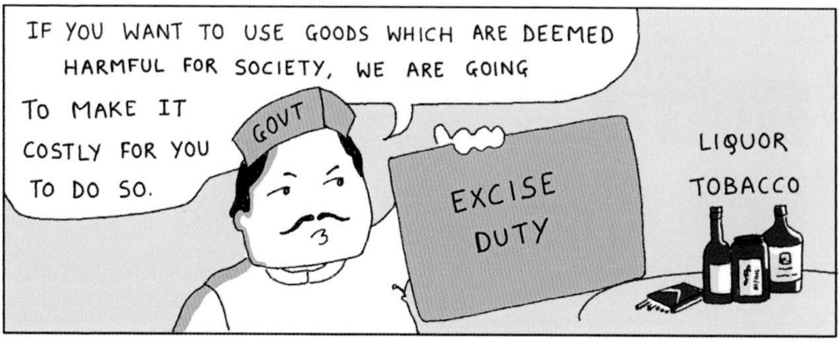
IF YOU WANT TO USE GOODS WHICH ARE DEEMED HARMFUL FOR SOCIETY, WE ARE GOING TO MAKE IT COSTLY FOR YOU TO DO SO.
GOVT
EXCISE DUTY
LIQUOR
TOBACCO

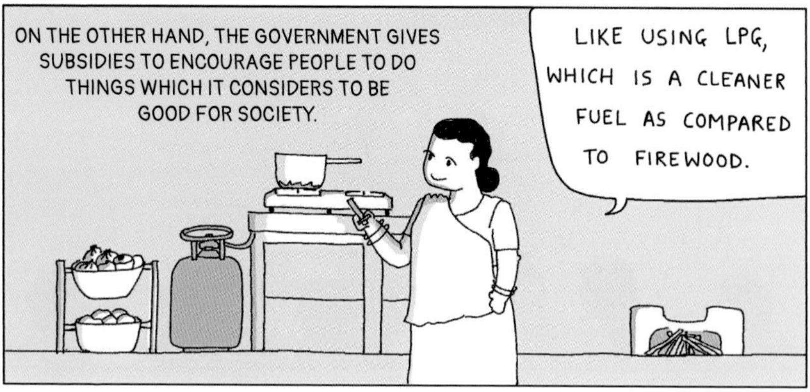
ON THE OTHER HAND, THE GOVERNMENT GIVES SUBSIDIES TO ENCOURAGE PEOPLE TO DO THINGS WHICH IT CONSIDERS TO BE GOOD FOR SOCIETY.
LIKE USING LPG, WHICH IS A CLEANER FUEL AS COMPARED TO FIREWOOD.

HOWEVER, CHANGING INCENTIVES CAN ALSO
CREATE MARKET DISTORTIONS.

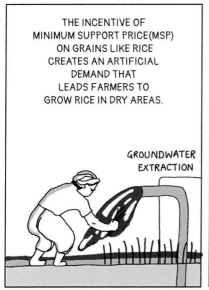

THE INCENTIVE OF
MINIMUM SUPPORT PRICE(MSP)
ON GRAINS LIKE RICE
CREATES AN ARTIFICIAL
DEMAND THAT
LEADS FARMERS TO
GROW RICE IN DRY AREAS.

GROUNDWATER
EXTRACTION

WITHOUT THIS ARTIFICIAL INCENTIVE,
FARMERS WOULD HAVE CHOSEN
TO GROW MORE LOCALLY SUITED
CROPS INSTEAD OF RICE.

WHICH CROP IS
SUITABLE HERE?

IS IT
HARDY?

WHAT
PRICE WILL
I GET?

THE RISK WITH THIS TOOL IS THAT THE LINE BETWEEN MARGINALLY CHANGING
INCENTIVES AND DRASTICALLY CHANGING INCENTIVES IS A VERY THIN ONE.

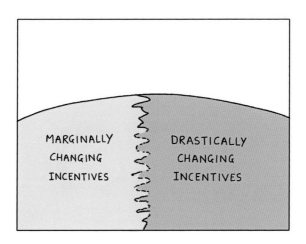

MARGINALLY
CHANGING
INCENTIVES

DRASTICALLY
CHANGING
INCENTIVES

#6. DRASTICALLY CHANGING INCENTIVES

WHEN THE GOVERNMENT WANTS TO DETER PEOPLE FROM DOING SOME THINGS, IT CAN GREATLY INCREASE THE COST OF DOING SO BY MAKING THEM A CRIME.

LIQUOR PROHIBITION
BEEF BAN
CRIMINALIZATION OF HOMOSEXUALITY

HOWEVER, DRASTICALLY CHANGING INCENTIVES REQUIRE SIGNIFICANTLY GREATER STATE CAPACITY FOR IMPLEMENTATION.

MORE POLICE
MORE JUDGES
MORE COURTS
MORE JAILS

SINCE STATE CAPACITY IS LIMITED, GOVERNMENTS NEED TO THINK IF THE ISSUE WARRANTS SPENDING THE ADDITIONAL RESOURCES ON IT.

IS THIS ALL WORTH IT FOR A VICTIMLESS CRIME?

REMEMBER, THERE IS AN OPPORTUNITY COST TO EVERYTHING. WOULDN'T THE SAME RESOURCES BE BETTER UTILIZED ON A MORE IMPORTANT ISSUE?

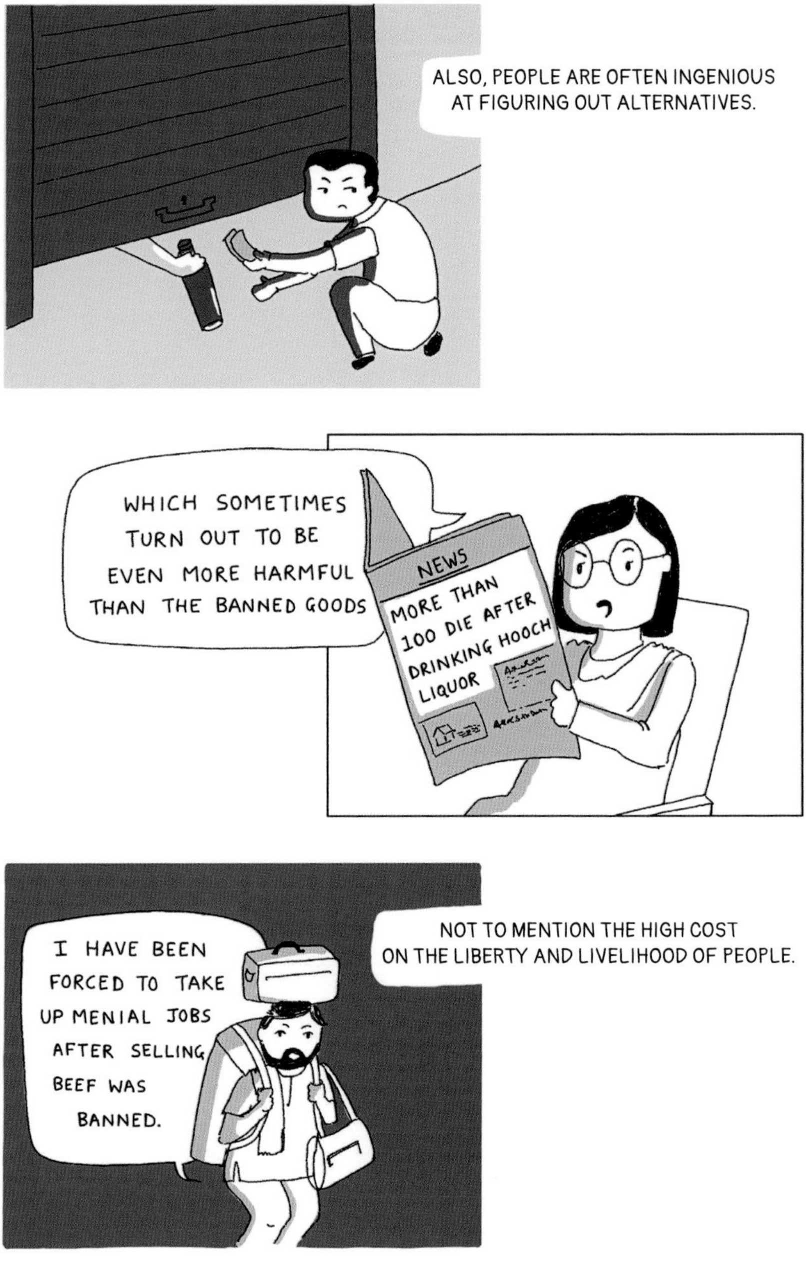
ALSO, PEOPLE ARE OFTEN INGENIOUS AT FIGURING OUT ALTERNATIVES.
WHICH SOMETIMES TURN OUT TO BE EVEN MORE HARMFUL THAN THE BANNED GOODS
NEWS
MORE THAN 100 DIE AFTER DRINKING HOOCH LIQUOR
NOT TO MENTION THE HIGH COST ON THE LIBERTY AND LIVELIHOOD OF PEOPLE.
I HAVE BEEN FORCED TO TAKE UP MENIAL JOBS AFTER SELLING BEEF WAS BANNED.

THIS MAKES IT AN INTERVENTION WITH HIGH ECONOMIC AND SOCIAL COST, AND IS A TOOL TO BE USED JUDICIOUSLY.

#7. DO IT YOURSELF

IN CASE OF MARKET FAILURES OR WHEN A MARKET IS ABSENT, THE GOVERNMENT MAY HAVE TO PRODUCE SOME GOODS AND SERVICES.

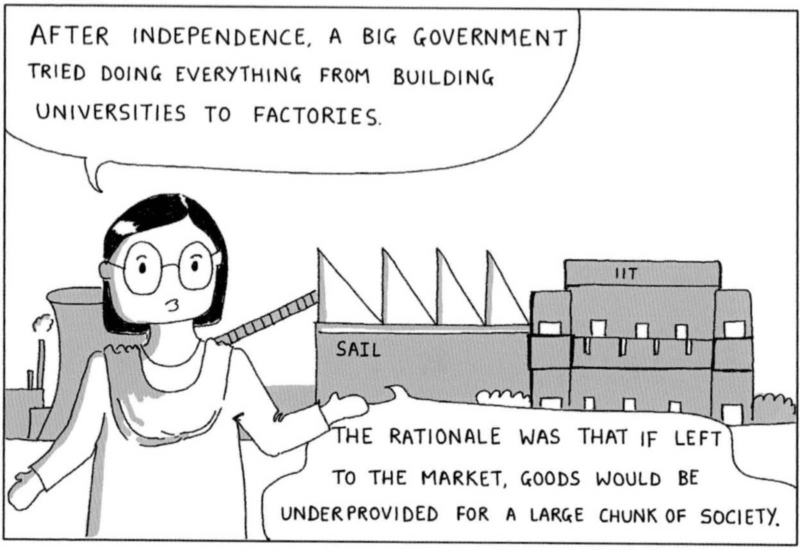
AFTER INDEPENDENCE, A BIG GOVERNMENT TRIED DOING EVERYTHING FROM BUILDING UNIVERSITIES TO FACTORIES.
IIT
SAIL
THE RATIONALE WAS THAT IF LEFT TO THE MARKET, GOODS WOULD BE UNDERPROVIDED FOR A LARGE CHUNK OF SOCIETY.

GOVERNMENT ALSO HAS TO PROVIDE FOR GOODS THAT CREATE A SAFETY NET IN SOCIETY, BUT IT'S AN INTERVENTION THAT REQUIRES HIGH STATE CAPACITY.

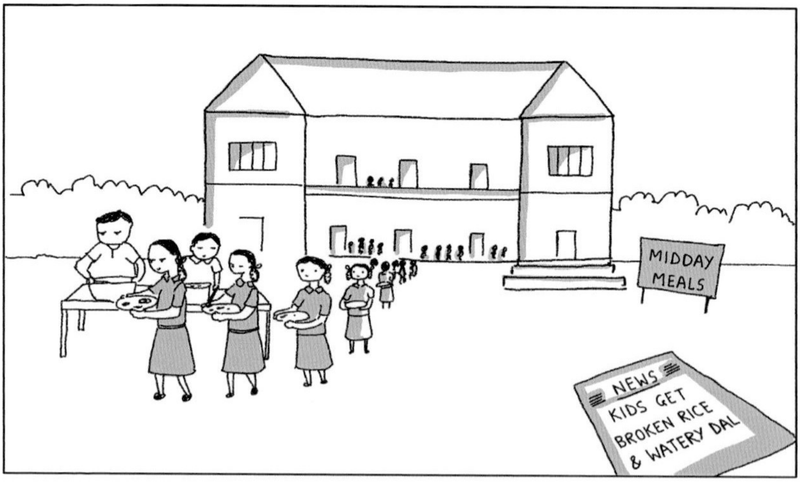
MIDDAY MEALS
NEWS
KIDS GET BROKEN RICE & WATERY DAL

THE DIY APPROACH REQUIRES AN ORGANIZATIONAL FOCUS ON EFFICIENCY WHICH GOVERNMENTS ACROSS THE WORLD ARE RELATIVELY WEAK AT.

ALSO, ONCE A GOVERNMENT PLAYER IS IN THE MARKET, THERE IS A STRONGER CHANCE OF MARKET DISTORTION, WHICH MAY IMPEDE OTHER PRIVATE PLAYERS FROM ENTERING THE MARKET.

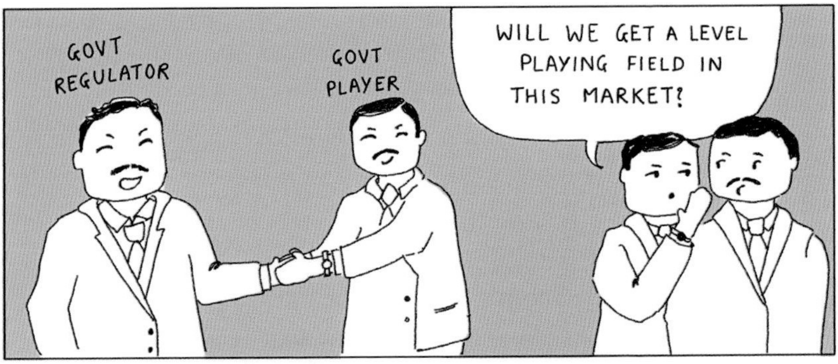
GOVT REGULATOR
GOVT PLAYER
WILL WE GET A LEVEL PLAYING FIELD IN THIS MARKET?

#8. CHANGE OWNERSHIP

SOMETIMES, THE GOVERNMENT CAN BRING ABOUT SWEEPING CHANGES BY SIMPLY CHANGING OWNERSHIPS, BUT THAT COMES WITH ITS OWN SET OF CHALLENGES.

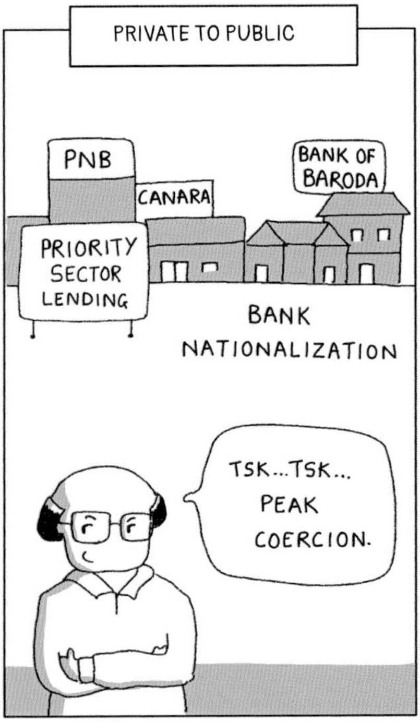
PRIVATE TO PUBLIC
PNB
CANARA
BANK OF BARODA
PRIORITY SECTOR LENDING
BANK NATIONALIZATION
TSK...TSK... PEAK COERCION.

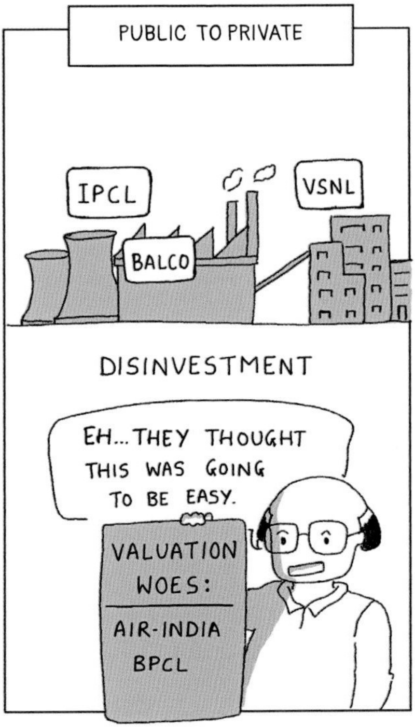
PUBLIC TO PRIVATE
IPCL
VSNL
BALCO
DISINVESTMENT
EH... THEY THOUGHT THIS WAS GOING TO BE EASY.
VALUATION WOES:
AIR-INDIA
BPCL

THIS MAY SEEM STRAIGHTFORWARD, BUT IT HAS ITS OWN SET OF CHALLENGES.

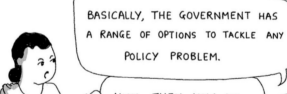

BASICALLY, THE GOVERNMENT HAS A RANGE OF OPTIONS TO TACKLE ANY POLICY PROBLEM.

HMM...THEN HOW DO WE DECIDE WHICH OF THE EIGHT THINGS IT SHOULD DO?

ONE WAY TO THINK ABOUT THIS IS TO KEEP IN MIND TWO FACTORS.

THINK INTERVENTION	THINK CAPACITY
TO WHAT EXTENT IS THE GOVERNMENT INTERVENING IN PEOPLE'S LIVES?	IS THERE ENOUGH STATE CAPACITY TO IMPLEMENT THE INTERVENTION?

HERE'S A FRAMEWORK TO THINK ABOUT THIS:

STATE CAPACITY
DO IT YOURSELF
UMPIRE
DRASTICALLY CHANGING INCENTIVE
MARGINALLY CHANGING INCENTIVE
CHANGE OWNERSHIP
NUDGE
ENGAGE IN RHETORIC
DO NOTHING
EXTENT OF INTERVENTION

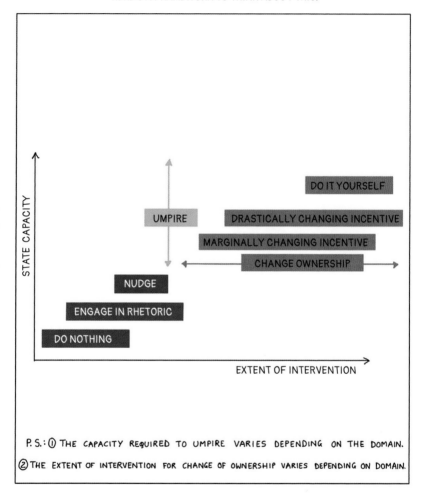

P. S.: ① THE CAPACITY REQUIRED TO UMPIRE VARIES DEPENDING ON THE DOMAIN.

② THE EXTENT OF INTERVENTION FOR CHANGE OF OWNERSHIP VARIES DEPENDING ON DOMAIN.

THE HIGHER THE EXTENT OF INTERVENTION AND
THE HIGHER THE STATE CAPACITY NEEDED TO IMPLEMENT IT,
THE HIGHER THE SOCIO-ECONOMIC COSTS TO IMPLEMENT THE POLICY.

TYPICALLY, EVERY PUBLIC POLICY WILL USE A COMBINATION OF ALL THESE TOOLS.

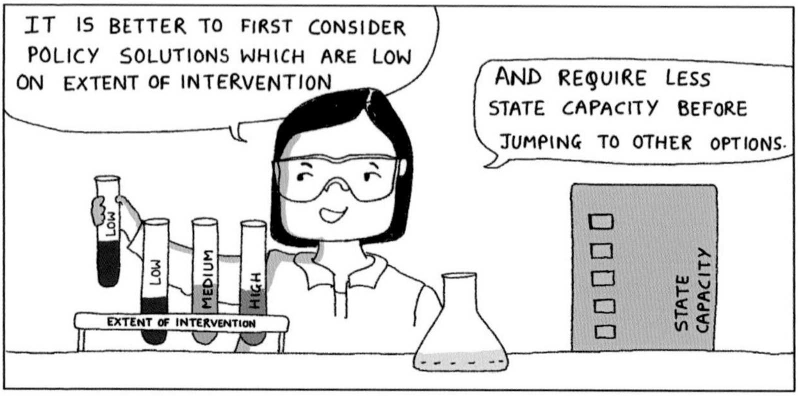
IT IS BETTER TO FIRST CONSIDER POLICY SOLUTIONS WHICH ARE LOW ON EXTENT OF INTERVENTION
AND REQUIRE LESS STATE CAPACITY BEFORE JUMPING TO OTHER OPTIONS.
LOW
LOW
MEDIUM
HIGH
EXTENT OF INTERVENTION
STATE CAPACITY

BE WARY OF SOLUTIONS WHICH ARE HIGH IN THE EXTENT OF INTERVENTION AND REQUIRE HIGH STATE CAPACITY.

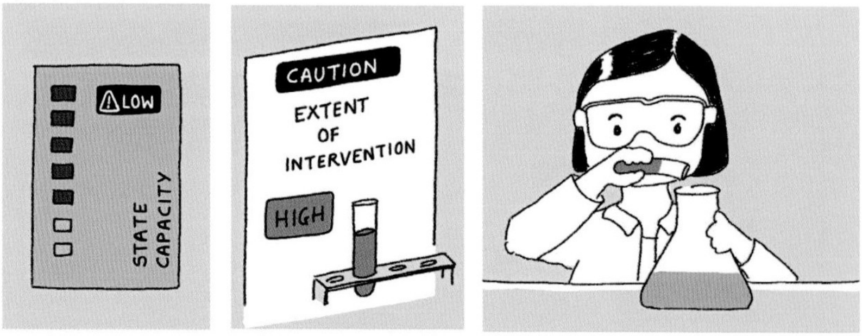
LOW
STATE CAPACITY
CAUTION
EXTENT OF INTERVENTION
HIGH

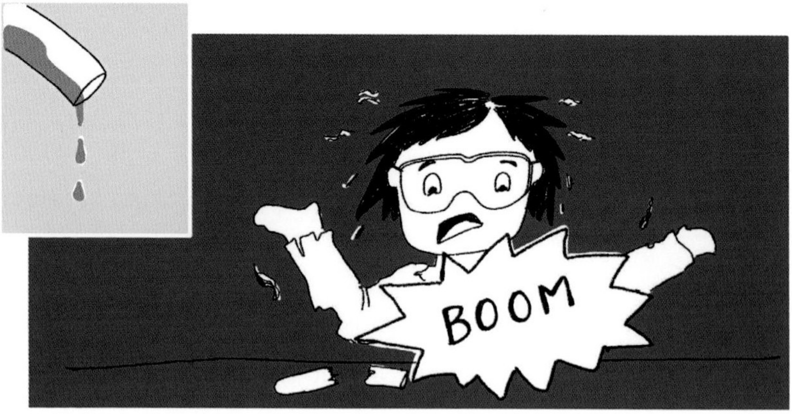
BOOM

BECAUSE A LOT CAN GO WRONG IF THE GOVERNMENT CANNOT IMPLEMENT THEM WELL.

Chapter 7

Caught Red-Handed with a Beer Bottle

Copycats beware

Once upon a time in colonial India,

Saheb, there are too many cobras in the city. Please do Something...
Don't worry. I have an idea. How about we give a prize to anyone who brings a dead cobra!
What an idea, Sirjee!

and so...

WIN A BOUNTY FOR EVERY DEAD COBRA

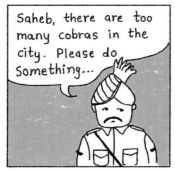

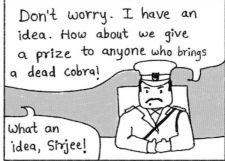

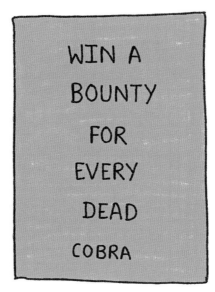

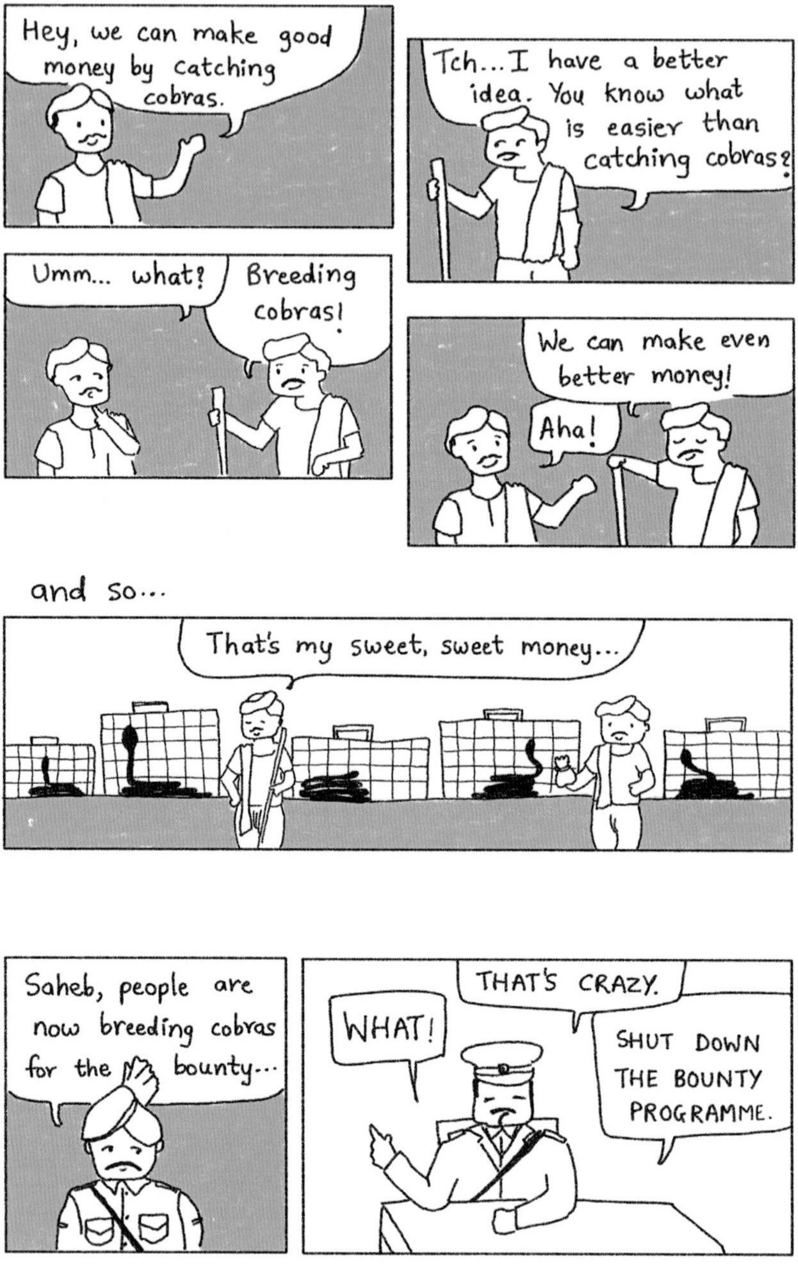
Hey, we can make good money by catching cobras.
Tch... I have a better idea. You know what is easier than catching cobras?
Umm... what?
Breeding cobras!
We can make even better money!
Aha!
and so...
That's my sweet, sweet money...
Saheb, people are now breeding cobras for the bounty...
WHAT!
THAT'S CRAZY.
SHUT DOWN THE BOUNTY PROGRAMME.

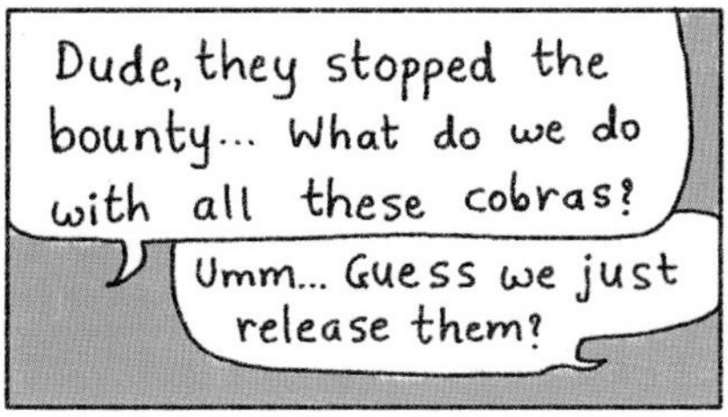
Dude, they stopped the bounty... What do we do with all these cobras?
Umm... Guess we just release them?

... and so ...

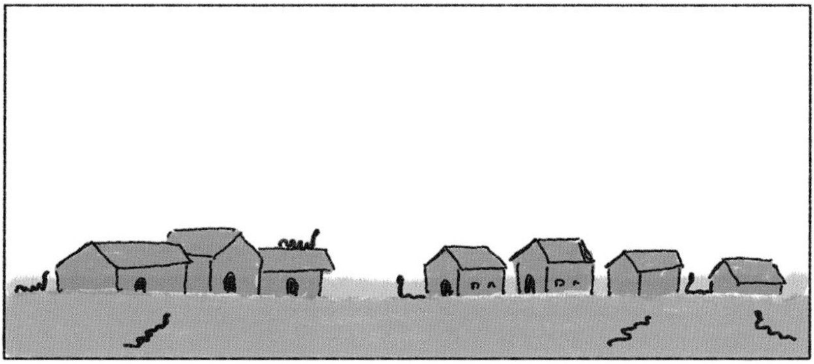

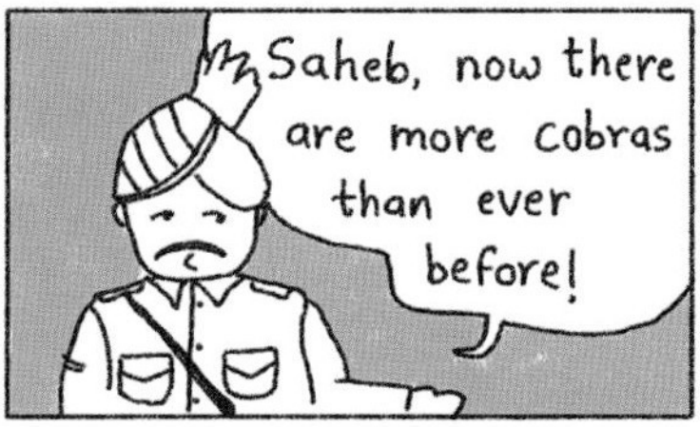
Saheb, now there are more cobras than ever before!

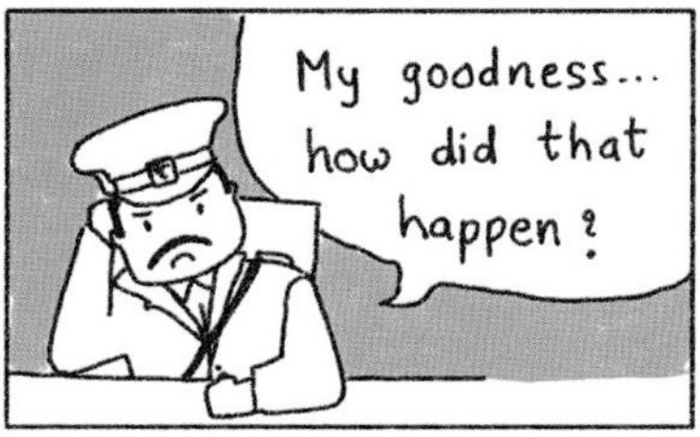
My goodness... how did that happen?

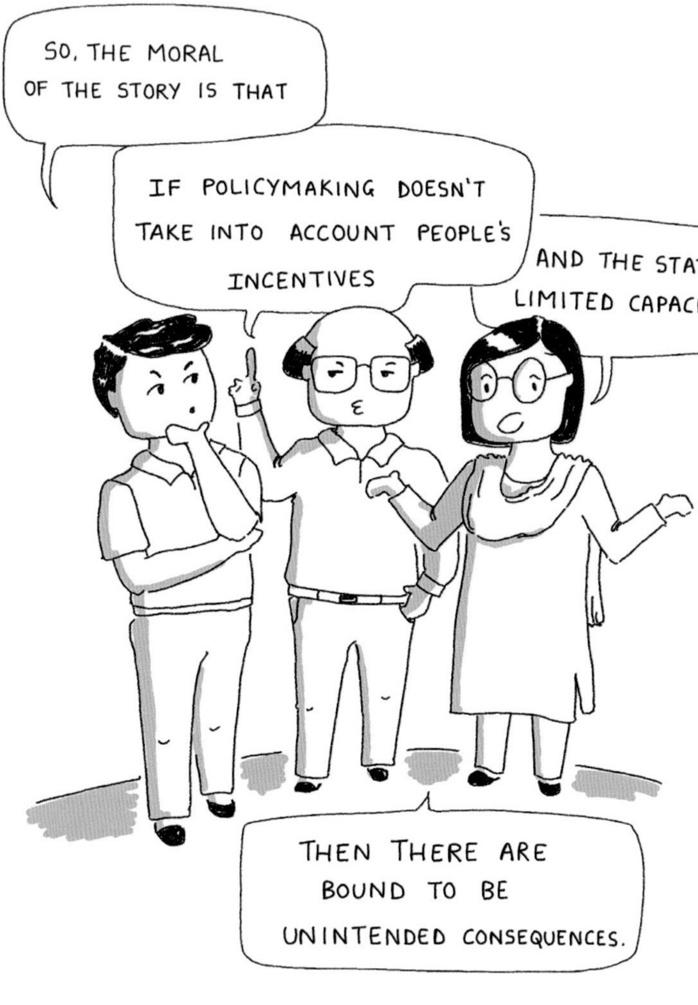

SO, THE MORAL OF THE STORY IS THAT
IF POLICYMAKING DOESN'T TAKE INTO ACCOUNT PEOPLE'S INCENTIVES
AND THE STATE'S LIMITED CAPACITY
THEN THERE ARE BOUND TO BE UNINTENDED CONSEQUENCES.

WE ALREADY TALKED ABOUT THE LOW CAPACITY OF
THE INDIAN STATE, PARTICULARLY AT THE LOCAL LEVEL.

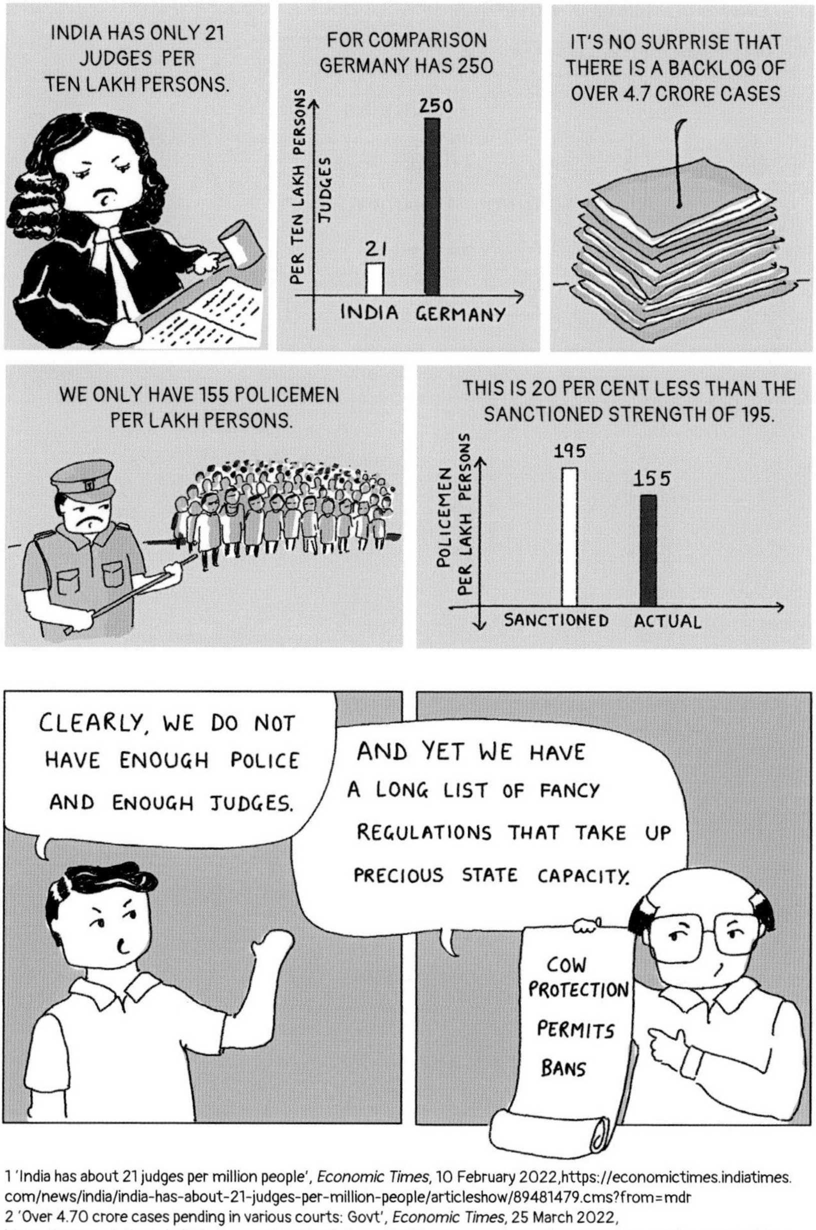
INDIA HAS ONLY 21 JUDGES PER TEN LAKH PERSONS.
FOR COMPARISON GERMANY HAS 250
PER TEN LAKH PERSONS
JUDGES
21
250
INDIA
GERMANY
IT'S NO SURPRISE THAT THERE IS A BACKLOG OF OVER 4.7 CRORE CASES
WE ONLY HAVE 155 POLICEMEN PER LAKH PERSONS.
THIS IS 20 PER CENT LESS THAN THE SANCTIONED STRENGTH OF 195.
POLICEMEN PER LAKH PERSONS
195
155
SANCTIONED
ACTUAL
CLEARLY, WE DO NOT HAVE ENOUGH POLICE AND ENOUGH JUDGES.
AND YET WE HAVE A LONG LIST OF FANCY REGULATIONS THAT TAKE UP PRECIOUS STATE CAPACITY.
COW PROTECTION
PERMITS
BANS

1 'India has about 21 judges per million people', *Economic Times*, 10 February 2022,https://economictimes.indiatimes.com/news/india/india-has-about-21-judges-per-million-people/articleshow/89481479.cms?from=mdr
2 'Over 4.70 crore cases pending in various courts: Govt', *Economic Times*, 25 March 2022, https://economictimes.indiatimes.com/news/india/over-4-70-crore-cases-pending-in-various-courts-govt/articleshow/90447554.cms?
3 https://www.mha.gov.in/MHA1/Par2017/pdfs/par2021-pdfs/rs-24032021/3266.pdf

CONSIDER THE LIQUOR PROHIBITION IN BIHAR.

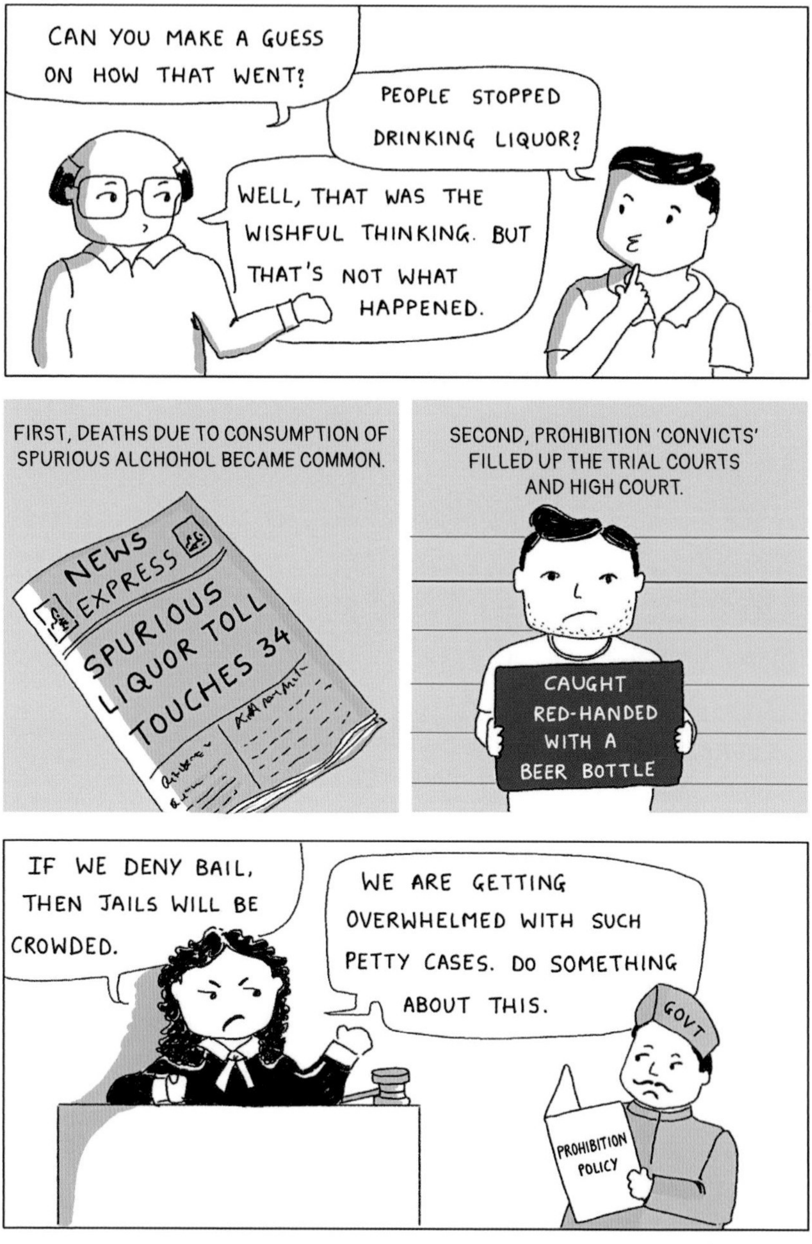
CAN YOU MAKE A GUESS ON HOW THAT WENT?
PEOPLE STOPPED DRINKING LIQUOR?
WELL, THAT WAS THE WISHFUL THINKING. BUT THAT'S NOT WHAT HAPPENED.
FIRST, DEATHS DUE TO CONSUMPTION OF SPURIOUS ALCHOHOL BECAME COMMON.
NEWS EXPRESS
SPURIOUS LIQUOR TOLL TOUCHES 34
SECOND, PROHIBITION 'CONVICTS' FILLED UP THE TRIAL COURTS AND HIGH COURT.
CAUGHT RED-HANDED WITH A BEER BOTTLE
IF WE DENY BAIL, THEN JAILS WILL BE CROWDED.
WE ARE GETTING OVERWHELMED WITH SUCH PETTY CASES. DO SOMETHING ABOUT THIS.
GOVT
PROHIBITION POLICY

FINALLY, THE BIHAR GOVERNMENT HAD TO RECONSIDER THE PUNISHMENT UNDER THE ACT. NOW, FIRST TIME OFFENDERS WILL BE FINED INSTEAD OF JAILED.

THIS AMENDMENT WILL SOLVE A SMALL PROBLEM FOR THE COURTS, BUT WOES WILL CONTINUE FOR THE PEOPLE.

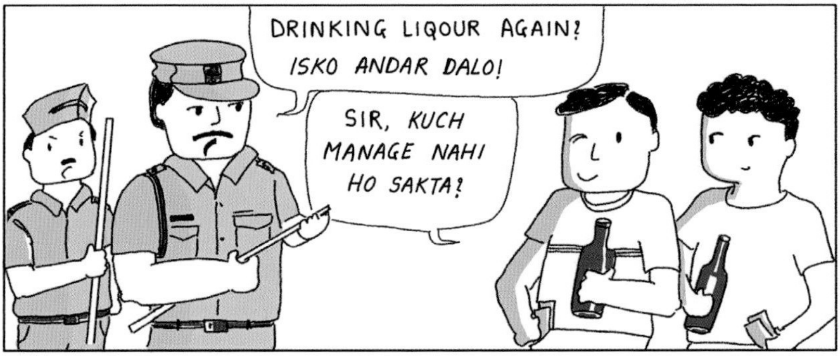
DRINKING LIQOUR AGAIN? *ISKO ANDAR DALO!*
SIR, *KUCH MANAGE NAHI HO SAKTA?*

THIS IS BOUND TO ENCOURAGE CORRUPTION. NOW, INSTEAD OF CATCHING CRIMINALS, THE POLICE HAS MORE INCENTIVES TO BE INTERESTED IN DRUNKARDS.

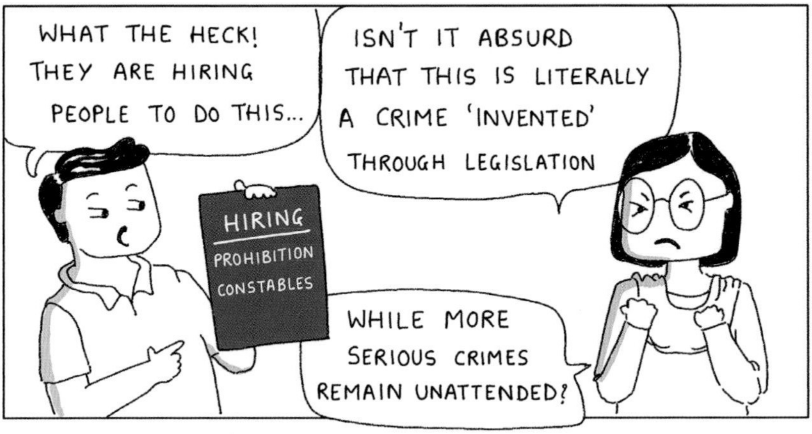
WHAT THE HECK! THEY ARE HIRING PEOPLE TO DO THIS...
HIRING
PROHIBITION CONSTABLES
ISN'T IT ABSURD THAT THIS IS LITERALLY A CRIME 'INVENTED' THROUGH LEGISLATION
WHILE MORE SERIOUS CRIMES REMAIN UNATTENDED?

ALL THIS IS NOT FREE OF COST. IT IS FUNDED BY PEOPLE'S MONEY.

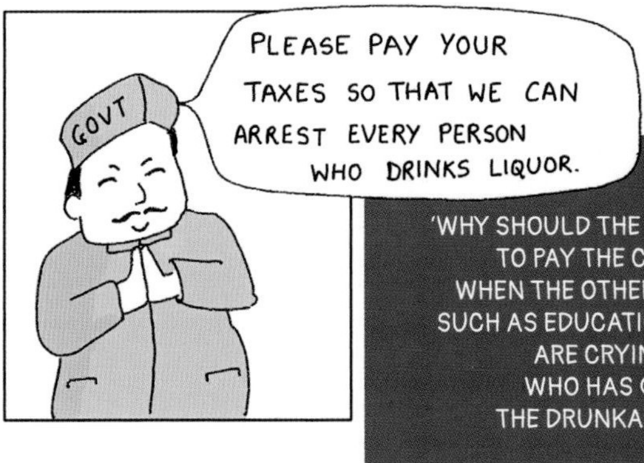
PLEASE PAY YOUR TAXES SO THAT WE CAN ARREST EVERY PERSON WHO DRINKS LIQUOR.
GOVT

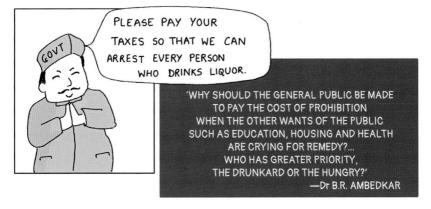

'WHY SHOULD THE GENERAL PUBLIC BE MADE TO PAY THE COST OF PROHIBITION WHEN THE OTHER WANTS OF THE PUBLIC SUCH AS EDUCATION, HOUSING AND HEALTH ARE CRYING FOR REMEDY?... WHO HAS GREATER PRIORITY, THE DRUNKARD OR THE HUNGRY?'

—Dr B.R. AMBEDKAR

IT DOES NOT HELP TO COPY AMBITIOUS LAWS FROM OTHER COUNTRIES WITHOUT HAVING THE ABILITY TO ENFORCE THEM.

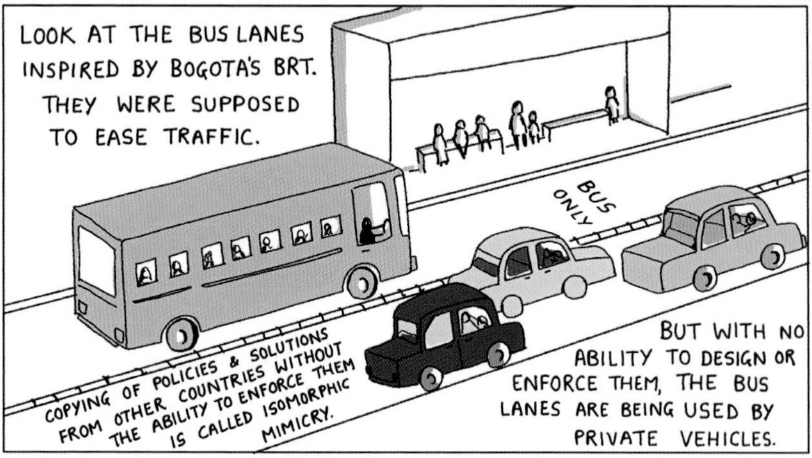
LOOK AT THE BUS LANES INSPIRED BY BOGOTA'S BRT. THEY WERE SUPPOSED TO EASE TRAFFIC.
BUS ONLY
COPYING OF POLICIES & SOLUTIONS FROM OTHER COUNTRIES WITHOUT THE ABILITY TO ENFORCE THEM IS CALLED ISOMORPHIC MIMICRY.
BUT WITH NO ABILITY TO DESIGN OR ENFORCE THEM, THE BUS LANES ARE BEING USED BY PRIVATE VEHICLES.

THE RULE-ABIDING CITIZENS ARE PENALIZED WITH ONE LESS LANE ON THE ROAD, WHILE THE RULE-BREAKING CITIZENS DASH THROUGH AS THERE IS NO ENFORCEMENT.

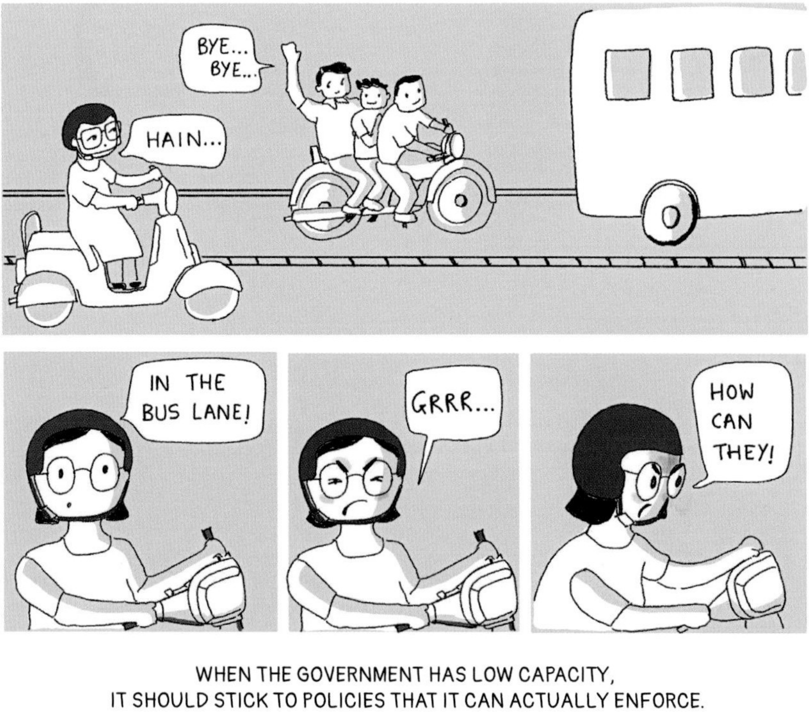
BYE... BYE...
HAIN...
IN THE BUS LANE!
GRRR...
HOW CAN THEY!

WHEN THE GOVERNMENT HAS LOW CAPACITY, IT SHOULD STICK TO POLICIES THAT IT CAN ACTUALLY ENFORCE.

OTHERWISE, RESPECT FOR LAW DIMINISHES IN THE LONG RUN.

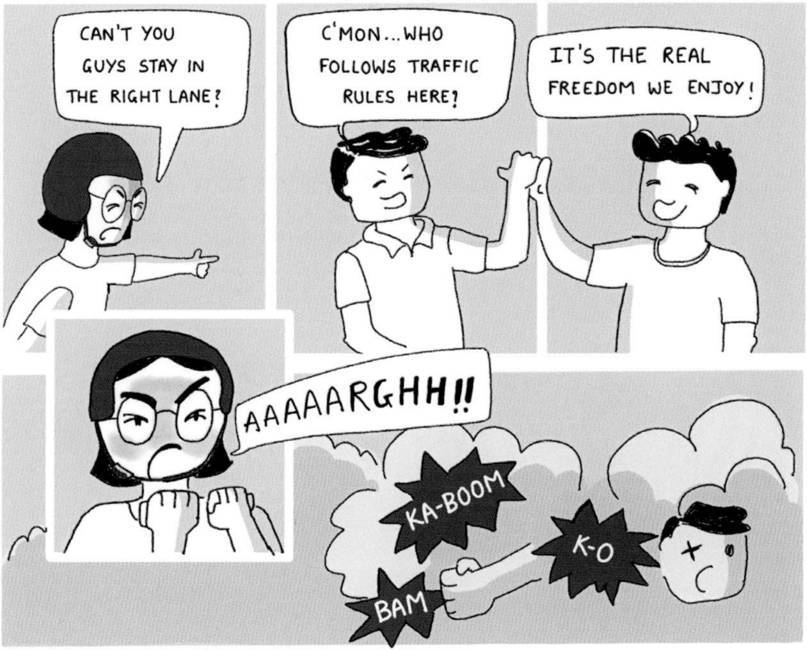
CAN'T YOU GUYS STAY IN THE RIGHT LANE?
C'MON...WHO FOLLOWS TRAFFIC RULES HERE?
IT'S THE REAL FREEDOM WE ENJOY!
AAAAARGHH!!
KA-BOOM
K-O
BAM

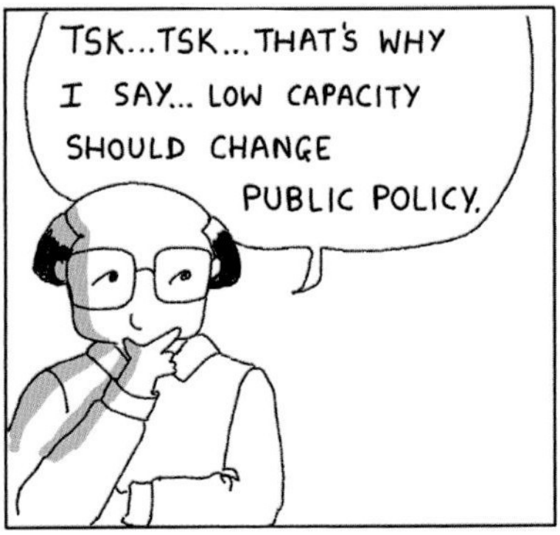
TSK...TSK...THAT'S WHY I SAY... LOW CAPACITY SHOULD CHANGE PUBLIC POLICY.

IT ALL COMES DOWN TO THE STATE CAPACITY.

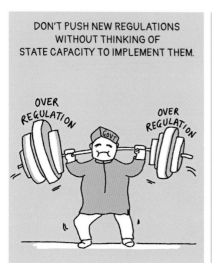

DON'T PUSH NEW REGULATIONS WITHOUT THINKING OF STATE CAPACITY TO IMPLEMENT THEM.
OVER REGULATION
GOVT
OVER REGULATION
INCREASE STATE CAPACITY IN CORE AREAS LIKE LAW AND ORDER, DEFENCE, AND PUBLIC GOODS.
LAW & ORDER
GOVT
PUBLIC GOODS
AS THE CHINESE SAYING GOES, 'DON'T ADD FEET TO SNAKES.'

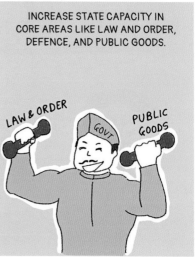

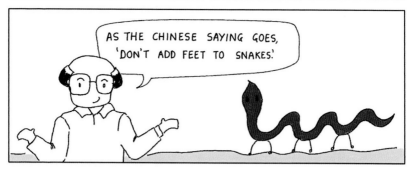

Chapter 8

When Getting a Phone Was a Five-Year Plan

When markets fail

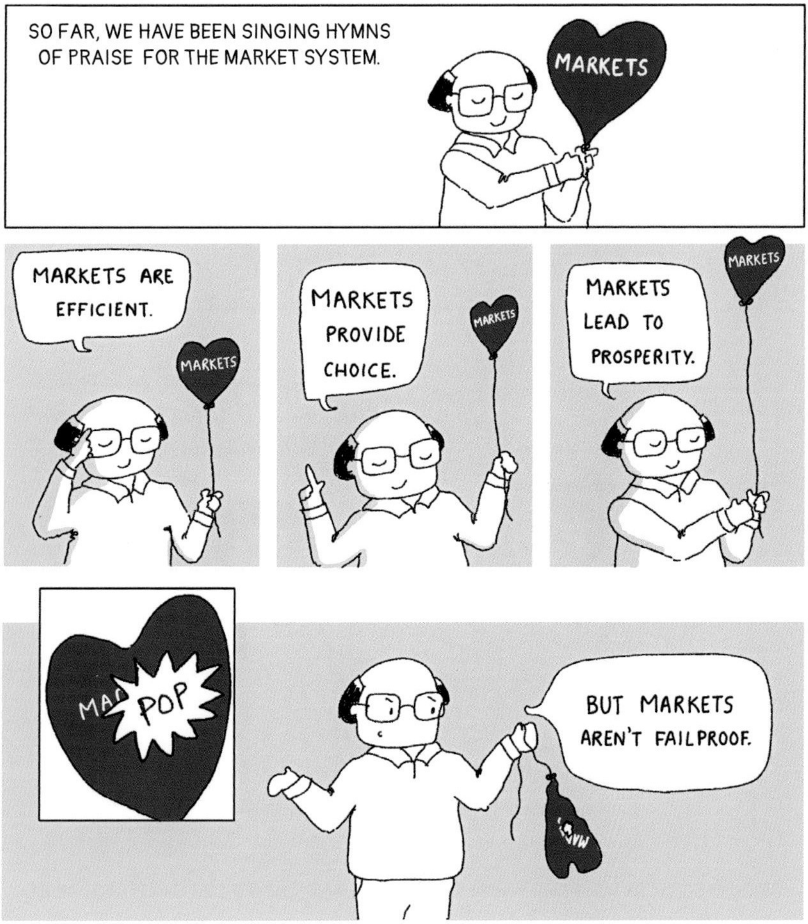
SO FAR, WE HAVE BEEN SINGING HYMNS OF PRAISE FOR THE MARKET SYSTEM.
MARKETS
MARKETS ARE EFFICIENT.
MARKETS
MARKETS PROVIDE CHOICE.
MARKETS
MARKETS LEAD TO PROSPERITY.
MARKETS
POP
BUT MARKETS AREN'T FAILPROOF.

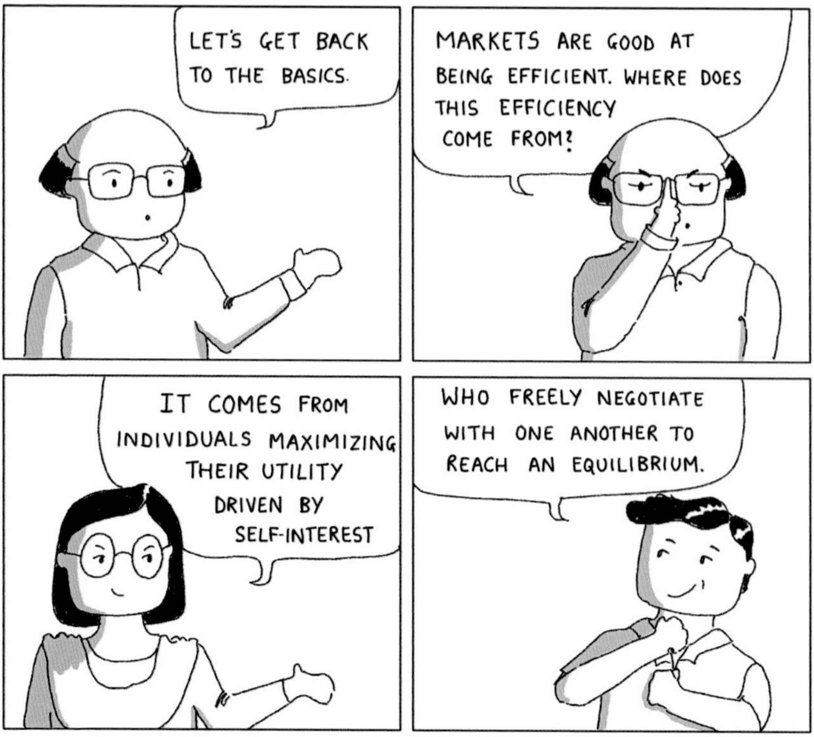
LET'S GET BACK TO THE BASICS.
MARKETS ARE GOOD AT BEING EFFICIENT. WHERE DOES THIS EFFICIENCY COME FROM?
IT COMES FROM INDIVIDUALS MAXIMIZING THEIR UTILITY DRIVEN BY SELF-INTEREST
WHO FREELY NEGOTIATE WITH ONE ANOTHER TO REACH AN EQUILIBRIUM.

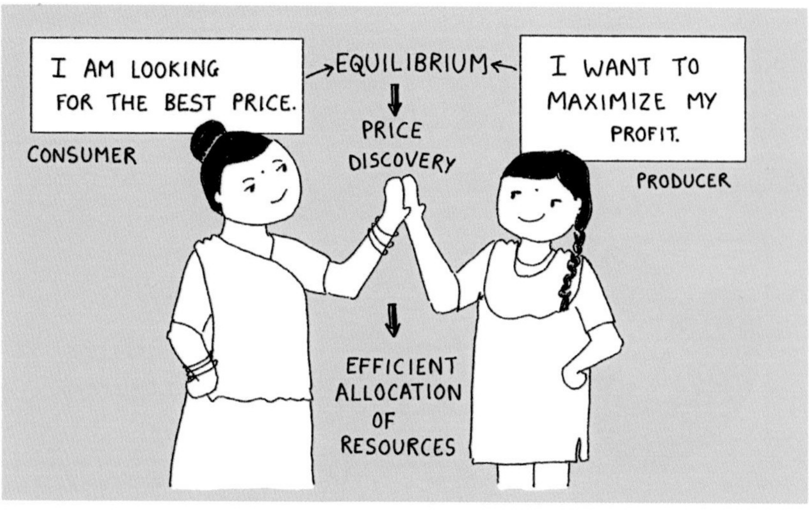
I AM LOOKING FOR THE BEST PRICE.
CONSUMER
EQUILIBRIUM
PRICE DISCOVERY
EFFICIENT ALLOCATION OF RESOURCES
I WANT TO MAXIMIZE MY PROFIT.
PRODUCER

PRICE DISCOVERY HAPPENS WHEN THE BUYER'S AND THE SELLER'S INTEREST MEET.

BUT, FOR THESE VOLUNTARY EXCHANGES TO BE SUCCESSFUL, FOUR CONDITIONS SHOULD BE MET.

TERMS
AND
CONDITIONS
DISCLAIMER

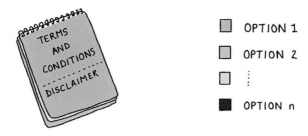

THERE IS PERFECT INFORMATION.

OPTION 1
OPTION 2
OPTION n

THERE IS PERFECT COMPETITION.

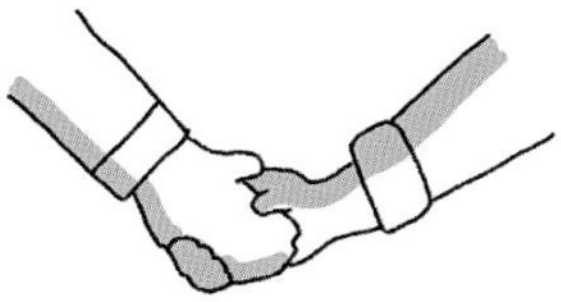

THERE IS NO TRANSACTION COST.

PROS
CONS

ALL COSTS AND BENEFITS ARE ACCOUNTED FOR.

BUT, IN REALITY...
NOTHING IS PERFECT
STILL, THESE CONDITIONS BROADLY HOLD TRUE UNDER MOST CIRCUMSTANCES.
BUT THERE ARE SITUATIONS IN WHICH THESE CONDITIONS ARE NOT MET, LEADING TO INEFFICIENT ALLOCATION OF RESOURCES. THESE ARE CALLED MARKET FAILURES.

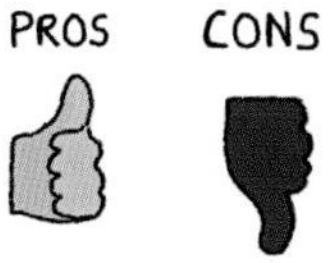

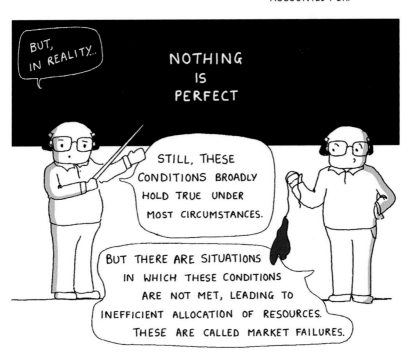

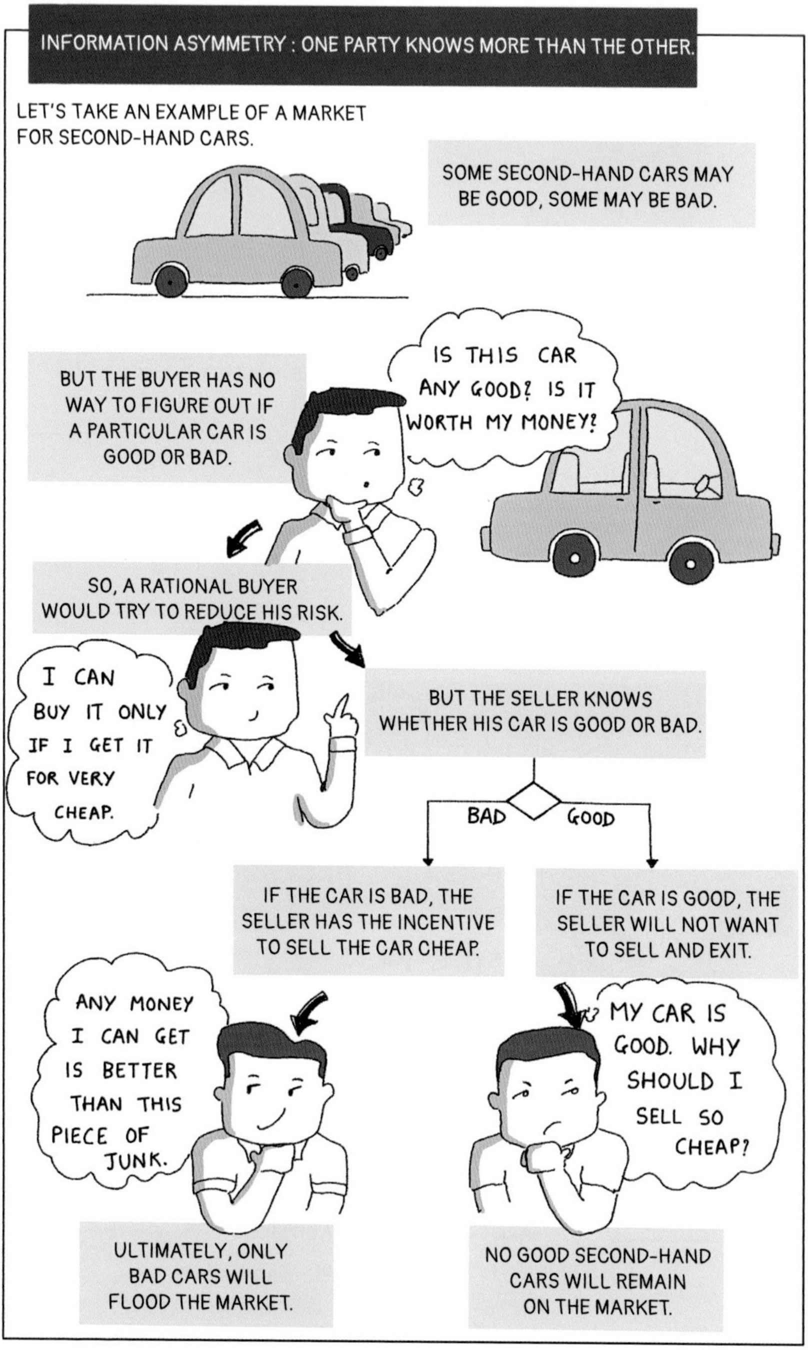
INFORMATION ASYMMETRY : ONE PARTY KNOWS MORE THAN THE OTHER.
LET'S TAKE AN EXAMPLE OF A MARKET FOR SECOND-HAND CARS.
SOME SECOND-HAND CARS MAY BE GOOD, SOME MAY BE BAD.
BUT THE BUYER HAS NO WAY TO FIGURE OUT IF A PARTICULAR CAR IS GOOD OR BAD.
IS THIS CAR ANY GOOD? IS IT WORTH MY MONEY?
SO, A RATIONAL BUYER WOULD TRY TO REDUCE HIS RISK.
I CAN BUY IT ONLY IF I GET IT FOR VERY CHEAP.
BUT THE SELLER KNOWS WHETHER HIS CAR IS GOOD OR BAD.
BAD
GOOD
IF THE CAR IS BAD, THE SELLER HAS THE INCENTIVE TO SELL THE CAR CHEAP.
IF THE CAR IS GOOD, THE SELLER WILL NOT WANT TO SELL AND EXIT.
ANY MONEY I CAN GET IS BETTER THAN THIS PIECE OF JUNK.
MY CAR IS GOOD. WHY SHOULD I SELL SO CHEAP?
ULTIMATELY, ONLY BAD CARS WILL FLOOD THE MARKET.
NO GOOD SECOND-HAND CARS WILL REMAIN ON THE MARKET.

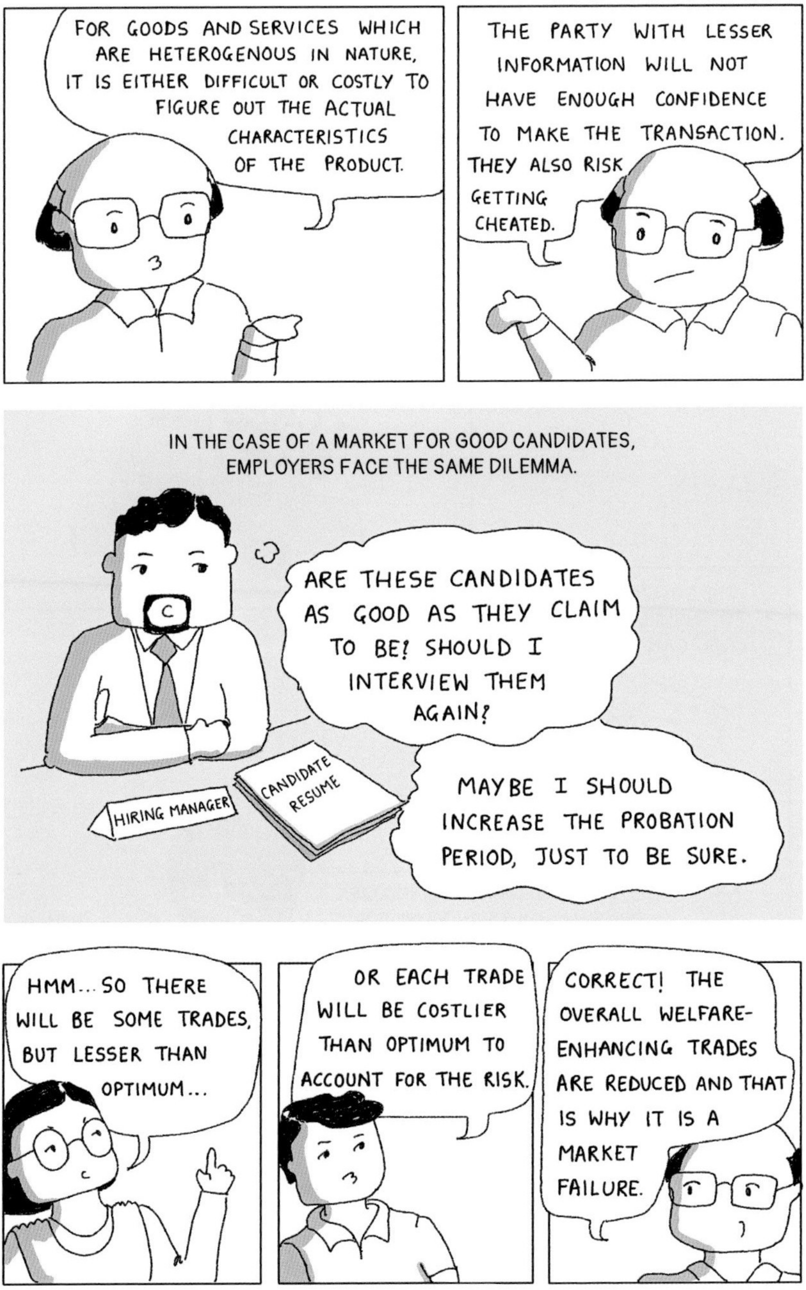
FOR GOODS AND SERVICES WHICH ARE HETEROGENOUS IN NATURE, IT IS EITHER DIFFICULT OR COSTLY TO FIGURE OUT THE ACTUAL CHARACTERISTICS OF THE PRODUCT.
THE PARTY WITH LESSER INFORMATION WILL NOT HAVE ENOUGH CONFIDENCE TO MAKE THE TRANSACTION. THEY ALSO RISK GETTING CHEATED.
IN THE CASE OF A MARKET FOR GOOD CANDIDATES, EMPLOYERS FACE THE SAME DILEMMA.
ARE THESE CANDIDATES AS GOOD AS THEY CLAIM TO BE? SHOULD I INTERVIEW THEM AGAIN?
MAYBE I SHOULD INCREASE THE PROBATION PERIOD, JUST TO BE SURE.
HIRING MANAGER
CANDIDATE RESUME
HMM... SO THERE WILL BE SOME TRADES, BUT LESSER THAN OPTIMUM...
OR EACH TRADE WILL BE COSTLIER THAN OPTIMUM TO ACCOUNT FOR THE RISK.
CORRECT! THE OVERALL WELFARE-ENHANCING TRADES ARE REDUCED AND THAT IS WHY IT IS A MARKET FAILURE.

THIS TYPE OF MARKET FAILURE IS CALLED INFORMATION ASYMMETRY.

THE SOLUTION IS TO INCREASE TRANSPARENCY AND BUILD TRUST.

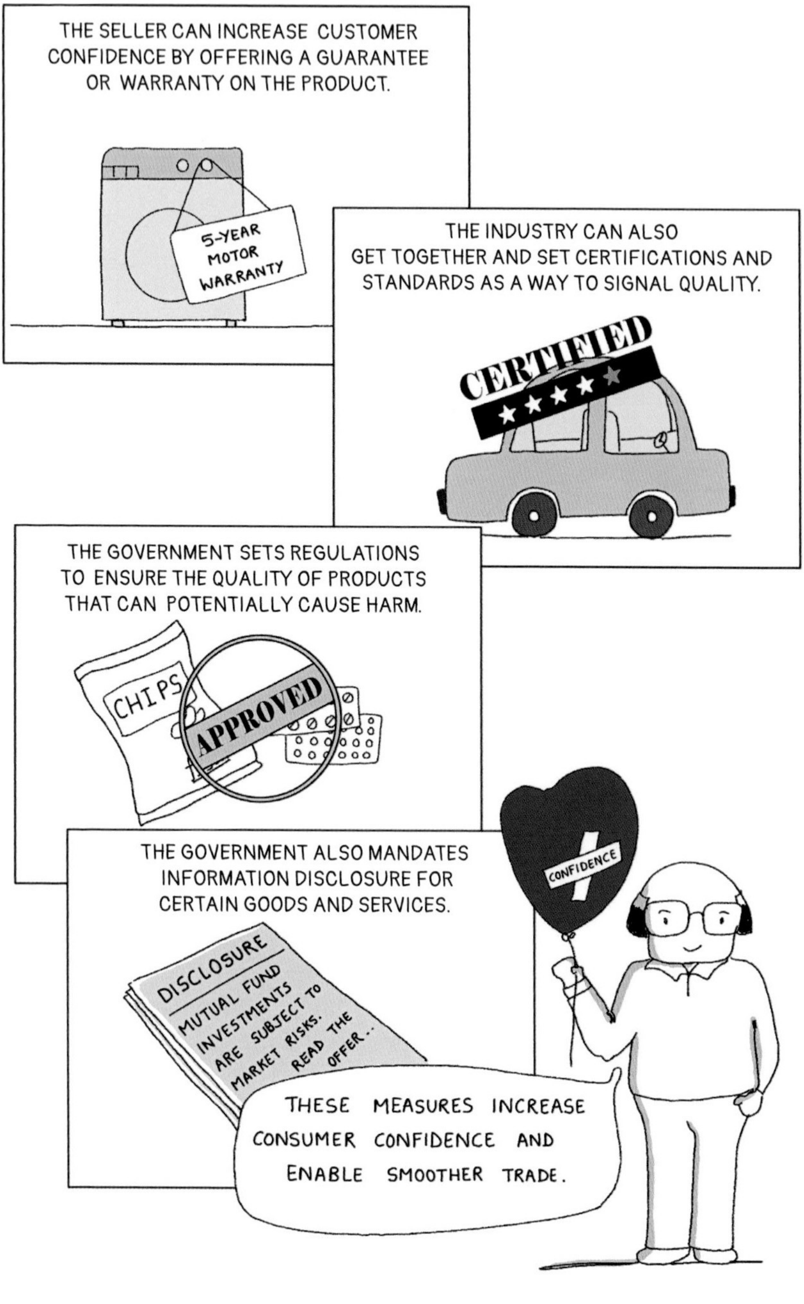
THE SELLER CAN INCREASE CUSTOMER CONFIDENCE BY OFFERING A GUARANTEE OR WARRANTY ON THE PRODUCT.
5-YEAR MOTOR WARRANTY
THE INDUSTRY CAN ALSO GET TOGETHER AND SET CERTIFICATIONS AND STANDARDS AS A WAY TO SIGNAL QUALITY.
CERTIFIED
THE GOVERNMENT SETS REGULATIONS TO ENSURE THE QUALITY OF PRODUCTS THAT CAN POTENTIALLY CAUSE HARM.
CHIPS
APPROVED
THE GOVERNMENT ALSO MANDATES INFORMATION DISCLOSURE FOR CERTAIN GOODS AND SERVICES.
DISCLOSURE
MUTUAL FUND INVESTMENTS ARE SUBJECT TO MARKET RISKS. READ THE OFFER..
CONFIDENCE
THESE MEASURES INCREASE CONSUMER CONFIDENCE AND ENABLE SMOOTHER TRADE.

CONCENTRATION OF MARKET POWER: ONE PARTY IN THE NEGOTIATION HAS MORE POWER THAN THE OTHER.

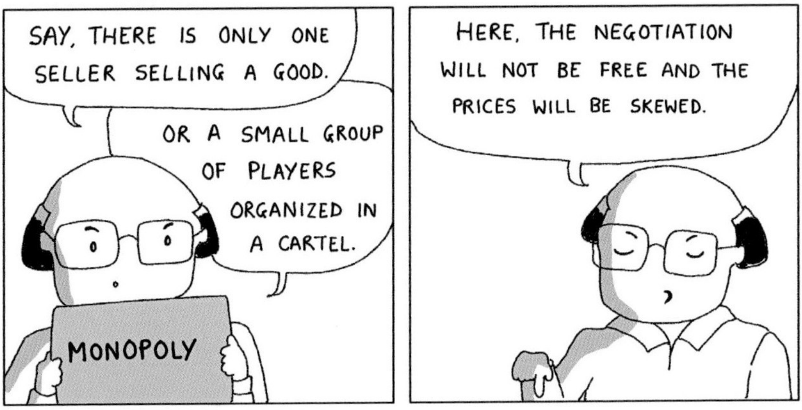
SAY, THERE IS ONLY ONE SELLER SELLING A GOOD.
OR A SMALL GROUP OF PLAYERS ORGANIZED IN A CARTEL.
MONOPOLY
HERE, THE NEGOTIATION WILL NOT BE FREE AND THE PRICES WILL BE SKEWED.

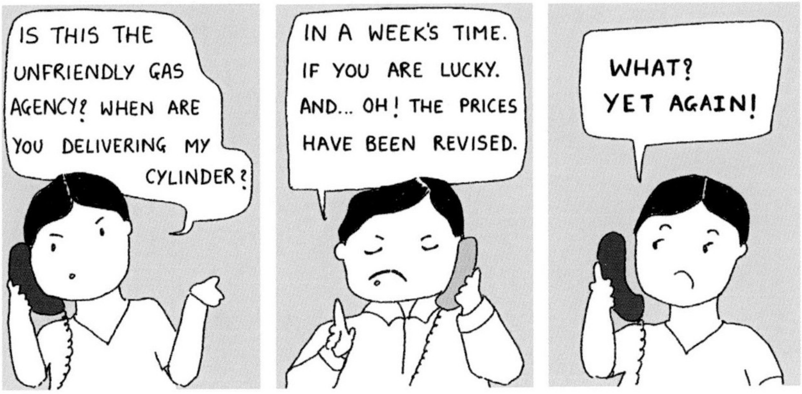
IS THIS THE UNFRIENDLY GAS AGENCY? WHEN ARE YOU DELIVERING MY CYLINDER?
IN A WEEK'S TIME. IF YOU ARE LUCKY. AND... OH! THE PRICES HAVE BEEN REVISED.
WHAT? YET AGAIN!

THE BUYER WILL HAVE NO OPTION BUT TO PURCHASE AT A HIGHER THAN OPTIMAL PRICE.

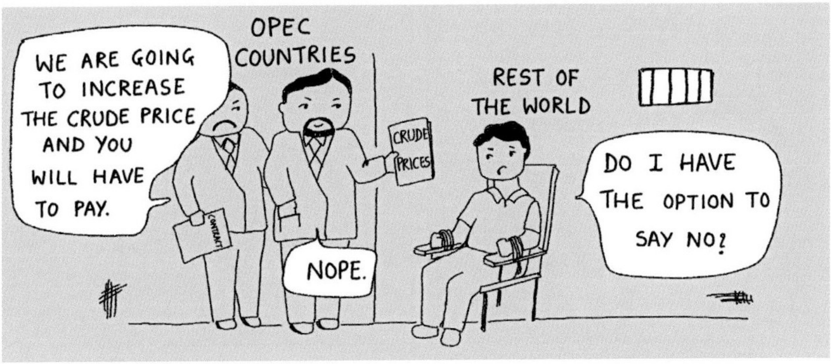
OPEC COUNTRIES
WE ARE GOING TO INCREASE THE CRUDE PRICE AND YOU WILL HAVE TO PAY.
CRUDE PRICES
CONTRACT
NOPE.
REST OF THE WORLD
DO I HAVE THE OPTION TO SAY NO?

THIS IS A MARKET FAILURE CALLED CONCENTRATION OF MARKET POWER.

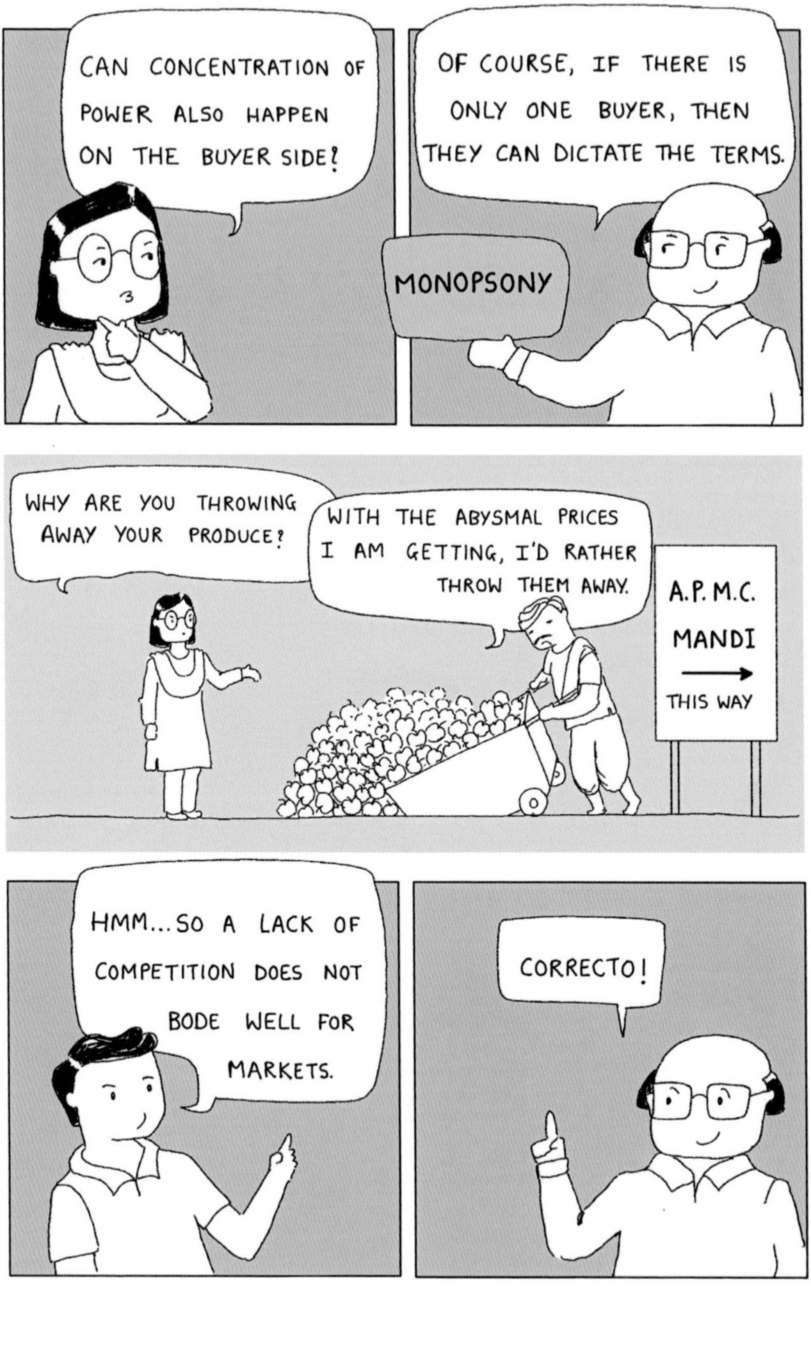
CAN CONCENTRATION OF POWER ALSO HAPPEN ON THE BUYER SIDE?
OF COURSE, IF THERE IS ONLY ONE BUYER, THEN THEY CAN DICTATE THE TERMS.
MONOPSONY
WHY ARE YOU THROWING AWAY YOUR PRODUCE?
WITH THE ABYSMAL PRICES I AM GETTING, I'D RATHER THROW THEM AWAY.
A.P.M.C. MANDI
THIS WAY
HMM...SO A LACK OF COMPETITION DOES NOT BODE WELL FOR MARKETS.
CORRECTO!

THE LOGIC IS SIMPLE—ANY PLAYER WITH TOO MUCH POWER HAS NO INCENTIVE TO INNOVATE.

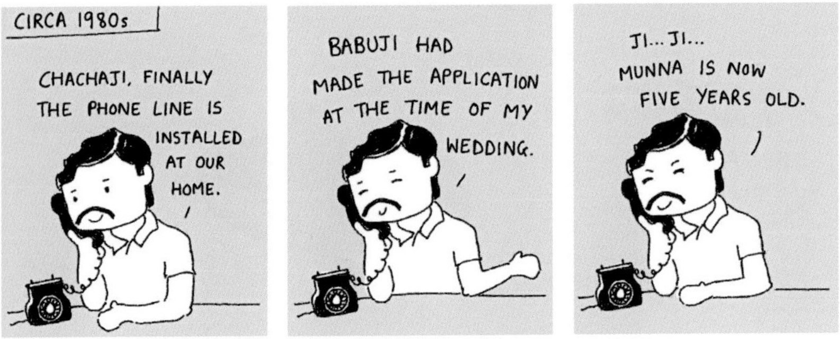
CIRCA 1980s
CHACHAJI, FINALLY THE PHONE LINE IS INSTALLED AT OUR HOME.
BABUJI HAD MADE THE APPLICATION AT THE TIME OF MY WEDDING.
JI... JI... MUNNA IS NOW FIVE YEARS OLD.

ULTIMATELY CONSUMERS WILL HAVE FEWER CHOICES AND LESSER THAN DESIRED QUANTITY OF GOODS AND SERVICES.

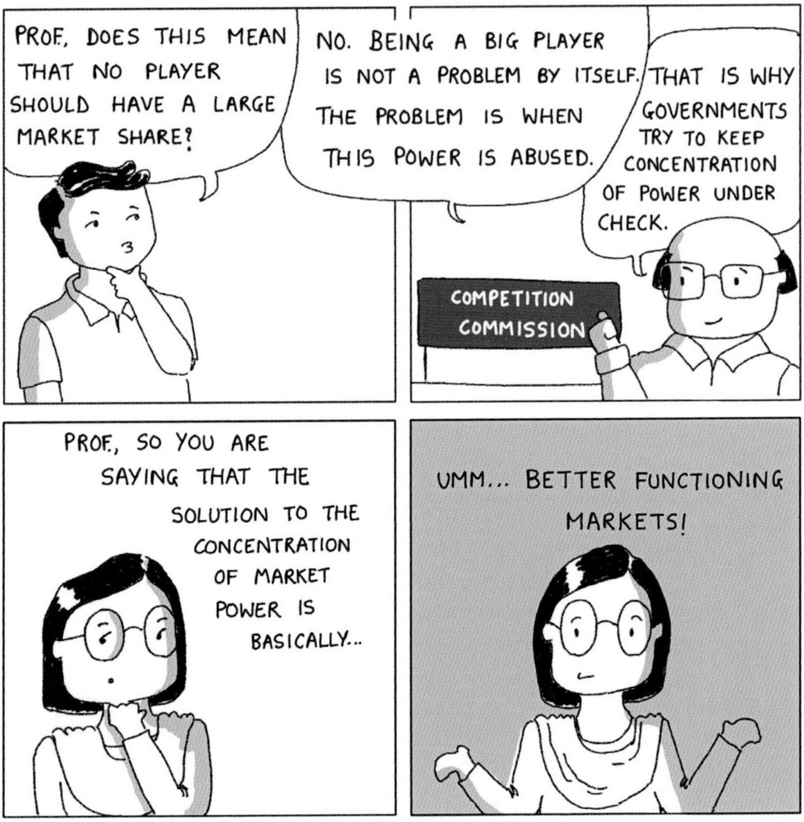
PROF., DOES THIS MEAN THAT NO PLAYER SHOULD HAVE A LARGE MARKET SHARE?
NO. BEING A BIG PLAYER IS NOT A PROBLEM BY ITSELF. THE PROBLEM IS WHEN THIS POWER IS ABUSED.
THAT IS WHY GOVERNMENTS TRY TO KEEP CONCENTRATION OF POWER UNDER CHECK.
COMPETITION COMMISSION
PROF., SO YOU ARE SAYING THAT THE SOLUTION TO THE CONCENTRATION OF MARKET POWER IS BASICALLY...
UMM... BETTER FUNCTIONING MARKETS!

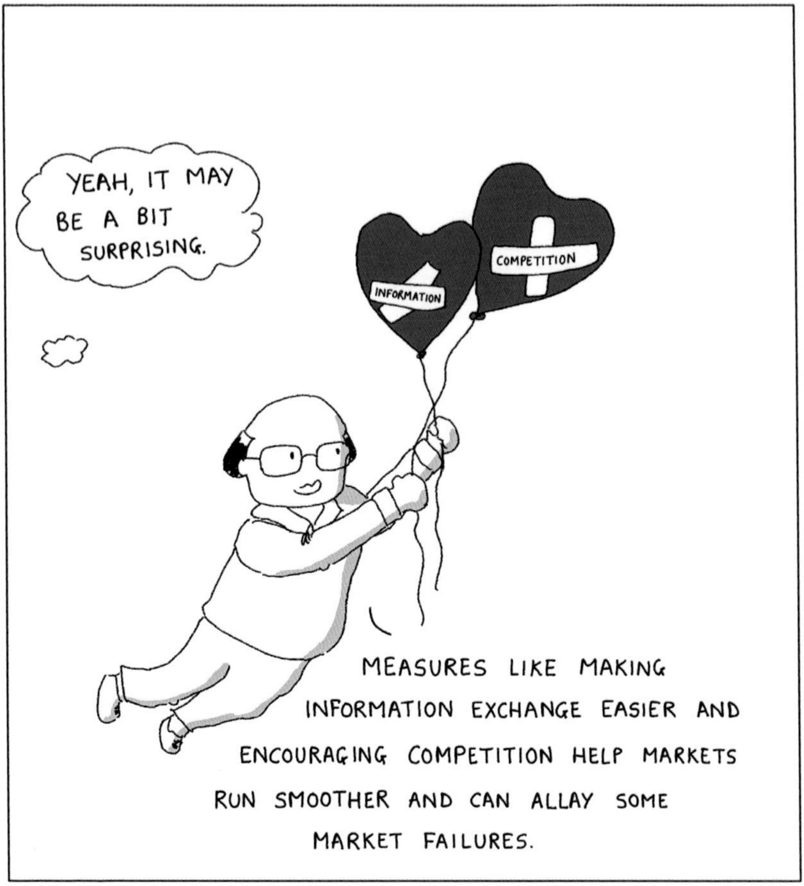
YEAH, IT MAY BE A BIT SURPRISING.
INFORMATION
COMPETITION
MEASURES LIKE MAKING INFORMATION EXCHANGE EASIER AND ENCOURAGING COMPETITION HELP MARKETS RUN SMOOTHER AND CAN ALLAY SOME MARKET FAILURES.

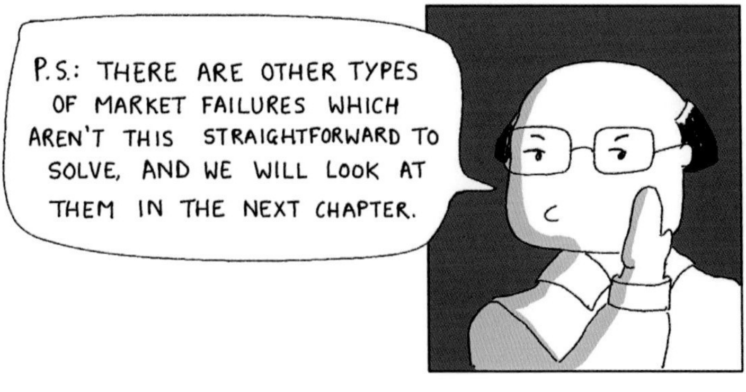
P.S.: THERE ARE OTHER TYPES OF MARKET FAILURES WHICH AREN'T THIS STRAIGHTFORWARD TO SOLVE, AND WE WILL LOOK AT THEM IN THE NEXT CHAPTER.

Chapter 9

Who Pays for the Lighthouse?

The tragedy of the commons

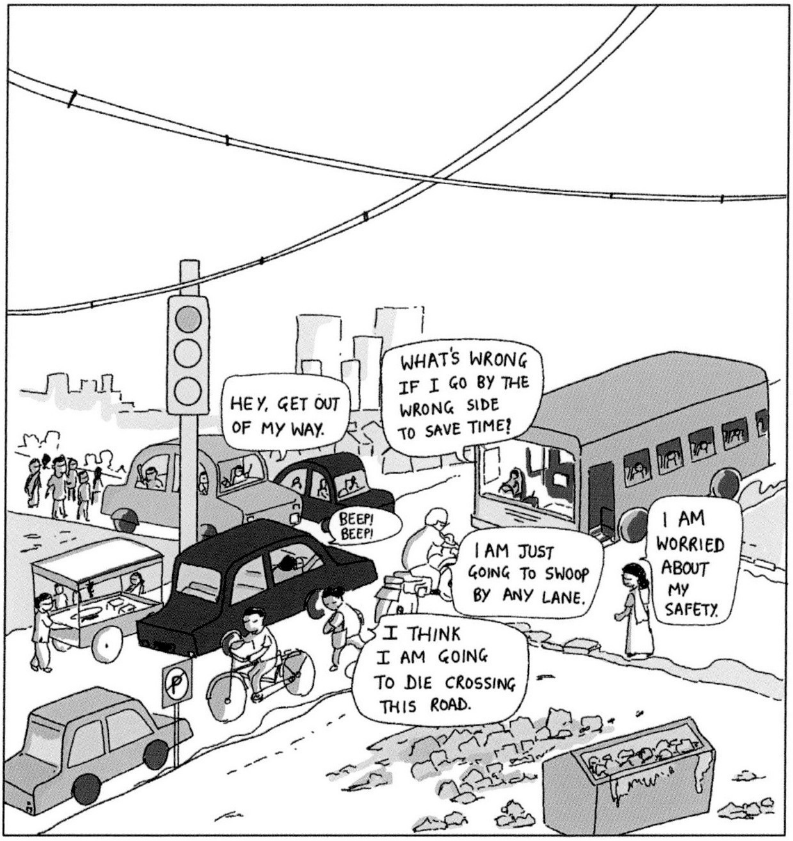
HEY, GET OUT OF MY WAY.
WHAT'S WRONG IF I GO BY THE WRONG SIDE TO SAVE TIME?
BEEP! BEEP!
I AM JUST GOING TO SWOOP BY ANY LANE.
I AM WORRIED ABOUT MY SAFETY.
I THINK I AM GOING TO DIE CROSSING THIS ROAD.

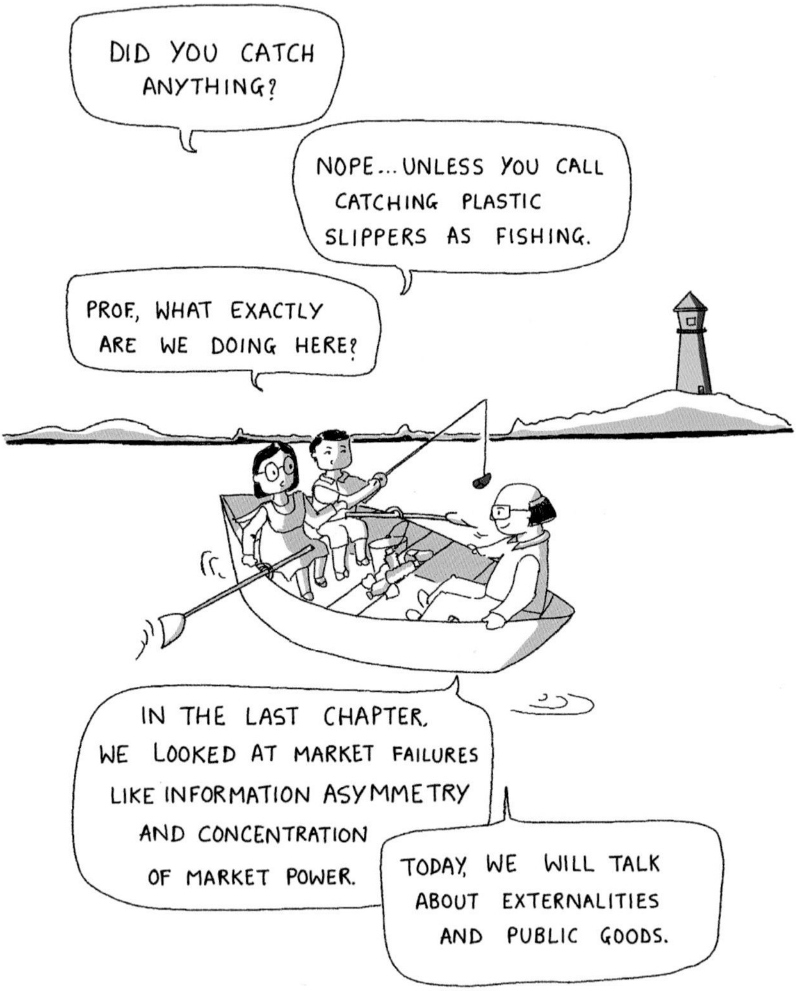
DID YOU CATCH ANYTHING?
NOPE... UNLESS YOU CALL CATCHING PLASTIC SLIPPERS AS FISHING.
PROF., WHAT EXACTLY ARE WE DOING HERE?
IN THE LAST CHAPTER, WE LOOKED AT MARKET FAILURES LIKE INFORMATION ASYMMETRY AND CONCENTRATION OF MARKET POWER.
TODAY, WE WILL TALK ABOUT EXTERNALITIES AND PUBLIC GOODS.

EXTERNALITIES

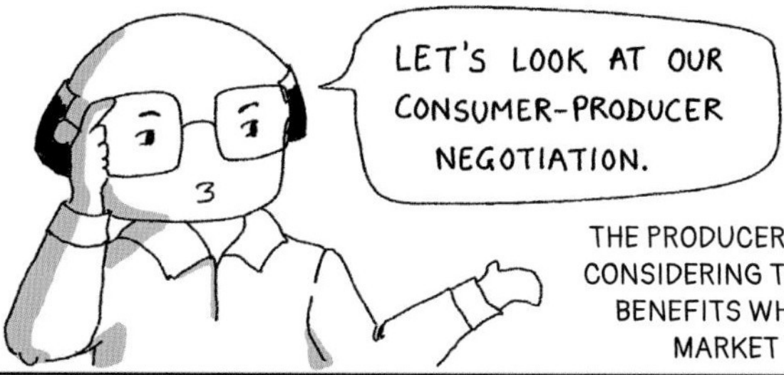
LET'S LOOK AT OUR CONSUMER-PRODUCER NEGOTIATION.

THE PRODUCER AND CONSUMER ARE CONSIDERING THEIR OWN COSTS AND BENEFITS WHILE ENGAGING IN A MARKET TRANSACTION.

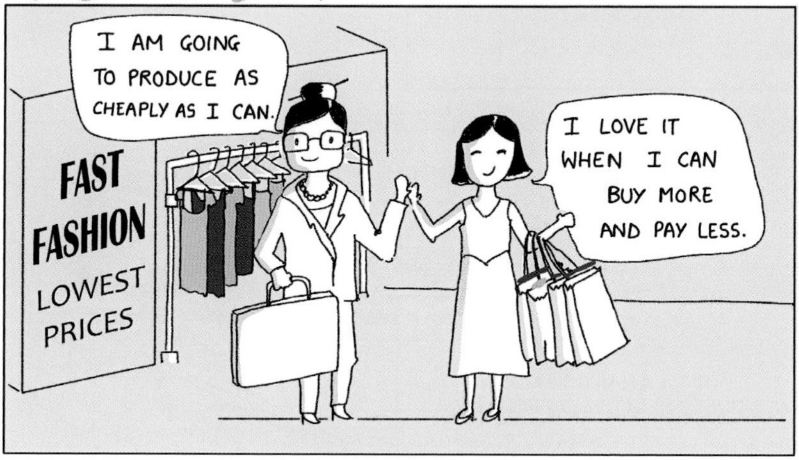
I AM GOING TO PRODUCE AS CHEAPLY AS I CAN.
FAST FASHION
LOWEST PRICES
I LOVE IT WHEN I CAN BUY MORE AND PAY LESS.

BUT WHAT IF THEIR ACTIONS HAVE AN EFFECT ON A BYSTANDER?

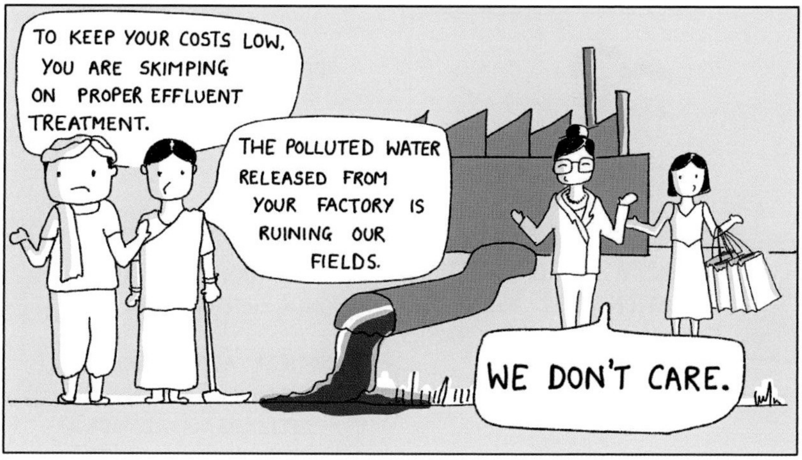
TO KEEP YOUR COSTS LOW, YOU ARE SKIMPING ON PROPER EFFLUENT TREATMENT.
THE POLLUTED WATER RELEASED FROM YOUR FACTORY IS RUINING OUR FIELDS.
WE DON'T CARE.

DOES THE PRODUCER-CONSUMER DEAL TAKE INTO ACCOUNT THE COST TO THIS BYSTANDER?

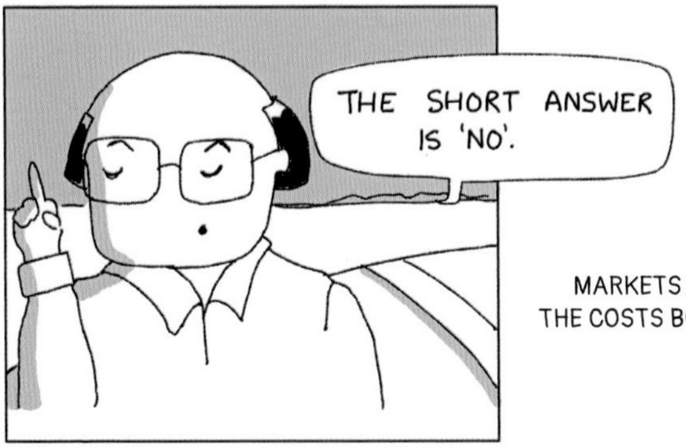
THE SHORT ANSWER IS 'NO'.

MARKETS DO NOT ACCOUNT FOR THE COSTS BORNE BY THE BYSTANDER.

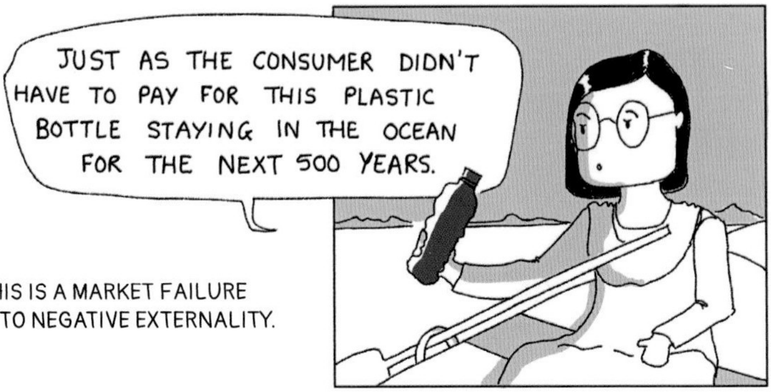
JUST AS THE CONSUMER DIDN'T HAVE TO PAY FOR THIS PLASTIC BOTTLE STAYING IN THE OCEAN FOR THE NEXT 500 YEARS.

THIS IS A MARKET FAILURE DUE TO NEGATIVE EXTERNALITY.

NOW, THERE CAN BE POSITIVE EXTERNALITIES TOO.

LIKE EDUCATION.

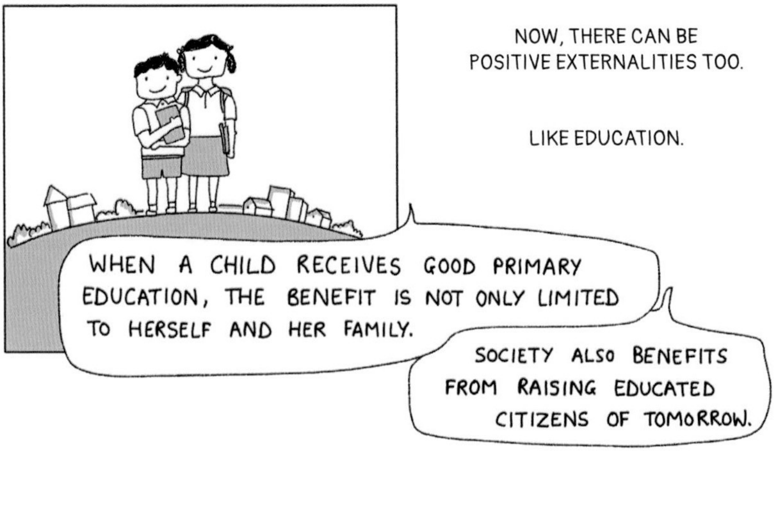
WHEN A CHILD RECEIVES GOOD PRIMARY EDUCATION, THE BENEFIT IS NOT ONLY LIMITED TO HERSELF AND HER FAMILY.
SOCIETY ALSO BENEFITS FROM RAISING EDUCATED CITIZENS OF TOMORROW.

BECAUSE MARKETS DO NOT TAKE INTO ACCOUNT
THE COSTS AND BENEFITS TO BYSTANDERS,

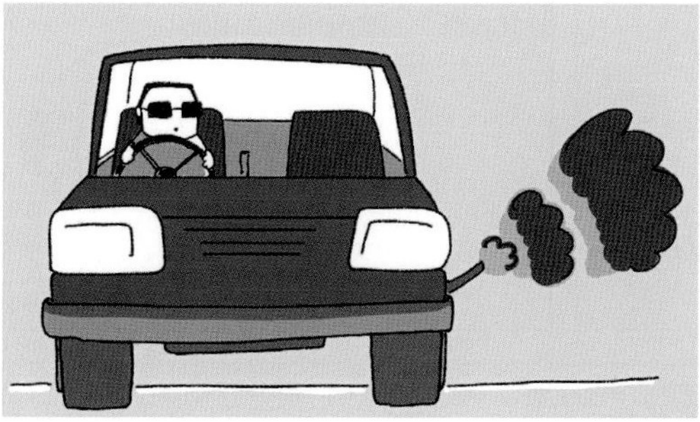

THEY TEND TO OVER-PRODUCE
GOODS AND SERVICES WITH
NEGATIVE EXTERNALITIES

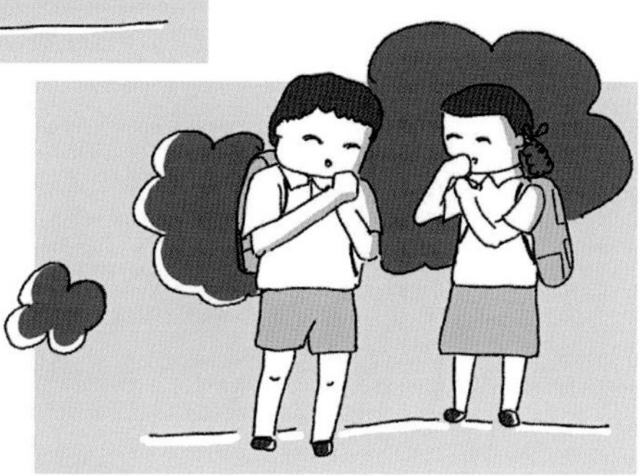

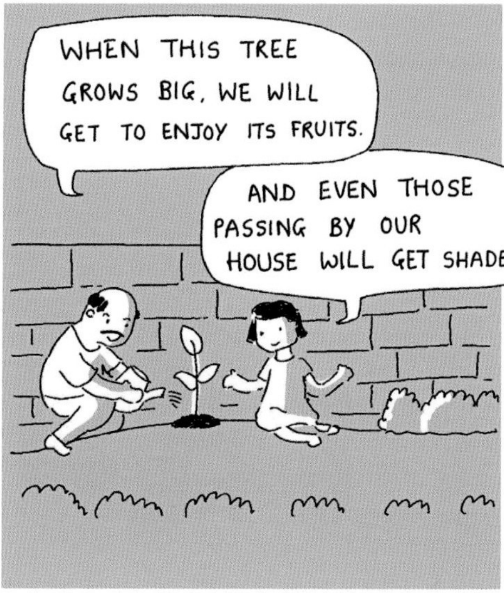
WHEN THIS TREE GROWS BIG, WE WILL GET TO ENJOY ITS FRUITS.
AND EVEN THOSE PASSING BY OUR HOUSE WILL GET SHADE.

AND UNDER-PRODUCE
GOODS AND SERVICES WITH
POSITIVE EXTERNALITIES.

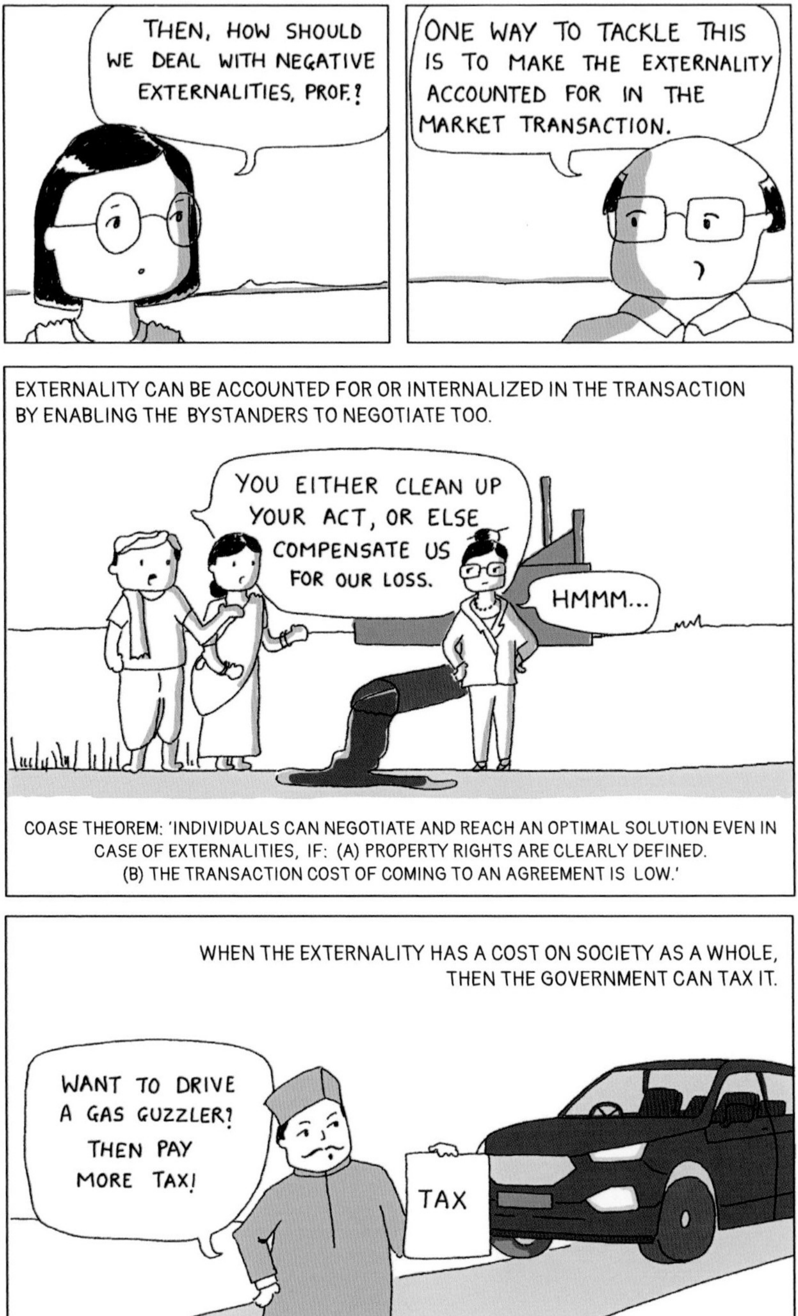
THEN, HOW SHOULD WE DEAL WITH NEGATIVE EXTERNALITIES, PROF.?
ONE WAY TO TACKLE THIS IS TO MAKE THE EXTERNALITY ACCOUNTED FOR IN THE MARKET TRANSACTION.
EXTERNALITY CAN BE ACCOUNTED FOR OR INTERNALIZED IN THE TRANSACTION BY ENABLING THE BYSTANDERS TO NEGOTIATE TOO.
YOU EITHER CLEAN UP YOUR ACT, OR ELSE COMPENSATE US FOR OUR LOSS.
HMMM...
COASE THEOREM: 'INDIVIDUALS CAN NEGOTIATE AND REACH AN OPTIMAL SOLUTION EVEN IN CASE OF EXTERNALITIES, IF: (A) PROPERTY RIGHTS ARE CLEARLY DEFINED. (B) THE TRANSACTION COST OF COMING TO AN AGREEMENT IS LOW.'
WHEN THE EXTERNALITY HAS A COST ON SOCIETY AS A WHOLE, THEN THE GOVERNMENT CAN TAX IT.
WANT TO DRIVE A GAS GUZZLER? THEN PAY MORE TAX!
TAX

REGULATION ALSO BECOMES INEVITABLE IN KEEPING NEGATIVE EXTERNALITIES WITHIN SAFE LIMITS.

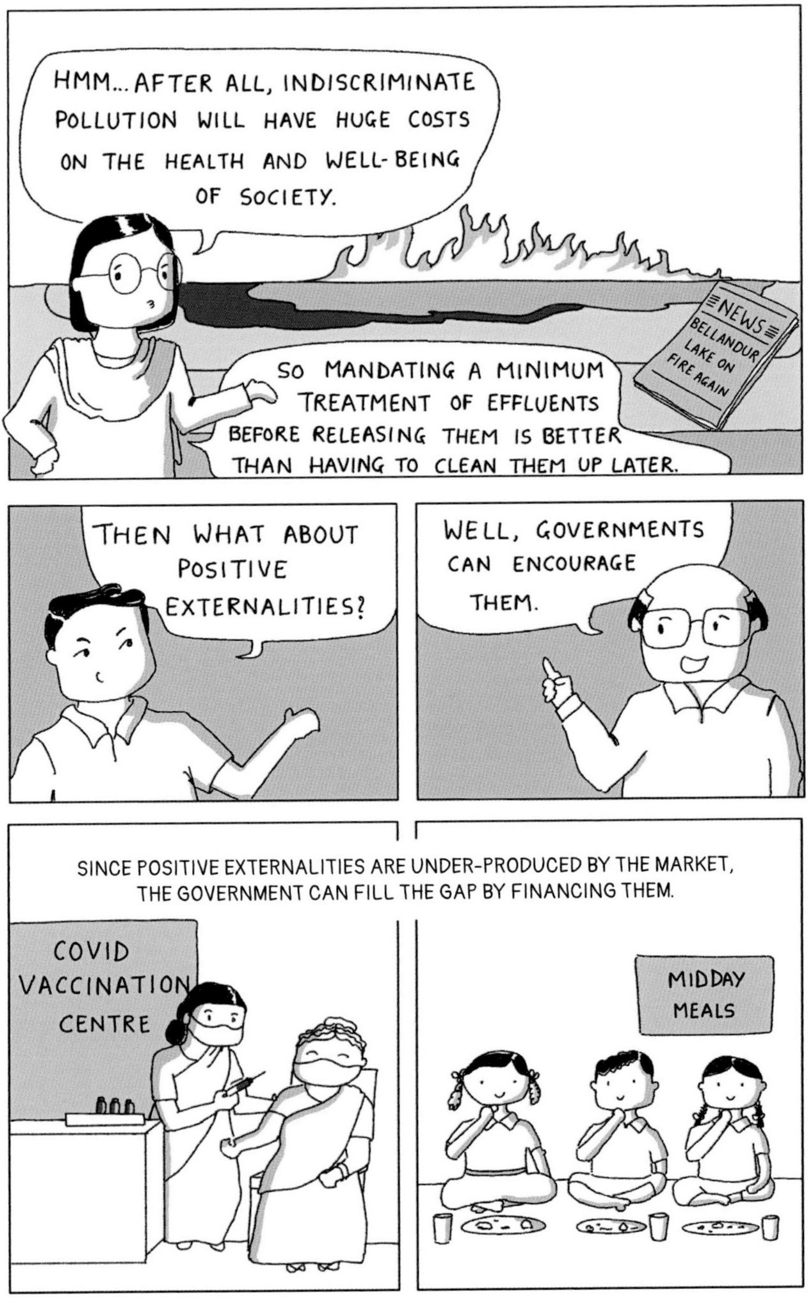
HMM... AFTER ALL, INDISCRIMINATE POLLUTION WILL HAVE HUGE COSTS ON THE HEALTH AND WELL-BEING OF SOCIETY.
NEWS
BELLANDUR LAKE ON FIRE AGAIN
SO MANDATING A MINIMUM TREATMENT OF EFFLUENTS BEFORE RELEASING THEM IS BETTER THAN HAVING TO CLEAN THEM UP LATER.
THEN WHAT ABOUT POSITIVE EXTERNALITIES?
WELL, GOVERNMENTS CAN ENCOURAGE THEM.
SINCE POSITIVE EXTERNALITIES ARE UNDER-PRODUCED BY THE MARKET, THE GOVERNMENT CAN FILL THE GAP BY FINANCING THEM.
COVID VACCINATION CENTRE
MIDDAY MEALS

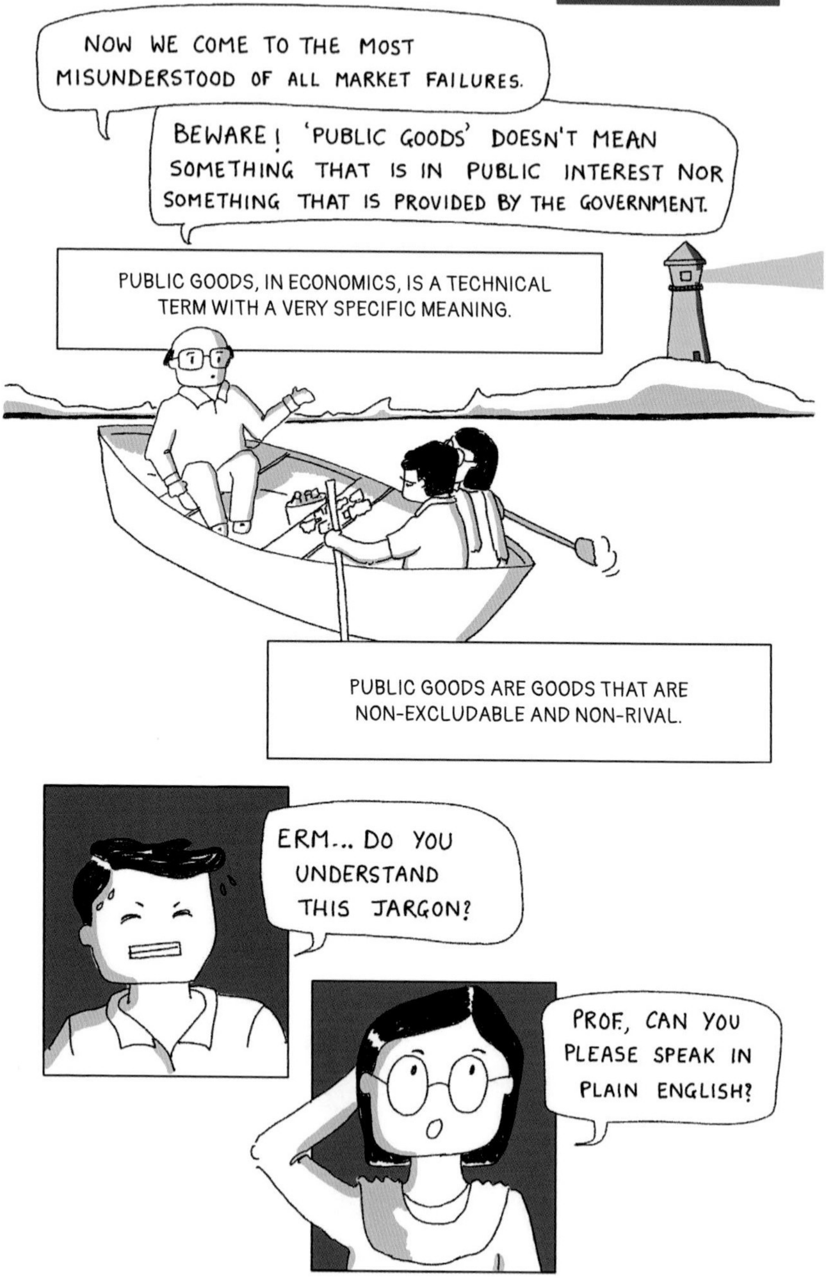
NOW WE COME TO THE MOST MISUNDERSTOOD OF ALL MARKET FAILURES.
BEWARE! 'PUBLIC GOODS' DOESN'T MEAN SOMETHING THAT IS IN PUBLIC INTEREST NOR SOMETHING THAT IS PROVIDED BY THE GOVERNMENT.
PUBLIC GOODS, IN ECONOMICS, IS A TECHNICAL TERM WITH A VERY SPECIFIC MEANING.
PUBLIC GOODS ARE GOODS THAT ARE NON-EXCLUDABLE AND NON-RIVAL.
ERM... DO YOU UNDERSTAND THIS JARGON?
PROF., CAN YOU PLEASE SPEAK IN PLAIN ENGLISH?

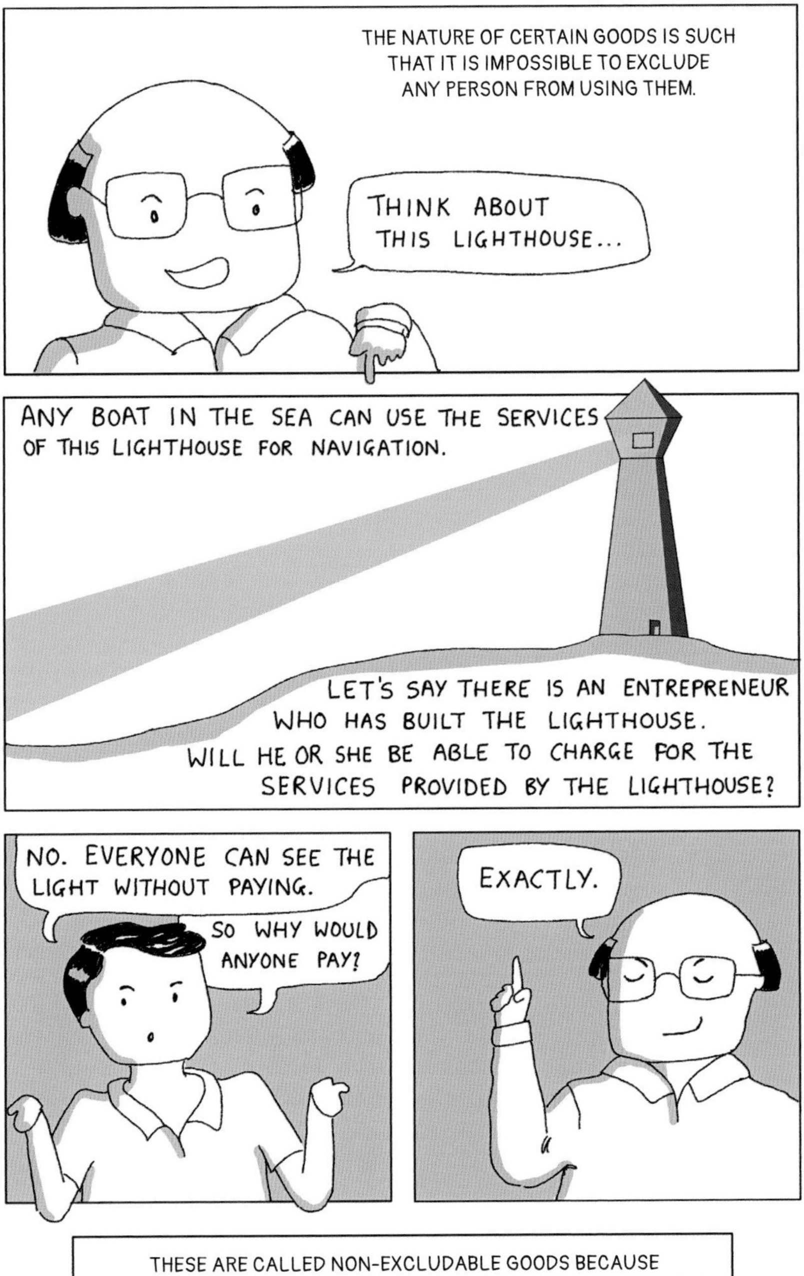
THE NATURE OF CERTAIN GOODS IS SUCH THAT IT IS IMPOSSIBLE TO EXCLUDE ANY PERSON FROM USING THEM.
THINK ABOUT THIS LIGHTHOUSE...
ANY BOAT IN THE SEA CAN USE THE SERVICES OF THIS LIGHTHOUSE FOR NAVIGATION.
LET'S SAY THERE IS AN ENTREPRENEUR WHO HAS BUILT THE LIGHTHOUSE. WILL HE OR SHE BE ABLE TO CHARGE FOR THE SERVICES PROVIDED BY THE LIGHTHOUSE?
NO. EVERYONE CAN SEE THE LIGHT WITHOUT PAYING.
SO WHY WOULD ANYONE PAY?
EXACTLY.

THESE ARE CALLED NON-EXCLUDABLE GOODS BECAUSE IT IS IMPOSSIBLE TO EXCLUDE ANY NON-PAYER FROM USING THEM.

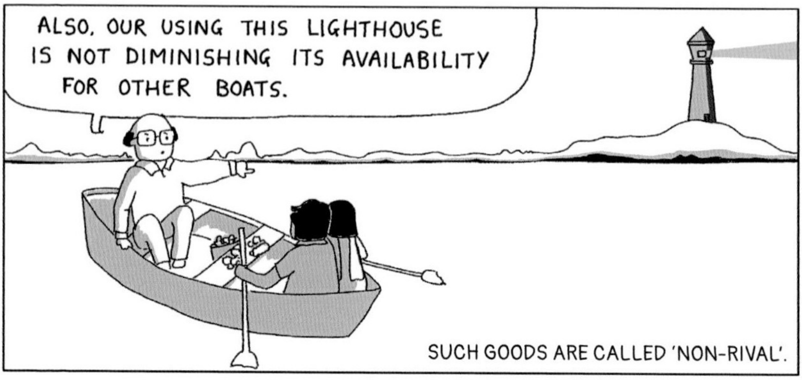
ALSO, OUR USING THIS LIGHTHOUSE IS NOT DIMINISHING ITS AVAILABILITY FOR OTHER BOATS.
SUCH GOODS ARE CALLED 'NON-RIVAL'.

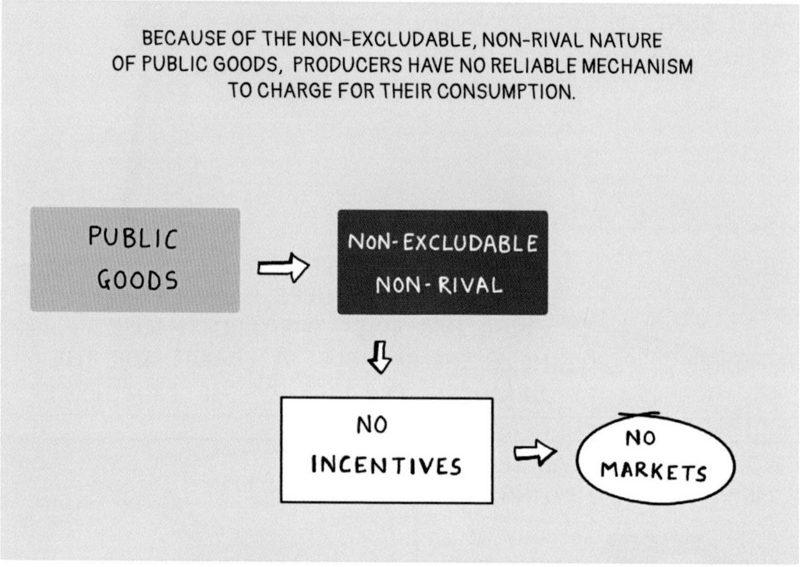
BECAUSE OF THE NON-EXCLUDABLE, NON-RIVAL NATURE OF PUBLIC GOODS, PRODUCERS HAVE NO RELIABLE MECHANISM TO CHARGE FOR THEIR CONSUMPTION.
PUBLIC GOODS
NON-EXCLUDABLE NON-RIVAL
NO INCENTIVES
NO MARKETS

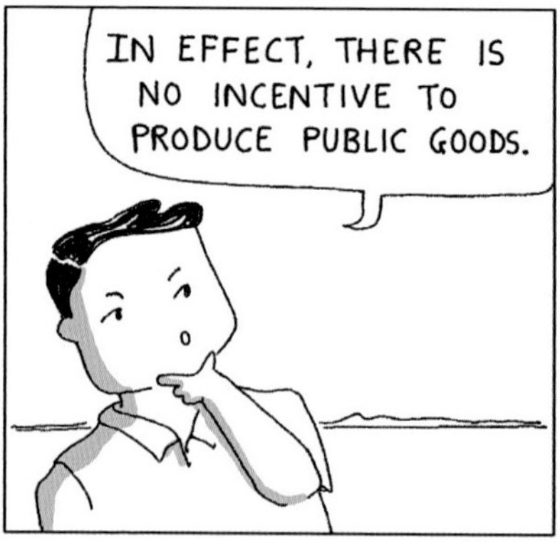
IN EFFECT, THERE IS NO INCENTIVE TO PRODUCE PUBLIC GOODS.

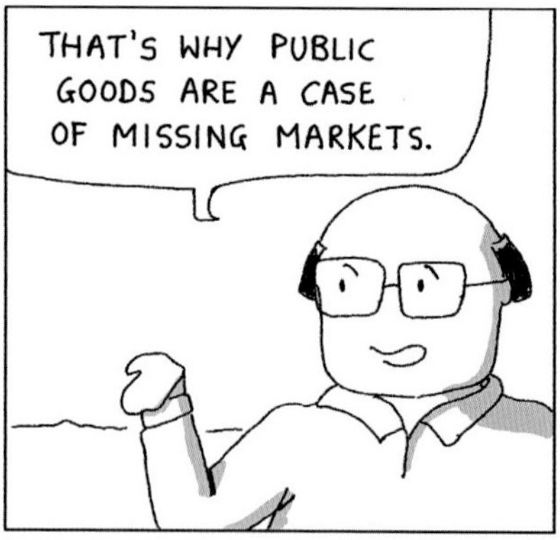
THAT'S WHY PUBLIC GOODS ARE A CASE OF MISSING MARKETS.

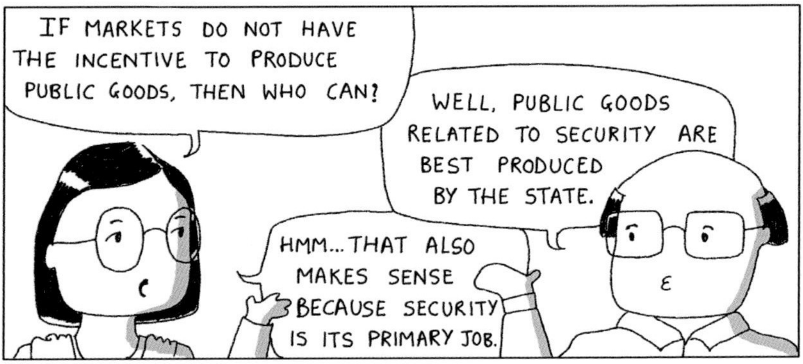
IF MARKETS DO NOT HAVE THE INCENTIVE TO PRODUCE PUBLIC GOODS, THEN WHO CAN?
WELL, PUBLIC GOODS RELATED TO SECURITY ARE BEST PRODUCED BY THE STATE.
HMM... THAT ALSO MAKES SENSE BECAUSE SECURITY IS ITS PRIMARY JOB.

ECONOMISTS AGREE THAT PUBLIC GOODS RELATED TO INTERNAL AND EXTERNAL SECURITY ARE BEST PROVIDED BY THE STATE.

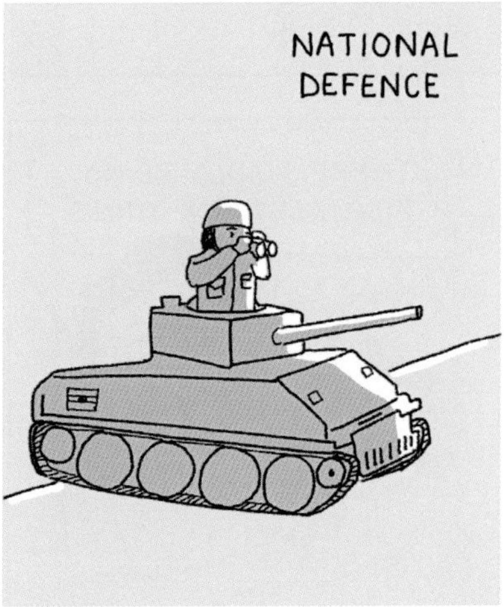
NATIONAL DEFENCE

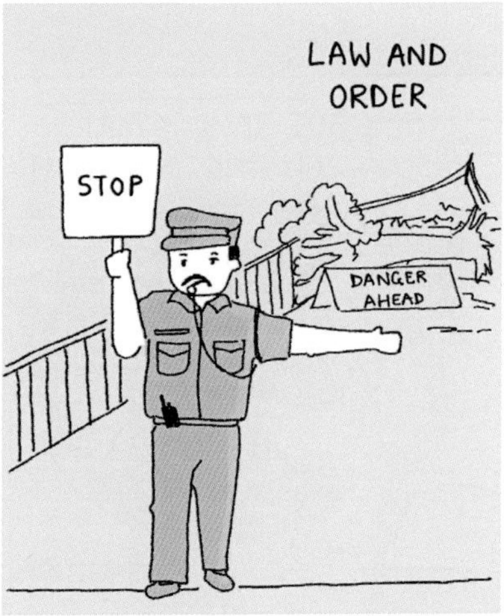
LAW AND ORDER
STOP
DANGER AHEAD

MORE LOCALIZED PUBLIC GOODS LIKE LIGHTHOUSES OR PUBLIC PARKS CAN ALSO BE BUILT BY LOCAL COMMUNITY EFFORTS OR PHILANTHROPIC ACTS.

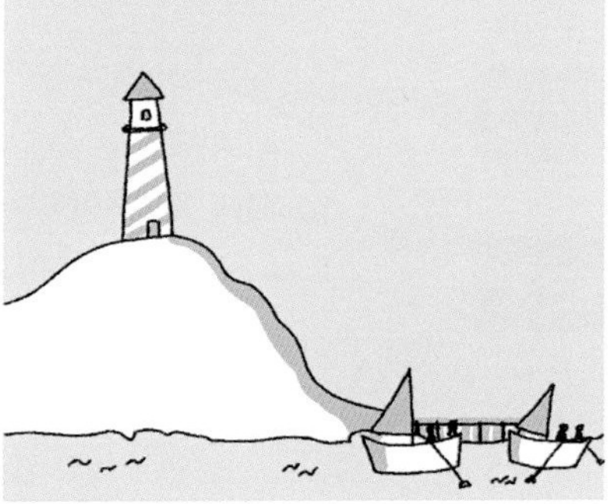

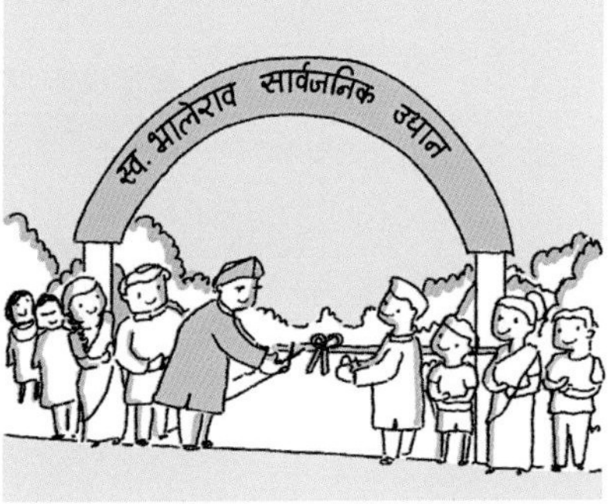
स्व. भालेराव सार्वजनिक उद्यान

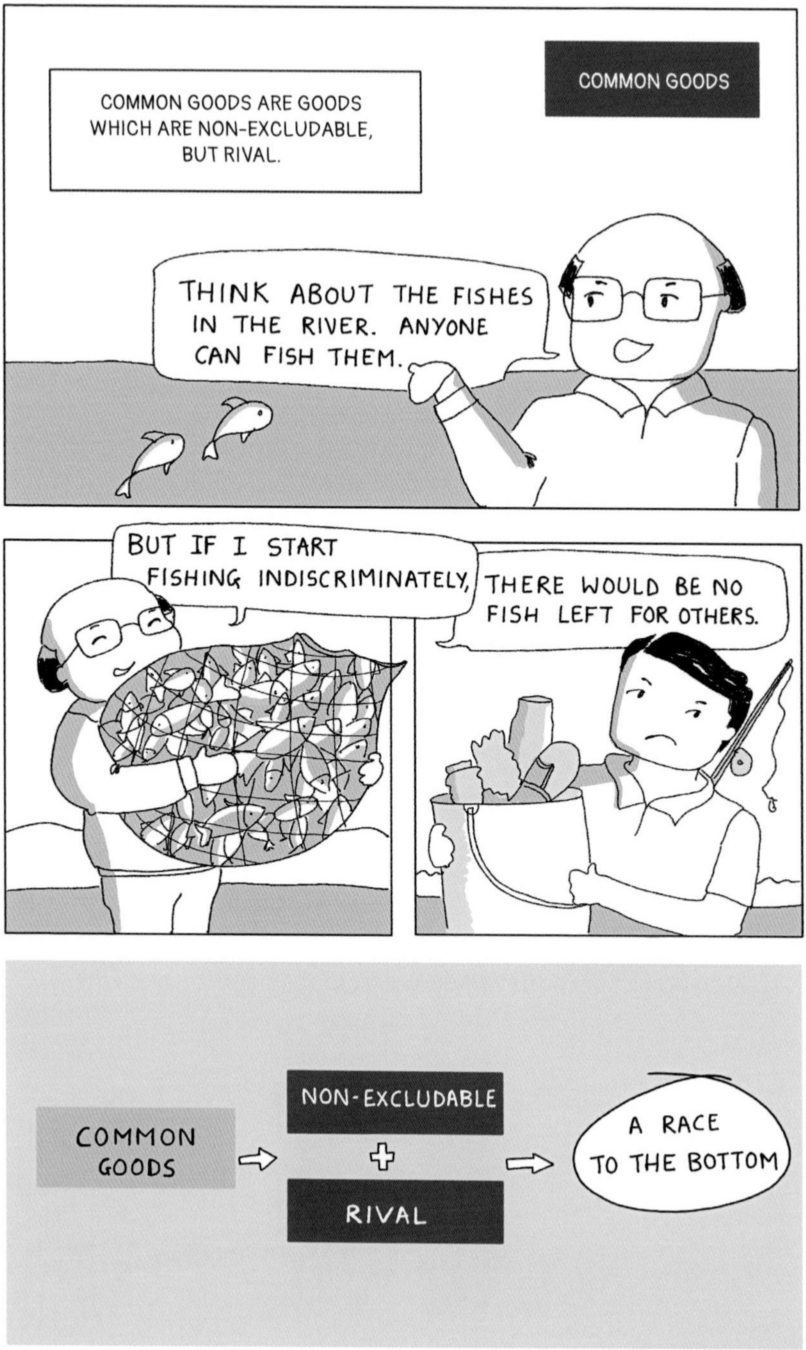
COMMON GOODS
COMMON GOODS ARE GOODS WHICH ARE NON-EXCLUDABLE, BUT RIVAL.
THINK ABOUT THE FISHES IN THE RIVER. ANYONE CAN FISH THEM.
BUT IF I START FISHING INDISCRIMINATELY,
THERE WOULD BE NO FISH LEFT FOR OTHERS.
COMMON GOODS
NON-EXCLUDABLE
+
RIVAL
A RACE TO THE BOTTOM

BECAUSE COMMON GOODS ARE RIVAL, BUT NON-EXCLUDABLE, INDIVIDUALS ACTING OUT OF SELF-INTEREST CAN EASILY DEPLETE THEM, LEADING TO A TRAGEDY FOR ALL.

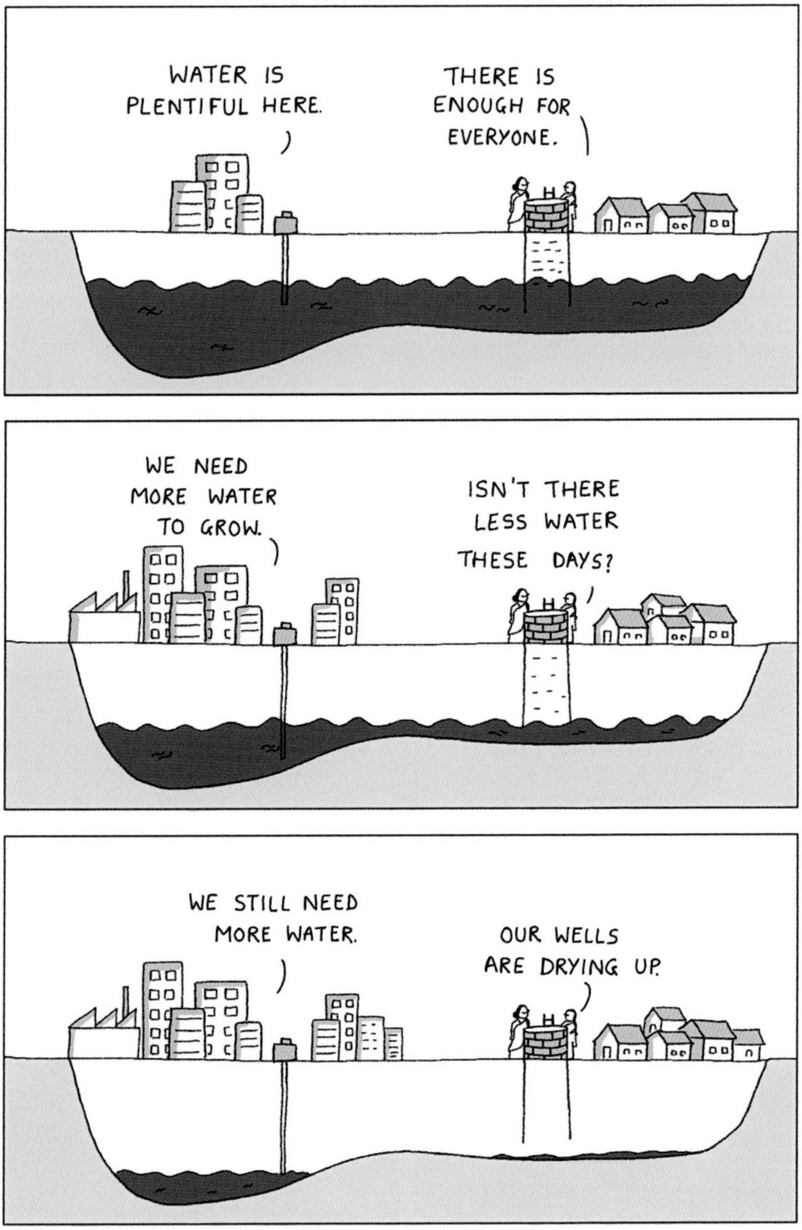
WATER IS PLENTIFUL HERE.
THERE IS ENOUGH FOR EVERYONE.
WE NEED MORE WATER TO GROW.
ISN'T THERE LESS WATER THESE DAYS?
WE STILL NEED MORE WATER.
OUR WELLS ARE DRYING UP.

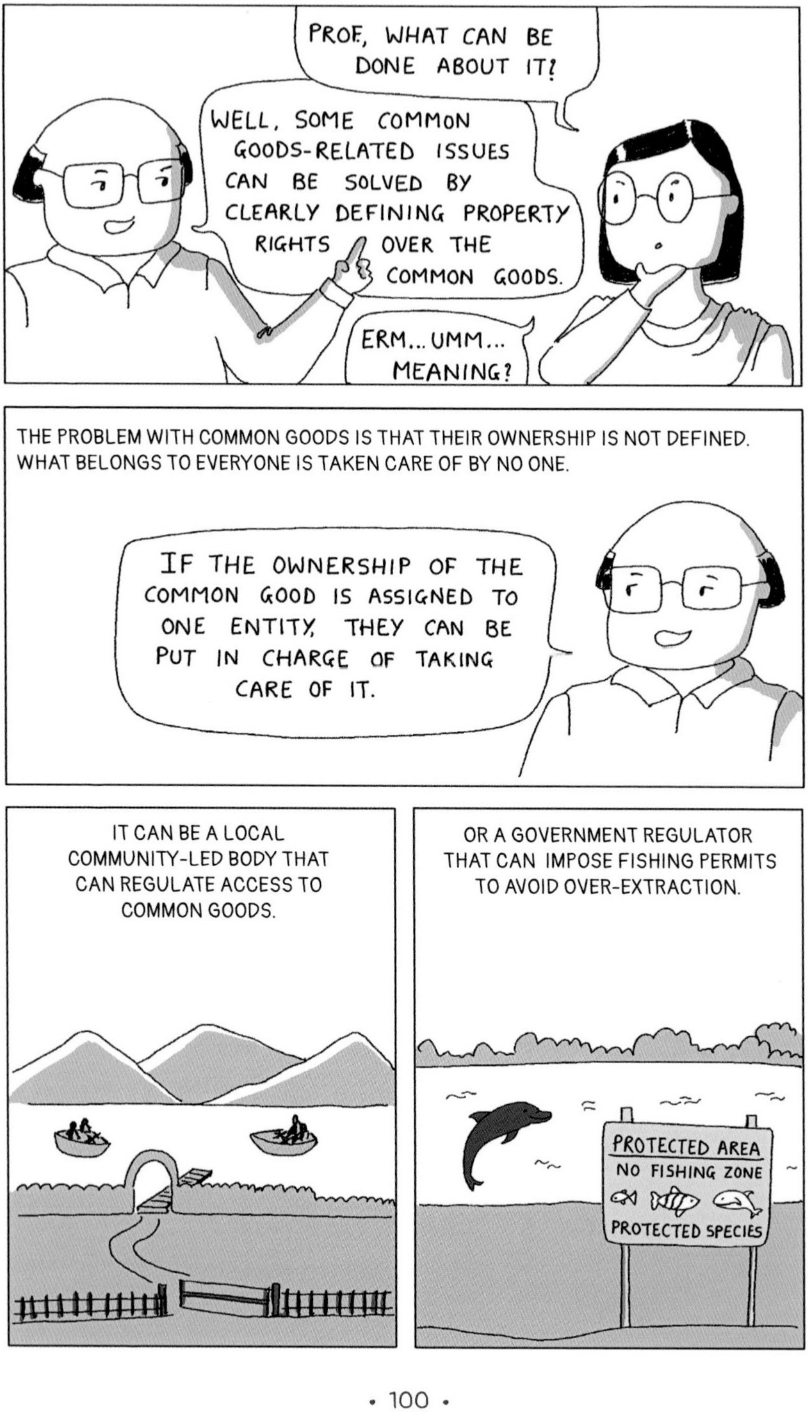
PROF, WHAT CAN BE DONE ABOUT IT?
WELL, SOME COMMON GOODS-RELATED ISSUES CAN BE SOLVED BY CLEARLY DEFINING PROPERTY RIGHTS OVER THE COMMON GOODS.
ERM... UMM... MEANING?
THE PROBLEM WITH COMMON GOODS IS THAT THEIR OWNERSHIP IS NOT DEFINED. WHAT BELONGS TO EVERYONE IS TAKEN CARE OF BY NO ONE.
IF THE OWNERSHIP OF THE COMMON GOOD IS ASSIGNED TO ONE ENTITY, THEY CAN BE PUT IN CHARGE OF TAKING CARE OF IT.
IT CAN BE A LOCAL COMMUNITY-LED BODY THAT CAN REGULATE ACCESS TO COMMON GOODS.
OR A GOVERNMENT REGULATOR THAT CAN IMPOSE FISHING PERMITS TO AVOID OVER-EXTRACTION.
PROTECTED AREA
NO FISHING ZONE
PROTECTED SPECIES

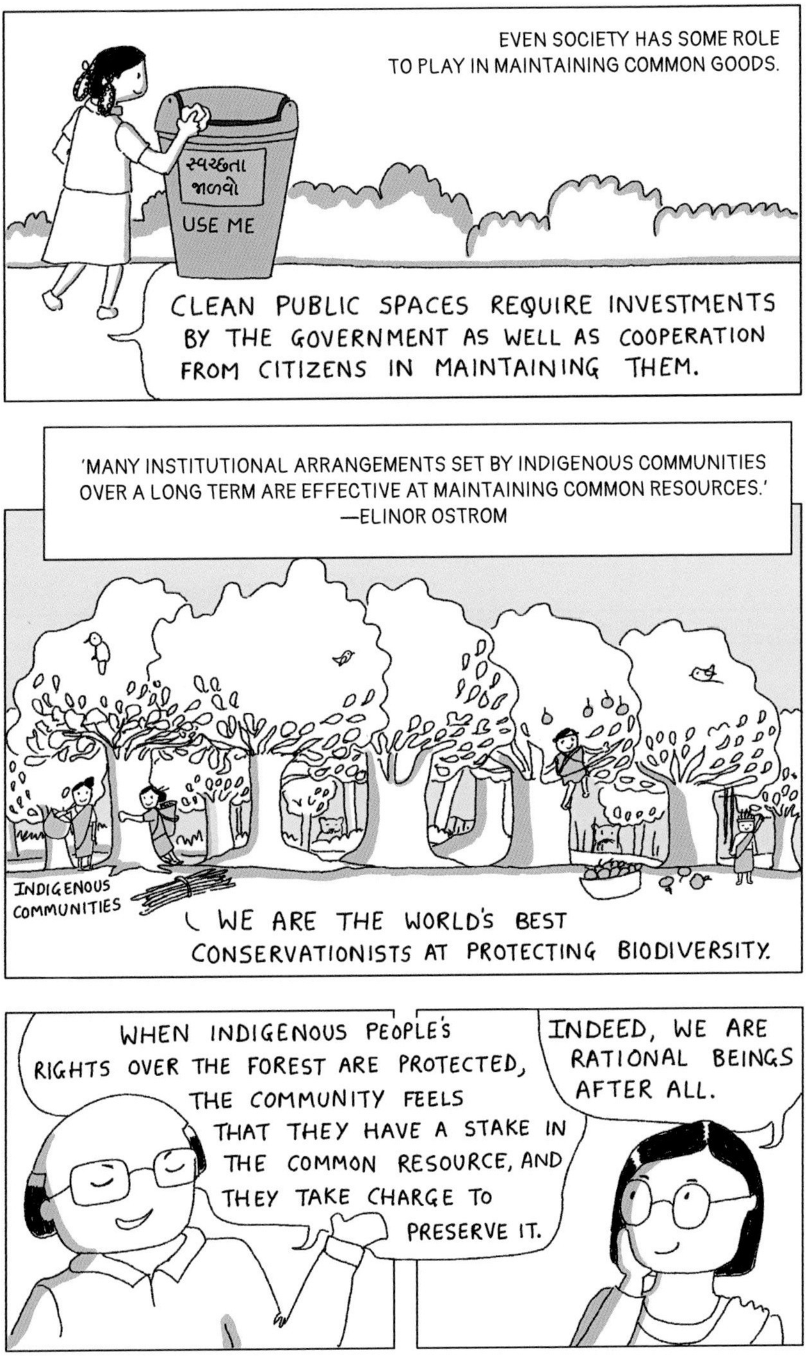
EVEN SOCIETY HAS SOME ROLE TO PLAY IN MAINTAINING COMMON GOODS.
સ્વચ્છતા જાળવો
USE ME
CLEAN PUBLIC SPACES REQUIRE INVESTMENTS BY THE GOVERNMENT AS WELL AS COOPERATION FROM CITIZENS IN MAINTAINING THEM.
'MANY INSTITUTIONAL ARRANGEMENTS SET BY INDIGENOUS COMMUNITIES OVER A LONG TERM ARE EFFECTIVE AT MAINTAINING COMMON RESOURCES.' —ELINOR OSTROM
INDIGENOUS COMMUNITIES
WE ARE THE WORLD'S BEST CONSERVATIONISTS AT PROTECTING BIODIVERSITY.
WHEN INDIGENOUS PEOPLE'S RIGHTS OVER THE FOREST ARE PROTECTED, THE COMMUNITY FEELS THAT THEY HAVE A STAKE IN THE COMMON RESOURCE, AND THEY TAKE CHARGE TO PRESERVE IT.
INDEED, WE ARE RATIONAL BEINGS AFTER ALL.

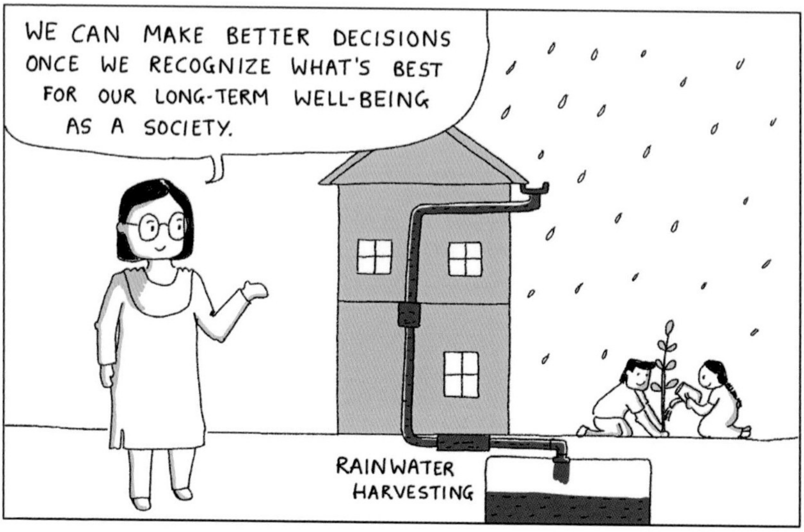
WE CAN MAKE BETTER DECISIONS ONCE WE RECOGNIZE WHAT'S BEST FOR OUR LONG-TERM WELL-BEING AS A SOCIETY.
RAINWATER HARVESTING

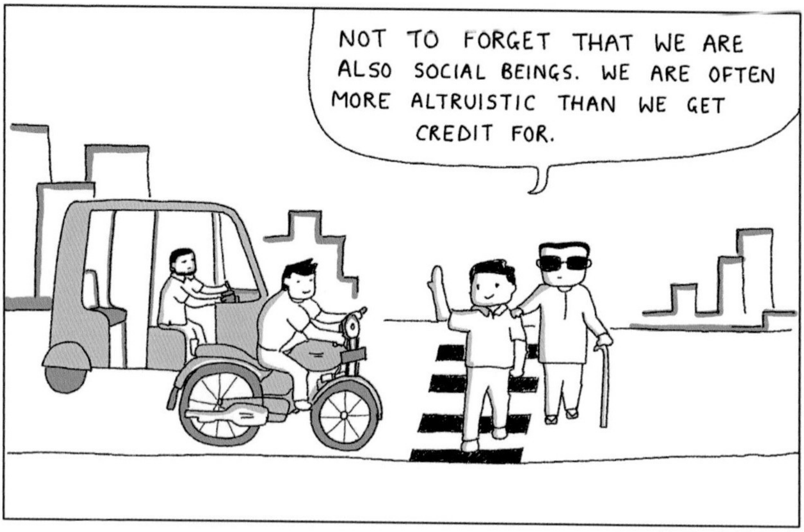
NOT TO FORGET THAT WE ARE ALSO SOCIAL BEINGS. WE ARE OFTEN MORE ALTRUISTIC THAN WE GET CREDIT FOR.

SO WHEN MARKETS FAIL...

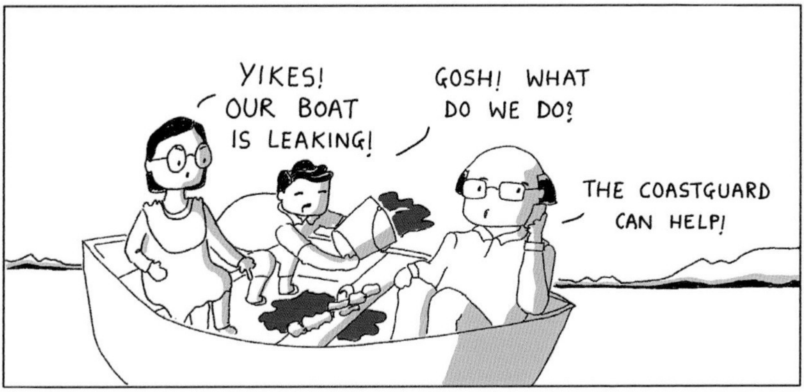
YIKES! OUR BOAT IS LEAKING!
GOSH! WHAT DO WE DO?
THE COASTGUARD CAN HELP!

THE STATE AND THE SOCIETY CAN ACT AS THE SAFETY NET.

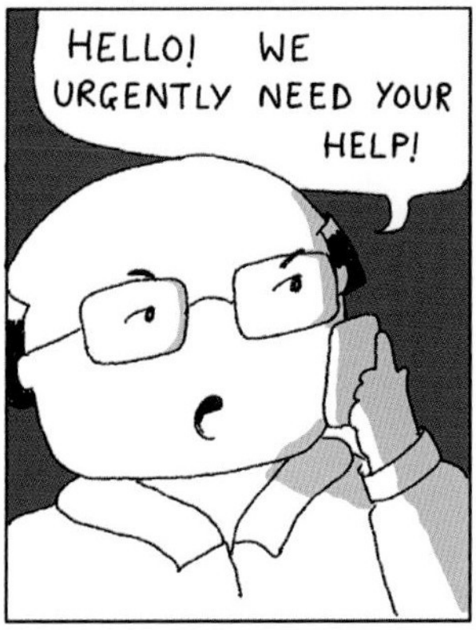
HELLO! WE URGENTLY NEED YOUR HELP!

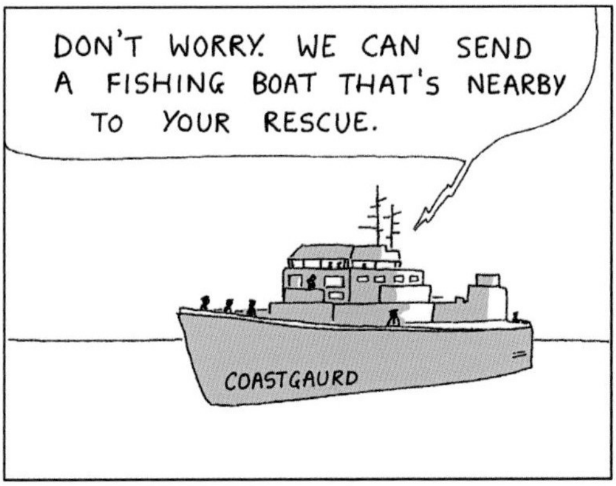
DON'T WORRY. WE CAN SEND A FISHING BOAT THAT'S NEARBY TO YOUR RESCUE.
COASTGAURD

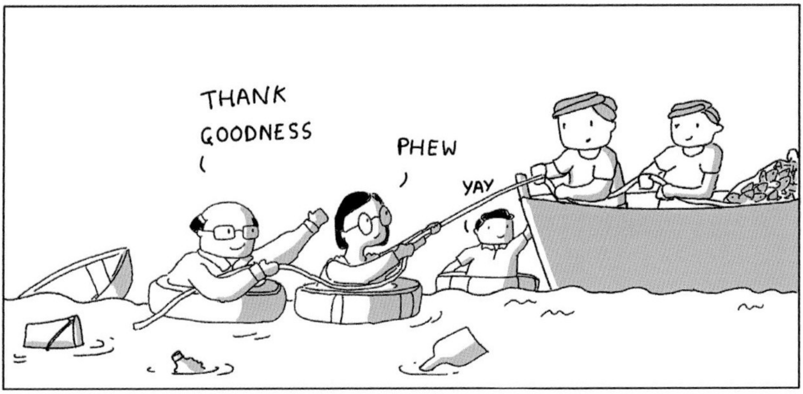
THANK GOODNESS
PHEW
YAY

AND THAT IS WHY WE NEED A WELL-FUNCTIONING STATE, MARKET AND SOCIETY.

Chapter 10

Minimum Coercion, Maximum Prosperity

The path of least coercion

IF THERE IS ONE LESSON TO BE LEARNT FROM THOUSANDS OF YEARS OF HUMAN HISTORY...

FIRE
AGRICULTURE
SETTLEMENT
INVENTIONS
PRINT PRESS
EXPLORATION
TRADE
MODERN MEDICINE
X-RAY
ANTI-BIOTICS
VACCINE
SPACE EXPLORATION
INTERNET

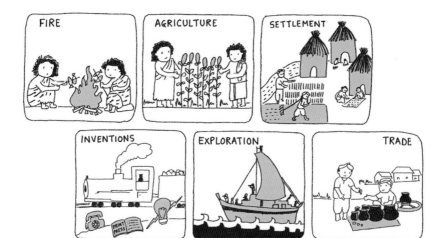

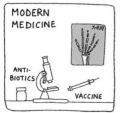

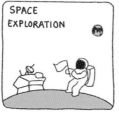

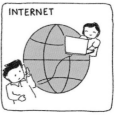

IT IS THAT WHEN HUMANS ARE FREE, PRETTY GOOD THINGS HAPPEN.

WHEN HUMANS WAKE UP FEELING FREE,
THEY EXUDE THE ENERGY THAT DRIVES ALL INNOVATION.

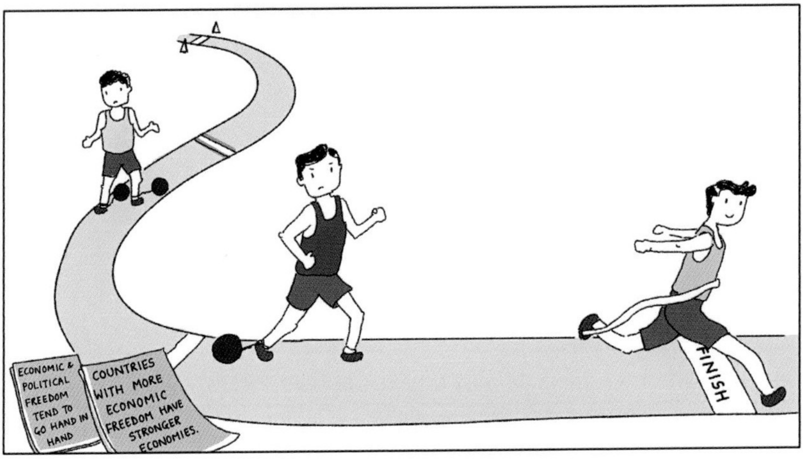
ECONOMIC & POLITICAL FREEDOM TEND TO GO HAND IN HAND
COUNTRIES WITH MORE ECONOMIC FREEDOM HAVE STRONGER ECONOMIES.
FINISH

THAT IS WHY FREER COUNTRIES DO WELL AND
NOT-SO-FREE COUNTRIES DO NOT DO SO WELL.

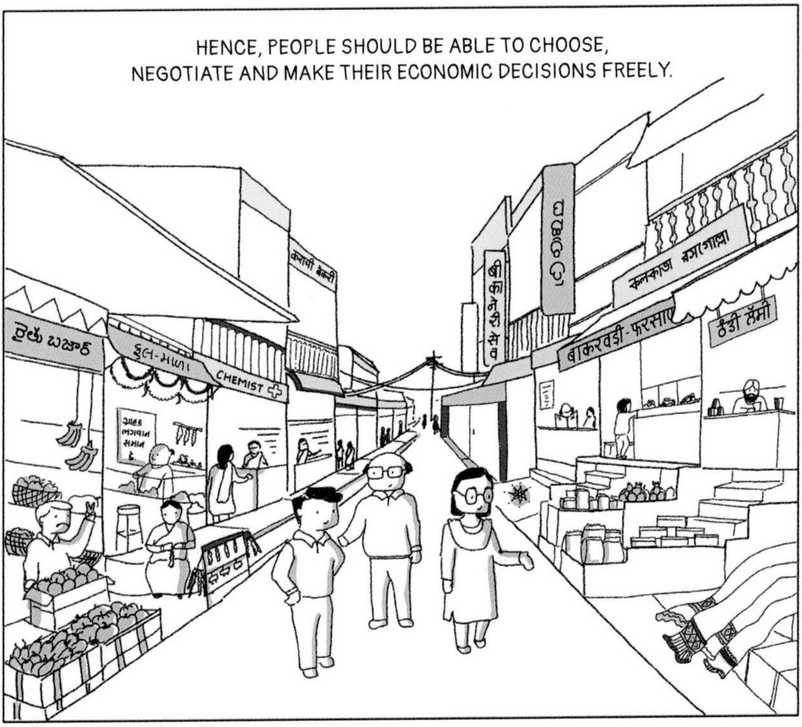
HENCE, PEOPLE SHOULD BE ABLE TO CHOOSE,
NEGOTIATE AND MAKE THEIR ECONOMIC DECISIONS FREELY.
CHEMIST

NOW, WHAT SHOULD THE STATE DO TO ENABLE THIS FREE MARKETPLACE?

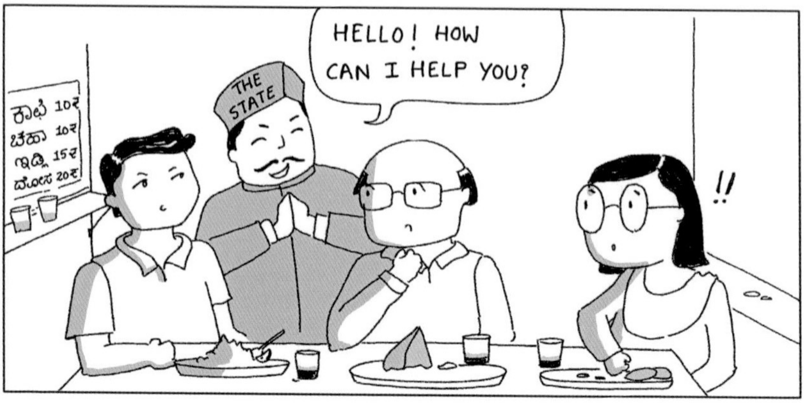
ಕಾಫಿ 10₹
ಚಹಾ 10₹
ಇಡ್ಲಿ 15₹
ದೋಸೆ 20₹
THE STATE
HELLO! HOW CAN I HELP YOU?
!!

WE OFTEN THINK OF THE STATE AS A BENEVOLENT PATRIARCH.

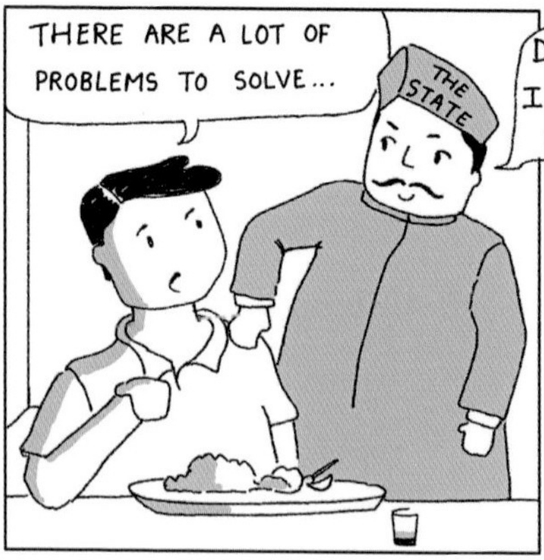
THERE ARE A LOT OF PROBLEMS TO SOLVE...
THE STATE
DON'T WORRY. I WILL TAKE CARE OF EVERYTHING.

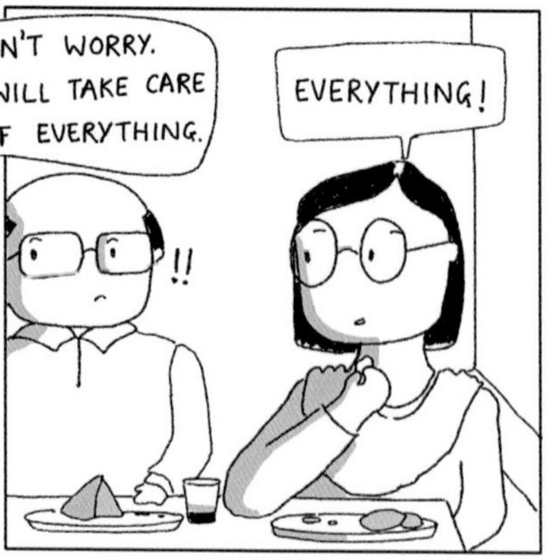
EVERYTHING!
!!

BUT THE BASIS OF ALL STATE ACTION IS COERCION.

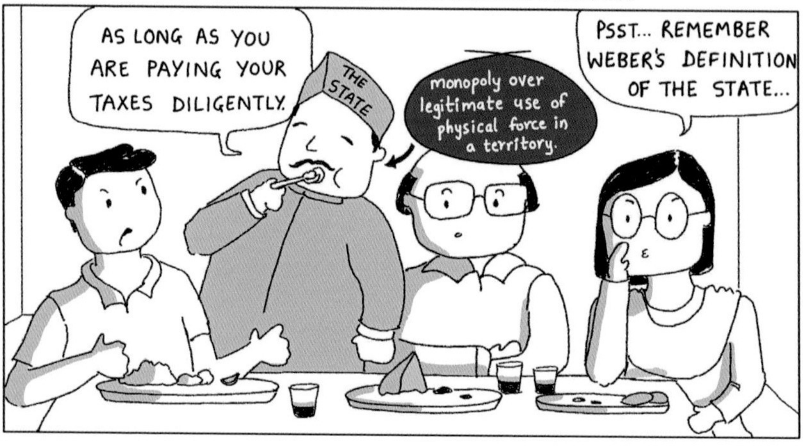
AS LONG AS YOU ARE PAYING YOUR TAXES DILIGENTLY.
THE STATE
monopoly over legitimate use of physical force in a territory.
PSST... REMEMBER WEBER'S DEFINITION OF THE STATE...

BUT THEN, THE STATE EXISTS FOR A REASON.

INDIVIDUALS MAXIMIZING FOR SELF-INTEREST CAN LEAD TO MARKET EFFICIENCY, BUT IT MAY NOT NECESSARILY LEAD TO EQUITABLE OUTCOMES FOR SOCIETY AS A WHOLE.

THE STATE
THAT'S WHERE I CAN MAKE A DIFFERENCE. BUT HOW DO I DO THIS WITH THE LEAST REDUCTION IN FREEDOMS?

NOW, THE STATE HAS ONLY TWO LEVERS OF COERCION.

#1.
REGULATE
#2.
COLLECT TAXES
FINANCE STUFF
PRODUCE STUFF

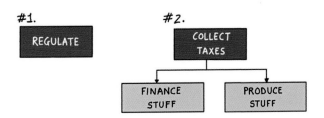

SO HOW DO WE NEGOTIATE THIS FINE LINE OF THE COERCIVE ASPECT OF THE STATE AND THE REALITY OF MARKET FAILURES ?

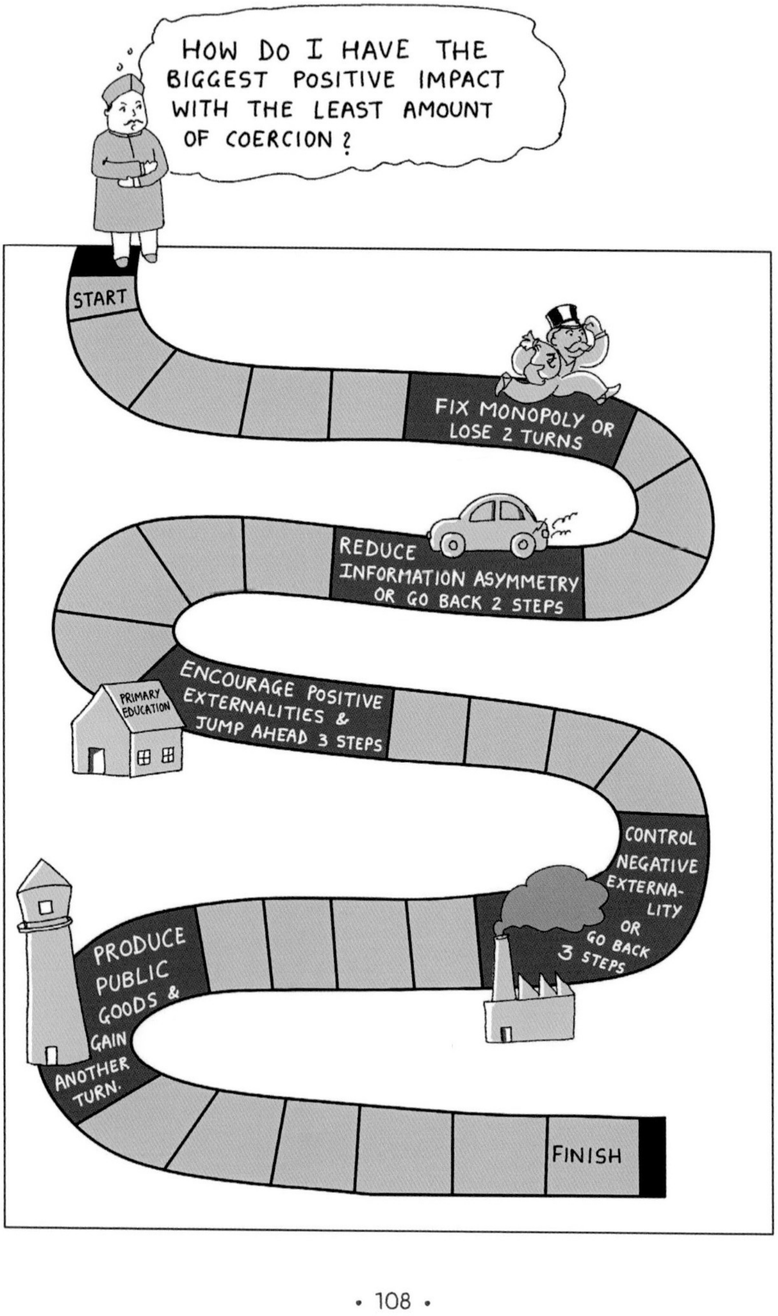
HOW DO I HAVE THE BIGGEST POSITIVE IMPACT WITH THE LEAST AMOUNT OF COERCION ?
START
FIX MONOPOLY OR LOSE 2 TURNS
REDUCE INFORMATION ASYMMETRY OR GO BACK 2 STEPS
PRIMARY EDUCATION
ENCOURAGE POSITIVE EXTERNALITIES & JUMP AHEAD 3 STEPS
CONTROL NEGATIVE EXTERNALITY OR GO BACK 3 STEPS
PRODUCE PUBLIC GOODS & GAIN ANOTHER TURN.
FINISH

THIS FRAMEWORK PROPOSED BY SHAH AND KELKAR IN THIS* BOOK CAN PROVIDE US WITH SOME GUIDANCE.
IN SERVICE OF THE REPUBLIC

REGULATE
MARKET POWER
MAKE SURE MARKETS RUN WELL
INFORMATION ASYMMETRY
REDUCE FRICTION
NEGATIVE EXTERNALITIES
KEEP WITHIN SAFE LIMITS
FINANCE
POSITIVE EXTERNALITIES
ENCOURAGE GOOD THINGS (but don't produce)
PRODUCE
ONLY
PUBLIC GOODS
BECAUSE NOBODY ELSE WILL!

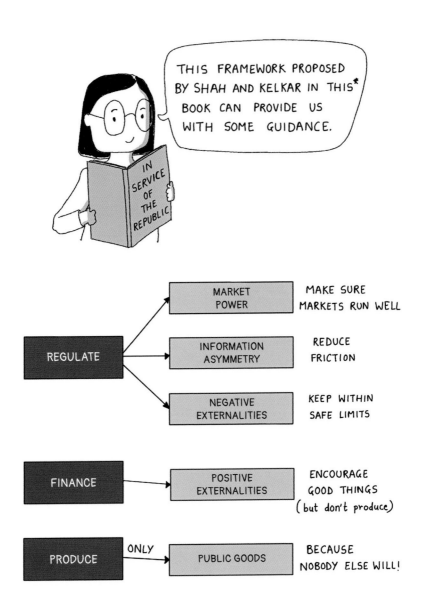

* Vijay Kelkar and Ajay Shah, *In Service of the Republic* (Penguin Random House India, 2019)

THE ANSWER LIES IN CHOOSING THE PATH OF LEAST COERCION AND MINIMIZING STATE INTERVENTION AS FAR AS POSSIBLE.

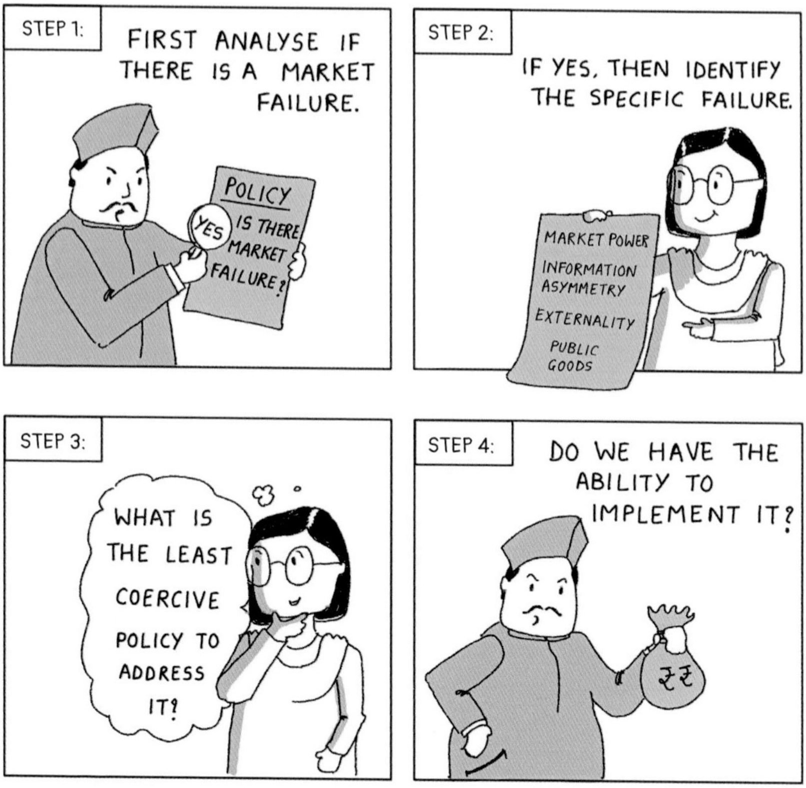
STEP 1:
FIRST ANALYSE IF THERE IS A MARKET FAILURE.
POLICY
IS THERE MARKET FAILURE?
YES
STEP 2:
IF YES, THEN IDENTIFY THE SPECIFIC FAILURE.
MARKET POWER
INFORMATION ASYMMETRY
EXTERNALITY
PUBLIC GOODS
STEP 3:
WHAT IS THE LEAST COERCIVE POLICY TO ADDRESS IT?
STEP 4:
DO WE HAVE THE ABILITY TO IMPLEMENT IT?
₹₹

REMEMBER THAT STATE INTERVENTION ALSO COMES AT A COST.

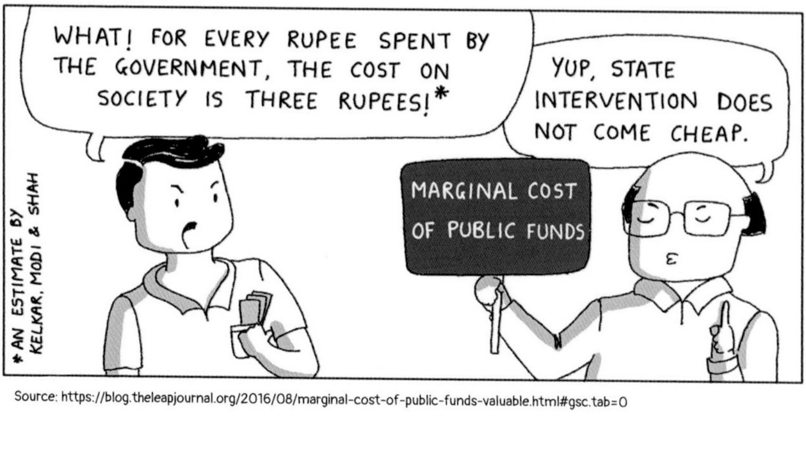
WHAT! FOR EVERY RUPEE SPENT BY THE GOVERNMENT, THE COST ON SOCIETY IS THREE RUPEES!*
YUP, STATE INTERVENTION DOES NOT COME CHEAP.
MARGINAL COST OF PUBLIC FUNDS
* AN ESTIMATE BY KELKAR, MODI & SHAH

Source: https://blog.theleapjournal.org/2016/08/marginal-cost-of-public-funds-valuable.html#gsc.tab=0

SO, IT SHOULD CHOOSE WELL ON
WHAT TO DO AND WHAT NOT TO DO.

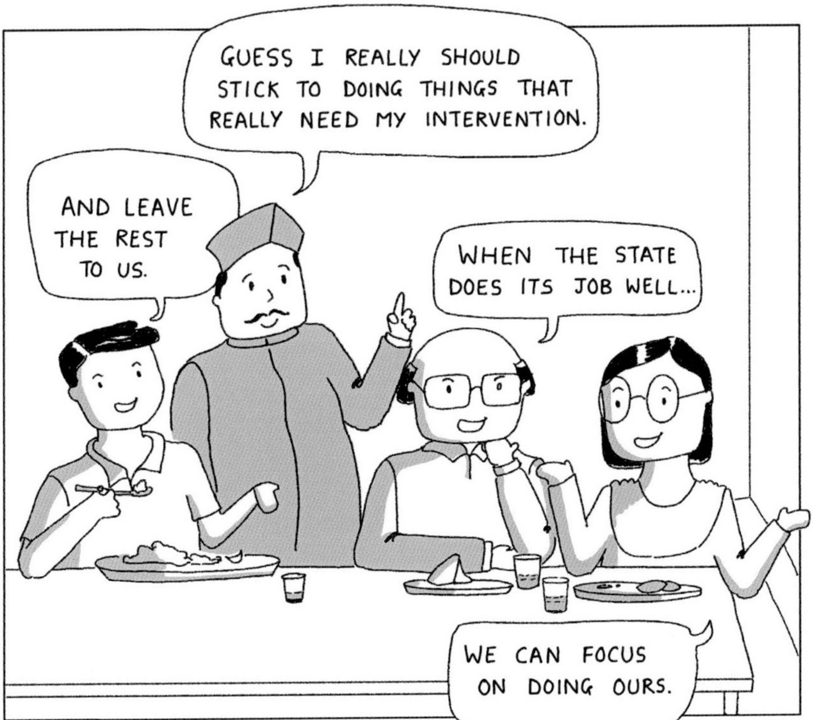
GUESS I REALLY SHOULD STICK TO DOING THINGS THAT REALLY NEED MY INTERVENTION.
AND LEAVE THE REST TO US.
WHEN THE STATE DOES ITS JOB WELL...
WE CAN FOCUS ON DOING OURS.

Chapter 11

There Is Just One Rajinikanth!

Why do governments fail?

MANY OF US ARE AWARE OF MARKET FAILURES AND THINK THAT THE SOLUTION LIES IN GOVERNMENT ACTION.

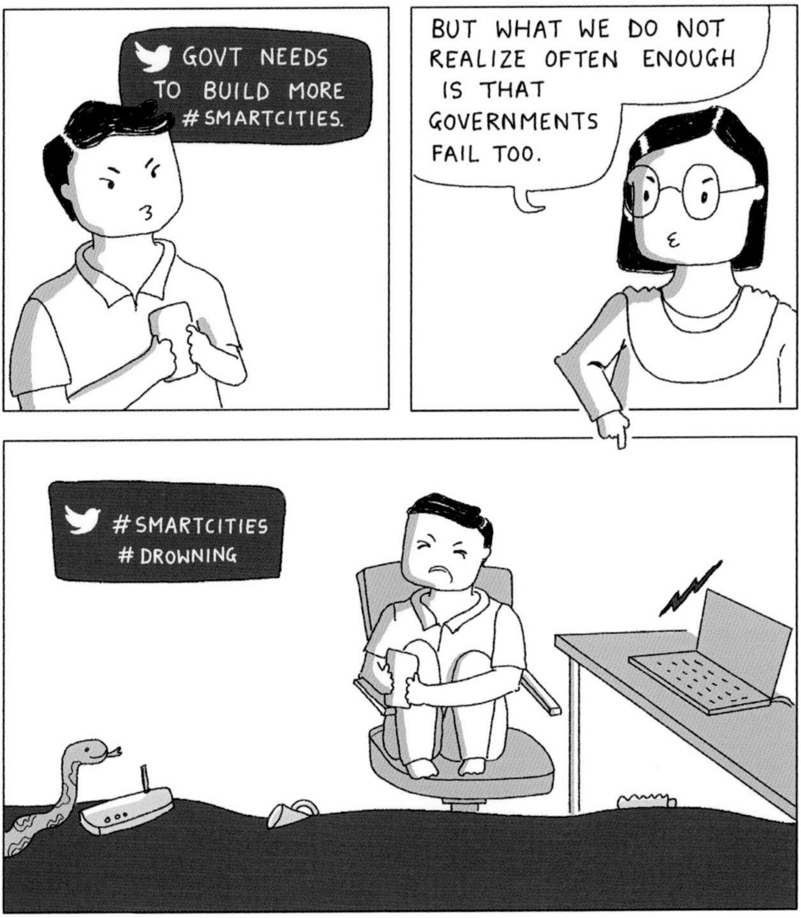
GOVT NEEDS TO BUILD MORE #SMARTCITIES.
BUT WHAT WE DO NOT REALIZE OFTEN ENOUGH IS THAT GOVERNMENTS FAIL TOO.
#SMARTCITIES #DROWNING

BECAUSE THE GOVERNMENT WIELDS MUCH MORE POWER THAN ANY OTHER ENTITY, GOVERNMENT FAILURES CAN HAVE EVEN MORE PERVASIVE AND LONG-LASTING CONSEQUENCES.

AND GOVERNMENTS CAN FAIL IN MANY WAYS...

1. MARKET DISTORTION

2. MISALIGNED INCENTIVES

3. RENT-SEEKING

4. REGULATORY CAPTURE

5. REGULATORY RISK

6. MORAL HAZARD

7. ONE POLICY, MANY GOALS

1. MARKET DISTORTION

WHEN THE GOVERNMENT INTERVENES BY CAPPING PRICES 'THINKING' THAT IT IS CORRECTING FOR A MARKET FAILURE, IT OFTEN ENDS UP INTRODUCING NEW MARKET DISTORTIONS.

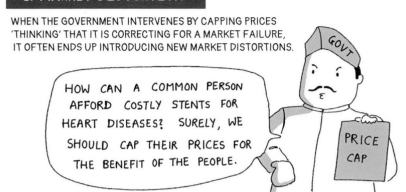

HOW CAN A COMMON PERSON AFFORD COSTLY STENTS FOR HEART DISEASES? SURELY, WE SHOULD CAP THEIR PRICES FOR THE BENEFIT OF THE PEOPLE.

THIS MAY BE DONE WITH GOOD INTENTIONS, BUT IT DOES NOT HELP THE CAUSE.

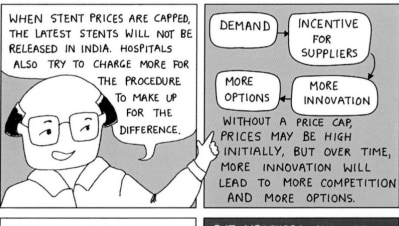

WHEN STENT PRICES ARE CAPPED, THE LATEST STENTS WILL NOT BE RELEASED IN INDIA. HOSPITALS ALSO TRY TO CHARGE MORE FOR THE PROCEDURE TO MAKE UP FOR THE DIFFERENCE.

DEMAND → INCENTIVE FOR SUPPLIERS

MORE OPTIONS ← MORE INNOVATION

WITHOUT A PRICE CAP, PRICES MAY BE HIGH INITIALLY, BUT OVER TIME, MORE INNOVATION WILL LEAD TO MORE COMPETITION AND MORE OPTIONS.

ULTIMATELY, THERE WILL BE MORE COST-EFFECTIVE OPTIONS IN THE MARKET AND PEOPLE WILL BENEFIT FROM THAT.

BUT MEASURES SUCH AS PRICE-CAPPING REDUCE THE INCENTIVE TO PRODUCE THESE GOODS, THEREBY REDUCING THE SUPPLY AND INNOVATION EVEN FURTHER.

HEY, BUT I WAS ONLY TRYING TO HELP!

IN A WELL-FUNCTIONING MARKET, HIGH PRICES CAN CORRECT THEMSELVES OVER TIME, BUT GOVERNMENTS ARE OFTEN NOT SO NIMBLE.

SO, MANY WELL-MEANING GOVERNMENT REGULATIONS WHICH MADE SENSE IN ONE ERA GO ON TILL THEY BECOME HARMFUL TO THE VERY CAUSE THEY ESPOUSED.

MARKET DISTORTION

WE CAN STILL SEE THE AFTER-EFFECTS OF THE BOMBAY RENT ACT OF 1947 IN THE FORM OF DILAPIDATED HOUSING.

WHEN HOMEOWNERS CANNOT INCREASE RENT, THERE IS NO INCENTIVE TO MAINTAIN THE PROPERTY. OVER TIME, THIS REDUCES THE AMOUNT OF HOUSING AVAILABLE.

GOVERNMENT ACTIONS THAT CREATE MARKET DISTORTIONS ARE BOUND TO FAIL IN THE LONG TERM.

WE OFTEN ASSUME THAT THE GOVERNMENT IS ONE MONOLITH AND HAS CLEARLY DEFINED GOALS THAT IT IS WORKING TOWARDS.

2. MISALIGNED INCENTIVES

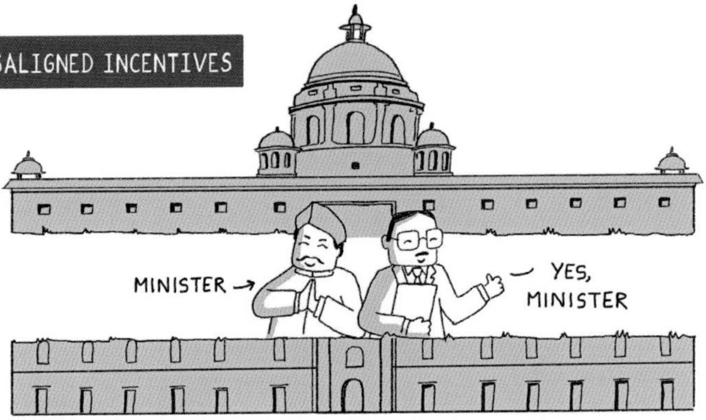
MINISTER
YES, MINISTER

HOWEVER, THE GOVERNMENT HAS VARIED AND COMPLEX GOALS, AND THE INCENTIVES OF THE PEOPLE IN THE GOVERNMENT ARE NOT NECESSARILY ALIGNED.

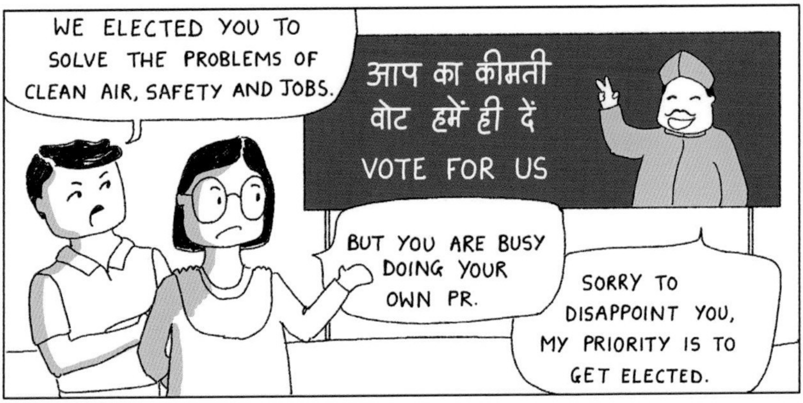
WE ELECTED YOU TO SOLVE THE PROBLEMS OF CLEAN AIR, SAFETY AND JOBS.
आप का कीमती वोट हमें ही दें
VOTE FOR US
BUT YOU ARE BUSY DOING YOUR OWN PR.
SORRY TO DISAPPOINT YOU, MY PRIORITY IS TO GET ELECTED.

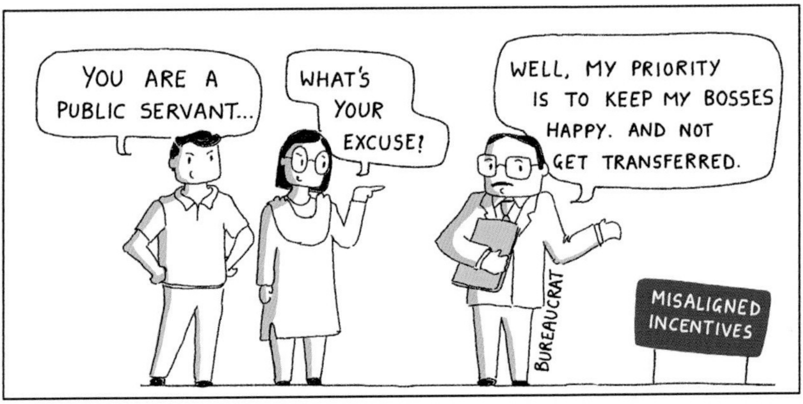
YOU ARE A PUBLIC SERVANT...
WHAT'S YOUR EXCUSE?
WELL, MY PRIORITY IS TO KEEP MY BOSSES HAPPY. AND NOT GET TRANSFERRED.
BUREAUCRAT
MISALIGNED INCENTIVES

IN BUSINESS, PROFIT PROVIDES A GOOD MEASURE OF THE SUCCESS OR FAILURE OF THE PRODUCT OR THE COMPANY.

WHILE IN GOVERNMENT, IT IS NOT AS EASY TO MEASURE SUCCESS. AND IT IS EVEN MORE DIFFICULT TO ATTRIBUTE THE SUCCESS TO ONE POLICY.

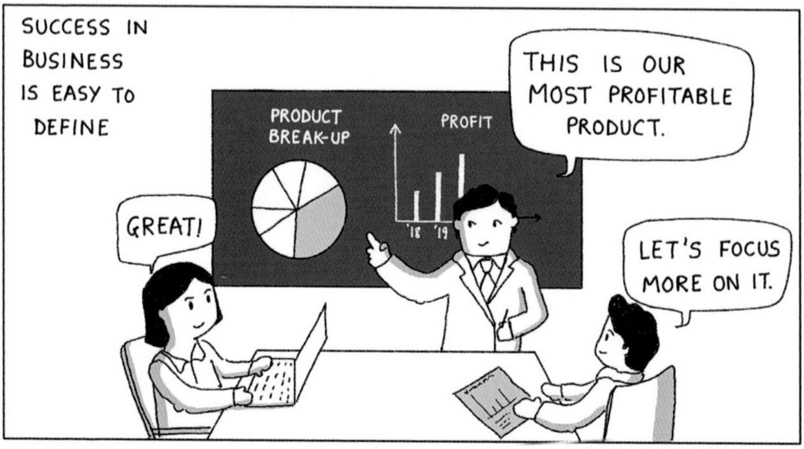
SUCCESS IN BUSINESS IS EASY TO DEFINE
PRODUCT BREAK-UP
PROFIT
'18 '19
THIS IS OUR MOST PROFITABLE PRODUCT.
GREAT!
LET'S FOCUS MORE ON IT.

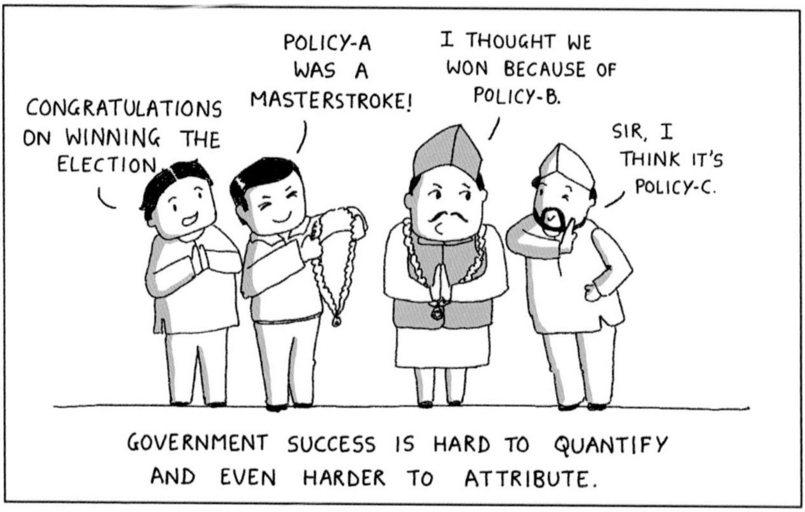
CONGRATULATIONS ON WINNING THE ELECTION
POLICY-A WAS A MASTERSTROKE!
I THOUGHT WE WON BECAUSE OF POLICY-B.
SIR, I THINK IT'S POLICY-C.
GOVERNMENT SUCCESS IS HARD TO QUANTIFY AND EVEN HARDER TO ATTRIBUTE.

IT DOES NOT HELP THAT ELECTIONS PROVIDE VERY FUZZY FEEDBACK, MAKING IT DIFFICULT TO READ WHAT PEOPLE REALLY WANT FROM THE GOVERNMENT.

POOR FEEDBACK MEANS THAT SELF-CORRECTION IS EITHER MISSING OR IS VERY DELAYED.

3. RENT-SEEKING

WHEN GOVERNMENTS HAVE A MONOPOLY IN SERVICE DELIVERY, IT LEADS TO RENT-SEEKING BEHAVIOUR.

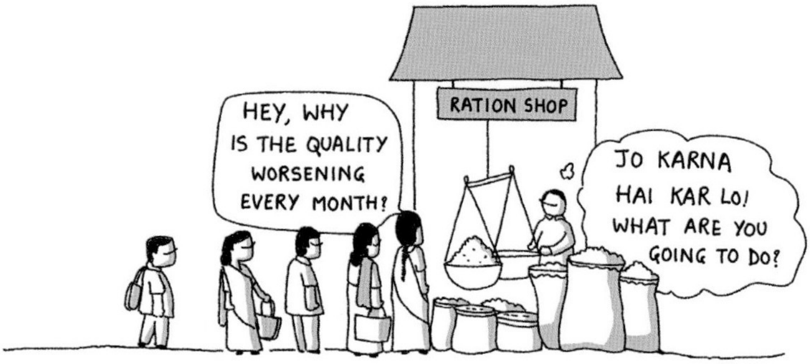
RATION SHOP
HEY, WHY IS THE QUALITY WORSENING EVERY MONTH?
JO KARNA HAI KAR LO! WHAT ARE YOU GOING TO DO?

CITIZENS CANNOT SIMPLY WALK TO THE NEXT ALTERNATIVE IF A PARTICULAR GOVERNMENT SERVICE IS POOR.

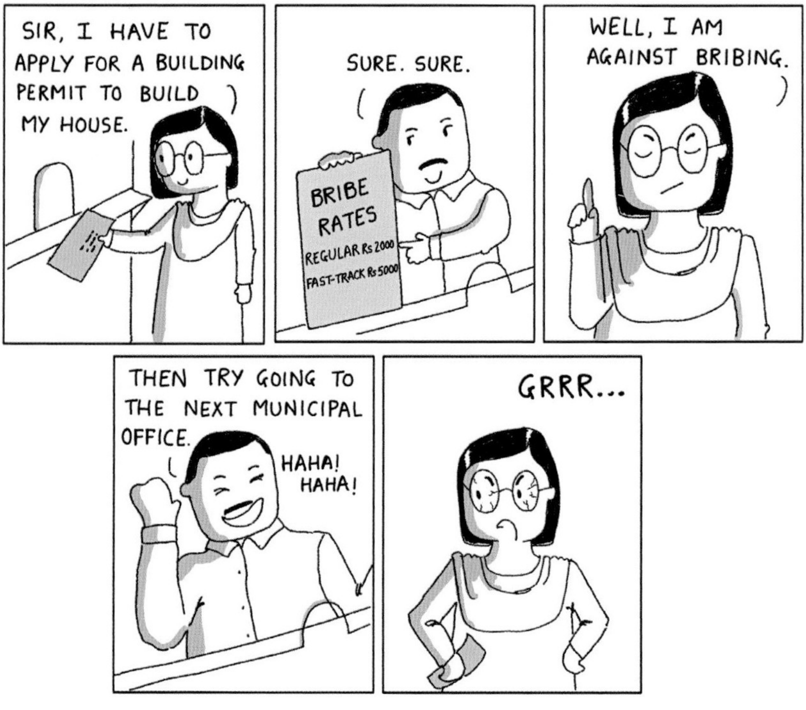
SIR, I HAVE TO APPLY FOR A BUILDING PERMIT TO BUILD MY HOUSE.
SURE. SURE.
BRIBE RATES
REGULAR Rs 2000
FAST-TRACK Rs 5000
WELL, I AM AGAINST BRIBING.
THEN TRY GOING TO THE NEXT MUNICIPAL OFFICE.
HAHA! HAHA!
GRRR...

THIS NOT ONLY LEADS TO CORRUPTION AND EXPLOITATION, BUT ALSO UNDERMINES THE STATE'S OBJECTIVE OF ENSURING SAFETY.

4. REGULATORY CAPTURE

IF GOVERNMENT DEPARTMENTS CAN BE CORRUPTED, REGULATORS CAN BE COMPROMISED TOO.

WHEN THE UMPIRE COLLUDES WITH A PLAYER, ONE PLAYER GETS UNFAIR ADVANTAGE OVER OTHERS.

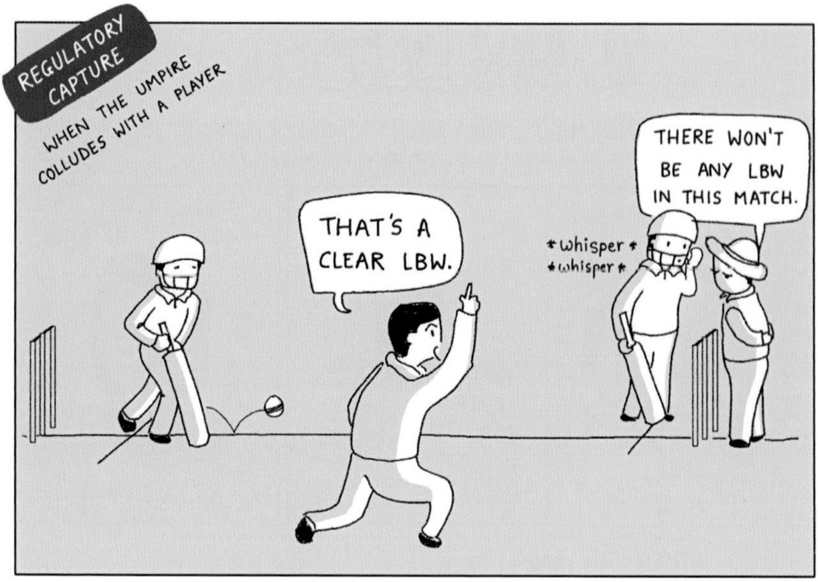
REGULATORY CAPTURE
WHEN THE UMPIRE COLLUDES WITH A PLAYER
THAT'S A CLEAR LBW.
THERE WON'T BE ANY LBW IN THIS MATCH.
whisper
whisper

THIS LEADS TO A MONOPOLY CREATED BY THE GOVERNMENT.

5. REGULATORY RISK

ANOTHER RELATED BUT EVEN BIGGER RISK IS AN UMPIRE WHO IS ARBITRARY AND CAPRICIOUS.

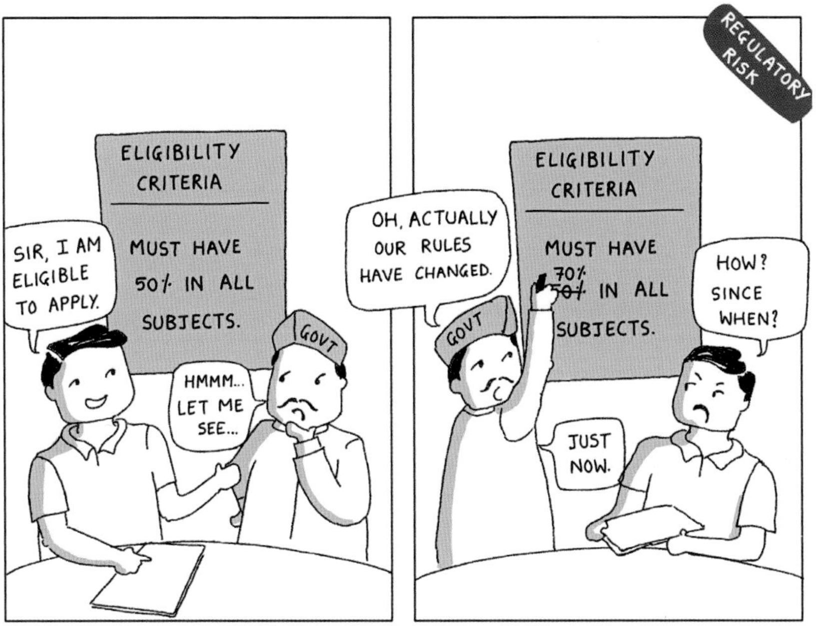

ELIGIBILITY CRITERIA
MUST HAVE 50% IN ALL SUBJECTS.
SIR, I AM ELIGIBLE TO APPLY.
GOVT
HMMM... LET ME SEE...
REGULATORY RISK
OH, ACTUALLY OUR RULES HAVE CHANGED.
ELIGIBILITY CRITERIA
MUST HAVE 70% 50% IN ALL SUBJECTS.
GOVT
HOW? SINCE WHEN?
JUST NOW.

THIS KIND OF UNCERTAIN REGULATORY ENVIRONMENT REDUCES THE CONFIDENCE OF ANY ENTREPRENEUR TO INVEST IN THE INDUSTRY.

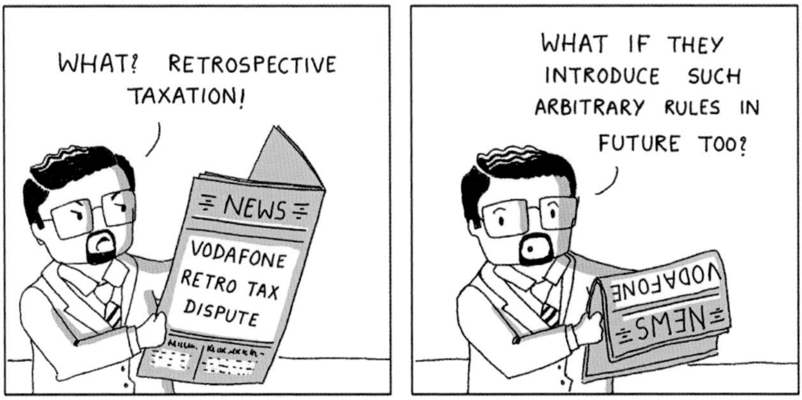

WHAT? RETROSPECTIVE TAXATION!
NEWS
VODAFONE RETRO TAX DISPUTE
WHAT IF THEY INTRODUCE SUCH ARBITRARY RULES IN FUTURE TOO?

6. MORAL HAZARD

SOMETIMES, THE GOVERNMENT TRIES TO RESCUE ENTERPRISES OR GROUPS FROM THE NEGATIVE CONSEQUENCES OF THEIR OWN ACTION. THIS ENDS UP CREATING A MORAL HAZARD, THEREBY CONTINUING POOR DECISION-MAKING.

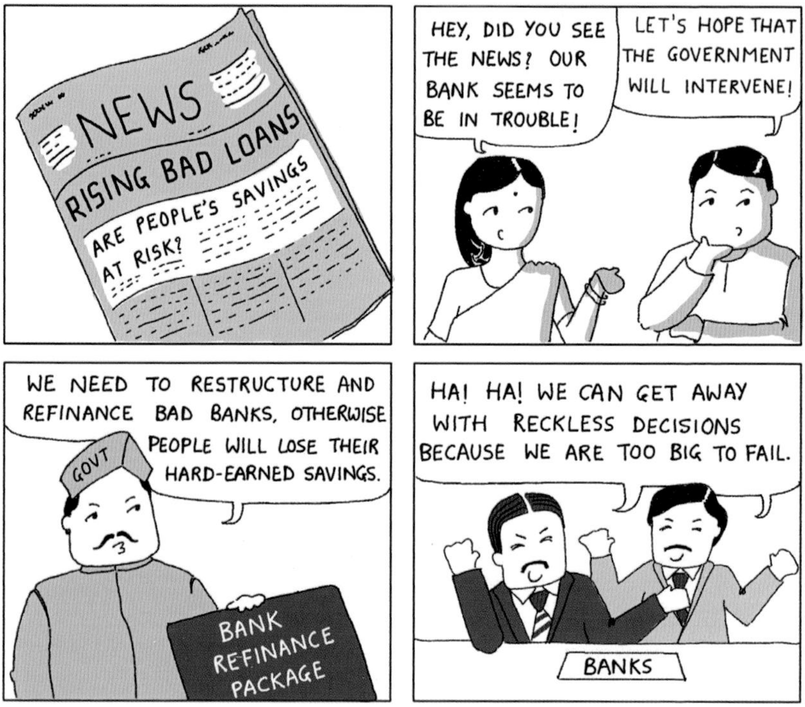
NEWS
RISING BAD LOANS
ARE PEOPLE'S SAVINGS AT RISK?
HEY, DID YOU SEE THE NEWS? OUR BANK SEEMS TO BE IN TROUBLE!
LET'S HOPE THAT THE GOVERNMENT WILL INTERVENE!
WE NEED TO RESTRUCTURE AND REFINANCE BAD BANKS, OTHERWISE PEOPLE WILL LOSE THEIR HARD-EARNED SAVINGS.
GOVT
BANK REFINANCE PACKAGE
HA! HA! WE CAN GET AWAY WITH RECKLESS DECISIONS BECAUSE WE ARE TOO BIG TO FAIL.
BANKS

ALSO, SUCH SHORT-TERM FIXES HINDER MORE LONG-TERM SOLUTIONS TO SYSTEMIC PROBLEMS.

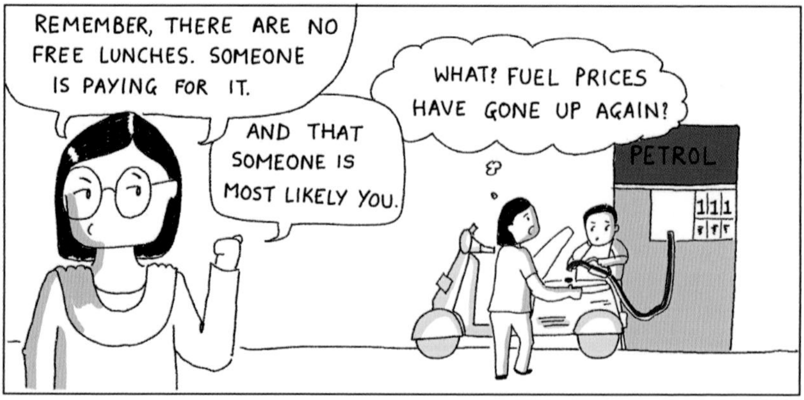
REMEMBER, THERE ARE NO FREE LUNCHES. SOMEONE IS PAYING FOR IT.
AND THAT SOMEONE IS MOST LIKELY YOU.
WHAT? FUEL PRICES HAVE GONE UP AGAIN?
PETROL

7. ONE POLICY, MANY GOALS

ANOTHER APPROACH THAT GOVERNMENTS OFTEN FOLLOW IS TO INTRODUCE ONE POLICY TO MEET MANY DIFFERENT OBJECTIVES.

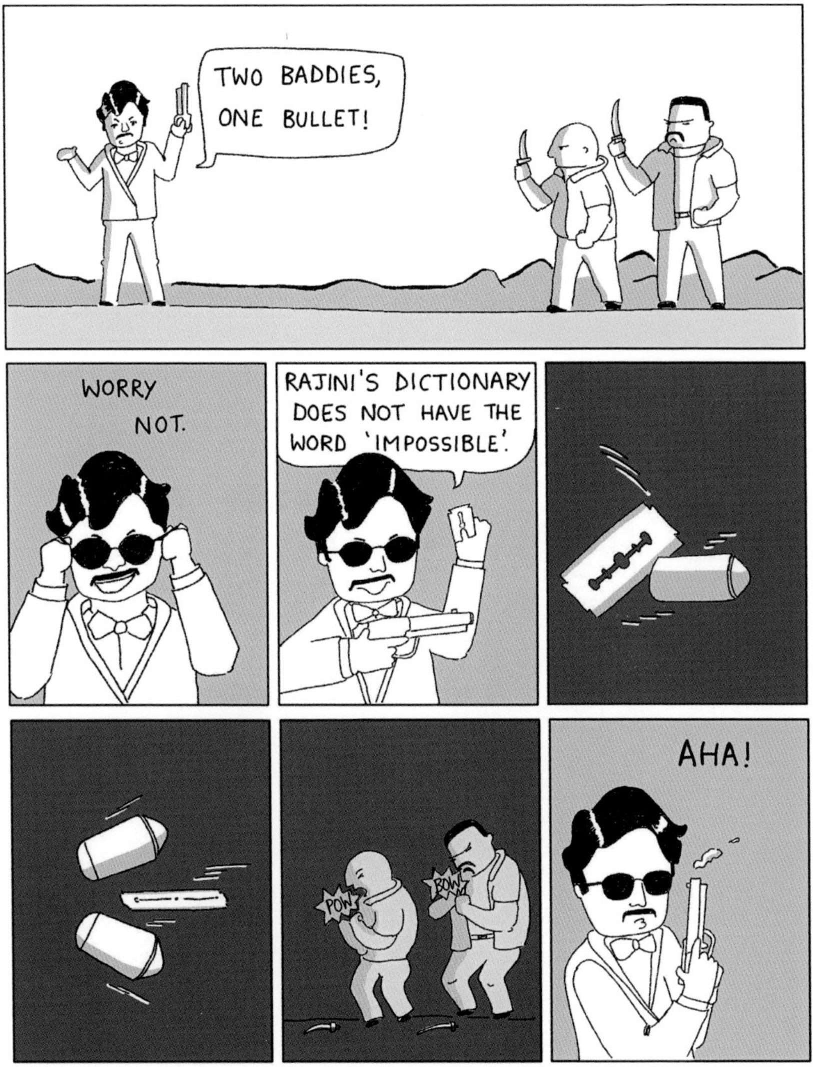

TWO BADDIES, ONE BULLET!
WORRY NOT.
RAJINI'S DICTIONARY DOES NOT HAVE THE WORD 'IMPOSSIBLE'.
POW
BOW
AHA!

THIS APPROACH MAY WORK IN MOVIES, BUT IN REALITY WE OFTEN END UP WITH A POLICY THAT FULFILS NONE OF THE INTENDED OBJECTIVES.

AN EXAMPLE OF THIS IS OUR TAX POLICY THAT TRIES TO ACHIEVE MANY OBJECTIVES, LEADING TO A COMPLICATED TAX STRUCTURE THAT LEAVES AVENUES FOR TAX EVASION AND CORRUPTION.

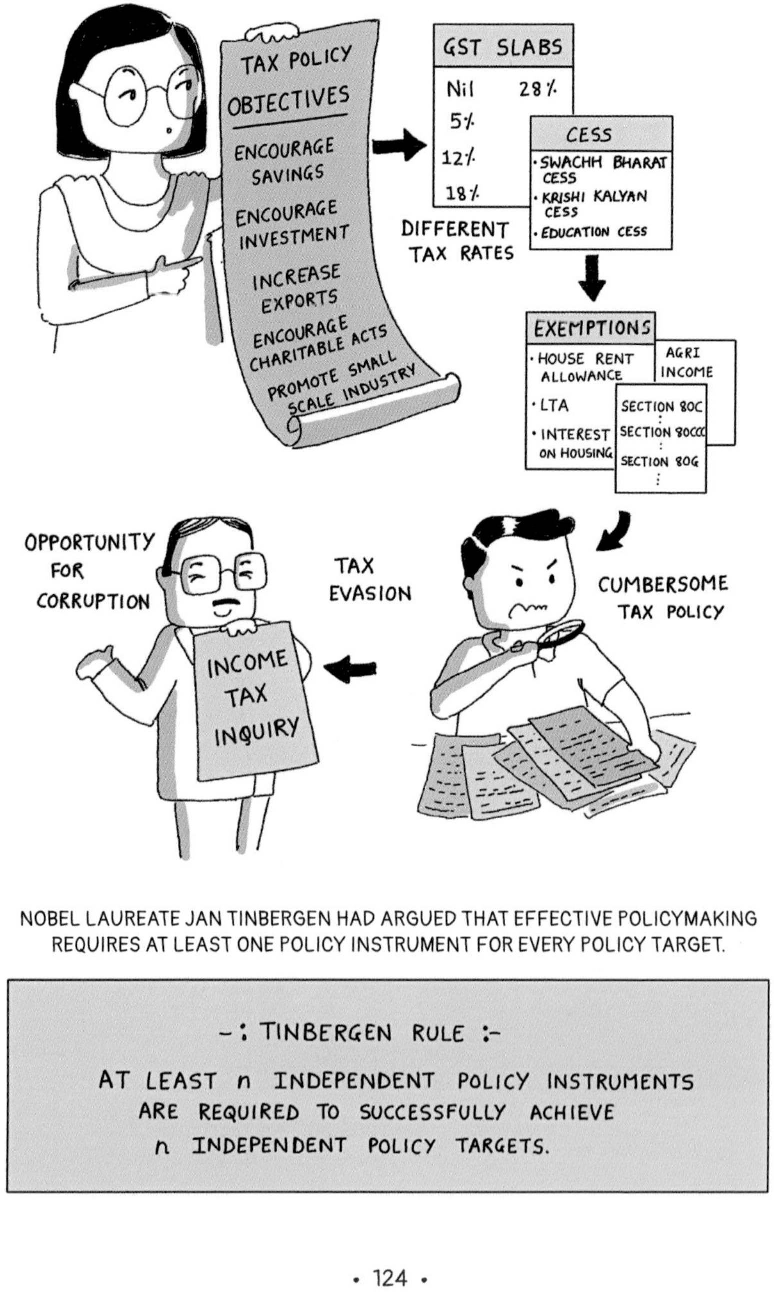

TAX POLICY
OBJECTIVES
ENCOURAGE SAVINGS
ENCOURAGE INVESTMENT
INCREASE EXPORTS
ENCOURAGE CHARITABLE ACTS
PROMOTE SMALL SCALE INDUSTRY
GST SLABS
Nil 28%
5%
12%
18%
DIFFERENT TAX RATES
CESS
• SWACHH BHARAT CESS
• KRISHI KALYAN CESS
• EDUCATION CESS
EXEMPTIONS
• HOUSE RENT ALLOWANCE
• LTA
• INTEREST ON HOUSING
AGRI INCOME
SECTION 80C
SECTION 80CCC
SECTION 80G
CUMBERSOME TAX POLICY
TAX EVASION
OPPORTUNITY FOR CORRUPTION
INCOME TAX INQUIRY

NOBEL LAUREATE JAN TINBERGEN HAD ARGUED THAT EFFECTIVE POLICYMAKING REQUIRES AT LEAST ONE POLICY INSTRUMENT FOR EVERY POLICY TARGET.

> –: TINBERGEN RULE :–
>
> AT LEAST *n* INDEPENDENT POLICY INSTRUMENTS ARE REQUIRED TO SUCCESSFULLY ACHIEVE *n* INDEPENDENT POLICY TARGETS.

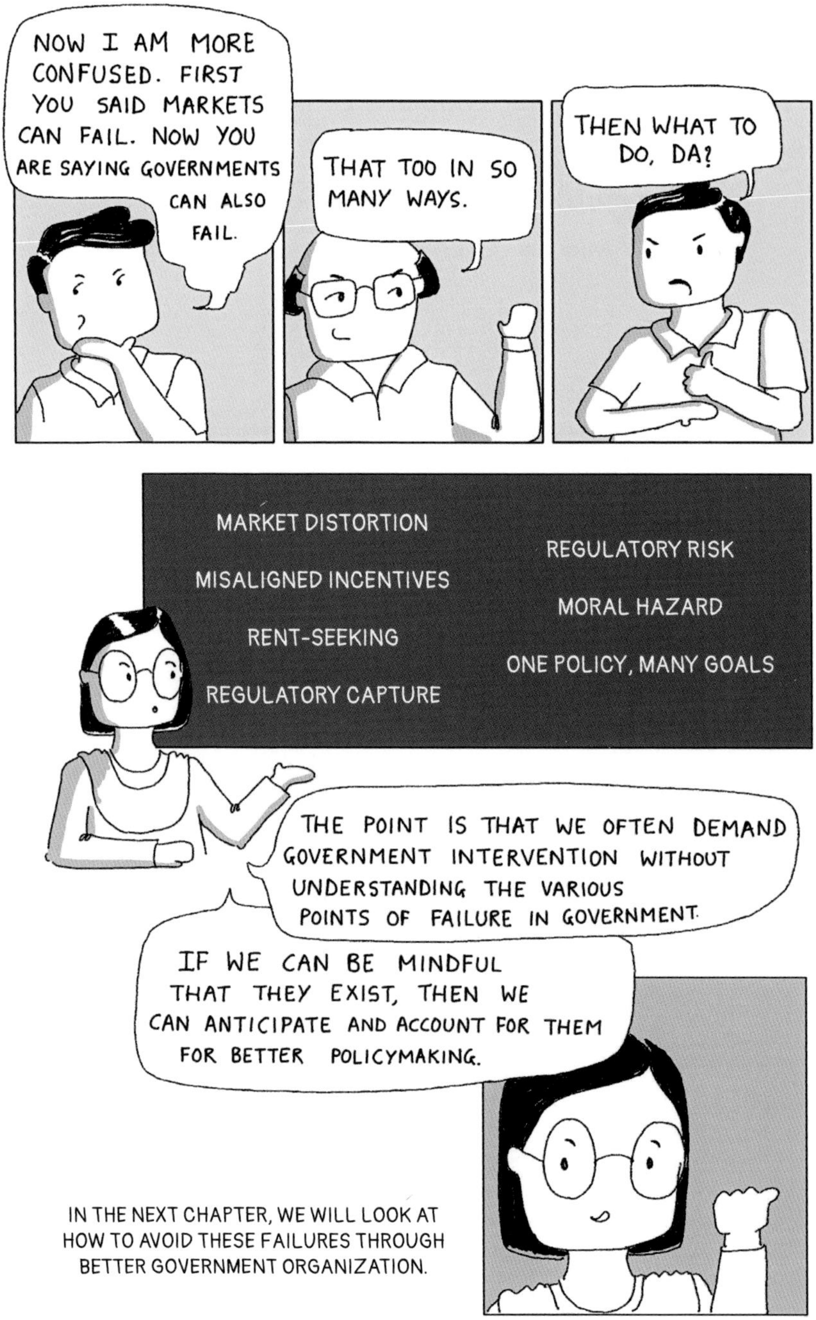
NOW I AM MORE CONFUSED. FIRST YOU SAID MARKETS CAN FAIL. NOW YOU ARE SAYING GOVERNMENTS CAN ALSO FAIL.
THAT TOO IN SO MANY WAYS.
THEN WHAT TO DO, DA?
MARKET DISTORTION
MISALIGNED INCENTIVES
RENT-SEEKING
REGULATORY CAPTURE
REGULATORY RISK
MORAL HAZARD
ONE POLICY, MANY GOALS
THE POINT IS THAT WE OFTEN DEMAND GOVERNMENT INTERVENTION WITHOUT UNDERSTANDING THE VARIOUS POINTS OF FAILURE IN GOVERNMENT.
IF WE CAN BE MINDFUL THAT THEY EXIST, THEN WE CAN ANTICIPATE AND ACCOUNT FOR THEM FOR BETTER POLICYMAKING.
IN THE NEXT CHAPTER, WE WILL LOOK AT HOW TO AVOID THESE FAILURES THROUGH BETTER GOVERNMENT ORGANIZATION.

Chapter 12

Constable Ganpat's Traffic Dilemma

Making governments work better

WHEN IT COMES TO GOVERNMENT REFORMS, WE OFTEN FALL BACK ON A FALSE BINARY—IT'S EITHER PRIVATIZATION OR NATIONALIZATION.

WHY ARE TAXPAYERS' MONEY BEING USED TO KEEP SICK PSUs ALIVE?
बेच दो इन्हें।
SELL THEM!
PRIVATIZE PSUs
WHY ARE OUR NATURAL RESOURCES BEING GIVEN INTO PRIVATE HANDS?
NATIONALIZE

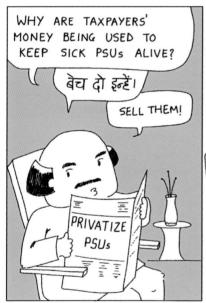

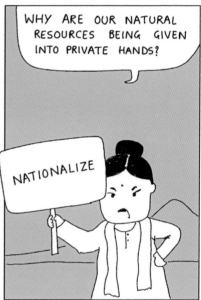

BUT IT IS OFTEN OVERLOOKED THAT THERE ARE OTHER MECHANISMS OF ORGANIZATIONAL REFORMS THAT CAN BRING MUCH NEEDED ACCOUNTABILITY AND EFFICIENCY IN GOVERNMENT FUNCTIONING.

MANY OF OUR GOVERNMENT AGENCIES OR
EVEN REGULATORS PERFORM MORE THAN ONE FUNCTION.

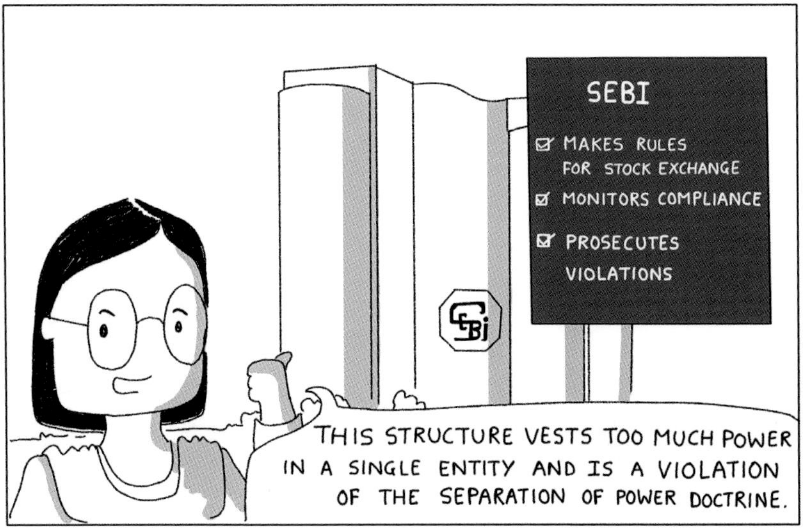
SEBI
MAKES RULES FOR STOCK EXCHANGE
MONITORS COMPLIANCE
PROSECUTES VIOLATIONS
THIS STRUCTURE VESTS TOO MUCH POWER IN A SINGLE ENTITY AND IS A VIOLATION OF THE SEPARATION OF POWER DOCTRINE.

WHEN THE SAME AGENCY IS RESPONSIBLE FOR MAKING RULES,
FOR MONITORING COMPLIANCE AND ALSO FOR PROSECUTING VIOLATIONS,
IT GETS TOO MUCH POWER AND TOO LITTLE ACCOUNTABILITY.

SEPARATION OF FUNCTIONS

AN IMPORTANT BUT LESSER KNOWN FRAMEWORK ON ORGANIZATIONAL REFORM IS TO SEPARATE GOVERNMENT ENTITIES BASED ON THEIR KEY FUNCTION.

'DRAFTING POLICIES' AND 'MAKING REGULATIONS' ARE STEERING FUNCTIONS. THESE ARE CRITICAL AT DRIVING GOVERNMENT POLICY IN THE RIGHT DIRECTION.

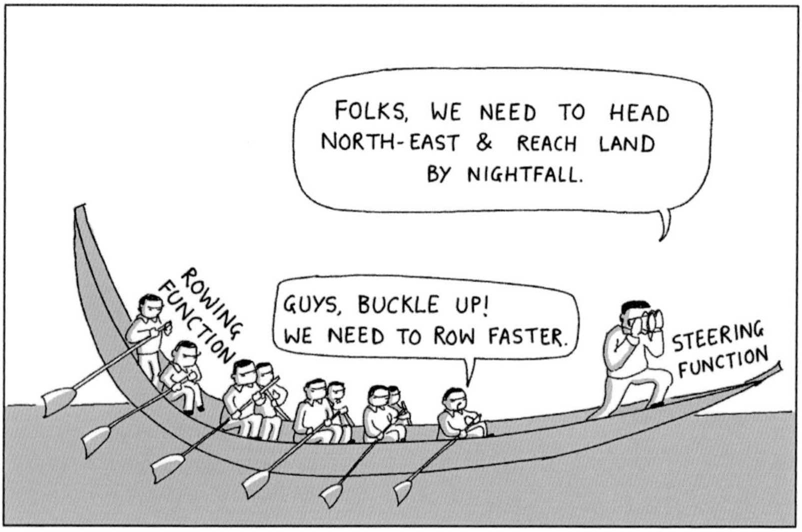
FOLKS, WE NEED TO HEAD NORTH-EAST & REACH LAND BY NIGHTFALL.
ROWING FUNCTION
GUYS, BUCKLE UP! WE NEED TO ROW FASTER.
STEERING FUNCTION

ON THE OTHER HAND, 'SERVICE DELIVERY' AND 'COMPLIANCE' ARE ROWING FUNCTIONS. ONCE A CLEAR TARGET IS SET BY THE STEERING ENTITY, THE ROWING ENTITY CAN WORK INDEPENDENTLY TOWARDS MEETING THE TARGET.

STEERING AND ROWING FUNCTIONS REQUIRE DIFFERENT MINDSETS, AND THEREFORE THEY SHOULD BE DONE BY DIFFERENT ENTITIES.

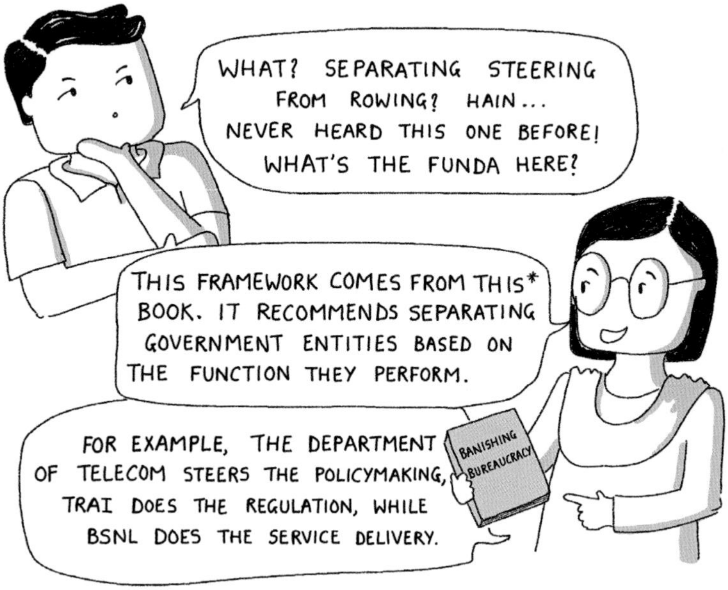
WHAT? SEPARATING STEERING FROM ROWING? HAIN... NEVER HEARD THIS ONE BEFORE! WHAT'S THE FUNDA HERE?
THIS FRAMEWORK COMES FROM THIS* BOOK. IT RECOMMENDS SEPARATING GOVERNMENT ENTITIES BASED ON THE FUNCTION THEY PERFORM.
FOR EXAMPLE, THE DEPARTMENT OF TELECOM STEERS THE POLICYMAKING, TRAI DOES THE REGULATION, WHILE BSNL DOES THE SERVICE DELIVERY.
BANISHING BUREAUCRACY

steering function	rowing function
POLICYMAKING MAKING LONG-TERM POLICY e.g. Department of Telecom	SERVICE DELIVERY PROVIDING GOVERNMENT SERVICES e.g. Public Distribution System
REGULATION MAKING RULES FOR IMPLEMENTATION e.g. Telecom Regulatory Authority of India	COMPLIANCE ENSURING RULES ARE BEING FOLLOWED e.g. Traffic Police

* David Osborne and Peter Plastrik, *Banishing Bureaucracy* (Basic Books, 1997)

THIS IS BECAUSE EACH FUNCTION HAS A DIFFERENT OBJECTIVE WHICH CAN BE AT ODDS WITH THE OBJECTIVES OF OTHER FUNCTIONS.

TAKE THE EXAMPLE OF TRAFFIC POLICE, THAT HAS TO PERFORM TWO JOBS.

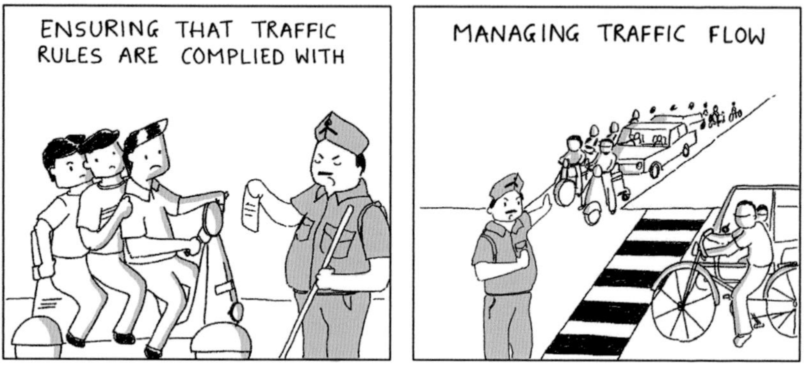
ENSURING THAT TRAFFIC RULES ARE COMPLIED WITH
MANAGING TRAFFIC FLOW

NOW THESE TWO FUNCTIONS ARE SOMETIMES IN CONFLICT WITH EACH OTHER

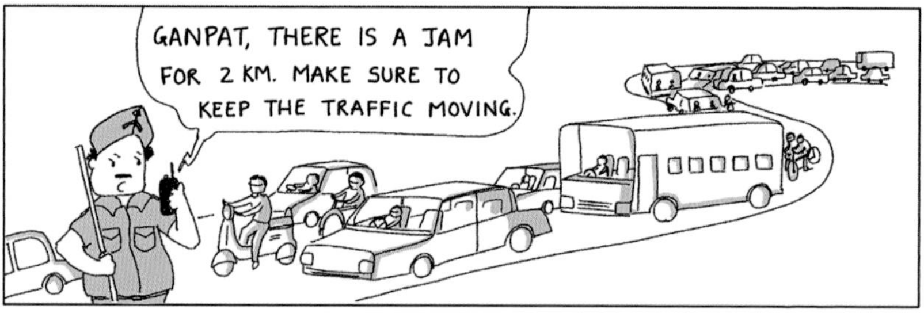
GANPAT, THERE IS A JAM FOR 2 KM. MAKE SURE TO KEEP THE TRAFFIC MOVING.

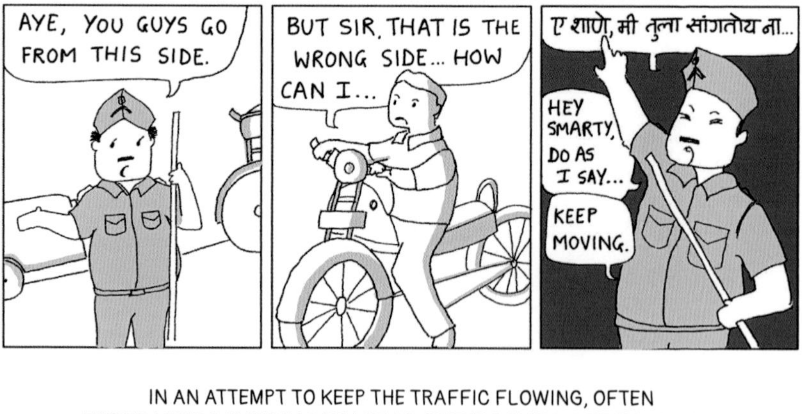
AYE, YOU GUYS GO FROM THIS SIDE.
BUT SIR, THAT IS THE WRONG SIDE... HOW CAN I...
ए शाणे, मी तुला सांगतोय ना...
HEY SMARTY, DO AS I SAY...
KEEP MOVING.

IN AN ATTEMPT TO KEEP THE TRAFFIC FLOWING, OFTEN THE TRAFFIC POLICE HAS TO LET GO OF THE COMPLIANCE FUNCTION.

IDEALLY, THE TWO FUNCTIONS SHOULD BE SEPARATED.

THE TRAFFIC POLICE SHOULD JUST STICK TO ENFORCING COMPLIANCE.
WHILE A MUNICIPAL DEPARTMENT CAN MANAGE TRAFFIC FLOW.
HMM... BUT WHAT'S THE ADVANTAGE OF THIS?

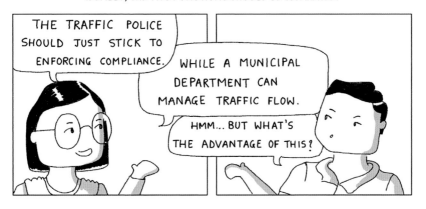

BY SEPARATING THE FUNCTIONS, EACH ENTITY CAN WORK ON A NARROW BUT WELL-DEFINED OBJECTIVE.

FUNCTION	ENTITY	OBJECTIVE
COMPLIANCE	TRAFFIC POLICE	ENFORCE TRAFFIC RULES
SERVICE DELIVERY	MUNICIPALITY	MANAGE TRAFFIC FLOW

AND THE INCENTIVES OF THE PEOPLE WORKING IN THAT ENTITY CAN NOW BE CLEARLY ALIGNED TO THAT FUNCTION.

TEAM, LET'S PLAN FOR A SMOOTHER FLOW FOR OUR BUSIEST ROUTES: BETTER TRAFFIC LIGHTS, FEWER CHOKE POINTS.
TEAM, LET'S ENSURE THAT NO ONE JUMPS THE RED LIGHT, AND BE VERY STRICT WITH DRIVING ON THE WRONG SIDE.

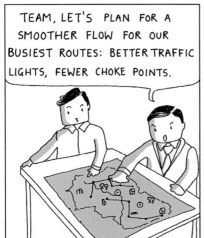

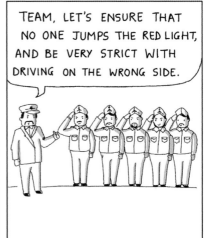

1. THE STEERING FUNCTION SHOULD ANTICIPATE AND PLAN FOR VARIOUS POINTS OF FAILURES WHILE MAKING POLICIES AND REGULATIONS.

THE GOVERNMENT'S MAIN JOB IS TO FOCUS ON MAKING POLICIES THAT AREN'T JUST WELL-INTENTIONED BUT ALSO WORK WELL.

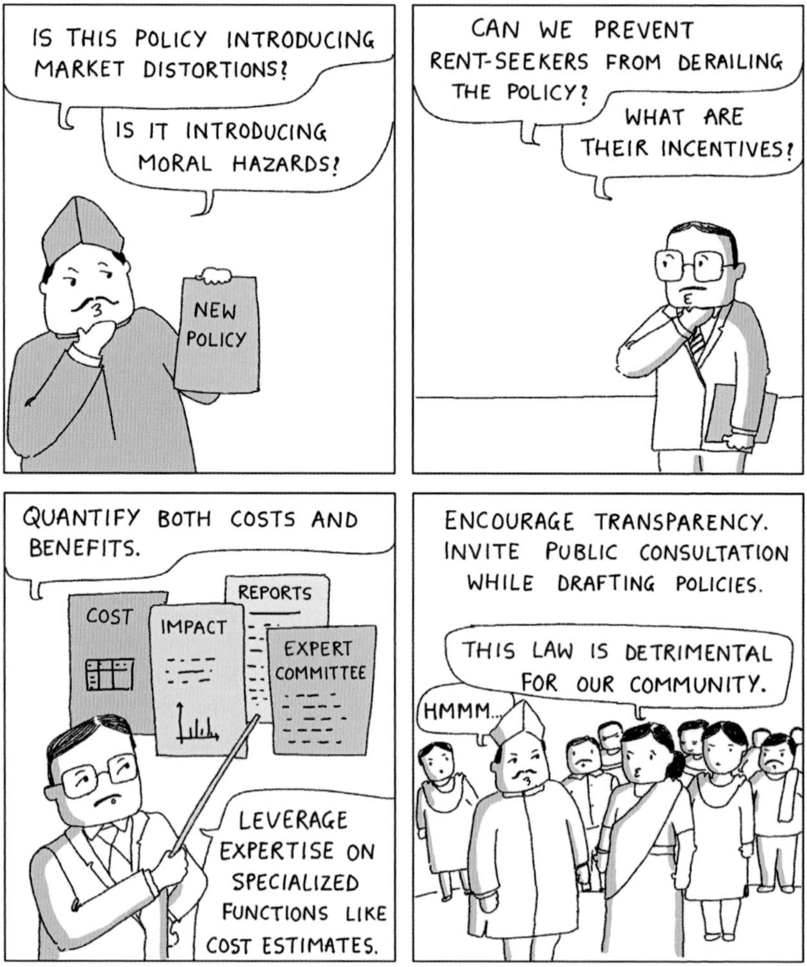

IS THIS POLICY INTRODUCING MARKET DISTORTIONS?
IS IT INTRODUCING MORAL HAZARDS?
NEW POLICY
CAN WE PREVENT RENT-SEEKERS FROM DERAILING THE POLICY?
WHAT ARE THEIR INCENTIVES?
QUANTIFY BOTH COSTS AND BENEFITS.
REPORTS
COST
IMPACT
EXPERT COMMITTEE
LEVERAGE EXPERTISE ON SPECIALIZED FUNCTIONS LIKE COST ESTIMATES.
ENCOURAGE TRANSPARENCY. INVITE PUBLIC CONSULTATION WHILE DRAFTING POLICIES.
THIS LAW IS DETRIMENTAL FOR OUR COMMUNITY.
HMMM...

AND FOR THAT TO HAPPEN, IT CAN CONSULT DOMAIN EXPERTS AND TAKE FEEDBACK FROM THE PEOPLE WHO MAY BE AFFECTED BY THE POLICY.

2. HAVING OUTLINED THE POLICY, THE STEERING ENTITY MUST NOW SET OUTCOME GOALS INSTEAD OF OUTPUT GOALS FOR THE ROWING ENTITY.

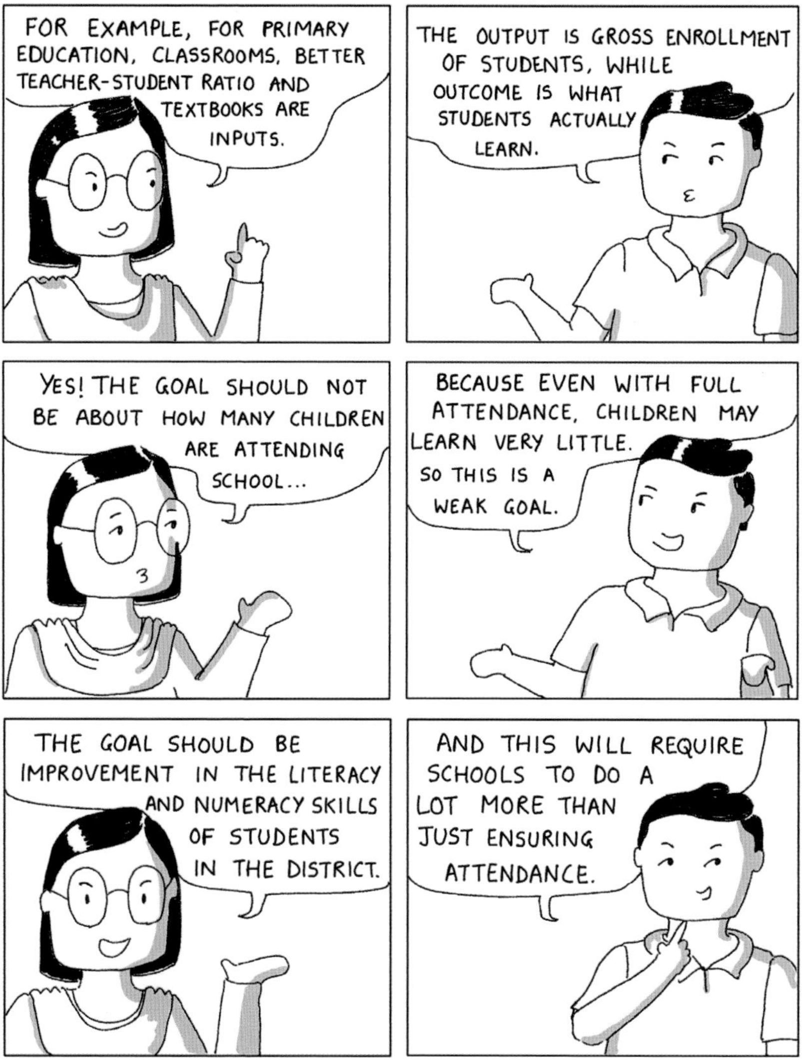
FOR EXAMPLE, FOR PRIMARY EDUCATION, CLASSROOMS, BETTER TEACHER-STUDENT RATIO AND TEXTBOOKS ARE INPUTS.
THE OUTPUT IS GROSS ENROLLMENT OF STUDENTS, WHILE OUTCOME IS WHAT STUDENTS ACTUALLY LEARN.
YES! THE GOAL SHOULD NOT BE ABOUT HOW MANY CHILDREN ARE ATTENDING SCHOOL...
BECAUSE EVEN WITH FULL ATTENDANCE, CHILDREN MAY LEARN VERY LITTLE. SO THIS IS A WEAK GOAL.
THE GOAL SHOULD BE IMPROVEMENT IN THE LITERACY AND NUMERACY SKILLS OF STUDENTS IN THE DISTRICT.
AND THIS WILL REQUIRE SCHOOLS TO DO A LOT MORE THAN JUST ENSURING ATTENDANCE.

ONCE QUANTIFIABLE AND OUTCOME-ORIENTED GOALS ARE SET, THE TASK CAN NOW BE DEVOLVED TO AN INDEPENDENT ROWING ENTITY.

OFCOURSE, THE GOVERNMENT MUST ALSO DEVOLVE ENOUGH POWER TO THE ROWING ENTITY SO THAT IT CAN DO EVERYTHING IT NEEDS TO IN ORDER TO ACHIEVE THE OUTCOME GOALS.

3. NOW THAT OUTCOME-ORIENTED GOALS ARE SET, COMPETITION CAN BE INTRODUCED IN THE ROWING FUNCTION.

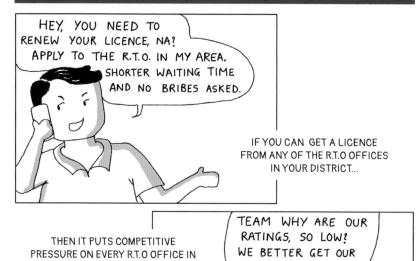

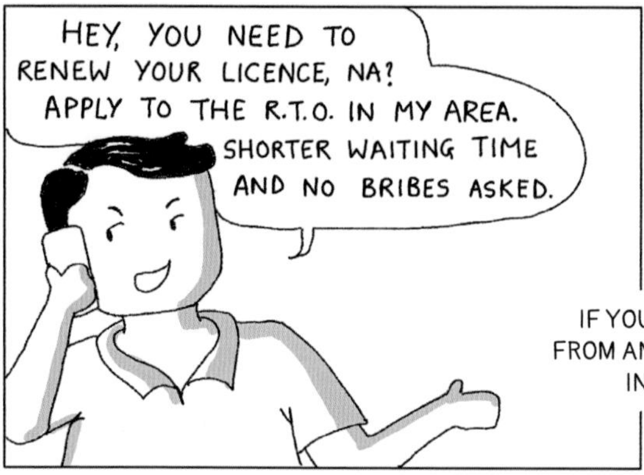
HEY, YOU NEED TO RENEW YOUR LICENCE, NA? APPLY TO THE R.T.O. IN MY AREA. SHORTER WAITING TIME AND NO BRIBES ASKED.

IF YOU CAN GET A LICENCE FROM ANY OF THE R.T.O OFFICES IN YOUR DISTRICT...

THEN IT PUTS COMPETITIVE PRESSURE ON EVERY R.T.O OFFICE IN THE DISTRICT TO PERFORM BETTER.

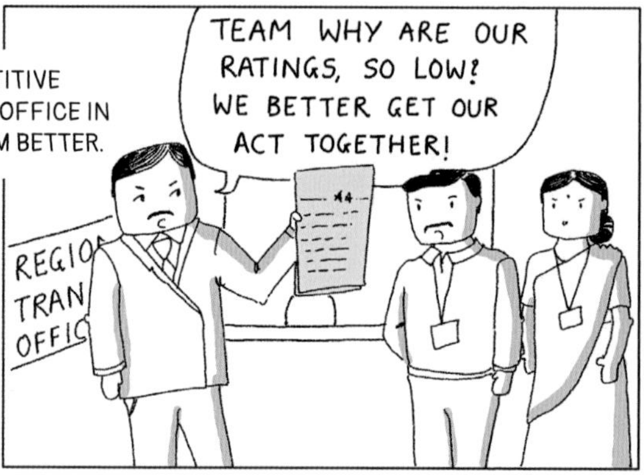
TEAM WHY ARE OUR RATINGS, SO LOW? WE BETTER GET OUR ACT TOGETHER!

THIS IS A WAY TO INTRODUCE COMPETITION AND EFFICIENCY IN SERVICE DELIVERY BY GOVERNMENT.

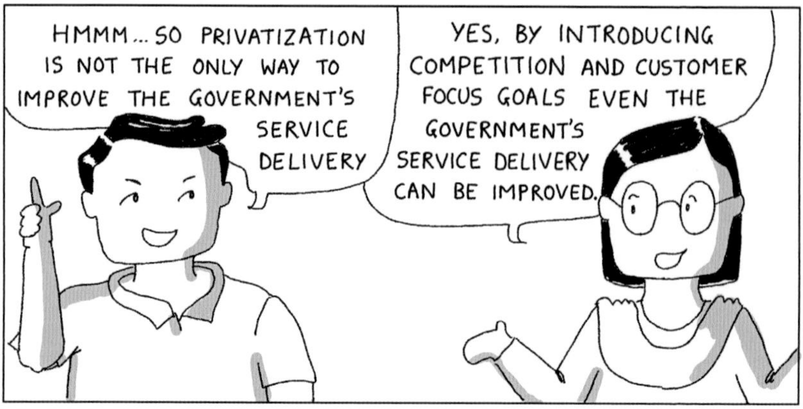
HMMM... SO PRIVATIZATION IS NOT THE ONLY WAY TO IMPROVE THE GOVERNMENT'S SERVICE DELIVERY
YES, BY INTRODUCING COMPETITION AND CUSTOMER FOCUS GOALS EVEN THE GOVERNMENT'S SERVICE DELIVERY CAN BE IMPROVED.

AFTER ALL, THE GOVERNMENT'S ROLE IS INDISPENSABLE IN CIVIC LIFE.

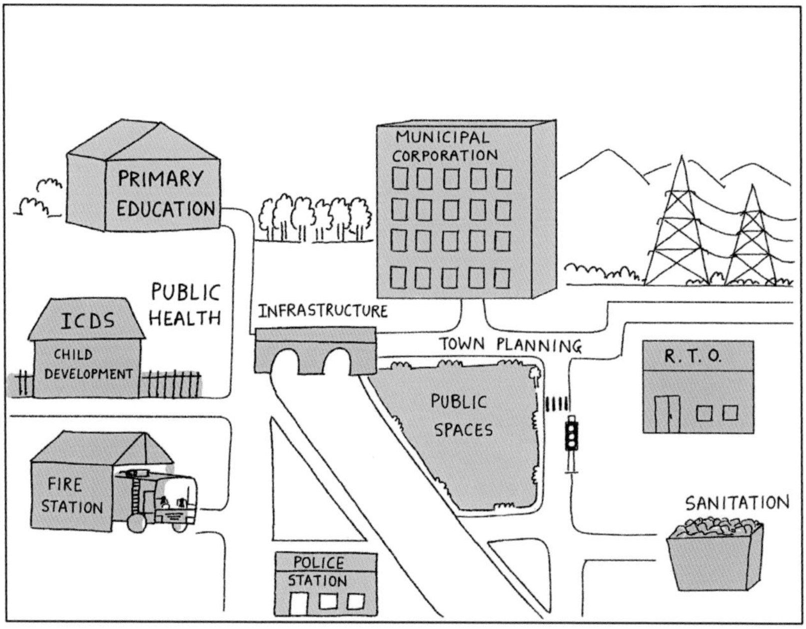
MUNICIPAL CORPORATION
PRIMARY EDUCATION
PUBLIC HEALTH
ICDS
CHILD DEVELOPMENT
INFRASTRUCTURE
TOWN PLANNING
R. T. O.
PUBLIC SPACES
FIRE STATION
SANITATION
POLICE STATION

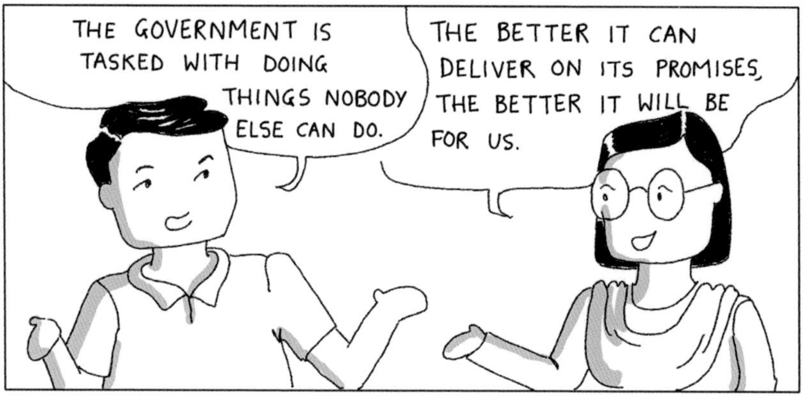
THE GOVERNMENT IS TASKED WITH DOING THINGS NOBODY ELSE CAN DO.
THE BETTER IT CAN DELIVER ON ITS PROMISES, THE BETTER IT WILL BE FOR US.

Chapter 13

'Mile Sur Mera Tumhara'

Society as a change maker

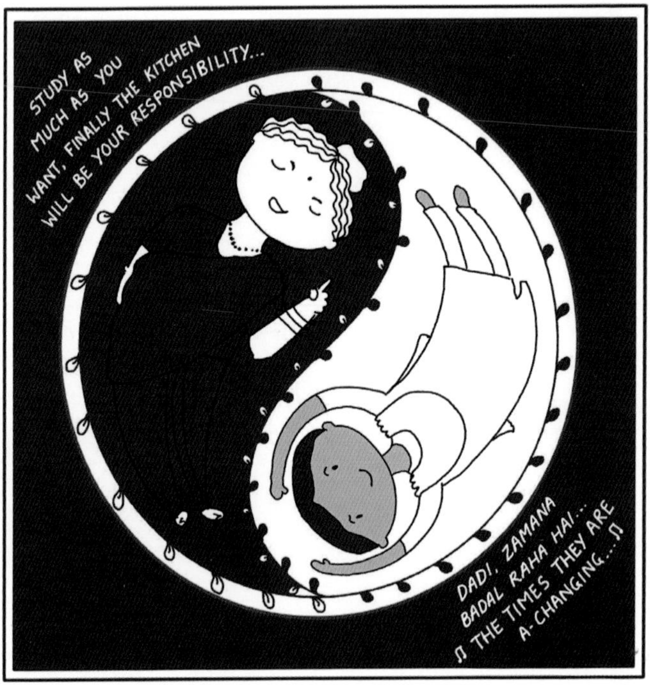
STUDY AS MUCH AS YOU WANT, FINALLY THE KITCHEN WILL BE YOUR RESPONSIBILITY...
DADI, ZAMANA BADAL RAHA HAI... ♫ THE TIMES THEY ARE A-CHANGING... ♫

INDIA'S FEMALE LABOUR FORCE PARTICIPATION RATIO IS A PUZZLE.

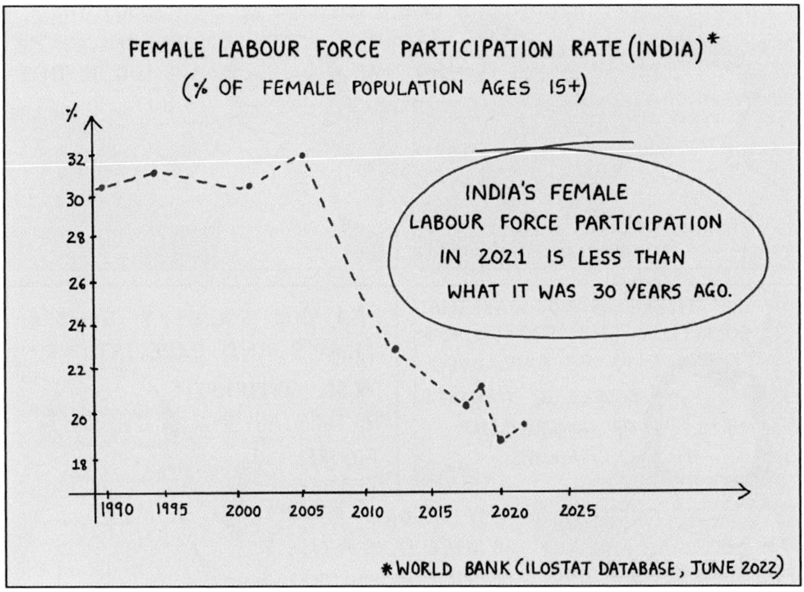
FEMALE LABOUR FORCE PARTICIPATION RATE (INDIA)*
(% OF FEMALE POPULATION AGES 15+)
%
32
30
28
26
24
22
20
18
1990
1995
2000
2005
2010
2015
2020
2025
INDIA'S FEMALE LABOUR FORCE PARTICIPATION IN 2021 IS LESS THAN WHAT IT WAS 30 YEARS AGO.
*WORLD BANK (ILOSTAT DATABASE, JUNE 2022)

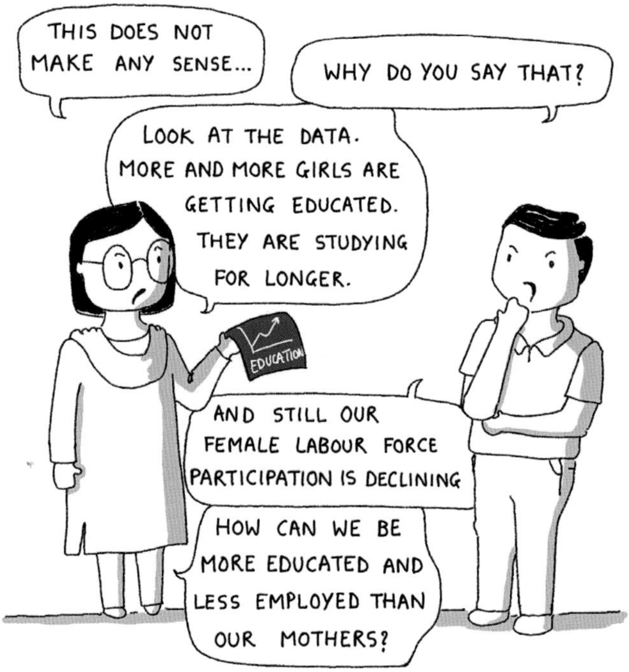
THIS DOES NOT MAKE ANY SENSE...
WHY DO YOU SAY THAT?
LOOK AT THE DATA. MORE AND MORE GIRLS ARE GETTING EDUCATED. THEY ARE STUDYING FOR LONGER.
EDUCATION
AND STILL OUR FEMALE LABOUR FORCE PARTICIPATION IS DECLINING
HOW CAN WE BE MORE EDUCATED AND LESS EMPLOYED THAN OUR MOTHERS?

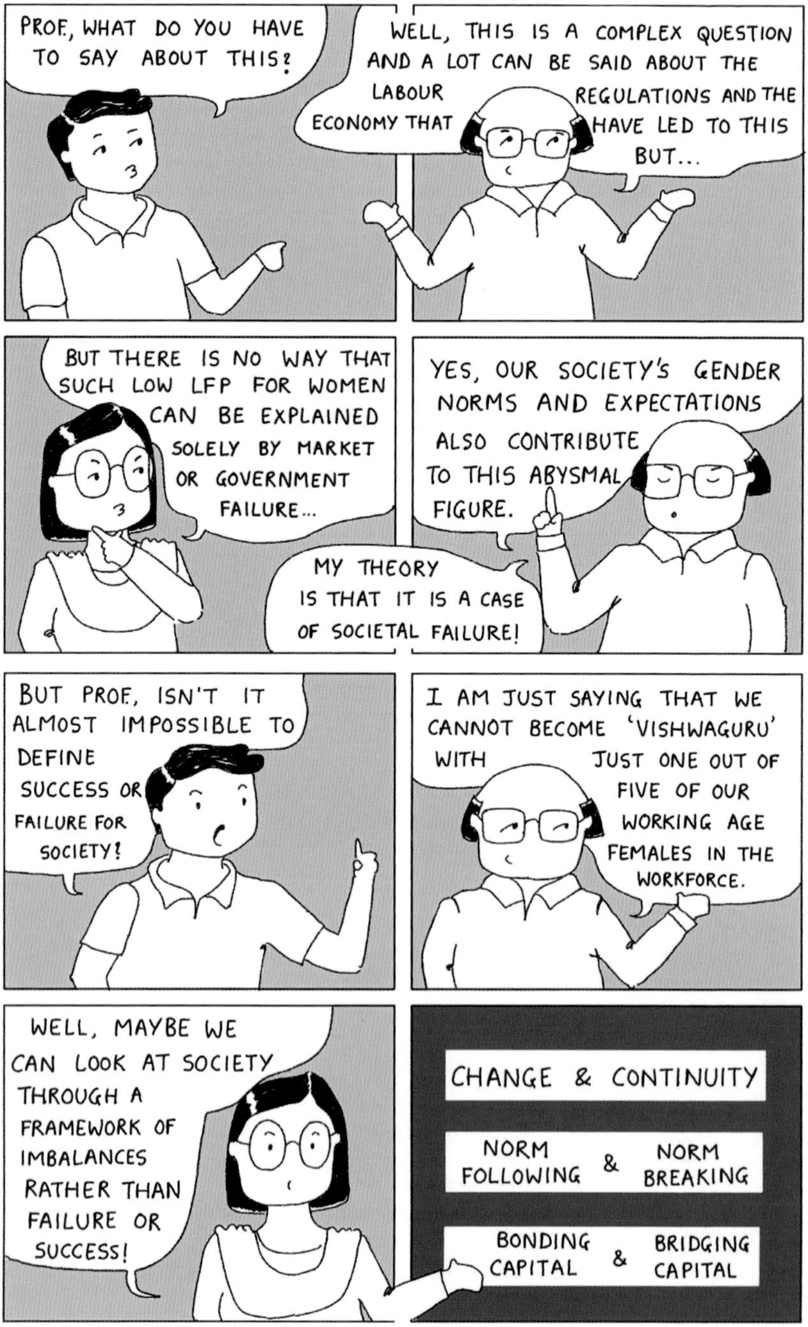
PROF., WHAT DO YOU HAVE TO SAY ABOUT THIS?
WELL, THIS IS A COMPLEX QUESTION AND A LOT CAN BE SAID ABOUT THE LABOUR ECONOMY THAT REGULATIONS AND THE HAVE LED TO THIS BUT...
BUT THERE IS NO WAY THAT SUCH LOW LFP FOR WOMEN CAN BE EXPLAINED SOLELY BY MARKET OR GOVERNMENT FAILURE...
YES, OUR SOCIETY'S GENDER NORMS AND EXPECTATIONS ALSO CONTRIBUTE TO THIS ABYSMAL FIGURE.
MY THEORY IS THAT IT IS A CASE OF SOCIETAL FAILURE!
BUT PROF., ISN'T IT ALMOST IMPOSSIBLE TO DEFINE SUCCESS OR FAILURE FOR SOCIETY?
I AM JUST SAYING THAT WE CANNOT BECOME 'VISHWAGURU' WITH JUST ONE OUT OF FIVE OF OUR WORKING AGE FEMALES IN THE WORKFORCE.
WELL, MAYBE WE CAN LOOK AT SOCIETY THROUGH A FRAMEWORK OF IMBALANCES RATHER THAN FAILURE OR SUCCESS!
CHANGE & CONTINUITY
NORM FOLLOWING & NORM BREAKING
BONDING CAPITAL & BRIDGING CAPITAL

THERE ARE DIFFERENT AXES OF IMBALANCE IN EVERY SOCIETY.

CHANGE AND CONTINUITY

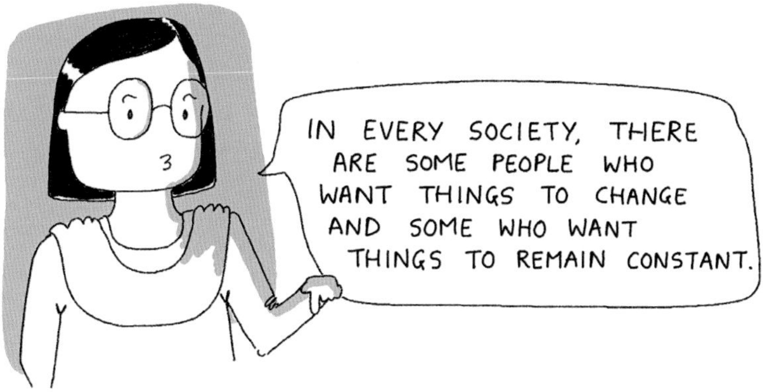
IN EVERY SOCIETY, THERE ARE SOME PEOPLE WHO WANT THINGS TO CHANGE AND SOME WHO WANT THINGS TO REMAIN CONSTANT.

HUMANS NATURALLY GRAVITATE TOWARDS CONTINUITY.
WE DON'T LIKE IT WHEN THINGS CHANGE.

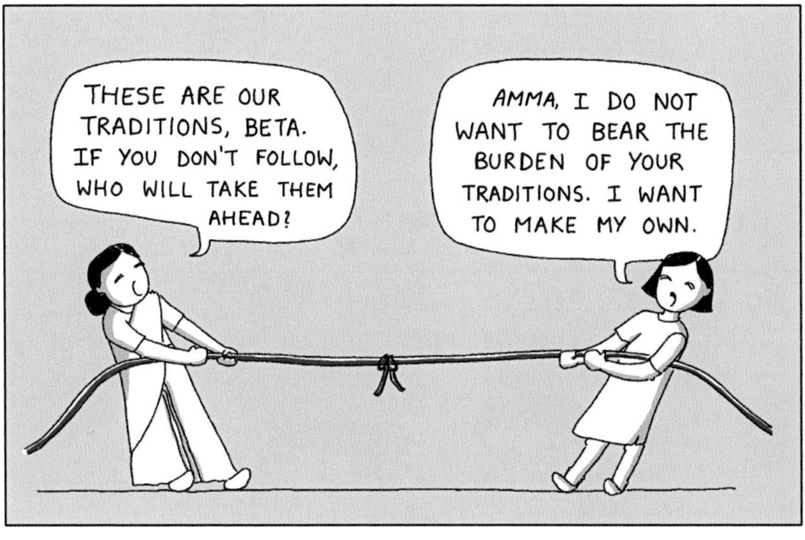
THESE ARE OUR TRADITIONS, BETA. IF YOU DON'T FOLLOW, WHO WILL TAKE THEM AHEAD?
AMMA, I DO NOT WANT TO BEAR THE BURDEN OF YOUR TRADITIONS. I WANT TO MAKE MY OWN.

AT THE SAME TIME, A SOCIETY THAT DOES NOT CHANGE WITH TIME,
RUNS THE RISK OF BEING OSSIFIED AND OUTDATED.

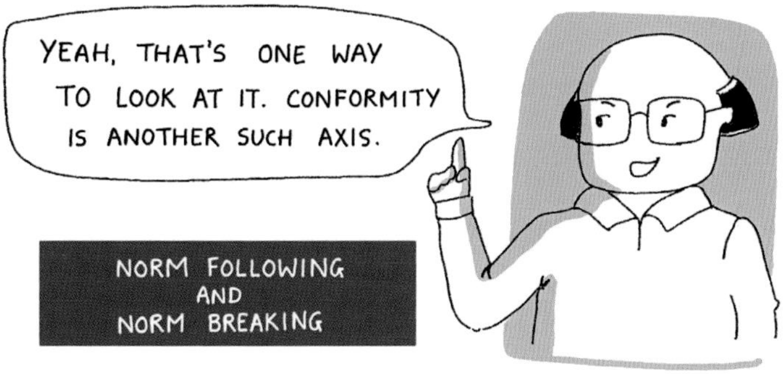
YEAH, THAT'S ONE WAY TO LOOK AT IT. CONFORMITY IS ANOTHER SUCH AXIS.
NORM FOLLOWING AND NORM BREAKING

SOME AMOUNT OF NORM FOLLOWING BRINGS STABILITY IN SOCIETY.

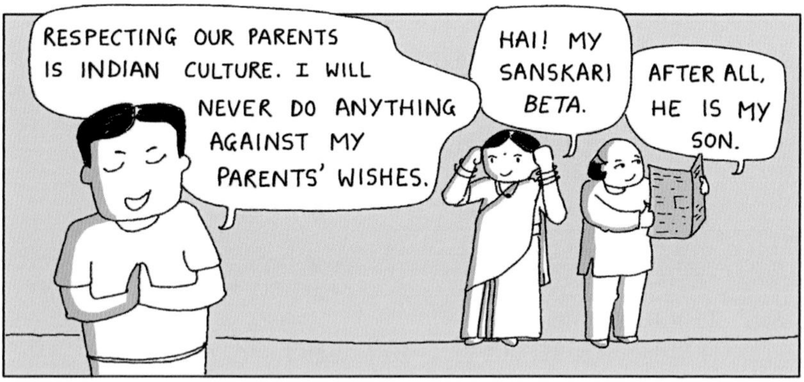
RESPECTING OUR PARENTS IS INDIAN CULTURE. I WILL NEVER DO ANYTHING AGAINST MY PARENTS' WISHES.
HAI! MY SANSKARI *BETA*.
AFTER ALL, HE IS MY SON.

BUT IF EVERYONE FOLLOWS ALL NORMS BLINDLY WITHOUT EVER QUESTIONING THEM, THEN IT REDUCES REAL CHOICES FOR INDIVIDUALS.

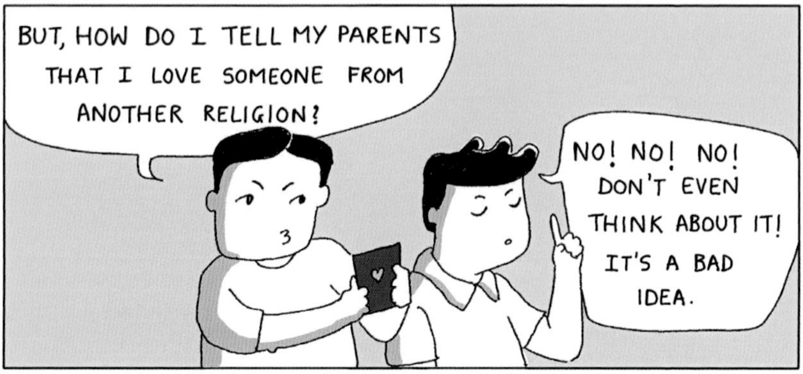
BUT, HOW DO I TELL MY PARENTS THAT I LOVE SOMEONE FROM ANOTHER RELIGION?
NO! NO! NO! DON'T EVEN THINK ABOUT IT! IT'S A BAD IDEA.

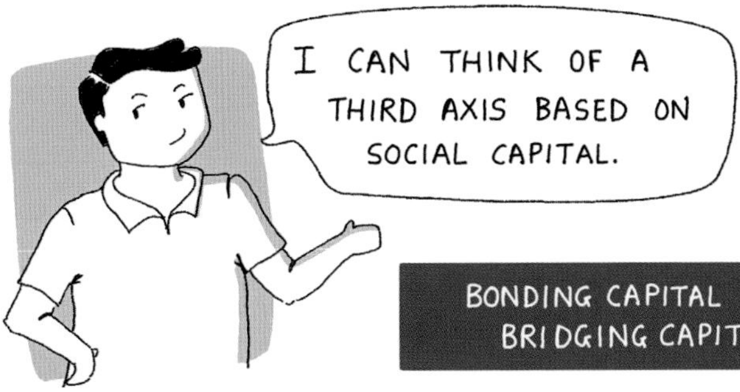
I CAN THINK OF A THIRD AXIS BASED ON SOCIAL CAPITAL.

BONDING CAPITAL AND BRIDGING CAPITAL

SOCIAL TRUST IS THE LUBRICANT THAT MAKES A SOCIETY RUN SMOOTHLY. INDIAN SOCIETY TRADITIONALLY HAD HIGH TRUST AND BONDING WITHIN IN-GROUPS, BUT LOW TRUST AND BRIDGING CAPITAL OUTSIDE OF TRADITIONAL IN-GROUPS.

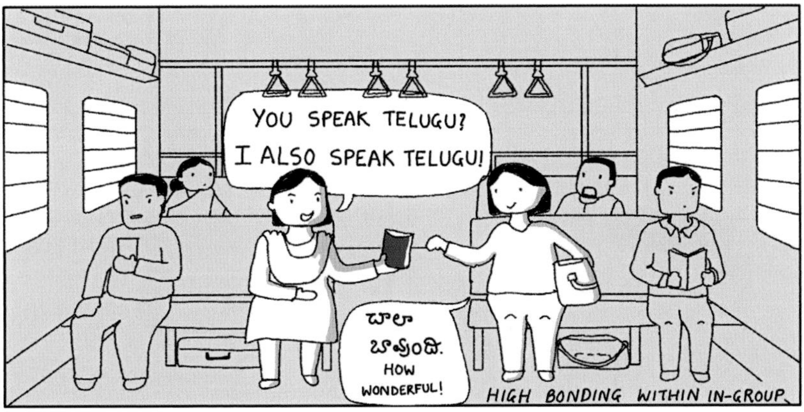
YOU SPEAK TELUGU? I ALSO SPEAK TELUGU!
చాలా బావుంది. HOW WONDERFUL!
HIGH BONDING WITHIN IN-GROUP

WHEN THERE IS A LACK OF TRUST, EVERYTHING ELSE BECOMES DIFFICULT.

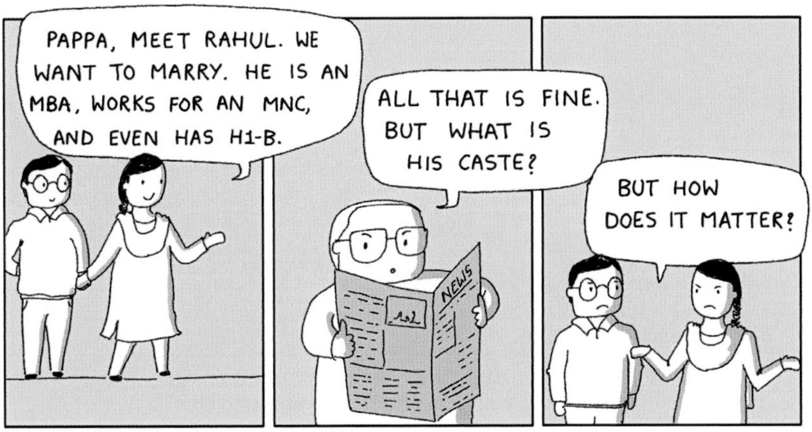
PAPPA, MEET RAHUL. WE WANT TO MARRY. HE IS AN MBA, WORKS FOR AN MNC, AND EVEN HAS H1-B.
ALL THAT IS FINE. BUT WHAT IS HIS CASTE?
NEWS
BUT HOW DOES IT MATTER?

A LACK OF BRIDGING CAPITAL MANIFESTS IN THE VARIOUS RIFTS WE SEE IN OUR SOCIETY ON THE LINES OF CASTE, RELIGION, LANGUAGE AND ETHNICITY.

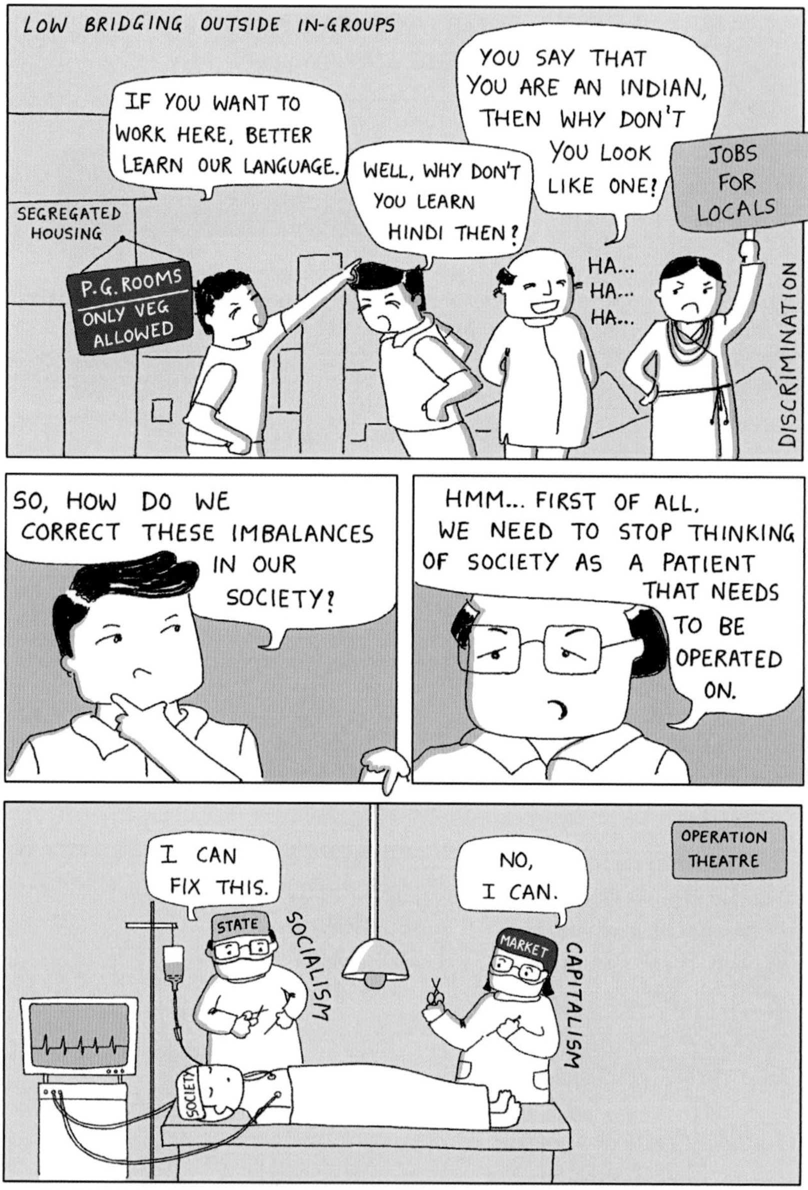
LOW BRIDGING OUTSIDE IN-GROUPS
SEGREGATED HOUSING
P.G. ROOMS ONLY VEG ALLOWED
IF YOU WANT TO WORK HERE, BETTER LEARN OUR LANGUAGE.
WELL, WHY DON'T YOU LEARN HINDI THEN?
YOU SAY THAT YOU ARE AN INDIAN, THEN WHY DON'T YOU LOOK LIKE ONE?
HA... HA... HA...
JOBS FOR LOCALS
DISCRIMINATION
SO, HOW DO WE CORRECT THESE IMBALANCES IN OUR SOCIETY?
HMM... FIRST OF ALL, WE NEED TO STOP THINKING OF SOCIETY AS A PATIENT THAT NEEDS TO BE OPERATED ON.
OPERATION THEATRE
I CAN FIX THIS.
STATE
SOCIALISM
NO, I CAN.
MARKET
CAPITALISM
SOCIETY

THIS DICHOTOMY ASSUMES THAT THE SOLUTIONS TO OUR PROBLEMS LIE EITHER WITH THE STATE OR THE MARKET.

BUT THERE IS A THIRD LEG IN THIS SYSTEM—SOCIETY ITSELF.

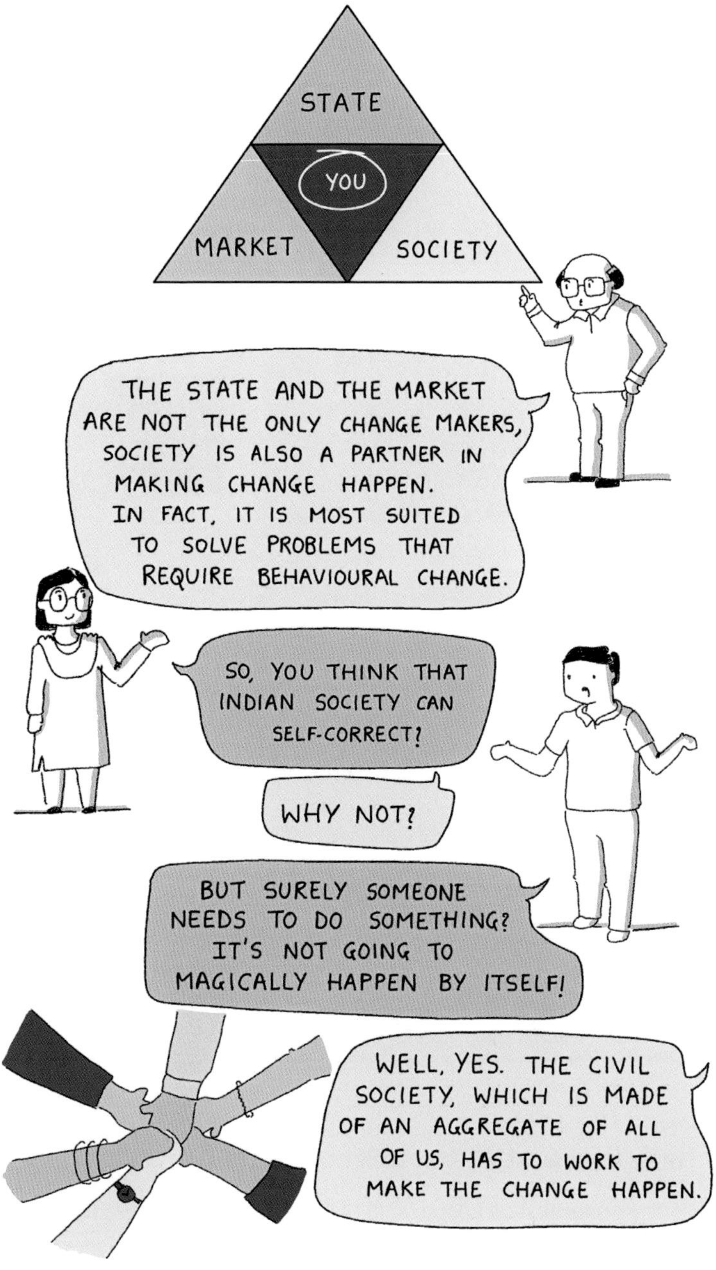
STATE
YOU
MARKET
SOCIETY
THE STATE AND THE MARKET ARE NOT THE ONLY CHANGE MAKERS, SOCIETY IS ALSO A PARTNER IN MAKING CHANGE HAPPEN. IN FACT, IT IS MOST SUITED TO SOLVE PROBLEMS THAT REQUIRE BEHAVIOURAL CHANGE.
SO, YOU THINK THAT INDIAN SOCIETY CAN SELF-CORRECT?
WHY NOT?
BUT SURELY SOMEONE NEEDS TO DO SOMETHING? IT'S NOT GOING TO MAGICALLY HAPPEN BY ITSELF!
WELL, YES. THE CIVIL SOCIETY, WHICH IS MADE OF AN AGGREGATE OF ALL OF US, HAS TO WORK TO MAKE THE CHANGE HAPPEN.

SOCIAL REFORM IS THE DOMAIN OF SOCIETY.
WE HAVE HAD VERY SUCCESSFUL REFORMS IN THE PRE-INDEPENDENCE ERA.

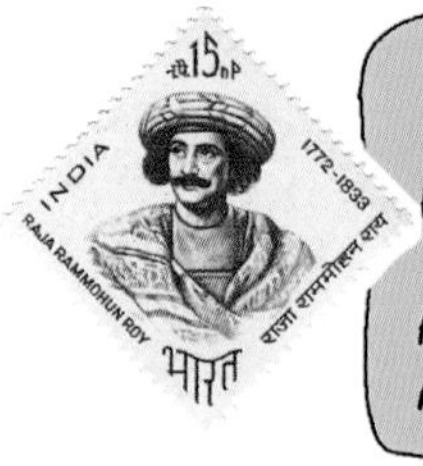
15 nP
INDIA
1772-1833
RAJA RAMMOHUN ROY
भारत

RAJA RAMMOHUN ROY WAS PERHAPS INDIA'S FIRST LIBERAL. HE WITNESSED HIS SISTER-IN-LAW BEING FORCED INTO SATI, AND LATER BECAME A CRUSADER AGAINST SATI AND CHILD MARRIAGE AND AN ADVOCATE FOR RATIONALISM.

SAVITRIBAI PHULE AND HER HUSBAND JYOTIRAO PHULE STARTED INDIA'S FIRST GIRLS' SCHOOL. SHE WAS OFTEN ATTACKED WITH DUNG FOR 'DARING' TO TEACH GIRLS.

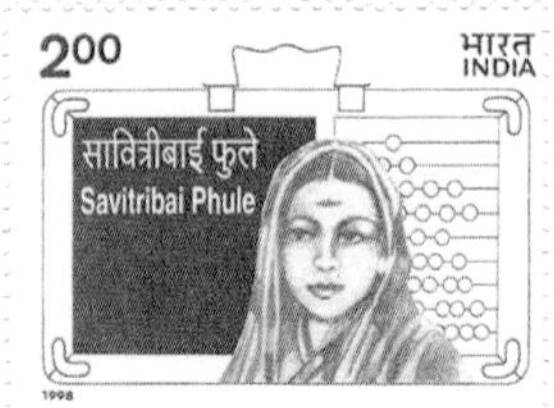
2.00
भारत
INDIA
सावित्रीबाई फुले
Savitribai Phule
1998

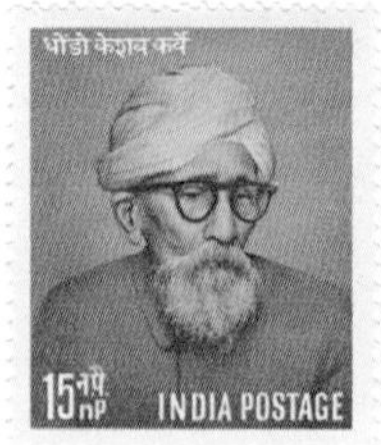
धोंडो केशव कर्वे
15 nP
INDIA POSTAGE

D. K. KARVE, ALSO KNOWN AS 'MAHARSHI KARVE', ADVOCATED FOR THE CAUSE OF WIDOW REMARRIAGE AND WIDOW EDUCATION. HE 'SHOCKED' PEOPLE BY MARRYING A WIDOW.

GANDHI WAS A BELIEVER IN SOCIETY'S ABILITY TO CHANGE ITSELF. HE TRAVELLED ACROSS THE COUNTRY ENGAGING WITH PEOPLE ON THE ISSUES RELATED TO UNTOUCHABILITY AND COMMUNAL HARMONY.

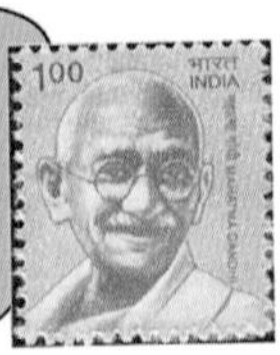
1.00
भारत
INDIA

THESE REFORMS WERE LED BY SOCIETY AND LATER SANCTIONED BY LAW.

THE GROUND FOR SOCIAL ACCEPTANCE OF THESE REFORMS WAS FIRST PREPARED THROUGH WIDESPREAD ENGAGEMENT BY CIVIL SOCIETY.

BUT WITH THE RISE OF A STRONG STATE, WE HAVE ABDICATED THE RESPONSIBILITY OF SOCIAL REFORMS TO THE STATE.

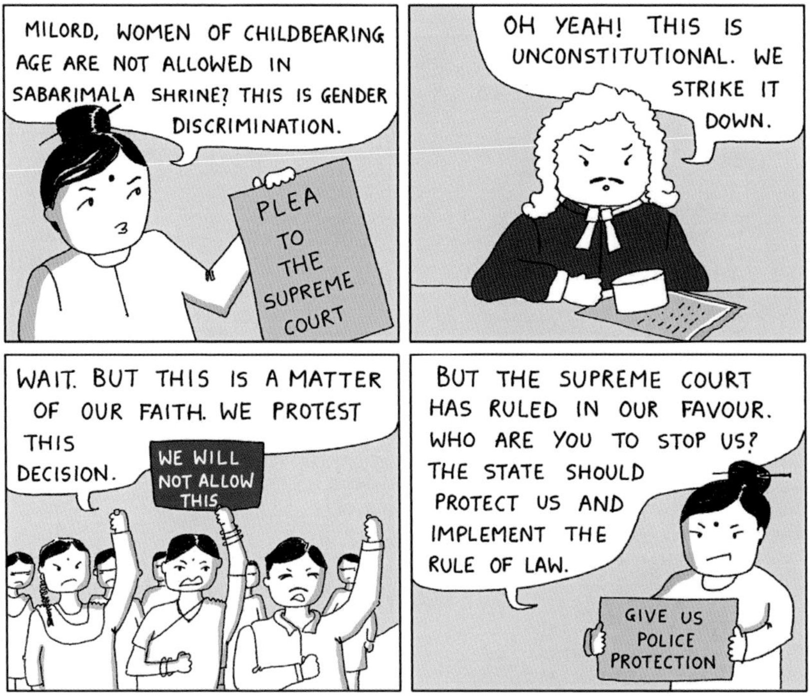
MILORD, WOMEN OF CHILDBEARING AGE ARE NOT ALLOWED IN SABARIMALA SHRINE? THIS IS GENDER DISCRIMINATION.
PLEA TO THE SUPREME COURT
OH YEAH! THIS IS UNCONSTITUTIONAL. WE STRIKE IT DOWN.
WAIT. BUT THIS IS A MATTER OF OUR FAITH. WE PROTEST THIS DECISION.
WE WILL NOT ALLOW THIS
BUT THE SUPREME COURT HAS RULED IN OUR FAVOUR. WHO ARE YOU TO STOP US? THE STATE SHOULD PROTECT US AND IMPLEMENT THE RULE OF LAW.
GIVE US POLICE PROTECTION

JUST BECAUSE THE COURT HAS PASSED AN ORDER, PEOPLE ARE NOT GOING TO CHANGE THEIR BELIEF OVERNIGHT.

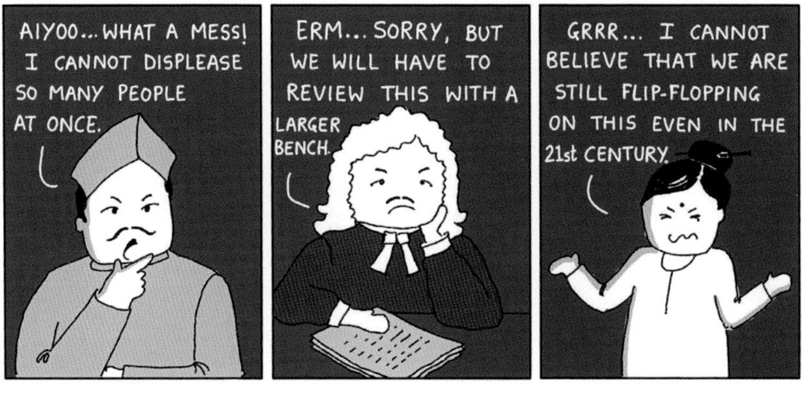
AIYOO... WHAT A MESS! I CANNOT DISPLEASE SO MANY PEOPLE AT ONCE.
ERM... SORRY, BUT WE WILL HAVE TO REVIEW THIS WITH A LARGER BENCH.
GRRR... I CANNOT BELIEVE THAT WE ARE STILL FLIP-FLOPPING ON THIS EVEN IN THE 21st CENTURY.

SOCIAL REFORMS SUCCEED WHEN THEY ARE DRIVEN GROUND UP RATHER THAN DICTATED TOP DOWN. THERE IS NO ALTERNATIVE TO ENGAGING WITH PEOPLE.

THE INDIAN STATE IS OVER-STRETCHED AND UNDER-RESOURCED. AFTER PROVIDING FOR THE PRESSING NEEDS OF POVERTY, NUTRITION, ETC., THE STATE IS NOT LEFT WITH MUCH FUNDS FOR ART, SPORT OR CULTURE.

MLA JI, THE YOUTH OF OUR DISTRICT WANT A DECENT SPORTS COMPLEX.
WE DON'T EVEN HAVE ENOUGH SCHOOLS IN OUR DISTRICT AND YOU WANT FUNDS FOR SPORTS?
FORGET ABOUT IT.
MLA

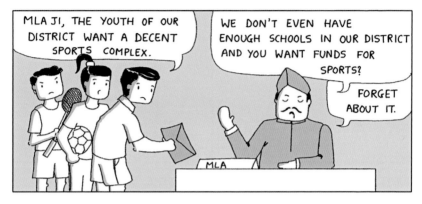

HERE, PHILANTHROPY CAN BE A WAY FOR THE SOCIETY TO PLUG IN THE GAPS LEFT BY THE STATE AND THE MARKET.

DID YOU KNOW? MAHARAJA SAYAJIRAO GAEKWAD OF BARODA PIONEERED INDIA'S FIRST PUBLIC LIBRARY MOVEMENT IN THE EARLY 20th CENTURY.

WE NEED A PUBLIC LIBRARY MOVEMENT LED BY COMMUNITIES AND SUPPORTED BY PHILANTHROPY.

WE ALSO NEED MORE PUBLIC AND CULTURAL SPACES WHERE PEOPLE CAN INTERACT WITH EACH OTHER FREELY.

DADA-DADI LAUGHING CLUB
HA... HA... HA...
HA... HA...
HA... HA...

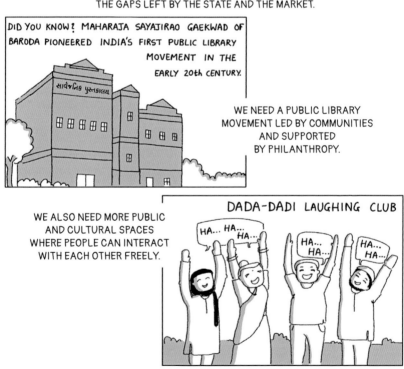

BECAUSE, WHEN PEOPLE FROM ALL WALKS OF LIFE CAN SHARE THE SAME SPACES AND EXPERIENCES, IT ENCOURAGES MORE BRIDGING CAPITAL.

SOCIETY CAN ALSO PLAY A PART IN CORRECTING MARKET FAILURES.

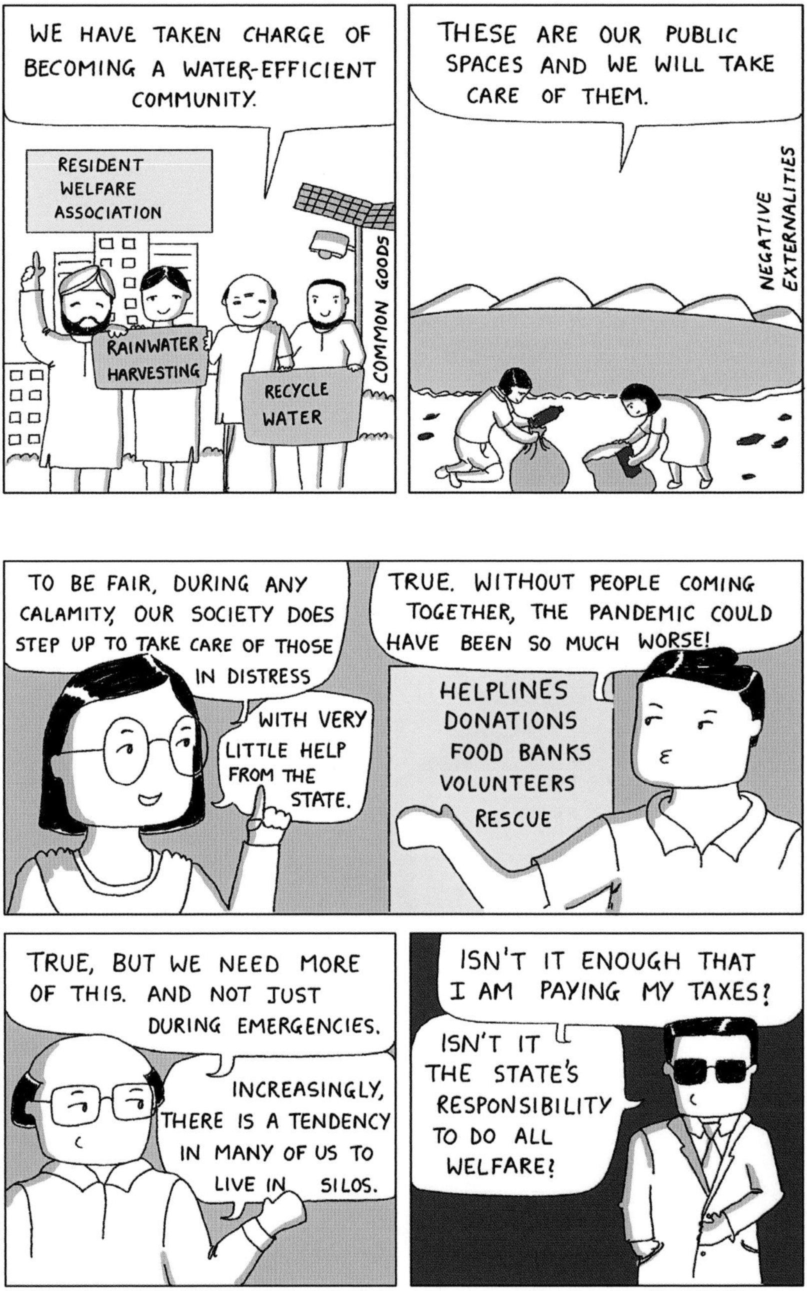
WE HAVE TAKEN CHARGE OF BECOMING A WATER-EFFICIENT COMMUNITY.
RESIDENT WELFARE ASSOCIATION
RAINWATER HARVESTING
RECYCLE WATER
COMMON GOODS
THESE ARE OUR PUBLIC SPACES AND WE WILL TAKE CARE OF THEM.
NEGATIVE EXTERNALITIES
TO BE FAIR, DURING ANY CALAMITY, OUR SOCIETY DOES STEP UP TO TAKE CARE OF THOSE IN DISTRESS
WITH VERY LITTLE HELP FROM THE STATE.
TRUE. WITHOUT PEOPLE COMING TOGETHER, THE PANDEMIC COULD HAVE BEEN SO MUCH WORSE!
HELPLINES
DONATIONS
FOOD BANKS
VOLUNTEERS
RESCUE
TRUE, BUT WE NEED MORE OF THIS. AND NOT JUST DURING EMERGENCIES.
INCREASINGLY, THERE IS A TENDENCY IN MANY OF US TO LIVE IN SILOS.
ISN'T IT ENOUGH THAT I AM PAYING MY TAXES?
ISN'T IT THE STATE'S RESPONSIBILITY TO DO ALL WELFARE?

WE NEED TO STRENGTHEN OUR SOCIETY.
AND THAT CANNOT HAPPEN IF WE ALL LIVE IN OUR BUBBLES.
OUR CONDO IS VERY SAFE. WE HAVE 24/7 SECURITY.
WE HAVE THE BEST AIR PURIFIER IN OUR HOUSE.
WE ORDER ONLY THE PUREST WATER IN OUR OFFICE.
THERE IS WFH + SWIGGY + ONLINE DELIVERY. WHY DOES ANYONE NEED TO STEP OUT OF THE HOUSE?

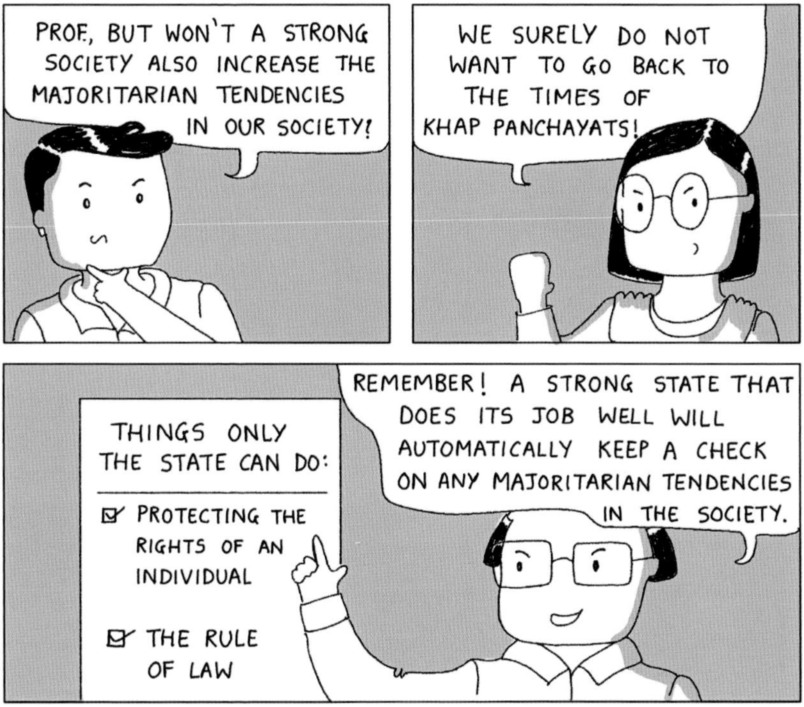
PROF, BUT WON'T A STRONG SOCIETY ALSO INCREASE THE MAJORITARIAN TENDENCIES IN OUR SOCIETY!
WE SURELY DO NOT WANT TO GO BACK TO THE TIMES OF KHAP PANCHAYATS!
THINGS ONLY THE STATE CAN DO:
PROTECTING THE RIGHTS OF AN INDIVIDUAL
THE RULE OF LAW
REMEMBER! A STRONG STATE THAT DOES ITS JOB WELL WILL AUTOMATICALLY KEEP A CHECK ON ANY MAJORITARIAN TENDENCIES IN THE SOCIETY.

AND FINALLY, WE NEED TO BUILD NEW WAYS OF CIVIL ENGAGEMENTS THAT TRANSCEND OUR TRADITIONAL GROUP IDENTITIES

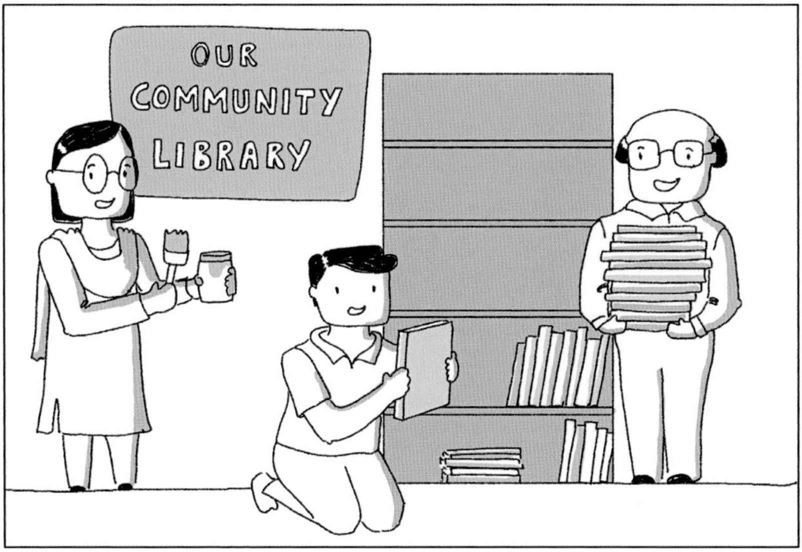
OUR COMMUNITY LIBRARY

AND HELP US FORGE NEW CIVIL IDENTITIES
THAT CONNECT US, RATHER THAN DIVIDE.

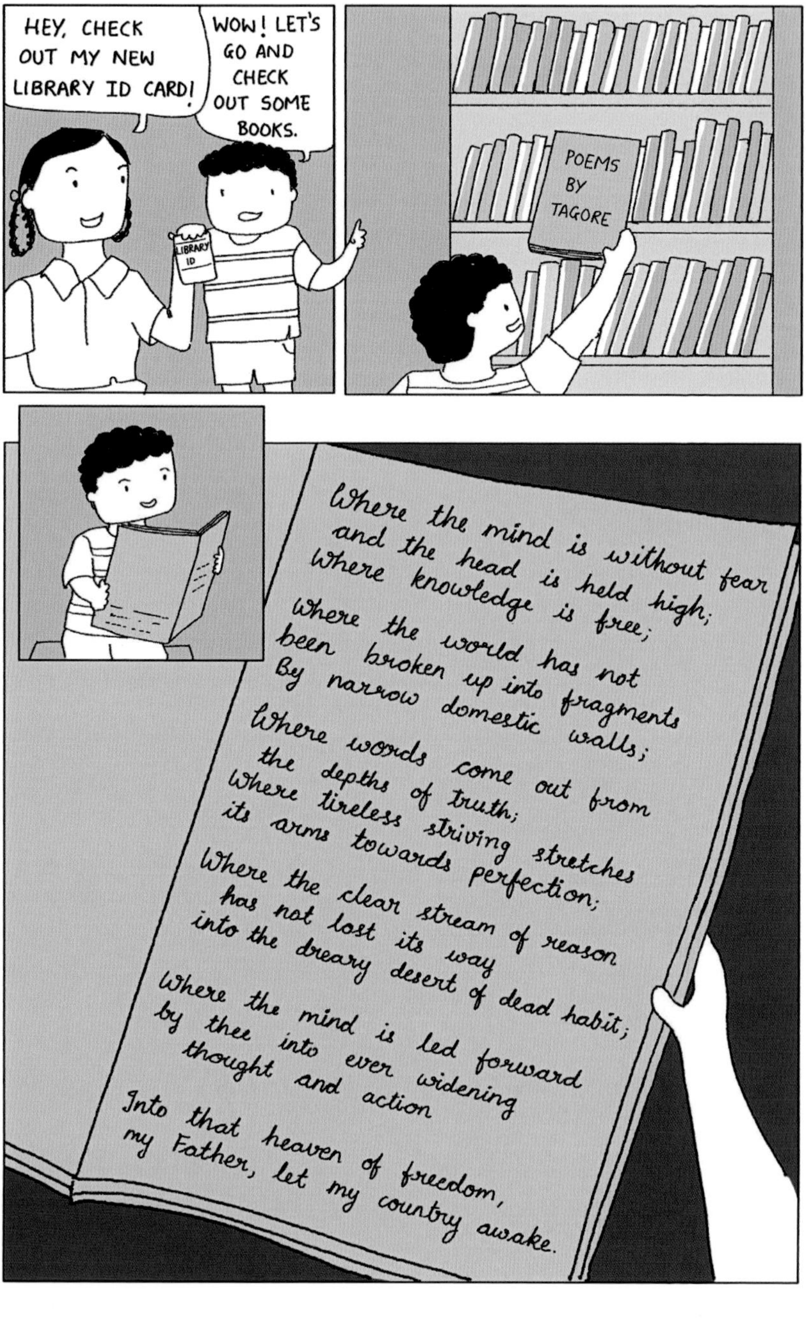
HEY, CHECK OUT MY NEW LIBRARY ID CARD!
WOW! LET'S GO AND CHECK OUT SOME BOOKS.
LIBRARY ID
POEMS BY TAGORE
Where the mind is without fear
and the head is held high;
Where knowledge is free;
Where the world has not
been broken up into fragments
By narrow domestic walls;
Where words come out from
the depths of truth;
Where tireless striving stretches
its arms towards perfection;
Where the clear stream of reason
has not lost its way
into the dreary desert of dead habit;
Where the mind is led forward
by thee into ever widening
thought and action
Into that heaven of freedom,
my Father, let my country awake.

Chapter 14

What Makes a Government File Move?

Making change happen

> 'NEVER DOUBT THAT A SMALL GROUP OF
> THOUGHTFUL, COMMITTED INDIVIDUALS
> CAN CHANGE THE WORLD.
> IN FACT, IT'S THE ONLY THING THAT EVER HAS.'
>
> —MARGARET MEAD

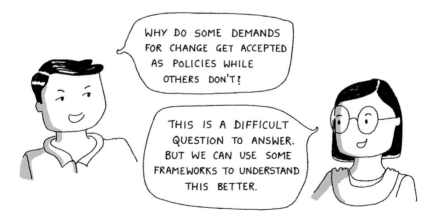

WHY DO SOME DEMANDS FOR CHANGE GET ACCEPTED AS POLICIES WHILE OTHERS DON'T?

THIS IS A DIFFICULT QUESTION TO ANSWER. BUT WE CAN USE SOME FRAMEWORKS TO UNDERSTAND THIS BETTER.

WHAT CHANGE IS MOST LIKELY TO HAPPEN?

OVERTON WINDOW IS A RANGE OF IDEAS THAT ARE SOCIALLY ACCEPTABLE AT ANY GIVEN TIME ON A PARTICULAR TOPIC.

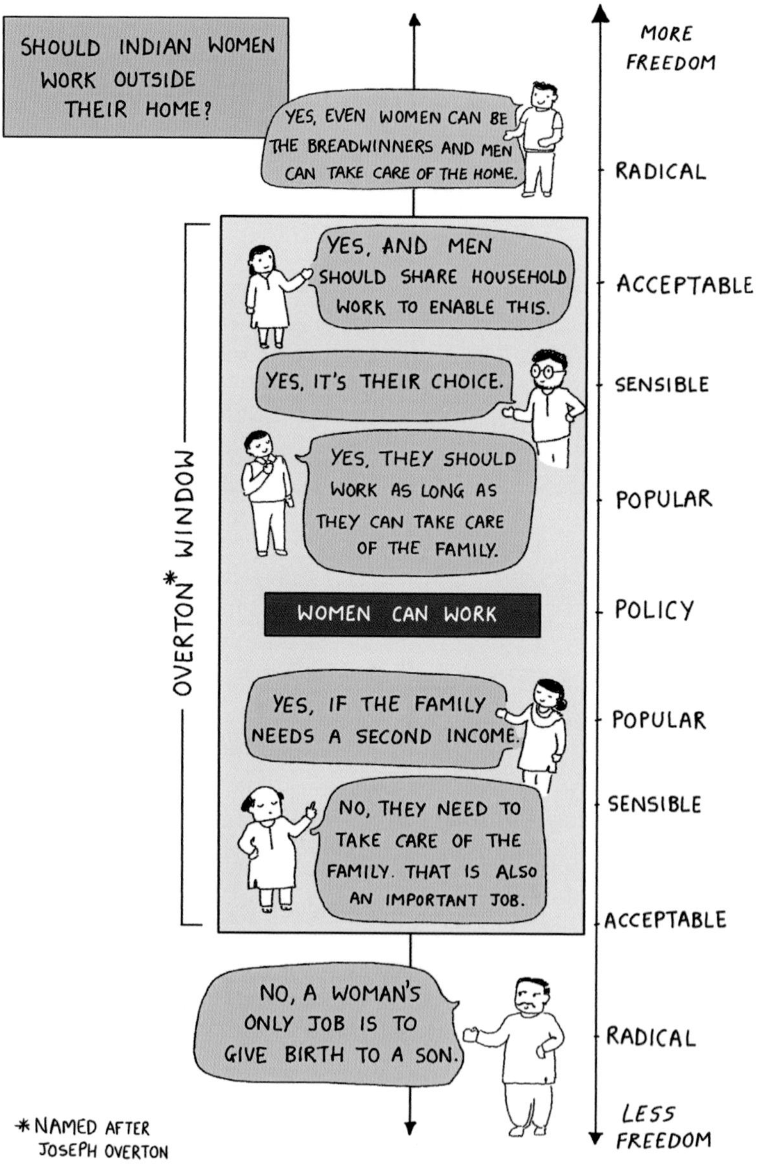

SHOULD INDIAN WOMEN WORK OUTSIDE THEIR HOME?
MORE FREEDOM
YES, EVEN WOMEN CAN BE THE BREADWINNERS AND MEN CAN TAKE CARE OF THE HOME.
RADICAL
YES, AND MEN SHOULD SHARE HOUSEHOLD WORK TO ENABLE THIS.
ACCEPTABLE
YES, IT'S THEIR CHOICE.
SENSIBLE
YES, THEY SHOULD WORK AS LONG AS THEY CAN TAKE CARE OF THE FAMILY.
POPULAR
WOMEN CAN WORK
POLICY
YES, IF THE FAMILY NEEDS A SECOND INCOME.
POPULAR
NO, THEY NEED TO TAKE CARE OF THE FAMILY. THAT IS ALSO AN IMPORTANT JOB.
SENSIBLE
ACCEPTABLE
OVERTON* WINDOW
NO, A WOMAN'S ONLY JOB IS TO GIVE BIRTH TO A SON.
RADICAL
LESS FREEDOM
* NAMED AFTER JOSEPH OVERTON

IT IS A SENSE CHECK OF WHERE THE PUBLIC OPINION LIES.

THE OVERTON WINDOW IS DYNAMIC AND IT SHIFTS AND STRETCHES OVER TIME, AS PEOPLE CHANGE THEIR PERSPECTIVE OVER AN ISSUE.

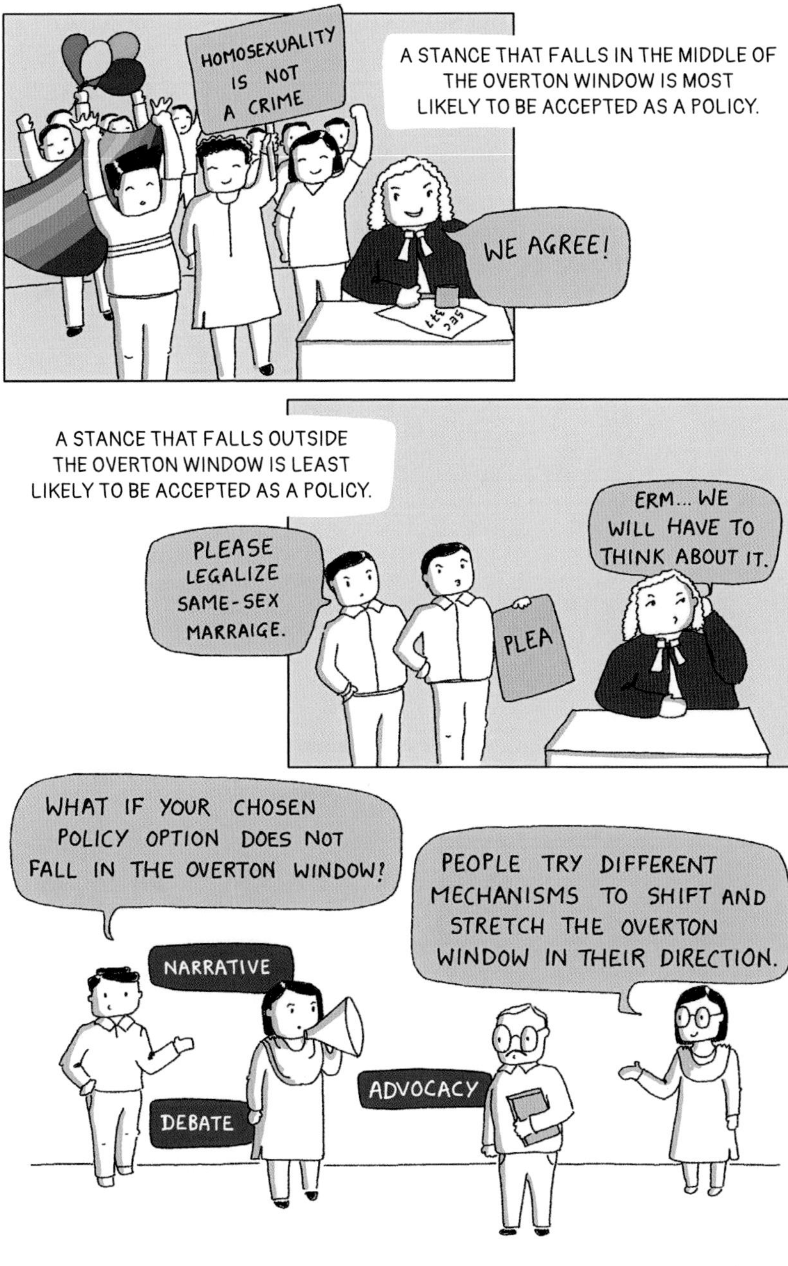
HOMOSEXUALITY IS NOT A CRIME
A STANCE THAT FALLS IN THE MIDDLE OF THE OVERTON WINDOW IS MOST LIKELY TO BE ACCEPTED AS A POLICY.
WE AGREE!
A STANCE THAT FALLS OUTSIDE THE OVERTON WINDOW IS LEAST LIKELY TO BE ACCEPTED AS A POLICY.
PLEASE LEGALIZE SAME-SEX MARRAIGE.
PLEA
ERM... WE WILL HAVE TO THINK ABOUT IT.
WHAT IF YOUR CHOSEN POLICY OPTION DOES NOT FALL IN THE OVERTON WINDOW?
PEOPLE TRY DIFFERENT MECHANISMS TO SHIFT AND STRETCH THE OVERTON WINDOW IN THEIR DIRECTION.
NARRATIVE
DEBATE
ADVOCACY

WITH CHANGING TIMES, THE OVERTON WINDOW MAY STRETCH AND POLICIES THAT WERE PREVIOUSLY NOT ACCEPTABLE MAY EVEN BECOME POPULAR.

BEFORE THE PANDEMIC
WHAT! WORK FROM HOME? YOU THINK YOU ARE MY SON-IN-LAW OR WHAT?
AFTER THE PANDEMIC
CONGRATS! WFH IS OUR NEW WORK POLICY.
PSST... AND WE ARE SAVING ON RENTAL COSTS.

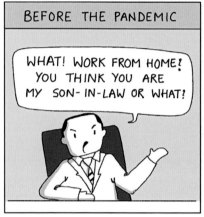

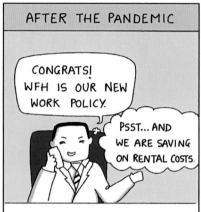

OR IT MAY SHIFT IN ONE DIRECTION, AND POLICIES THAT WERE EARLIER ACCEPTABLE MAY BECOME UNACCEPTABLE.

SLAVERY
RACIAL DISCRIMINATION
SATI
UNTOUCHABILITY
HUMAN RIGHTS
WOMEN'S RIGHTS
LGBTQ+ RIGHTS

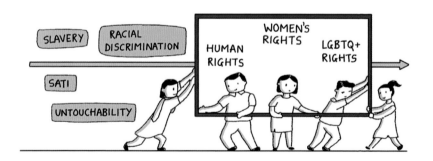

OVER A LONG TERM, THE OVERTON WINDOW ON THE TOPIC OF HUMAN RIGHTS HAS SHIFTED IN FAVOUR OF MORE FREEDOM AND RIGHTS FOR INDIVIDUALS.

COLLECTIVE ACTION FRAMEWORK

WHO WILL WIN WHEN SOME PEOPLE WANT CHANGE, WHILE OTHERS DON'T?

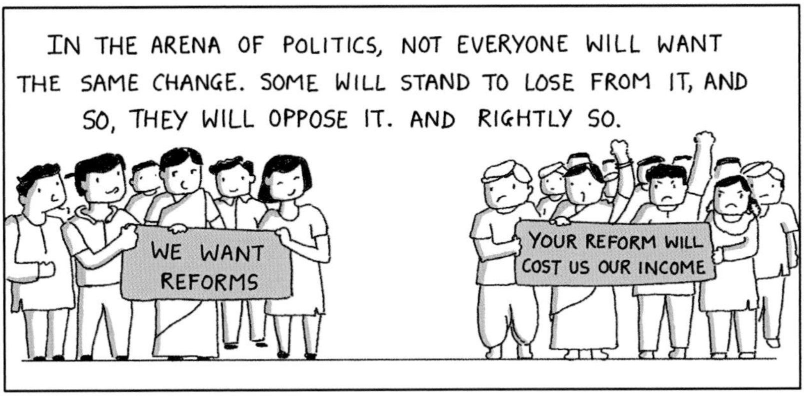
IN THE ARENA OF POLITICS, NOT EVERYONE WILL WANT THE SAME CHANGE. SOME WILL STAND TO LOSE FROM IT, AND SO, THEY WILL OPPOSE IT. AND RIGHTLY SO.
WE WANT REFORMS
YOUR REFORM WILL COST US OUR INCOME

THERE ARE COSTS AND BENEFITS ASSOCIATED WITH ANY CHANGE.

THE STRENGTH OF SUPPORT OR OPPOSITION TO THE CHANGE WILL DEPEND ON WHETHER THE COSTS AND BENEFITS ARE CONCENTRATED IN A SMALL GROUP OR DISPERSED OVER A LARGE GROUP.

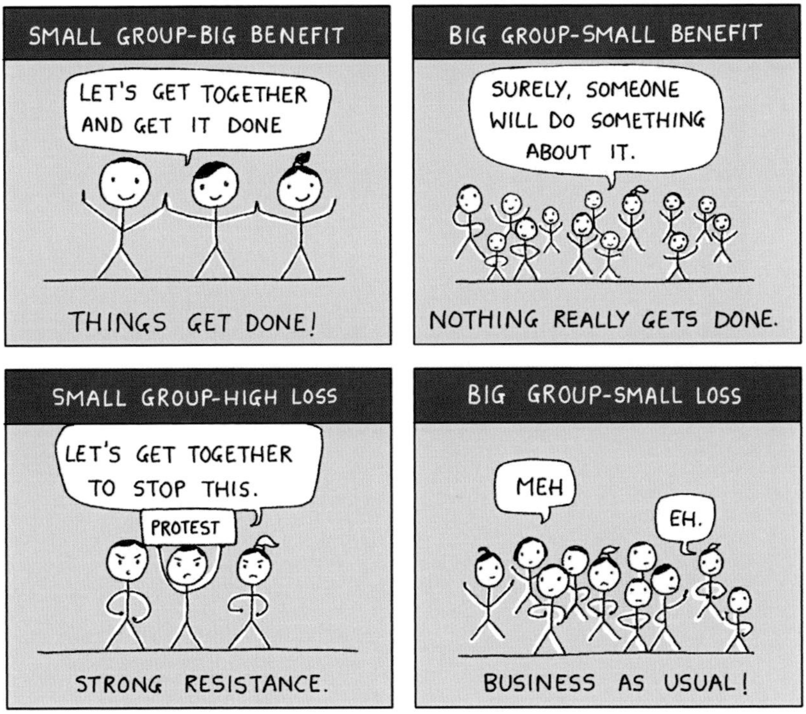
SMALL GROUP-BIG BENEFIT
LET'S GET TOGETHER AND GET IT DONE
THINGS GET DONE!
BIG GROUP-SMALL BENEFIT
SURELY, SOMEONE WILL DO SOMETHING ABOUT IT.
NOTHING REALLY GETS DONE.
SMALL GROUP-HIGH LOSS
LET'S GET TOGETHER TO STOP THIS.
PROTEST
STRONG RESISTANCE.
BIG GROUP-SMALL LOSS
MEH
EH.
BUSINESS AS USUAL!

DEPENDING ON WHETHER THE COSTS AND BENEFITS OF A POLICY ARE
CONCENTRATED IN A SMALL GROUP OR WIDELY SPREAD OVER A LARGE GROUP,
FOUR DIFFERENT TYPES OF POLITICS MAY EMERGE.

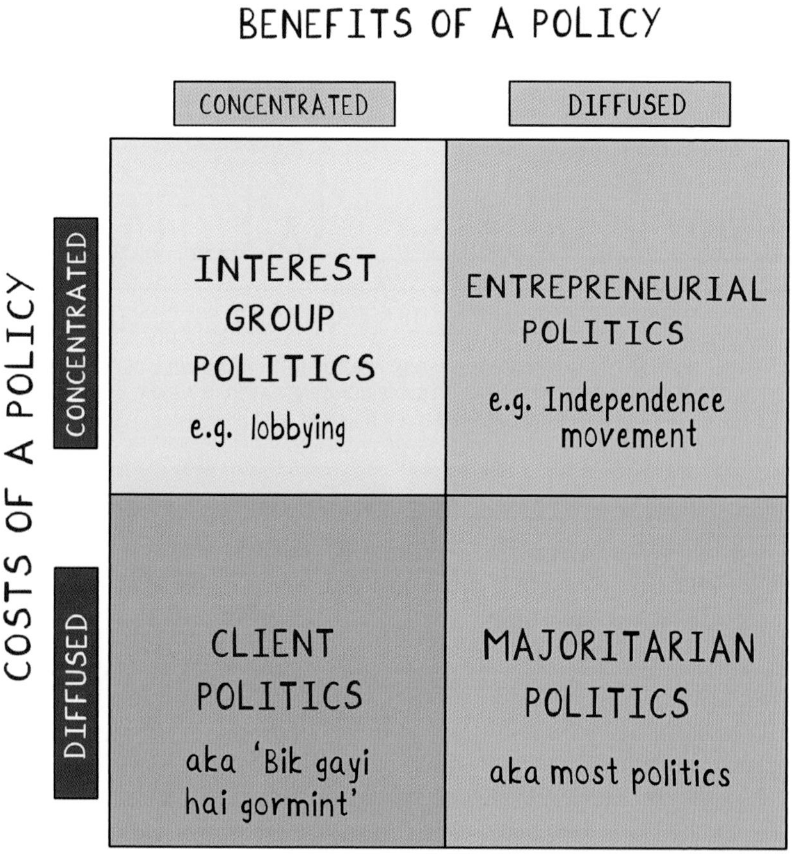

BENEFITS OF A POLICY

	CONCENTRATED	DIFFUSED
CONCENTRATED	INTEREST GROUP POLITICS e.g. lobbying	ENTREPRENEURIAL POLITICS e.g. Independence movement
DIFFUSED	CLIENT POLITICS aka 'Bik gayi hai gormint'	MAJORITARIAN POLITICS aka most politics

COSTS OF A POLICY

WILSON-LOWI MATRIX

DIFFUSED BENEFITS, DIFFUSED COSTS

MAJORITARIAN POLITICS

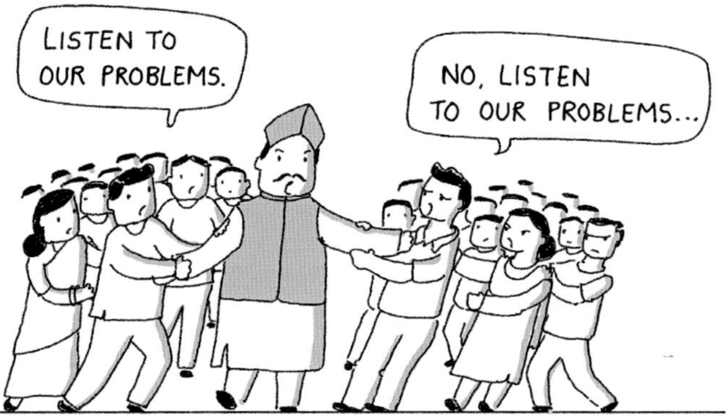
LISTEN TO OUR PROBLEMS.
NO, LISTEN TO OUR PROBLEMS...

WHO WINS? WHICHEVER SIDE CAN CONSOLIDATE BETTER. IN SHORT, MAJORITY WINS.

CONCENTRATED BENEFITS, CONCENTRATED COSTS

INTEREST GROUP POLITICS

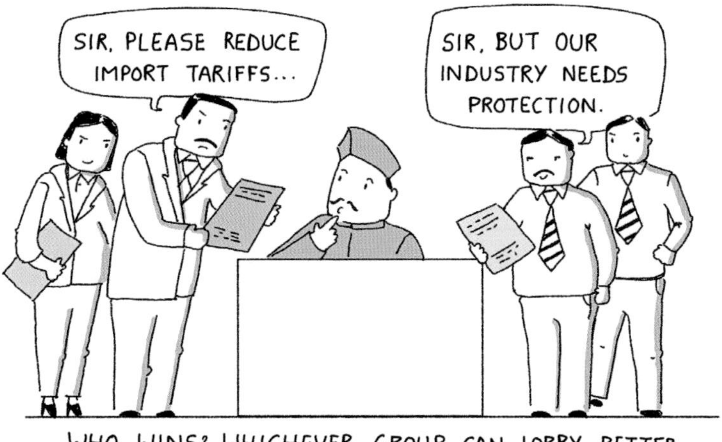
SIR, PLEASE REDUCE IMPORT TARIFFS...
SIR, BUT OUR INDUSTRY NEEDS PROTECTION.

WHO WINS? WHICHEVER GROUP CAN LOBBY BETTER.

CONCENTRATED BENEFITS, DIFFUSED COSTS

CLIENT POLITICS

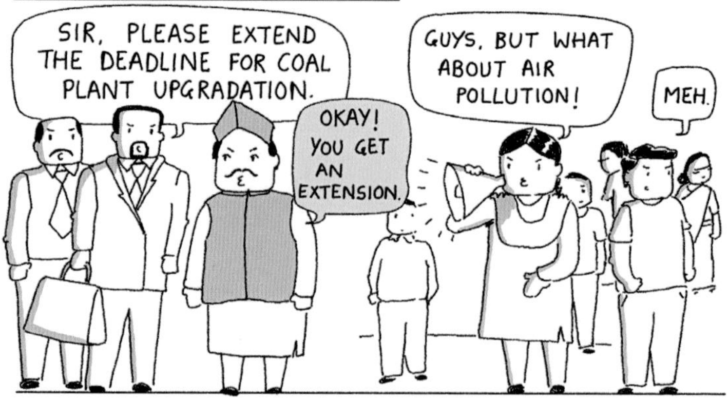
SIR, PLEASE EXTEND THE DEADLINE FOR COAL PLANT UPGRADATION.
OKAY! YOU GET AN EXTENSION.
GUYS, BUT WHAT ABOUT AIR POLLUTION!
MEH.

PEOPLE WHO BENEFIT WILL ORGANIZE, PEOPLE WHO BEAR THE COST WON'T.

DIFFUSED BENEFITS, CONCENTRATED COSTS

ENTREPRENEURIAL POLITICS

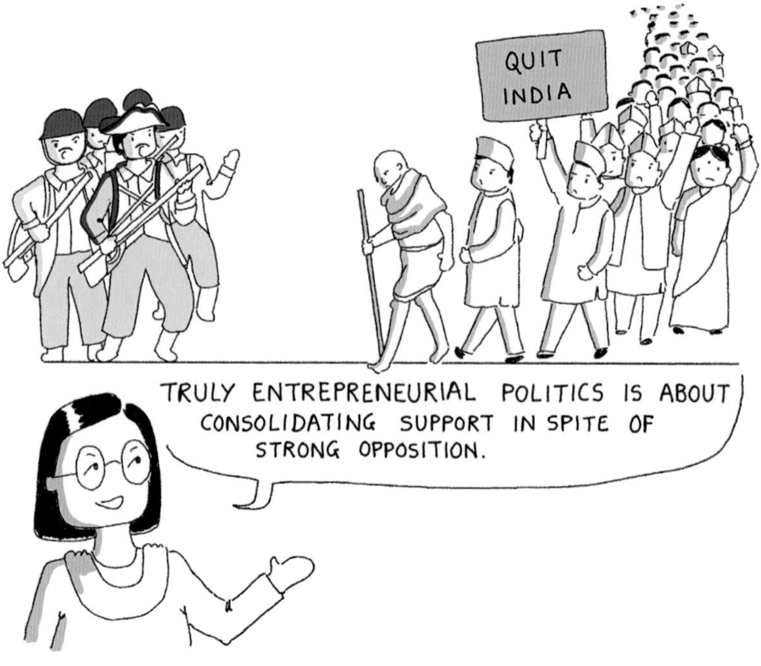
QUIT INDIA
TRULY ENTREPRENEURIAL POLITICS IS ABOUT CONSOLIDATING SUPPORT IN SPITE OF STRONG OPPOSITION.

USING THESE FRAMEWORKS, ONE CAN TRY TO UNDERSTAND THE DYNAMICS OF A PARTICULAR ISSUE AND PREDICT WHAT CHANGE IS LIKELY TO HAPPEN.

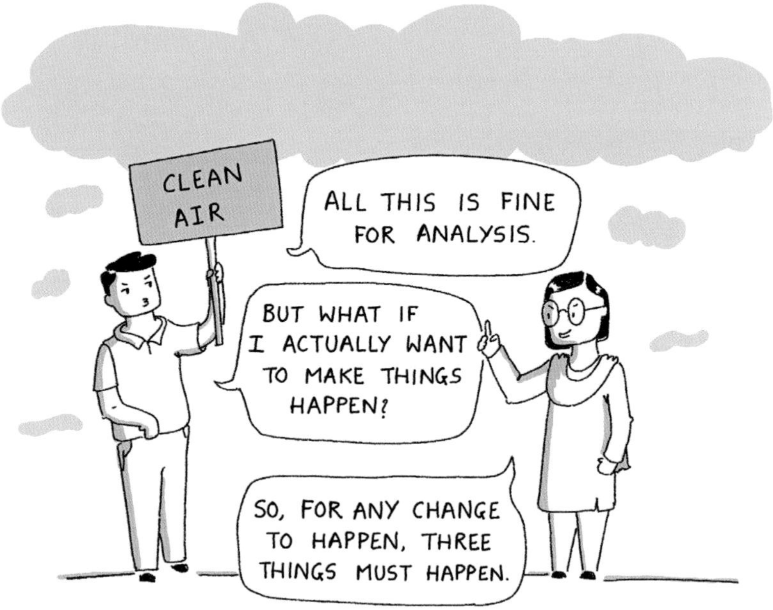
CLEAN AIR
ALL THIS IS FINE FOR ANALYSIS.
BUT WHAT IF I ACTUALLY WANT TO MAKE THINGS HAPPEN?
SO, FOR ANY CHANGE TO HAPPEN, THREE THINGS MUST HAPPEN.

WHEN DOES CHANGE HAPPEN?

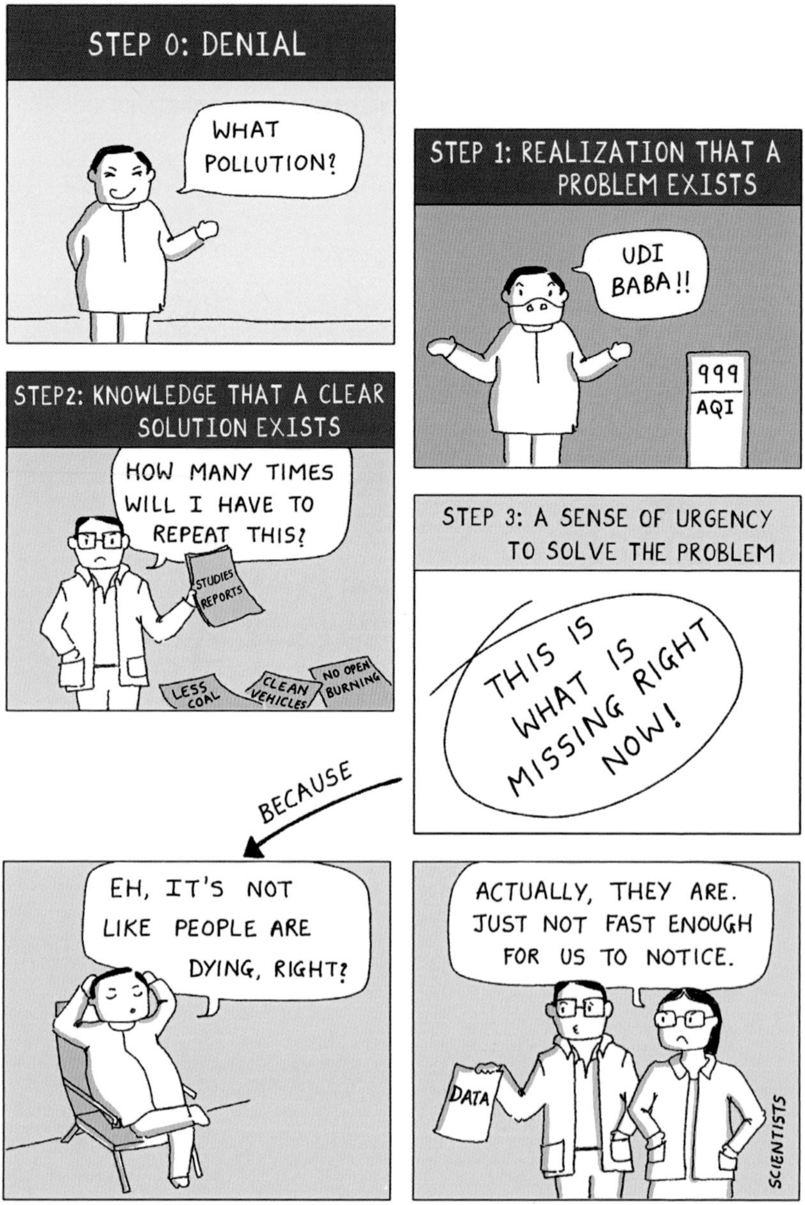
STEP 0: DENIAL
WHAT POLLUTION?
STEP 1: REALIZATION THAT A PROBLEM EXISTS
UDI BABA!!
999
AQI
STEP2: KNOWLEDGE THAT A CLEAR SOLUTION EXISTS
HOW MANY TIMES WILL I HAVE TO REPEAT THIS?
STUDIES
REPORTS
LESS COAL
CLEAN VEHICLES
NO OPEN BURNING
STEP 3: A SENSE OF URGENCY TO SOLVE THE PROBLEM
THIS IS WHAT IS MISSING RIGHT NOW!
BECAUSE
EH, IT'S NOT LIKE PEOPLE ARE DYING, RIGHT?
ACTUALLY, THEY ARE. JUST NOT FAST ENOUGH FOR US TO NOTICE.
DATA
SCIENTISTS

CHANGE WILL HAPPEN WHEN THERE IS REALIZATION
THAT THE PROBLEM EXISTS,
THERE IS A CLEAR SOLUTION IN SIGHT, AND
THERE IS AN URGENCY TO SOLVE THE PROBLEM.

WHEN CHANGE
WILL HAPPEN

☑ REALIZATION

☑ SOLUTION

☑ URGENCY

KINGDON SCHEMA

NOW, IT'S NOT ALWAYS UNDER OUR CONTROL TO PREDICT WHEN A PARTICULAR PROBLEM WILL BECOME URGENT.

BUT IT IS IN OUR CONTROL TO WORK ON THE PROBLEMS THAT WE WISH TO SEE RESOLVED.

YES!

SO THAT WHEN THE URGENCY TO SOLVE THE PROBLEM ARISES, WE HAVE A WELL-THOUGHT-OUT SOLUTION TO OFFER.

HOW TO EFFECT CHANGE?

ONE WAY TO EFFECT CHANGE IS TO WORK ON CREATING SOLUTIONS BEFORE THEY BECOME URGENT. VIJAY KELKAR AND AJAY SHAH IN THEIR BOOK *IN SERVICE OF THE REPUBLIC* EXPLAIN THIS CONCEPT AS A POLICY PIPELINE.

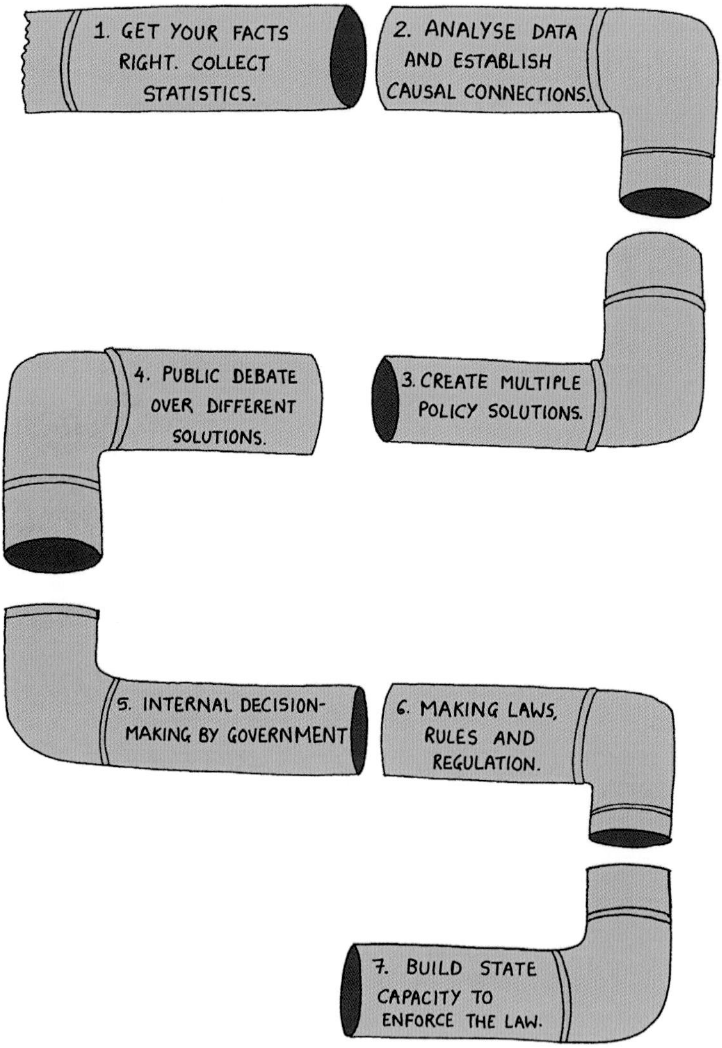

1. GET YOUR FACTS RIGHT. COLLECT STATISTICS.
2. ANALYSE DATA AND ESTABLISH CAUSAL CONNECTIONS.
3. CREATE MULTIPLE POLICY SOLUTIONS.
4. PUBLIC DEBATE OVER DIFFERENT SOLUTIONS.
5. INTERNAL DECISION-MAKING BY GOVERNMENT
6. MAKING LAWS, RULES AND REGULATION.
7. BUILD STATE CAPACITY TO ENFORCE THE LAW.

Vijay Kelkar and Ajay Shah, *In Service of the Republic* (Penguin Random House India, 2019), p. 207

IF WE LOOK AT THE POLICY SUCCESSES IN THE PAST, WE CAN SEE THAT ACADEMICIANS AND POLICYMAKERS WERE WORKING ON THE POLICY PIPELINE WAY BEFORE THE CRISIS AROSE.

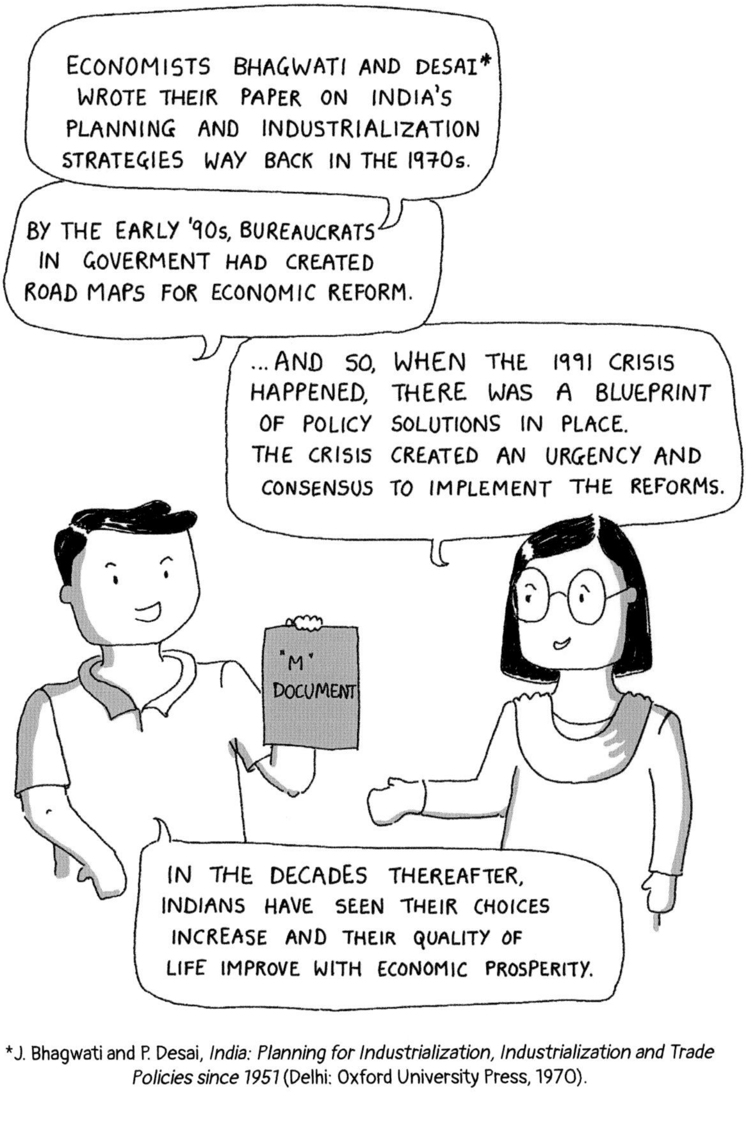

ECONOMISTS BHAGWATI AND DESAI* WROTE THEIR PAPER ON INDIA'S PLANNING AND INDUSTRIALIZATION STRATEGIES WAY BACK IN THE 1970s.
BY THE EARLY '90s, BUREAUCRATS IN GOVERMENT HAD CREATED ROAD MAPS FOR ECONOMIC REFORM.
...AND SO, WHEN THE 1991 CRISIS HAPPENED, THERE WAS A BLUEPRINT OF POLICY SOLUTIONS IN PLACE. THE CRISIS CREATED AN URGENCY AND CONSENSUS TO IMPLEMENT THE REFORMS.
"M" DOCUMENT
IN THE DECADES THEREAFTER, INDIANS HAVE SEEN THEIR CHOICES INCREASE AND THEIR QUALITY OF LIFE IMPROVE WITH ECONOMIC PROSPERITY.

*J. Bhagwati and P. Desai, *India: Planning for Industrialization, Industrialization and Trade Policies since 1951* (Delhi: Oxford University Press, 1970).

WE, AS CITIZENS, ALSO NEED TO REFLECT, EDUCATE OURSELVES AND DISCUSS POSSIBLE SOLUTIONS IN THE ARENA OF POLICY AND POLITICS.

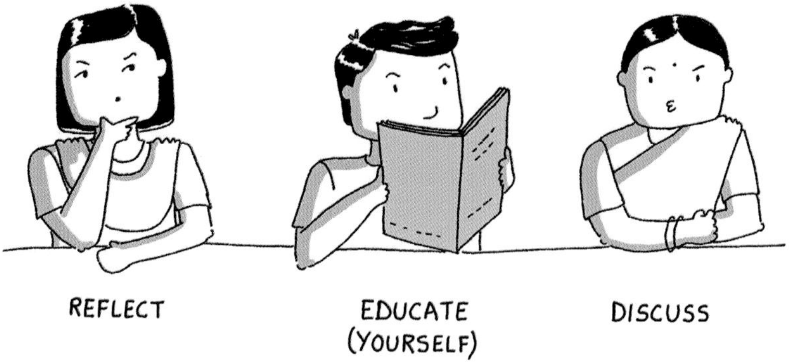
REFLECT
EDUCATE (YOURSELF)
DISCUSS

FINALLY, THERE IS NO ALTERNATIVE TO PARTICIPATING IN THE DISCOURSE, AND ADVOCATING FOR THE CHANGES WE WISH TO SEE.

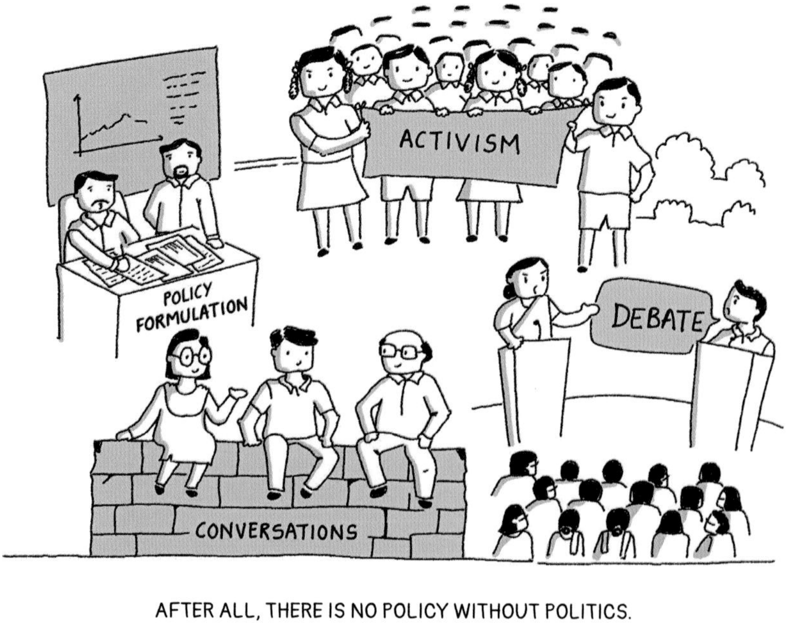
ACTIVISM
POLICY FORMULATION
DEBATE
CONVERSATIONS

AFTER ALL, THERE IS NO POLICY WITHOUT POLITICS.

Chapter 15

We Shall Overcome

The Indian Republic is our best hope

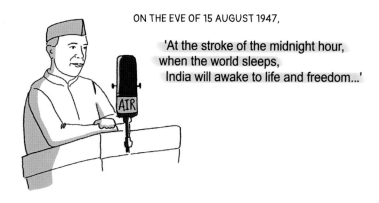

ON THE EVE OF 15 AUGUST 1947,

'At the stroke of the midnight hour,
when the world sleeps,
India will awake to life and freedom...'

IT WAS A NEW BEGINNING FILLED WITH HOPE.

'... a moment comes, which comes but rarely in history,
When we step out from the old to the new, when an age ends,
And when the soul of a nation, long suppressed, finds utterance...'

—Jawaharlal Nehru

BUT THE ROAD AHEAD WAS NOT EASY.
NOBODY WAS BETTING ON INDIA'S SUCCESS.

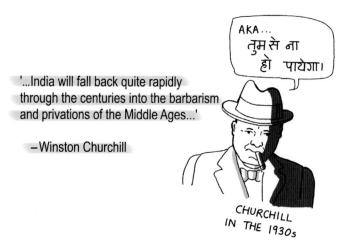

'...India will fall back quite rapidly through the centuries into the barbarism and privations of the Middle Ages...'

–Winston Churchill

AKA...
तुम से ना हो पायेगा।
CHURCHILL IN THE 1930s

INDEED, THE BEGINNING WAS TUMULTUOUS.

RIGHT AT INDEPENDENCE, THE NATION WAS SPLIT INTO TWO,
AND RIOTS HAD BROKEN OUT ON THE STREETS.

ENOUGH OF THIS MADNESS!

HUNDREDS OF PRINCELY STATES WERE STILL
BEING STITCHED INTO ONE COUNTRY.

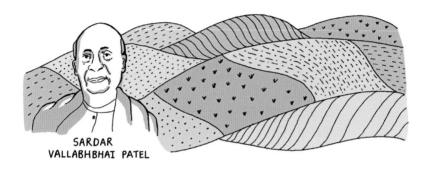

SARDAR
VALLABHBHAI PATEL

THE FRAMERS OF THE INDIAN
CONSTITUTION WERE AWARE
OF THE CHALLENGES AHEAD
OF THEM.

CONSTITUENT
ASSEMBLY
DEBATES

THEY WERE EQUALLY
WORRIED WHETHER INDIA
WOULD BE ABLE TO HOLD ON
TO ITS NEW-FOUND FREEDOM.

BUT IT SAYS SOMETHING ABOUT THE AUDACITY OF THEIR DREAM...

THAT THEY CHOSE TO WRITE A CONSTITUTION THAT PROMISED EQUAL RIGHTS TO EVERY INDIAN, IRRESPECTIVE OF THE MANY DIVISIONS IN OUR SOCIETY.

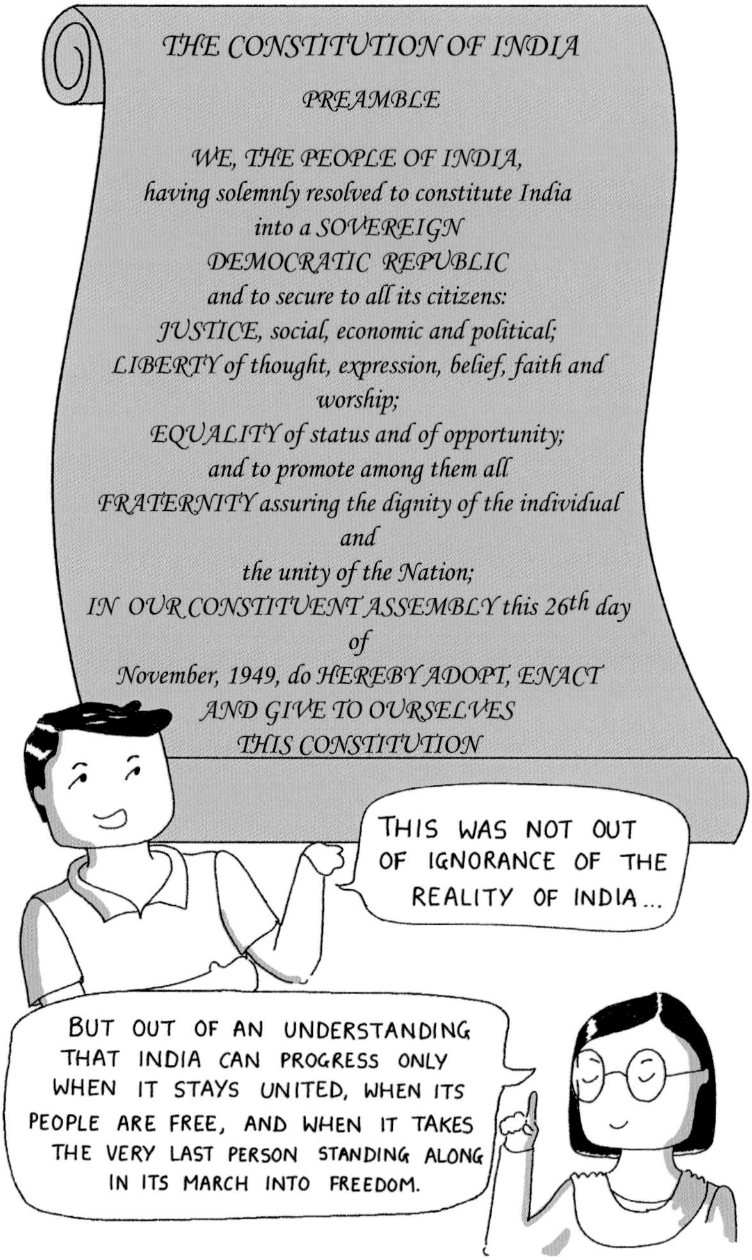
THE CONSTITUTION OF INDIA
PREAMBLE
WE, THE PEOPLE OF INDIA,
having solemnly resolved to constitute India
into a SOVEREIGN
DEMOCRATIC REPUBLIC
and to secure to all its citizens:
JUSTICE, social, economic and political;
LIBERTY of thought, expression, belief, faith and
worship;
EQUALITY of status and of opportunity;
and to promote among them all
FRATERNITY assuring the dignity of the individual
and
the unity of the Nation;
IN OUR CONSTITUENT ASSEMBLY this 26th day
of
November, 1949, do HEREBY ADOPT, ENACT
AND GIVE TO OURSELVES
THIS CONSTITUTION
THIS WAS NOT OUT OF IGNORANCE OF THE REALITY OF INDIA...
BUT OUT OF AN UNDERSTANDING THAT INDIA CAN PROGRESS ONLY WHEN IT STAYS UNITED, WHEN ITS PEOPLE ARE FREE, AND WHEN IT TAKES THE VERY LAST PERSON STANDING ALONG IN ITS MARCH INTO FREEDOM.

THE CONSTITUENT ASSEMBLY HAD PEOPLE FROM ALL SECTIONS OF THE INDIAN SOCIETY. IT WAS A CONSTITUTION WRITTEN BY INDIANS.

AND THEY WERE NOT CONTENT WITH MERE POLITICAL DEMOCRACY.

'...We must make our political democracy a social democracy as well. Political democracy cannot last unless there lies at the base of it social democracy. What does social democracy mean? It means a way of life which recognizes liberty, equality and fraternity as the principles of life...'

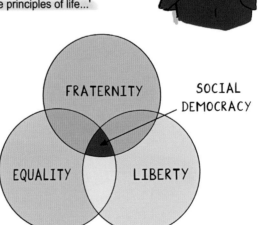

FRATERNITY

SOCIAL DEMOCRACY

EQUALITY

LIBERTY

'...Without equality, liberty would produce the supremacy of the few over the many. Equality without liberty would kill individual initiative. Without fraternity, liberty and equality could not become a natural course of things...'

–Dr B.R. Ambedkar

IN THE PAST 75 YEARS, INDIA HAS MADE MUCH PROGRESS...

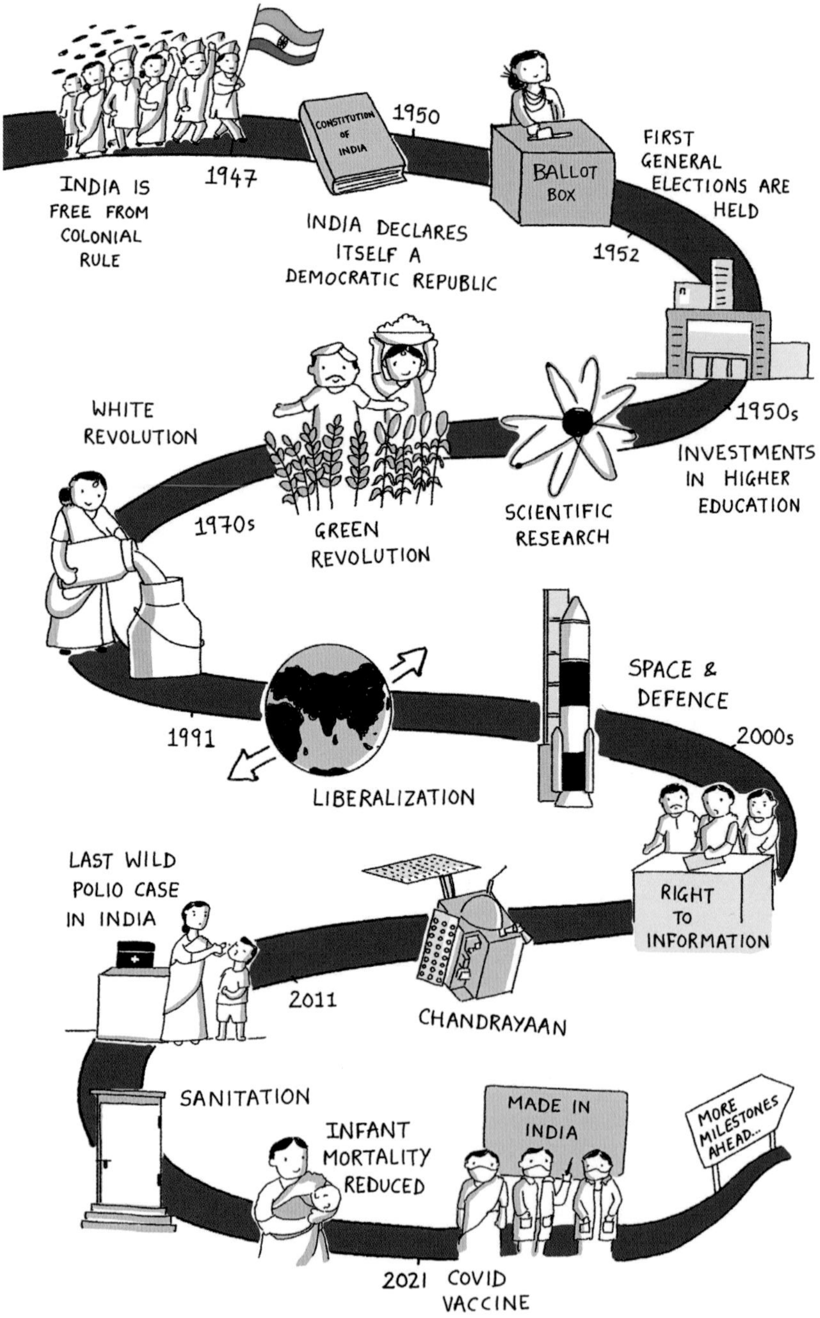

1947
INDIA IS FREE FROM COLONIAL RULE
CONSTITUTION OF INDIA
1950
INDIA DECLARES ITSELF A DEMOCRATIC REPUBLIC
BALLOT BOX
FIRST GENERAL ELECTIONS ARE HELD
1952
1950s
INVESTMENTS IN HIGHER EDUCATION
SCIENTIFIC RESEARCH
GREEN REVOLUTION
1970s
WHITE REVOLUTION
1991
LIBERALIZATION
SPACE & DEFENCE
2000s
RIGHT TO INFORMATION
CHANDRAYAAN
2011
LAST WILD POLIO CASE IN INDIA
SANITATION
INFANT MORTALITY REDUCED
2021
COVID VACCINE
MADE IN INDIA
MORE MILESTONES AHEAD...

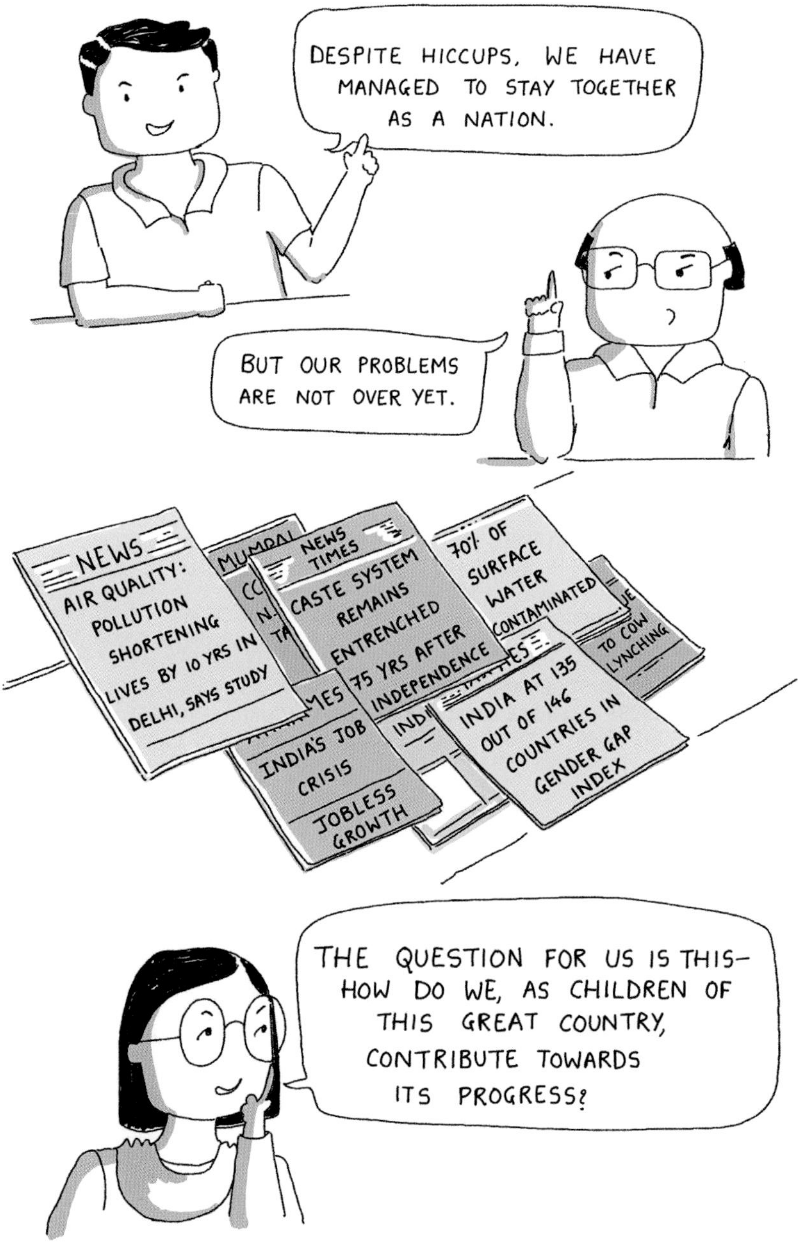
DESPITE HICCUPS, WE HAVE MANAGED TO STAY TOGETHER AS A NATION.
BUT OUR PROBLEMS ARE NOT OVER YET.
NEWS
AIR QUALITY: POLLUTION SHORTENING LIVES BY 10 YRS IN DELHI, SAYS STUDY
NEWS TIMES
CASTE SYSTEM REMAINS ENTRENCHED 75 YRS AFTER INDEPENDENCE
70% OF SURFACE WATER CONTAMINATED
TO COW LYNCHING
INDIA'S JOB CRISIS
JOBLESS GROWTH
INDIA AT 135 OUT OF 146 COUNTRIES IN GENDER GAP INDEX
THE QUESTION FOR US IS THIS— HOW DO WE, AS CHILDREN OF THIS GREAT COUNTRY, CONTRIBUTE TOWARDS ITS PROGRESS?

HOW DO WE HELP IN CREATING A BETTER INDIA OF TOMORROW?

STATE
MARKET
SOCIETY
REMEMBER, WE ARE HERE.

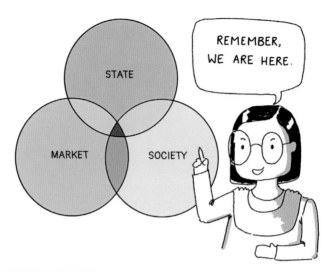

WE LIVE AT THE INTERSECTION OF THE STATE, MARKET AND SOCIETY. SO, WE MUST ENGAGE WITH ALL THREE OF THEM.

FIRSTLY, WE MUST DEMAND THAT THE STATE DELIVERS IN AREAS WHERE IT IS UNSUBSTITUTABLE SUCH AS PROVIDING SECURITY, PROTECTING FUNDAMENTAL RIGHTS AND UPHOLDING THE RULE OF LAW.

RULE OF LAW
ACCOUNTABILITY
CITIZENS, NOT SUBJECTS
CITIZEN RIGHTS
STATE

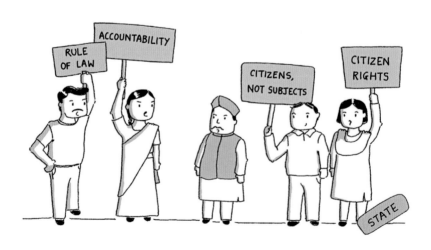

SECONDLY, AS INDIVIDUALS, WE MUST COLLABORATE AND PARTICIPATE WITH ALL OUR ENERGY IN THE GLOBAL MARKETPLACE.

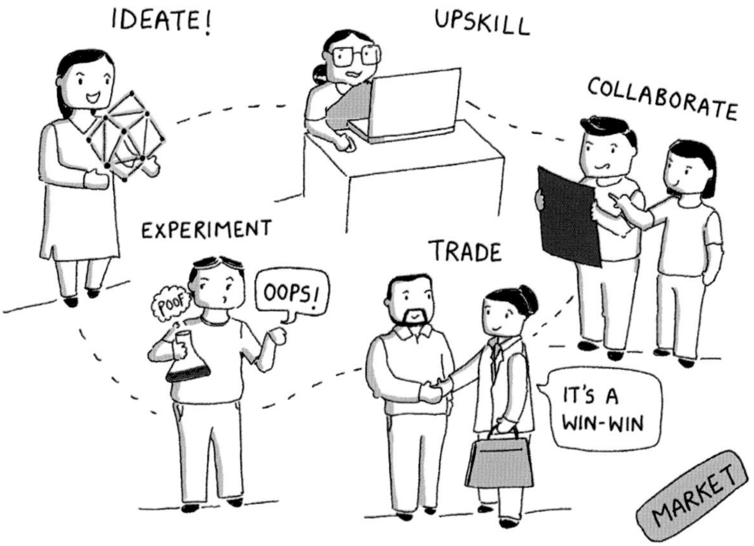
IDEATE!
UPSKILL
COLLABORATE
EXPERIMENT
POOF
OOPS!
TRADE
IT'S A WIN-WIN
MARKET

THIRDLY, WE MUST STEP OUT OF OUR IMMEDIATE SILOS AND BUILD COMMUNITIES THAT BRING TOGETHER PEOPLE FROM ALL WALKS OF LIFE.

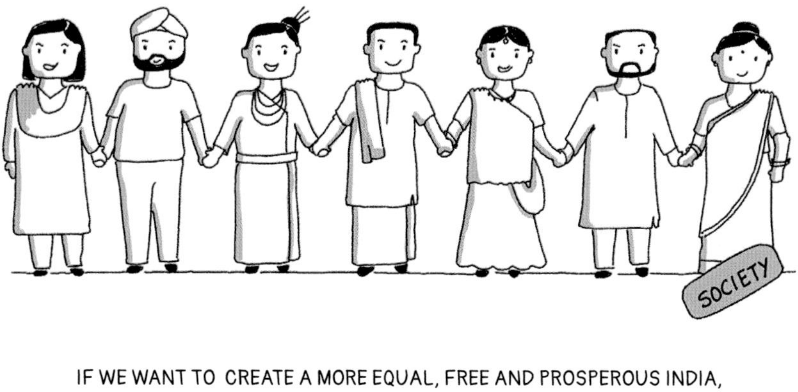
SOCIETY

IF WE WANT TO CREATE A MORE EQUAL, FREE AND PROSPEROUS INDIA, THERE IS NO ALTERNATIVE TO RUNNING THIS SISYPHEAN MARATHON.

ON THE EVE OF 15 AUGUST 1947,
PM NEHRU CONCLUDED HIS SPEECH WITH THE FOLLOWING LINES:

'The future beckons to us.
Whither do we go and what shall be our endeavour?
To bring freedom and opportunity to the common man,
to the peasants and workers of India; to fight and end poverty
and ignorance and disease; to build up a prosperous,
democratic and progressive nation, and to create
social, economic and political institutions which will ensure
justice and fullness of life to every man and woman.
We have hard work ahead.'

–Jawaharlal Nehru

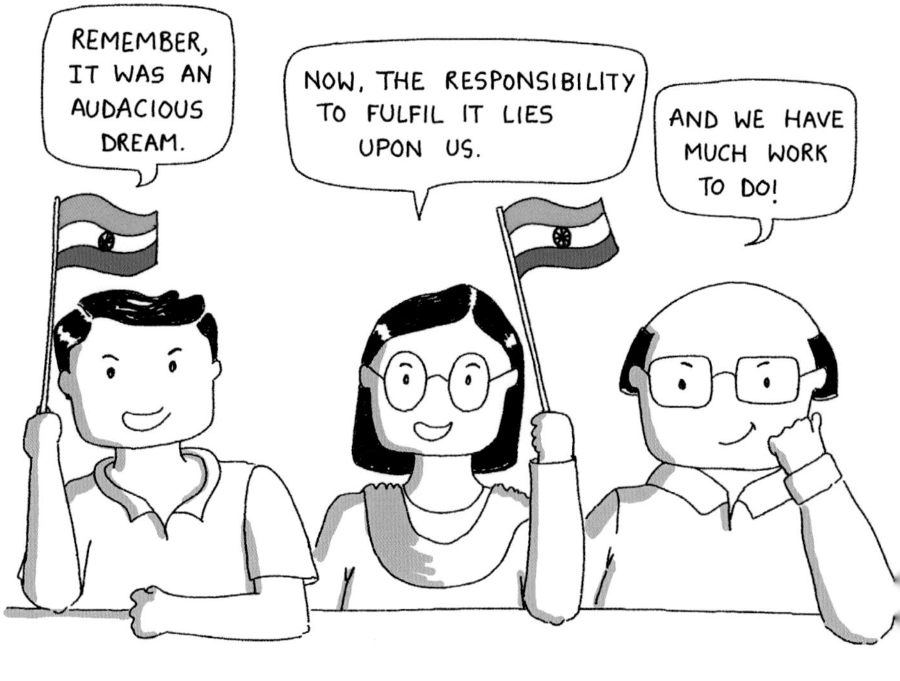
REMEMBER, IT WAS AN AUDACIOUS DREAM.
NOW, THE RESPONSIBILITY TO FULFIL IT LIES UPON US.
AND WE HAVE MUCH WORK TO DO!

WE HAVE MUCH WORK TO DO.

Acknowledgements

When we conceptualized this book, we had no clarity on its shape or form. We thank the good folks at the Takshashila Institution for their motivation and support, and for fostering an environment where such a book can be imagined.

Without Nitin Pai, this book would not have been possible. Much of the GCPP curriculum, which we heavily borrow from, was conceptualized by him.

We also thank Ajay Shah, Vijay Kelkar, Sowmya Prabhakar and Pratap Bhanu Mehta for their encouragement.

We thank our editor, Karthik Venkatesh, for his support and guidance in bringing this book to life.

Finally, we want to thank Takshashila's student community, which pushes us to make teaching public policy awesome and engaging.

—Khyati, Anupam, Pranay

* * *

Thanks to Avisha for being the first reader of every chapter and providing quick feedback and constant cheerleading at every stage.

Thanks to Ma-Pappa, Amma-Dad, Neel, Harsh, Apuroop and Umika for their encouragement and support. Thanks to Peeyush Sekhsaria for his guidance.

—Khyati

* * *

Thanks to Baishu, perhaps the only person to read all my writings (as she claims) and for patiently listening to my rants against price controls during romantic dinners.

Thanks to my parents, Satya and Vani, for encouraging me to study economics instead of engineering or medicine (and for duly forwarding all my writings on their WhatsApp groups). Finally, thanks to Anshu and Shyama for their constant love and support.

—Anupam

* * *

Without Asha's encouragement and support, I wouldn't have taken on this project.

—Pranay